'Race' in Britain
Continuity and change

TO BE
DISPOSED
BY
AUTHORITY

'Race' in Britain
Continuity and change

Edited by Charles Husband

Hutchinson

London Melbourne Sydney Auckland Johannesburg

Hutchinson Education

An imprint of Century Hutchinson Ltd

62–65 Chandos Place, London WC2N 4NW

Century Hutchinson Australia Pty Ltd
PO Box 496, 16–22 Church Street, Hawthorn,
Victoria 3122, Australia

Century Hutchinson New Zealand Ltd
PO Box 40–086, Glenfield, Auckland 10,
New Zealand

Century Hutchinson South Africa (Pty) Ltd
PO Box 337, Berglvei 2012, South Africa

First published 1982
Reprinted 1982, 1984, 1985, 1986
Second edition first published 1987

© Charles Husband 1982, 1987

Set in IBM Press Roman

Printed and bound in Great Britain by
Mackays of Chatham Ltd

British Library Cataloguing in Publication Data

ISBN 0 09 173158 5

Contents

Tables

Figures

Acknowledgements

The editor and publisher wish to thank the following for permission to reproduce the material listed below:

V. G. Kiernan and George Weidenfeld and Nicolson Ltd for extracts from *The Lords of Human Kind* (1969); Winthrop D. Jordan and the University of North Carolina Press for 'First impressions: initial English confrontations with Africans' from *The White Man's Burden* (1974); James Walvin and Penguin Books Ltd for 'Black caricature: the roots of racialism' from *Black and White: The Negro and English Society 1555–1945* (1973); Michael and Ann Dummett and Sheed and Ward for 'The role of government in Britain's racial crisis' from Lewis Donnelly (ed.), *Justice First* (1969); Gideon Ben-Tovim, John Gabriel, Sage Publications, and the Institute of Race Relations, London, for 'The politics of race in Britain 1962–79' from *Sage Race Relations Abstracts*, vol. 4, no. 4 (November 1979), pp. 1–56; Janet Cohen and the BBC for extracts from *File on 4*; Henri Tajfel and the Minority Rights Group, London, for *The Social Psychology of Minorities* (1978).

In addition, the editor would like to acknowledge the varying forms of support and assistance which have been critical in contributing to the development of this book; I would like to thank Derrick Anderson, Peter Braham, Jagdish Chouhan, Amrah Darr, Rob Jeffcoate, Barbara Mayor, Bill Prescott, and Robert Ramdhanie. I would also like to acknowledge the patience and skill of Win Healey for typing the manuscripts. Finally, and in no sense least deserving of thanks, I would like to acknowledge my considerable debt to Claire L'Enfant, and her colleagues at Hutchinson, who have been exceptionally helpful in facilitating the production of both the first edition, and this second edition of this book.

Preface

This book examines the place of the concept of 'race' in contemporary British society and culture. Through an historical examination of its origins, the cultural habit of placing people into 'races' based on skin colour or ancestral lineage is placed in perspective as a social rather than a *natural* or inevitable phenomenon. The significance of this way of defining people and 'explaining' the nature of the relationships between them is analysed in the context of the response to immigration into Britain. The pattern of migration into Britain and social change within Britain is identified as the particular context within which historical images of 'race' and of nationality have had relevance for shaping individual experience and public policy. Indeed, it is argued that the politics of the last three decades cannot be adequately understood without an analysis of the ways in which 'race' has cultural meaning for white Britons and has become central to party politics. 'Race' as a way of defining others and experiencing our own identity requires careful analysis, and this book explores the relations between social identity and social structure in order to unravel some of its power in shaping events in Britain now.

Produced as a set reader for the Open University course 'Ethnic minorities and community relations', this book inevitably reflects the concerns and content of that course. While intended to complement the course units for Open University students, the chapters in this book have also been deliberately compiled so as to provide a broadly based introduction to contemporary 'race relations' for all concerned to understand ethnic relations and British politics. As an *introduction* it must be hoped that all readers will be stimulated to follow up the many references and arguments which are presented here.

Introduction: 'Race', the continuity of a concept

Charles Husband

'As a way of categorising people, race is based upon a delusion because popular ideas about racial classification lack scientific validity and are moulded by political pressures rather than by the evidence from biology.' (Banton and Harwood, 1975, p. 8.) In identifying the fallacious nature of racial classification Banton and Harwood very appropriately refer to its use as delusionary; for like very many other delusions racial categorization is remarkably resistant to change and extinction. I would like to propose that one reason for its continuing vitality is that beneath its apparently simple reduction of complex individuals and societies to self-evidently basic units there lies a highly complex body of emotive ideas. These are ideas which reach out in their reference and significance beyond the immediate forms of racial categorization as such. Rather they invoke a rich matrix of values and images referring to purity–pollution, Christianity–Heathen, national–alien, amongst others. 'Race', like 'love', is a word often used with innocent spontaneity, and yet it remains highly problematic to determine adequately the boundaries of its denotative and connotative meanings.

That this should be so is not surprising when the development of the concept of race is understood. There will be no adequate way in which this may be reviewed in an introductory chapter such as this and the reader must follow the general reviews of Barzun (1965), Banton and Harwood (1975), and the more specific accounts of Jordan (1969), and Walvin (1971). As Banton and Harwood state:

It [race] has to be studied historically, for the various meanings the word has acquired can be understood in no other way. Current notions of race are an integral part of the history of western Europe, drawing upon many aspects of that story. These notions cannot be separated from the rest of that history and attributed to single 'factors' like capitalism, colonialism, biological error or personal prejudice. The sources of popular imagery concerning race are very diverse and the interrelations between their growth and contemporary political affairs are far too complex for the whole historical sequence to be explicable in simple terms. [1975, p. 9]

This book is itself somewhat distorted by a bias towards 'contemporary political affairs' in its emphasis upon 'race relations' defined in terms of colour. Walvin and Jordan in this book are specifically intended to aid an understanding of the emergence of racial categorization along colour lines. Yet this should not be interpreted as equating race with colour. Racial distinctions along colour lines may be the dominant expression of racial thinking in contemporary Britain, but it is not the only form of racial categorization, and has not historically always been predominant. It may be a useful initial corrective to note this racial observation of 1860:

> But I am haunted by the human chimpanzees I saw along that hundred miles of horrible country. I don't believe they are our fault. I believe there are not only many more of them than of old, but that they are happier, better, more comfortably fed and lodged under our rule than they ever were. But to see white chimpanzees is dreadful; if they were black, one would not feel it so much, but their skins, except where tanned by exposure, are as white as ours. [Cited in Curtis, 1968, p. 84]

No, not some imperialist reference to an exotic tribe of albino Africans; but Charles Kingsley, author of *Hereward the Wake*, writing in a letter to his wife about his visit to Ireland. Given the colour = race equation of contemporary times it can be quite startling to observe the ape-like caricatures of *white* Irish reproduced in Curtis (1971) *Apes and Angels: The Irishman in Victorian Caricature.* Yet it is only something more than a century since virulent racial categorization clearly set the Irish aside from, and inferior to, the English. As Curtis summarized the situation in his 'Study of anti-Irish prejudice in Victorian England':

> The gist of many observations made about the Irish people by Victorian Englishmen was that the fundamental differences between English and Irish character were largely, if not exclusively, based on the racial factor. In the conventional language of the day the Celtic blood of the Irish and the Saxon blood of the English determined their contrasting patterns of behaviour, and any mixture of the two peoples invariably resulted in the corruption or adulteration of the better (Anglo-Saxon) blood by the baser (Celtic) blood. [Curtis, 1968, p. 36]

In considering 'race' we should therefore be aware of the emergence of a tradition of categorical assortment of people into groupings by 'race', variously defined; and the more specific case of applying 'racial' categorization in relations to the historical imagery of colour. The latter case is a particularly powerful fusion of historically distinct traditions.

'Race' is first recorded in the English language in 1508 in a poem by William Dunbar and through the seventeenth and eighteenth centuries 'race' was essentially a literary word devoid of scientific aura, denoting a class of persons or things. Throughout the eighteenth and nineteenth centuries there was increasing contact with Africa, India, 'the Orient', and other 'exotic' places where the variety of *Homo sapiens'* physical and cultural forms were a continuing source of wonder. Not only of wonder but also of enquiry for, in centuries when the empirical triumph of the natural sciences was being developed in Europe, such observations could not remain aesthetic novelties and explanation was essential. With the growth of *systematic* science in biology, zoology, chemistry and physics, the willingness to see such phenomena as simply further demonstrations of God's creative order was being eroded. From the sixteenth century the variety of human form had demanded an explanation, not least the variation in colour. Scriptural answers were sought which had the difficult task of leaving intact the monogenist view of a common descent of all from Adam and Eve. In referring to the Bible for an answer contradictory explanations could be found by selective interpretation of scripture. As Jordan illustrates in this book some accounts attributed variation in colour to the effect of the sun, thus leaving the essential commonality of all persons intact. Others, however, saw blackness as being a consequence of God's curse upon Ham the son of Noah. This account, whilst not challenging the monogenist view of human origins as depicted in Genesis, did invoke God's intervention to account for fixed differences between groups of people. This opposition between accounts of human variation in terms of physical cause and environment or culture echoed through the debates of the seventeenth and eighteenth centuries. With the ascendancy of science in the nineteenth century, physical cause emerged as a predominant model and was encapsulated in the transition of 'race' from signifying in its literary sense a line of descent — a group defined by historical continuity — to its scientific sense of 'race' as a zoologically defined group.

It is useful to note here Jordan's comment on the significance of colour:

> In the long run, of course, the Negro's colour attained greatest significance not as a scientific problem but as a social fact. Englishmen found blackness in human beings a peculiar and important point of difference. The Negro's colour set him radically apart from Englishmen. [Jordan, 1969, p. 20]

Colour then became the means of distinguishing groups of people and of identifying the behaviour to be expected of them. 'Race' provided the theory which accounted for the consistency between sign of category membership, colour; and the characteristic behaviour of members of the category. The 'social fact' of colour and the theory of 'race' do not have a single origin and the unique development of each must therefore be treated independently.

Banton identifies the writing of French anatomist Cuvier as particularly significant in the development of 'race' theory. Cuvier as the nineteenth century opened presented a strong statement of the physical causation of culture. In a series of lectures in 1805 he postulated the existence of three major 'races' which were the white, the yellow and the black. He also indicated that there was an ordering from superior to inferior in this typology. Cuvier's view of pure types of 'race' was highly influential and was reflected and developed in such works as Charles Hamilton Smith's *The Natural History of the Human Species* published in 1848; Robert Knox's *The Races of Man* (1850), Gobineau's *Essai sur l'inégalité des Races humaines* (1853) and in Nott and Gliddon's *Types of Mankind* published in 1854. Banton observes that the doctrine of racial typology developed in this literature had four chief features:

> First, that variations in the constitution and behaviour of individuals were to be explained as the expression of different underlying biological types of a permanent kind; secondly, differences between these types explained variations in the cultures of human populations; thirdly, the distinctive nature of the types explained the superiority of Europeans in general and Aryans in particular; fourthly, the friction between nations and individuals of different type arose from innate characters. [Banton, 1979, p. 18]

Significantly Banton notes that in Europe the social origins of such racial typologies had little to do with relations between blacks and whites; rather writers like Knox and Gobineau were more influenced by the revolutionary events in Europe of 1848 wherein the authors saw evidence for their theories of racial conflict. In adducing this 'evidence' they were able to draw upon pre-existing imagery of competing national lineages located in pristine Saxon, Frankish or Aryan origins. Such mythic imagery has persisted for centuries (Poliakov, 1974), but without the systematic scientific theory of 'race'. It had been previously theorized in relation to 'race' as lineage. Now it proved equally amenable to 'race' conceptualized within the rigour of nineteenth-century science.

The simple clarity of 'race' conceived in pure types was rapidly superseded by the implications of Darwin's *Origin of Species* (1859). Through the process of selection Darwin introduced a mechanism whereby there might be change within and between races. One implication was that the superior pure races may be contaminated through contact with inferior races resulting in racial degeneration. On the other hand, for those of a more optimistic philosophic bent, this same mechanism held out the possibility of deliberate human intervention in order to maximize the benefits of selection and advance the emergence of pure races. Implicit in both the pessimistic and optimistic interpretation of Darwinian racial theory was the responsibility of the superior race (Anglo-Saxon?) to resist the dangers of degeneration or to promote the emergence of a pure and proper order. Darwin's contribution to 'race', zoologically defined, was to provide the theory of 'race' with a motor for change in natural selection; and where there is change there is the possibility, for some the necessity, of control. This imperative for planned racial development emerged as a central tenet of the school of thought that became known as Social Darwinism.

In Social Darwinism it is again possible to see how developments in 'racial' theory co-opt established 'social facts'. Thus, not only was the Aryan superiority and colour stereotyping given new vitality when incorporated into Social Darwinist theory, but the social facts of class were equally amenable to new illumination. Thus at the end of the nineteenth and beginning of the twentieth century, British imperial expansion was happily able to view the subordination, at times genocide (e.g. Tasmania), of inferior peoples as not only a necessary, but a laudable unfolding of natural law. (The application of this perspective in the British occupation and control of Egypt is given detailed analysis in Said's (1978) brilliant review in *Orientalism*.) At home the same Social Darwinist philosophy was expressed in anxiety about the terrifying fecundity of the inferior classes. The development of intelligence-testing in Britain and America was, for example, intimately related to eugenics movements in Britain and the United States. Kamin (1977) has detailed the nature of this relationship in American politics and psychology, and Evans and Waites (1981) provide an account with a British focus.

In the early decades of the twentieth century 'race' continued to acquire legitimacy through the 'scientific' study of 'racial' variation particularly in psychology and anthropology. It is perhaps worth noting that race theory was, in the first half of the twentieth century, a specific expression of a more general acceptance in Britain of the physical determination of abilities. For example, in the 1930s and 1940s, when the state education system was being developed, the received wisdom was that intellectual ability was due to genetic endowment and hence not subject to change. Thus the divided and hierarchical secondary school system with streaming and selection at eleven plus was envisaged as being the appropriate means for maximizing the achievement of given abilities. Within this general perspective 'race' continued, in the 1930s and later, to have the self evident veracity of a concept given legitimacy as a 'scientific fact'. That is, not just a 'social fact', but an incontestable social fact.

After the horror of the Second World War and particularly the slaughter of millions of Jews, but also of Slavs, Poles and Gypsies on racial grounds, the international academic community challenged the 'scientific' basis of race and racial difference. Indicative of this change, and particularly influential, were the UNESCO *Statements on Race and Race Prejudice* of 1950, 1951, 1964 and 1967. As an undergraduate in the mid 1960s I remember the 1951 UNESCO *Statement of the Nature of Race and Race Differences* as having almost unimpeachable authority. Yet by the early 1970s such was the resurgence of scientific 'race' theory, particularly stimulated by Jensen's 1969 paper that again popular racism based on colour was able to draw upon 'scientific' justification for the reasonableness of discriminating between 'races' because of their innately different characteristics. For the academic and wider audience, this theoretical development in psychology and sociology took on a special pertinence because of the immediate relevance this academic literature had for ethnic conflict in the United States and Britain. In America the long hot summers of rioting in the late 1960s, Black Nationalism and the Black Panthers put 'Civil Rights' at the forefront of the political agenda. In Britain the successful growth of

grass roots colour prejudice and the Parliamentary capitulation into discriminatory legislation (see Dummett and Dummett in this book) represented the
racialization of the British political scene in less than a decade. The physical
causation versus environment, nature–nurture, debate was again enjoined;
and particularly violently in the specific area of 'race'. Just looking at my
bookshelf, I observe Eysenck's 1971 *Race, Intelligence and Education* which
very strongly presented the case for racial differences in intelligence; and hence
a defence of both 'race' as a real category and intelligence as a genetically
determined characteristic. On the same shelf is the 1972 Richardson and Spears
Race, Culture and Intelligence which critically reviewed the assumptions of the
Jensen–Eysenck position. This latter book published by Penguin Education
was accompanied by *Race and Social Difference* edited by Baxter and Sansom
for the same imprint in the same year; and was followed in 1973 by *Psychology
and Race*. All of these are paperbacks and are indicative of the centrality of
'race' for informed debate in the 1970s. The burgeoning of books on aspects
of 'race' also contributed to the emergence of downmarket 'popular' pieces in
magazines and the press. In this domain of communicating with 'the wider
audience' few can have matched Eysenck in flair and productivity. Throughout
the 1970s there has been a flow of information from academic production to
the lay public, which has helped to sustain *race* rather than *ethnicity* as the
unity of debate. This is an important observation in that 'race' retains a biological
–scientific sense of permanency characterized by genetic determination and
transmission, rather than the plasticity inherent in ethnicity with its basis in
culture (see Saifullah Khan in this book). In a more specific way Billig (1978 and
1979) has pointed out the benefit which fascist groups like the National Front
have derived from exploiting the writings of Jensen and Eysenck. That we have
in Britain politics defined in terms of race relations rather than ethnic relations
is not a minor semantic oddity. 'Race' as a means of categorizing people theorizes
the 'social facts' of colour difference in a rigid and absolute way which carries all
the implicit naturalness and authority of centuries of 'race'-thinking.

Just as the race theory of the 1930s and 1940s was embedded in a larger
movement of ideas, so we can discern the contemporary legitimacy of 'race' as
being part of a wider development in scientific theory.

In the 1960s there was an upsurge of biological thinking about human behaviour and social organization. The writings of authors such as Ardrey (1961,
1966, 1970), Lorenz (1966, 1974) and Morris (1967, 1969) presented a view of
individual behaviour as being largely controlled by powerful ancient instincts.
Human culture could at best develop mechanisms for moderating these
instinctual forces but could never override them, since cultures were themselves in the last instance shaped by the biological imperatives of *Homo sapiens*.
The arguments of neo-biologists such as these, usefully reviewed by Reynolds
(1976), received wide mass exposure through paperback sale in non-academic
bookshops, through television feature programmes arising from their work and
through magazine and newspaper articles. In the liberal and affluent 'Age of

Aquarius' of the late 1960s and early 1970s this expert confirmation of the simplicities of 'human nature' had its own grateful audience in a period of apparent sophistication and of rapid social change. It was also consistent with the simple truths of 'race', in both its literal and scientific forms. In a period that Hall *et al.* (1978) have portrayed as a crisis of political consensus, the immediate moral panics over industrial or political violence were rendered less threatening when viewed in the time-scale of English racial continuity. It was potentially comforting for the insecure to know that beneath the raging variety of contemporary fashions 'Old Adam' reigned unchanged. For example, in a period of growing feminist assaults on male privilege and on female acceptance of their inferior status, the academic writings of Bowlby (1952), Hutt (1972) or Tiger (1969), which in differing ways argued for the biological determination of male and female behaviour, were guaranteed at least one large and willing audience. The point to note is that the same scientific perspective, namely, the biological determination of behaviour, did not exist for the population at large only in its incorporation into their view on race; it was also at the heart of sexual politics (see Chetwynd and Hartnett, 1978, Lomax *et al.* , 1978). The 'social facts' of colour stereotyping were theorized in a conception of 'race' that shared very centrally a perspective which was widely represented elsewhere in the dominant debates of the time.

The neo-biologism of the 1960s has led to a much more sophisticated and apparently scientifically rigorous restatement in the 1970s in the form of socio-biology. Sociobiology represents a fusion of Darwinian evolutionary theory with modern population genetics, and whilst within it there exist theorectical differences, it has in the last five years and more had a major impact upon academic debate in a range of disciplines. Combining the principles of survival with sophisticated models of genetic transmission, sociobiology views individual behaviour, and indeed cultures, as being the end products of biological selection processes; everything from altruism to the assumed greater promiscuity of males is thus capable of explanation in biological—evolutionary terms. It has been seriously debated as possibly providing a scientific basis for determining moral values by psychologists and sociologists (see *American Sociological Review* vol. 39, 1974 and *American Psychologist* vol. 31, no. 5, 1976 for special editions of learned journals given over to discussion of the implications of this new theory). Sociobiology has penetrated further into the heartland of academic respectability than its 1960s precursors, but like them it has its popularizers; in Britain the most successful being Dawkins whose (1976) *The Selfish Gene* had very wide exposure. Whilst Sahlins (1977) has, as an anthropologist, fiercely attacked the evidence and ideology of sociobiology and Barker (1981) has argued the relation between modern racism and sociobiological theory, its significance should be seen in historical context. It is not novel in hypothesizing a biological determination of behaviour; though it has a novel apparatus of ideas to support this familiar view. Its significance for the analysis of contemporary 'race' thinking lies in the backdrop of academic legitimacy it lends to the analysis of behaviour and society in biological terms. It is hardly reasonable to expect people in Britain to cease to interpret the 'social facts' of colour in the language of biological race, if scientists are prepared to view such abstract entities as altruism as being biologically determined.

It is perhaps time to move to a discussion of what the 'everyday person in the street' means by 'race', since I am certainly not suggesting that they are all highly informed regarding the niceties of sociobiological theory; nor indeed that each individual has available for ready communication to an enquirer, an articulate theory of 'race'. I started by asserting that I believe people experience 'race' as a highly complex body of emotive ideas. Let me now develop that.

Jacques Barzun in a book first published in 1937, but which I still find immensely relevant today, describes race thinking in the following terms:

> In short, race-thinking is a habit. It is not confined to the anthropologists and ethnologists, the historians and publicists who make up systems or preach discrimination; race-thinking occurs whenever someone, in a casual or considered remark, implies the truth of any of the following propositions:
>
> 1 That mankind is divided into unchanging natural types, recognizable by physical features, which are transmitted 'through the blood' and that permit distinctions to be made between 'pure' and 'mixed' races.
> 2 That the mental and moral behaviour of human beings can be related to physical structure, and that knowledge of the structure or of the racial label which denotes it provides a satisfactory account of the behaviour.
> 3 That individual personality, ideas, and capacities, as well as national culture, politics, and morals, are the products of social entities variously termed race, nation, class, family, whose causative force is clear without further definition or inquiry into the connection between the group and the spiritual 'product'.
>
> These three types of race-thinking naturally merge into one another. Few writers limit themselves to any one type and mankind at large uses all three with equal readiness according to the occasion. The formal rejection of the fallacy in one guise does not protect against its other guises. [Barzun, 1937, 1965 ed, p. 12-14]

Barzun's criteria may seem surprisingly wide given the discussion of biological determination which has prevailed above; that would seem to relate only to the first two of his propositions. However, it is precisely the diversity and flexibility of race-thinking which Barzun identifies that I would wish to reiterate. It is the deterministic association of category of person with type of behaviour which is at the core of race-thinking. Whether the theoretical justification for this linkage is accomplished by reference to theories of biological or cultural determinism is a secondary, though not unimportant, issue. As Rex (1970, pp. 144-60) has pointed out theories which refer to sociological or historical factors in order to justify the identification of an out group and discrimination against its members have the same function as if they had referred to biological factors. It is clear, in for example Poliakov's (1974) account of the Aryan myth, that the pre-scientific literary theory of race was able to exploit lineage and shared history as just as potent a determining force as a post-Darwinian biological theory. In this sense twentieth-century biologism has not so much usurped earlier 'literary' theories of 'race', but has rather reinforced a powerful tradition of deterministic thinking. Barzun is right to emphasize the ease with which people flow from one proposition to another in sustaining their race-thinking. After all race-thinking usually occurs in the context of off-the-top-of-the-head, spontaneous utterance. Its success lies in the common sense status of its assumptions.

Up to now I have attempted not to use the term racism but perhaps I can clarify my discussion of 'race' by developing the relation between 'race' and racism. To paraphrase Phizacklea and Miles (1980, p. 22): racism refers to a system of beliefs held by the members of one group which serve to identify and set apart the members of another group who are assigned to a 'race' category on the basis of some biological or other invariable, 'natural seeming', characteristic which they are believed to possess, membership of this category then being sufficient to attribute other fixed characteristics to all assigned to it. 'Race' is a socially constructed categorization which specifies rules for the identification of members. Racism is the application of 'race' categories in social contexts with an accompanying attribution of invariable characteristics to category members. Historically the development of 'race' categories and the deterministically associated characteristics have rendered these two elements inseparable. As Kiernan, Jordan, and Walvin indicate in this book, when we operate with 'race' categories based on colour we evoke imagery with centuries of meaning — meaning which taps notions of purity, sexuality and Christian virtue dating to at least Elizabethan England, and notions of superiority embedded in centuries of British colonial rule. It is the many interconnections with important values and beliefs existing in other domains of individuals' lives that makes race-thinking so tenacious. As Miles argues, in this book, any understanding of 'race' in Britain must examine the interrelations between the imagery evoked by 'race' and the values and beliefs which underlie nationalism. Just as 'race' theory developed, and exists, in the context of a broader realm of competing ideas, so for individuals 'race' is not a finite part of their understanding which, like their 6 times table, they can draw upon when necessary. It is a much more diffuse patterning of beliefs and images which permeates the range of their consciousness in differing ways, each individual having a unique pattern constructed from many common elements, shaped by their particular context and experience.

As Hall *et al.* (1978) and Downing (1980, ch. 7) have stressed there is no single monolithic ideology shared by all Britons. The interlocking imagery and values which dominate the experience of any one group defined by class, region, ethnicity or gender is not the same as that prevailing in another group. And the same image or value found to be present in two different groups does not necessarily have the same range of meaning. An understanding of group identity requires a sensitivity to the interrelation of symbols and values within specific groups (see Saifullah Khan in this book). It is the unique interaction of values, and their supporting imagery, which gives each value its particular significance. Hence Downing's insistence that there are many ideological elements in contemporary British society which cannot be reduced to a single core. Whilst arguing that in sum the dominant ideas are oppressive in that they serve the interests of capital, he offers no simple conspiracy model of political control. Rather he emphasizes the contradictory and dynamic interactions which are to be found in the experience of individuals within particular contexts.

Thus I am making explicit the requirement to evaluate images and values within the context of group identity and inter-group relations (see Tajfel in this book). Of course there is likely to be considerable overlap with individuals having membership of different groups and thus it is probable that:

1 The same values may have different nuances for the same person in different situations, where different group memberships are invoked.
2 The same individuals may find themselves switching between values which in principle are opposed and which therefore they may ultimately have to 'do some work on'. The flexibility and illogical agility which Barzun identified in 'race-thinking' should not therefore be seen as unique to racist thought. What may be special to race-thinking in Britain is the frequency of cross-referencing to 'race' imagery which takes place throughout disparate areas of an individual's experience.

Let me develop this last point. Having argued the uniqueness of individual experience what then is left of racism as a general feature of contemporary Britain? Certainly any simple cultural contagion theory of racism will not suffice; namely an argument which identifies British culture as intrinsically racist and therefore Britain as perpetually racist. I have argued elsewhere, (Husband, 1975, 1977), that British culture is suffused with 'race' imagery and racist reference. That is not the same as arguing that racism is a uniform entity. The way in which this imagery is taken up and employed has to be analysed in the context of the economic and social processes of contemporary urban Britain, (see Billig, 1978, and Phizacklea and Miles, 1980, for recent attempts at such an analysis). However, to say that ideology is not monolithic is not to say that there are no recurrent themes to be traced, woven into the texture of white British consciousness — themes which may generate somewhat different nuances in different sub-cultures, but which remain none the less common to a white British consciousness. Hall *et al.* have made a comparable point elsewhere:

> We would argue that all social ideologies contain powerful images of society at their heart. These images may be diffuse, quite untheorized in any elaborate sense; but they serve to condense and order the view of society in which the ideologies are active, and they constitute both its unquestioned substratum of truth — what carries conviction — and the source of its collective emotional force and appeal. Together, these images produce and sustain an uncodified but immensely powerful conservative sense of Englishness, of an English

'way of life', of an 'English' viewpoint which – by its very density of reference – everyone shares to some extent. [Hall *et al.*, 1978, p. 140]

As Troyna has indicated in this book, the imagery and values of 'race' are negotiated in relation to other recurrent images of democracy, fairness, tolerance and rationality. In his analysis of the press reporting of the National Front it is possible to see racism emerging in the news as, at worst, a relative evil to be opposed within the agreed boundaries of social democratic processes and the rule of law, embodied in the right of free speech. Dummett and Dummett, also in this book, have painfully demonstrated how British Governments in defending 'the national interest', in maintaining 'British tolerance' and in seeking to gain electoral support have refused to challenge the racism of the electorate but have rather sought to submerge this in choosing to identify the black immigrant population as the problem to be contained. The press, too, in the 1960s whilst parading the tolerant virtues of British society simultaneously defined the political storm building around the response to black immigration as an 'immigration problem' (see Hartmann and Husband, 1974). Thus the British press, along with the majority of British academics in the 1960s, concluded that the 'race' of the immigrant population was the problem rather than the racism of the white society. As Bourne (1980) has pointed out, academics and politicians colluded in defining and studying 'race relations' in preference to identifying and opposing racism. The essential part of race-thinking is the common sense assumption that 'race' is a real and self-evidently neutral fact, not to be confused with racism which is a special condition of a few disturbed bigots who abuse reality with their prejudice. Thus liberal commitment to justice and equity became subverted to a concern for 'good race relations' and a concern for tolerance. Once the conceptual language of 'race' is invoked the assumptions of inferiority–superiority, national–alien, and us–them are inevitably at the heart of any judgements. As Barker (1979) has indicated, Parliamentary discussion remains larded with references to Anglo-Saxon heritage and other significant racial metaphors. Race-thinking also remains evident in apparently more innocuous contexts to any who maintain vigilance in listening to sports commentary, discussions of indigenous ethnic minorities, the Irish, Welsh and Scots, or in watching television entertainment. On the streets of Britain members of black ethnic communities need no particular vigilance to note the extent of race-thinking in contemporary Britain.

In the context of the recession of the 1970s and the economic crisis of the 1980s with its attendant massive unemployment, and in the context of a general erosion of civil liberties (Thompson, 1980), racism is not some legacy of a colonial era which has merely failed to fade and die. It has a specific vitality and is daily regenerated in the perceptions of white Britons. 'Race' has its immediate continuity and existence in individual consciousness; it has its political and ideological genesis in the contradictions of British society. In any analysis of 'race' these two domains must be related.

References

Ardrey, R. (1961), *African Genesis*, Collins
Ardrey, R. (1966), *The Territorial Imperative*, Collins
Ardrey, R. (1970), *The Social Contract*, Collins
Banton, R. (1979), 'The idea of race and the concept of race', in G. K. Verma and D. Bagley (eds.), *Race, Education and Identity*, Macmillan
Banton, M. and Harwood, J. (1975), *The Race Concept*, David & Charles
Barker, M. (1979), 'Racism — the new inheritors', *Radical Philosophy*, no. 21 (Spring), pp. 2-17
Barker, M. (1981), *The New Racism*, Junction Books
Barzun, J. (1965), *Race: A Study in Superstition*, New York: Harper & Row
Baxter, P. and Sansom, B. (1972), *Race and Social Difference*, Penguin
Billig, M. (1978), *Fascists: A Social Psychological View of the National Front*, Harcourt Brace Jovanovich
Billig, M. (1979), *Psychology, Racism and Fascism*, Searchlight Booklet, A F & R Publications
Bourne, J. (1980), 'Cheerleaders and ombudsmen: the sociology of race relations in Britain', *Race and Class*, vol. 21, no. 4, pp. 331-52
Bowlby, J. (1952), *Maternal Care and Mental Health*, World Health Organization, Geneva
Chetwynd, J. and Hartnett, O. (1978), *The Sex Role System*, Routledge & Kegan Paul
Curtis, L. P. (1971), *Apes and Angels: The Irishman in Victorian Caricature*, David & Charles
Curtis, L. P., Jr (1968), *Anglo-Saxons and Celts*, New York University Press
Dawkins, R. (1976), *The Selfish Gene*, Oxford University Press
Downing, J. (1980), *The Media Machine*, Pluto Press
Evans, B. and Waites, B. (1981), *IQ and Mental Testing*, Macmillan
Eysenck, H. J. (1971), *Race, Intelligence and Education*, Temple Smith
Hall, S. *et al.* (1978), *Policing the Crisis*, Macmillan
Hartmann, P. and Husband, C. (1974), *Racism and the Mass Media*, Davis-Poynter
Husband, C. (1975), 'Racism in society and the mass media: a critical interaction', in C. Husband (ed.), *White Media and Black Britain*, Arrow Books, pp. 15-38
Husband, C. (1977), 'News media, language and race relations: a case study in identity maintenance', in H. Giles (ed.), *Language, Ethnicity and Intergroup Relations*, Academic Press, pp. 211-40
Hutt, C. (1972), *Males and Females*, Penguin
Jensen, A. R. (1969), 'How much can we boost IQ and scholastic achievement?', *Harvard Educational Review*, vol. 39, pp. 1-123
Jordan, W. D. (1969), *White Over Black*, Penguin
Kamin, L. J. (1977), *The Science and Politics of IQ*, Penguin

Lomax, E. M. R., Kagan, J., and Rosenkrantz, B. G. (1978), *Science and Patterns of Child Care*, San Francisco: W. H. Freeman

Lorenz, K. (1966), *On Aggression*, Methuen

Lorenz, K. (1974), *Civilised Man's Eight Deadly Sins*, Methuen

Morris, D. (1967), *The Naked Ape*, Cape

Morris, D. (1969), *The Human Zoo*, Cape

Phizacklea, A. and Miles, R. (1980), *Labour and Racism*, Routledge & Kegan Paul

Poliakov, L. (1974), *The Aryan Myth*, Heinemann

Rex, J. (1970), *Race Relations in Sociological Theory*, Weidenfeld & Nicolson

Reynolds, V. (1976), *The Biology of Human Action*, San Francisco: W. H. Freeman

Richardson, K. and Spears, D. (1972), *Race, Culture and Intelligence*, Penguin

Sahlins, M. (1977), *The Use and Abuse of Biology*, Tavistock

Said, E. W. (1978), *Orientalism*, Routledge & Kegan Paul

Thompson, E. P. (1980), *Writing by Candlelight*, Merlin

Tiger, L. (1969), *Men in Groups*, New York: Random House

Walvin, J. (1971), *The Black Presence*, Orback & Chambers

Watson, P. (1973), *Psychology and Race*, Penguin

Part One
'Race' in Britain: the historical context

It is the purpose of this section to underline forcefully the necessity of adopting an historical perspective as the proper basis for any analysis of 'race relations'. The broad picture sketched by Kiernan usefully reminds us that British ideas of colour, 'race', nationality and empire developed in a particular context. He invites us to note the significance of competition with European neighbours as an influence upon the pattern of British imperial expansion. Kiernan shows how in European countries ideas about other cultures and people developed in the context of the particular ideas which were predominant in each country at specific times. And importantly he also indicates how such ideas were themselves reciprocally influenced by the different degree and kind of colonial activity prevalent in each country. The reciprocal relation between ideas and actions is echoed in the more specific focus of Jordan and Walvin upon the development of attitudes towards the Negro. Their analyses reject the possibility of viewing such attitudes as somehow ossified cultural legacies. Rather they show how attitudes to the Negro both shaped and were influenced by events. Complementing Jordan's analysis of the initial contact with Africans, Walvin indicates how common images of the Negro were given different significance in different eras. As 'race' theory developed so the imagery of 'inferior' groups metamorphosized. Historically established images tend not to be radically edited, rather they are re-ordered and re-worked.

Victorian ideas on 'race' are explored in Christine Bolt, *Victorian Attitudes to Race*, Routledge 1979, and D. A. Lorimer, *Class, Colour and the Victorians*, Leicester University Press 1978. A variety of Victorian race-thinking not based on colour imagery is discussed in L. P. Curtis, Jr, *Apes and Angels: The Irishman in Victorian Caricature*, David & Charles 1971. Colin Holmes provides a valuable comparative analysis of British responses to the immigration of differing ethnic groups in *Immigrants and Minorities in British Society*, George Allen and Unwin 1978; which is itself complemented by Kenneth Lunn (ed.), *Hosts, Immigrants and Minorities: Historical Responses to Newcomers in British Society 1870–1914*, Dawson 1980.

Peter Fryer in his book *Staying Power: The History of Black People in Britain*, Pluto Press 1984, has provided an essential complement to many of the above texts in recording the black experience and response to their situation in Britain. His book spans the period from Roman Britain to the opening of the 1980s and in doing so exposes the development of racism in Britain, and the extent to which the continuing black presence *in Britain* has been expunged from official histories, and British consciousness. However, as the chapters in this section show there has been no absence of images of alien 'races'. David Dabydeen has illustrated their transmission through literature in his edited text, *The Black Presence in English Literature*, Manchester University Press 1985. As we shall see in later sections these historically derived images are not passively reiterated in contemporary Britain, but are selectively incorporated into current contexts.

1 European attitudes to the outside world *

V. G. Kiernan

The shape of modern Europe

In the couple of centuries after 1450 Europe underwent a thorough stirring and shaking up, as if being plunged for rejuvenation into a cauldron of Medea. It was again a more radical transformation than any of the other big regions ever experienced, the stormy passage, full of changes good and ill, from medieval to modern. Internal pressures had slowly built up, and Europe's collisions with the other continents helped to release them. One facet of the process was the Renaissance. Revived memories of antiquity, the Turkish advance, the new horizons opening beyond, all encouraged Europe to see itself afresh as civilization confronting barbarism. But the Renaissance was an affair of aristocracy and intelligentsia, confronting also their own illiterate masses, and secularism was a false dawn in an age when the masses could still only act and be acted upon through religious feeling. Social crisis, the threatened breakdown of the whole feudal order, found expression in religious schism, the strife of Reformation and Counter-Reformation. Christianity was always the religion most given to schism and persecution, because Europe was the region most subject to change, growth, social tension. The old division between eastern and western, Greek and Latin Churches was promptly succeeded by a new division between Catholic and Protestant, broadly between south and north.

Class division and class consciousness, the driving-force of modern European evolution, were contained in and regulated by the national State, now fully developed in the West. Germany and Italy failed to coalesce into nations, and fell behind. A new type of government, absolute monarchy, managed the reorganization and modernization of feudal society, and then went on until overthrown by revolution: in the 1640s in England, in 1917 in Russia. This absolutism always differed from Asiatic monarchy, because it rested on other foundations; and even at the height of Bourbon power Frenchmen could feel that they were under a sort of 'constitutional', not merely arbitrary, régime. But it may be asked whether the monarchs' desire for unrestricted authority was not whetted by emulation of the Sultan, whom all Europe called 'the Grand

* Reprinted from *The Lords of Human Kind* (Penguin 1972), pp. 12-30.

Signior' much as the Greeks used to call the ruler of Persia 'the King'. Conversely, the more a Western people progressed the more it came to think of all personal despotism as 'Asiatic' and degrading.

Against its enemies, Muslim and Protestant as well as fellow-Catholic, Spain and consequently the Counter-Reformation which it championed received immense reinforcement from colonial tribute. Without this Europe might have emerged still further truncated by Turkish expansion, but more homogeneous. The tribute weakened Spain later on by inducing parasitism, and by strengthening all its conservative interests, Crown, nobility and Church, against the rest. It was then the turn of southern and south-western Europe to drop behind, while the north drew ahead. Russia and Sweden were both on the horizon, but the real growing-point was the north-west. The revolt of the Netherlands against Spain was also an early version of a bourgeois revolution, and in free Protestant Holland the explosive economic force of the coming age, capitalism, was maturing. England was moving in the same direction, and these two with northern France formed the vital area, a surprisingly small part of the continent as a whole, the truly 'European' area in terms of future development.[1] *

National states in competition gave deliberate encouragement to the economic and technical progress that was ushering in industrial capitalism, with industrial revolution or mechanization to follow; the old cumbrous empires always stifled experiment. Protestantism changed and moved with the times, and helped to change the times, more than any religion had ever done. It was in this capacity to evolve that Europe was most unique. It grew less 'European' towards the east; or rather there were two dynamic Europes of the north, as well as the inert south and the Turkish south-east. How far Russia belonged to Europe was a question, as it has never altogether ceased to be. It had cast off Tartar overlordship in the fifteenth century and come together under the lead of Moscow, a defeat of Islam comparable with its expulsion from most of Spain long before. But Moscow lay four hundred miles further east than Stamboul, and morally often looked not less remote. 'Russia is a European State', Catherine the Great laid it down in her programme of government,[2] but this German woman might be taken as stating an aspiration rather than a fact. A French aristocrat of the next generation habitually thought of the Russians he saw as 'Tartars' or savages, though he could at the same time predict a brilliant future for them.[3] Many of the formative experiences of Europe had not been shared by this country: Rome, hierarchical feudalism, Reformation. It represented one of those borderlands, such as Macedon was to Greece, close to an elder neighbour in race and speech, but newer, cruder, and capable therefore on occasion of more rapid adaptation, of taking up ideas conceived but not carried out in the more advanced region.

Politically, untrammelled autocracy at one end of northern Europe contrasted with the early stirrings of modern politics, and their paraphernalia of parties, elections, newspapers, in the north-west. Socially, legal freedom here, with

* Superior figures refer to the Notes which appear at the end of chapters.

contractual relations and wage labour, contrasted with the serfdom still prevalent in the east — in Russia intensifying down to 1800, after being introduced
by the ruling class under foreign tutelage to meet the costs of modernization
just when more developed countries were moving away from it. Western armies,
though not always navies, were manned by volunteers, often foreign professionals;
eastern more by conscripts. Conscription goes logically with serfdom or slavery,
and had died out along with it in most of Asia since ancient times. It spread
from east to west Europe after the French Revolution (and thence later on to
Asia), while industrialism travelled from west to east; a reminder that Europe's
east was not a mere torpid hinterland, but had its own energy, its contribution
to a future amalgam. It was on the cards, down to the defeat of the German
army in 1918, that the future Europe would be more 'eastern' than 'western'.
That this did not happen was due in good measure to the ability of the north-
western area to draw on the resources of other continents, as Spain had done
— though not without being coarsened and worsened in various ways in the
process.

There were unifying influences as well. In military technology northern
Europe was all one. Economically it was a compound, representing a division
of labour. Serfdom was geared to a new 'feudal capitalism', producing surpluses
of food and raw materials for sale to western countries in exchange for manu-
factures and luxuries. Western liberty and progress were buttressed on two sides
by unfree labour, serfdom in Europe and slavery in colonies. In terms of
sentiment, the break-up of the little Latin Christendom of old days into the
'*Europe des patries*' was a stage in the growth of popular consciousness, and
indirectly in the long run of European consciousness. Even in the course of
fighting one another Europeans were recognizing their differentness from
anyone else. As the sulphur and brimstone of the religious wars drifted away,
there was a broader revival of the Renaissance consciousness of a common
civilization, with rational, secular, scientific interests, much more vigorous
though these might be in some countries than in others.

One aspect of the trend towards secular thinking was that colour, as well
as culture, was coming to be a distinguishing feature of Europe. Part of the
Christian world now lay beyond the Atlantic, but any kinship felt with it would
be with Spanish colonists, as offspring of Europe, not with Indians as converts
to Christianity. It was an important element in Europe's collective consciousness
that its peoples all looked much alike. If Swede and Neapolitan differed, it was
not more than northern and southern Chinese, less than northern and southern
Indian, and there was every physical gradation in between. Between east and
west physical though not social similarity was even closer. Europeans gave the
impression, to themselves as well as to outsiders, of being one race. That Magyars
or Basques spoke, like Turks, languages not of the European family was something Europe was hardly conscious of before the nineteenth century, and in any
case counted for far less than physical appearance. In odd corners of the continent
remnants of very primitive peoples could still be found; the Highlanders whom

Dr Johnson met were nearly as alien to him as the Tahitians he read about. Yet a Highlander taught English and the minuet was at once European. Apart from a sprinkling of new African arrivals, only Jews and Gypsies, both of Asiatic origin, represented elements sometimes felt to be intrusive to Europe. In general all Europeans could intermarry, if not prevented by class or cult. Royalty always intermarried.

Europe and the world

The seventeenth-century interval

While the new Europe discovered itself, most of the outside world it had discovered was being given a breathing-space. Spain and Portugal, the pioneers, were in decline by 1600; Holland and England were both small; all of them were chiefly occupied at home, and with Europe's incessant wars. The Thirty Years' War, and the conflicts of Louis XIV's epoch that followed, were European civil wars, and meant a respite for other continents, as the war of 1914-19 did later. They were, on the other hand, stimulating military science and spirit to a point where Europe would be crushingly superior to the rest when they did meet. A Brussels tapestry of the late seventeenth century depicting the Four Continents displayed Europe's emblems as a victory monument and a pile of pikes and guns, lances and drums.[4] At least its feuds meant, fortunately for itself and the world, that there would not be a united Europe going out to conquer the other continents. Napoleon brought this possibility near at one moment, Hitler at another.

Africa, the weakest, was not left alone. The Islamic lands had been drawing slaves from it for many centuries; like them Europe wanted not African territory but African men and women. They were wanted for all the parts of America where intensive cultivation was growing up, and most of all for the West Indian islands whose sugar plantations became in the eighteenth century the richest colonial prizes, much fought over by Britain and France. Elsewhere expansion was chiefly into the nearly empty spaces of northern Asia and America, whose accessibility carried the northern countries of Europe further into the lead. French, English and Dutch settlers were moving into north America above the limits of Spanish occupation. Russian explorers and trappers were drifting across Siberia towards the Pacific. Russia was the first country to open diplomatic relations with China — in Latin, of all languages, because there were Jesuits at Peking as interpreters.[5] A shipwrecked Japanese was brought to court to be scrutinized by Peter the Great.[6]

Interest in the outer world at large was nourished by travellers' tales, missionary reports, accounts from Spanish America and other colonies. One expression of such interest was the collecting of exotic curiosities. The Tradescant family collection now in the Ashmolean Museum had a printed catalogue as early as 1642, and included Red Indian hunting-shirts, Turkish slippers, Indian daggers.

One has only to compare the cock-and-bull stories that Othello told Desdemona — and that Shakespeare may have taken as seriously as Raleigh took similar nonsense in America — with the matter-of-fact travel-tales of Defoe, to see how knowledge had accumulated in a little over a century. Othello had one foot in the world of Sinbad the Sailor, Captain Singleton in the world of the *Morning Post*.

Today when Europe is no longer in the lead it is tempted to think, or to agree with others, that the civilization it was incubating was no unique property of its own but a stage of progress that other regions were moving towards. India on this view would have had cotton-mills, Japan would have come by submarines, whether Europe had brought them or not. This is of course possible, but may be regarded as exceedingly unlikely on any time-scale of centuries rather than millennia. An intricate set of interacting factors is required to bring about any significant historical transition, and there is small sign anywhere else (most perhaps in Japan) of anything like the complex of material and psychological forces then at work in north-west Europe. No other part of Europe itself could have made an Industrial Revolution. It is even doubtful whether any Asian country would have modernized itself by imitation of the West, if not forced by the West to do so as India, Japan, China all in different ways were.

At some earlier points the meeting of Europe with other civilizations had been friendly and promising. Queen Elizabeth's contemporary Akbar, greatest of the Mogul emperors, was eager to meet English envoys or Italian missionaries, and hear their ideas. He was at the head of an empire strong enough to command respect, still expanding, and as a result self-confident, and interested in other people's religions and artillery. In Japan too, where Europeans — Portuguese, then Dutch and English — had been coming since 1542, Iyeyasu who in 1603 founded the new Tokugawa dynasty of Shoguns, or feudal overlords, had the same kind of omnivorous interest. But for many reasons the meeting of minds between East and West was broken off, or petered out. Missionaries in the Far East were, then as later, in close league with European governments capable of hostile designs. Most other Westerners had no ideas to offer, and few goods that the East wanted, so that they were always tempted to take what they could by force. Their irruption, and their firearms, worsened the disorderliness always endemic in Asia. This intermediate period was plagued by a vast swarming of pirates over the seas of the world, a state of nature on the waves, the result of wars and social dislocation and the endeavours of Europeans to break into one another's colonies. Western freebooters, or the half-caste Portuguese who infested the Bay of Bengal, rubbed shoulders, or exchanged broadsides, with Arakanese, Malay, Chinese buccaneers. Some Robin Hoods among them started a model settlement in the Indian Ocean which they christened Libertatia:[7] few joined them.

In addition, Asian governments were often less confident now, less inclined to expose their subjects' loyalty to foreign contagion. More receptive than India or China because smaller, and an island, Japan was likewise first and most vigorous in reaction. In 1637 began a savage persecution of missionaries and their numerous converts, and Japan was sealed off for two centuries, except for the small peep-hole of the Dutch warehouse allowed to remain at Nagasaki. It was to become a European gibe at the mercenary Dutch that they consented to humiliate themselves and perform the annual trampling on the cross that Gulliver narrowly avoided when he landed in Japan from Laputa.[8] With the Manchu conquest in the 1640s China came under alien rule, and the new government embarked at once on a policy of exclusion, actually depopulating a long stretch of the southern coast, ostensibly to repel pirates but really, it must be suspected, to keep the restive southern Chinese from contact with the outside. China was thus insulated, while its rulers, barbarians at the outset, turned back into the blind alley of inner Asia to subdue Mongolia and eastern Turkestan. A few Jesuits at Peking provided the sole point of contact, as the Dutch traders did in Japan; they were tolerated for their astronomy, useful to official calendar-makers, but the converts they made soon got into serious trouble with the authorities.

India was never under such effective control as China, and its rulers cared little about sea or coast; but with Aurangzeb in the later seventeenth century, before the Mogul empire fell into confusion, Akbar's open-minded eclecticism was abandoned in favour of narrow Islamic orthodoxy, anti-Hindu and impervious to any fresh ideas from outside. Turkey and the other great Muslim power, Persia, which had a national revival in the early sixteenth century under the new Safavid dynasty, were both most receptive when strongest; but both were soon drying up. Forced on to the defensive in Europe after a second failure to capture Vienna in 1683, Turkey began to be pressed back by Austria and Russia, and to fall into a more negative mood, a siege mentality. All in all, during the interval between Europe's first and later bursts of expansion Asia's biggest countries were curling up like hedgehogs, failing to realize how Europe's technology was going ahead and how much they needed to learn from it. Their failure was deepened by their increased isolation from each other, partly through their own introversion, partly because the seas were controlled by Western ships or flayed by pirates. No great merchant fleets came to India from Ch'ing or Manchu China, as they had come in the time of the previous Ming dynasty. Turkey and Persia, Persia and India, still had contacts, but these mostly took the form of forays with old-fashioned armies or, from Persia, of old-fashioned poets.

The eighteenth-century outlook

Gulliver was a satire on how Europeans thought of and behaved to others, as well as on humanity as a whole. After his homecoming the traveller was told that he ought to have notified the English Government of all his discoveries, but he felt no wish to enlarge European domination, too often merely 'a free licence given to all acts of inhumanity and lust' — starting with a boat-load of pirates landing somewhere, killing some people, setting up 'a rotten plank, or a stone, for memorial' and getting a free pardon for their services to the empire.[9]

What was known about the earlier history of the Spanish American empire confirmed such criticism. Las Casas's book on *The Destruction of the Indies* had been translated into many languages, partly but not only for purposes of anti-Spanish propaganda. Similar crimes were heard of from Bengal after the fateful skirmish of Plassey in 1757 put it at the mercy of the East India Company. Adam Smith thought of Europe as the *magna virum mater*, the mighty mother of men, and of the European character as uniquely capable of grand designs. That the result of its conquests for the peoples subdued by it had hitherto been unmitigated evil seemed to him too obvious for argument.[10] Europe's crimes had indeed been, and were to be again, as gigantic as its achievements, and some of them as unparalleled.

At home inside Europe, too, aggression and bloodshed were too common. In the later eighteenth century thinking men were in a chastened mood over the spectacle of its blighting wars, which often seemed to have no reason but royal ambition. Anti-war feeling grew in France and Europe after the Seven Years' War of 1756-63, when Canada and the French foothold in India were lost to Britain; and in Britain and Europe after the War of American Independence, which brought on another European conflict. The mood was strongest among the French. They had no new possession like Bengal to make up for what they had lost, and as their belated revolution of 1789 drew nearer they were conscious of how far they had fallen, politically and economically, behind the English. Many of the most perceptive travellers of the age were Frenchmen, whereas Dutchmen and Englishmen in Asia were apt to look at native peoples with boorish contempt or indifference.[11] Frenchmen could look at Asians as interesting foreigners, instead of looking down on them, because France owned no colonies worth mentioning in Asia until the later nineteenth century.

This was not unconnected with the fact that in Europe Frenchmen were the leading spirits in the Enlightenment of the eighteenth century. One feature of it was a willingness to recognize civilizations outside Europe as fellow-members of a human family, equal or even superior to Europe in some of their attainments. The *Philosophes* thought, or liked to think they did, as citizens of the world, bounded by no narrower frontiers than those of all humanity.[12] In material achievement Europe was not yet vastly ahead of the most advanced countries of Asia, though already further ahead than most men realized. Asia was known to have its barbarians, its illiterate masses, its swarms of beggars, but so had Europe. What these intellectuals of an aristocratic society were predisposed to look for and to admire was something resembling themselves, a class of men of enlarged minds and sympathies benevolently guiding ordinary mankind.

There was nothing of the kind in neighbouring Turkey, which was only too much like unreformed Europe, warlike and unintellectual. But far away in little-known China there did appear to be a class of enlightened men, occupying a higher station than in Europe — with power to direct and control, not merely advise, as intellectuals always feel they ought to have. On the strength of Jesuit reports from Peking, somewhat rose-coloured in complexion, the Celestial

Empire was taken almost at its own valuation, as a model of how a vast region could be peacefully guided by a high-minded administration.[13] Tranquil and unwarlike, it made an attractive contrast with army-trampled Europe. Even its exports, tea, silk and porcelain, breathed the blandness and suavity of its supposed life.

In a more modest way China enjoyed a vogue in tea-drinking England too. When Goldsmith wanted to expound the creed of reason and benevolence he took as his mouthpiece an itinerant Chinese sage, who had seen many lands and learned 'to find nothing truly ridiculous but villainy and vice'. All civilization was one at heart, just as savages everywhere had only 'one character of imprudence and rapacity.'[14] England was more concerned with India, and for a time the Brahmin was looked upon as a personage of the same order as the scholar-magistrate of China. Sterne was surprised to see a monk at Calais with a noble, lofty countenance — 'but it would have suited a Brahmin, and had I met it upon the plains of Indostan, I had reverenced it'.[15] Brahmins were supposed to be the repository of a profound philosophy; their learned language, Sanskrit, was being studied and vastly admired, and its affinities with the classical languages of Europe revealed. Lord Monboddo convinced himself that the Greeks got their language from Egypt, which probably got it from India.[16] It was only eight years after Plassey when Sterne saw his monk. As the occupation of India proceeded, familiarity bred contempt, both because the average Brahmin was not after all a very admirable being, and because his English masters were no longer in a humour to admire anything Indian. In Asia at large Englishmen rummaging in search of profits were coming to see it more crudely, but in some ways more realistically, than the French theorists. A novelist out to extol the hard-working bourgeois decried the lounging English aristocrat as one of a great fraternity of drones including 'the monks of every country, the Dervishes of Persia, the Bramins of India, the Mandarins of China and the Gentlemen of these free and polished nations'.[17]

At the opposite end of the scale from the polished idler was the Noble Savage, another figure who haunted that age, and another compound of its open-mindedness and self-deception. It too originated in France, with Rousseau's essay of 1753 on Inequality, and it too suited the mood of a middle class pining for 'freedom', a Europe burdened with its own complexities. Commonly the ordinary man, in or out of Europe, was regarded as a born Caliban, only redeemable by paternal control. But perhaps on the contrary what he was suffering from was too much control, too much artificiality and class division. If so, man in his primitive condition might be expected to exhibit naturally the virtues that civilized men had to toil painfully for. The idea went through many metamorphoses, and Noble Savages turned up in all sorts of places, like the lost tribes of Israel; at this stage the Red Indian was a favourite candidate. Another English novelist had a hero reared among Red Indians, though (like Tarzan) heir to a noble estate in England, who brought back with him from the forests their simple and natural good feeling.[18] Disillusionment soon crept in here too.

Again Europe might partly have itself to blame, by its interference with other peoples; but at any rate primitive man was to prove as little able to resist European brandy as India or China to resist European batteries.

The nineteenth century

World domination

Between 1792 and 1815 Europe was engrossed with the wars of the French Revolution and Napoleon, and most of it was cut off from the outer world. Russia went on foraging eastward, and Britain, to make up for the loss of its American colonies and its exclusion from Europe, had a free run of every-one else's colonies, besides pushing on in India. Britain thus got a long lead over all rivals, which it kept through the century. The wars were followed by a second and greater loss of European power abroad, the winning of indepen-dence by Spanish America and the peaceful severance of Brazil from Portugal. In this case too the absence of European unity was important. Three countries had helped Washington to defeat George III; and when Ferdinand VII of Spain begged for combined assistance against his rebels, and Alexander of Russia was eager to strengthen the Holy Alliance by giving it, Britain had its own motives for frustrating the scheme.

Europe had lost two empires, but the European race had lost nothing, and the other continents now seemed positively to invite attack. Their feebleness must have done as much as European ambition to cause fresh empires to spring up. Asia had to all appearance lost the faculty of self-renewal. Obstacles that retarded technology in Western lands like Spain were exaggeratedly present there: rigid ideologies and social patterns, governments suspicious of change, absence of a bourgeois middle class. Westerners impregnated with their new ethos of change, progress, energy, invested Commerce with the same divine right that monarchy formerly claimed, and were irresistibly tempted to resort to force. They could feel that by doing so they were doing right, as the French Revolutionary armies marching over Europe and carrying liberty on their bay-onets had felt. To knock down decrepit régimes was to liberate peoples from the crushing burden of their past. In the first stage of European expansion Spain and Portugal thought of making a return to benighted regions for what they took from them, by giving them Christianity. Now there was again a feeling that expansion ought to have some ideal purpose, a goal beyond sordid greed, which came to be expressed in the phrase 'civilizing mission'. Backward lands would be given civilization, in return for the products wanted by Europe; Christianity might be part of it, though a subsidiary one. The idea of Europe's 'mission' dawned early,[19] but was taken up seriously in the nineteenth century. Turkey, China, and the rest would some day be prosperous, wrote Winwood Reade, one of the most sympathetic Westerners. 'But those people will never begin to advance . . . until they enjoy the rights of man; and these they will never obtain except by means of European conquest.'[20]

The idea was not entirely fallacious, but Europeans in Asia or Africa, like French armies in Europe, more than half falsified it by their other, more squalid motives. This happened all the more blatantly because often official Europe was preceded by private adventurers, rude pioneers of free enterprise, who hung on the skirts of decaying kingdoms or pressed into the wide areas where there was little settled rule. They might be under loose authority of distant governments, as in Siberia or on the American prairies; or bodies of men acknowledging some rough authority of their own like the Boer trekkers in South Africa. Some were individuals who took service with one faction against another, like the Frenchmen from Pondicherry who helped the last dynasty of Vietnam to get into the saddle, or the Americans employed in China against the Taiping rebellion, who dreamed of a principality of their own. Worst of all were the men under no kind of authority, successors to the buccaneers of the previous age. Piracy as a full-time profession was being left to Malays and other races, but these Europeans were pirates, traders, grabbers and settlers, by turns.

They spread far and wide, round Africa, among the Pacific islands, and gave the world a picture of Western civilization very much like the picture of Islam that Arab slave-dealers gave. Yet Europe's conviction of being the only really civilized region was becoming so strong that even its offscourings, these Ishmaels of the seven seas, carried it with them, and were fortified by it in their lawlessness. Whatever a white man did must in some grotesque fashion be 'civilized'. An opium smuggler, who could not help feeling shocked when he saw the 'shrivelled and shrunken carcasses' produced by the drug, landed on one occasion on Formosa with his men, had a fight, burned a village, plundered a junk, and removed its ammunition because 'there was no knowing how much they might yet require, before the natives were brought into submission to our superior civilization.'[21] Ruskin complained that some of the bigger men who had been selling opium at the point of the cannon were buying respectable estates in England.[22] At the end of the century the whole mob of adventurers had an apotheosis in King Leopold of the Belgians, building a private empire in central Africa with blood and iron.

India itself, the Mexico and Peru of the modern world, and the bridge between earlier and later imperialism, was acquired by a joint-stock company, whose morals before it was gradually brought under public control were not much better than the vagrant trader's with his glass beads and gun. It was a startling illustration of how haphazard, how unthinking, was Europe's approach to the world, in spite of the civilizing mission. Only by slow degrees was reckless plundering tempered by something closer to the better ideals of the Roman empire, so much a part of western Europe's education and consciousness. The conquest of India, spread over the century from Plassey to the Mutiny, was the main stride towards European domination of Asia, and most of the others followed from it. British power there radiated from India; other territories were taken with the help of Indian troops, often at the expense of the Indian taxpayer. Psychologically the effect was even greater. Wherever else the Briton went he felt and spoke as representative of the power at whose feet crouched a hundred million Hindus; he saw other 'natives' as so many crouching Hindus in different disguises.

So much of Britain's attention was drawn off to the East that from the fall of Napoleon in 1815 to the Anglo-French *Entente* of 1904 it was more often than not an absentee from European affairs, except for Palmerstonian games of bluff to amuse middle-class voters and, more seriously, engagement in the tangle of Turkish problems that were known as the Eastern Question. If Russia was sometimes held to belong rather to Asia, and Africa was humorously said to begin at the Pyrenees, Britain often appeared to belong to all the other continents more than to Europe; or appeared to itself, with its growing family of White colonies, a continent of its own. Empire meant for Britain a turning away from the rest of Europe as well as a turning towards the rest of the world. It was through most of the century Turkey's prop against Russia, and in 1902 it set a new precedent — followed later by Hitler — by an alliance with Japan.

France and Russia were Britain's chief rivals. Both looked alternately, as Spain had done, inward on Europe and outward on the world. Between Russia and Britain there was a trail of jealousies and recriminations from the Black Sea to the Pacific. Quarrels arose almost everywhere between France and Britain. Napoleon would have liked an empire beyond Europe too; after his Egyptian campaign of 1799 the East always fascinated him, as the grandest field of action for men like Alexander or himself. But he and France were faithful to the tradition of Louis XIV, and put Europe first. After Waterloo the French began to pick up crumbs in Africa for consolation; again after 1870, when Europe was bestridden by its new Colossus, the German army. Even then French interest in colonies had to be nursed by assiduous propaganda, chiefly by financial interests, and the old belief that power or influence outside Europe was something second-rate never entirely faded.

Hardly any European countries had significant connections, other than imperial, with any continent except America. Towards the end of the century, the 'age of imperialism' proper, a craze for annexations seized on everyone who had any chance, and Italy, Germany, Belgium all got shares, with the USA joining in. Individual businessmen were obviously doing well out of colonies; nations were easily tutored into believing (nearly always mistakenly) that they could do equally well, especially when they saw that all their neighbours believed it. The civilizing mission was now all the rage, whereas in earlier years it had often been rejected as too expensive. It was easiest of all to believe that what was good for Europe must be even better for the 'natives'. But now the white man had worked himself into a high state of self-conceit; but all through the century his reaction to any natives who tried to reject the blessings of civilized rule was that of Dr Johnson to the rebel Americans: 'They are a race of convicts, and ought to be thankful for any thing we allow them short of hanging'.[23]

Only those countries were able to cling to their independence that already had some national tradition and consciousness, besides some advantage of size or situation. Turkey had the rudiments of nationhood, partly from intercourse with Europe, though only at the end of the Great War did a true Turkish nation crystallize out of a lost Ottoman empire. Persia hung on precariously; but neither of these two made much internal progress, and practically all the rest of Islam, with its medley of peoples and its non-national structure, went under. It kept its identity by wrapping itself round and round in religion, as Hindu India under Muslim rule had done, thus falling still further behind. Africa, nibbled at from early in the century, was swallowed up entirely in the final scramble, with the exception of the ancient and mountainous kingdom of Abyssinia. It was in the Far East that nationality was best developed, and there modern nationalism could be grafted most successfully on to it, and modern technology adopted. Japan alone accomplished this in any radical way before 1914. China owed its survival partly to its vastness, though this helped to make it a slow and painful learner compared with Japan. But China's national unity was another factor, which delayed armed attack on it until 1839 when the conquest of India was almost at an end. In the Far East there was also the advantage that rival Western ambitions counteracted one another. Siam owed its survival to this.

In the course of their rivalries Europeans exchanged many hard words, and sometimes abused each other in order to please a non-European people. An Englishman in Haiti was indignant at the 'John Bull with the large and taloned hands, the creation of the French caricaturists'.[24] An Englishman in China, no admirer of that country, declared that China was 'certainly far more civilized than Russia'.[25] Russians deplored Britain's parasitic rule in India, directed as one wrote to 'profit and not civilization'.[26] They might all sympathize with one another's 'rebels'. But when it came to any serious colonial upheaval, white men felt their kinship, and Europe drew together. In 1857 its sympathies were mostly with Britain against the Indian sepoys;[27] it heard of course only of atrocities on one side. In 1900 there was united military action to put down the 'Boxers' in China. Above all, and very remarkably, despite innumerable crises over rival claims the European countries managed from the War of American Independence onward to avoid a single colonial war among themselves. (The Crimean War was fought partly in and because of Asia, and in the Russo-Japanese War Britain was a sleeping partner.) To this degree Europe had grown more solid than in its earlier days of chronic colonial wars, and better able to come before the world as one civilization.

Meanwhile, thanks in part to the resources it drew from other continents, it was able to expand in another way, building up its population to an unprecedented height without running into serious famines except at its two wretched extremities, Russia at one end, Ireland and Spain at the other. Facility of emigration was another safeguard, and the USA, free from Britain, attracted emigrants from all lands and became a second Europe instead of, like Australia, a second Britain. When its overseas members are counted in, it can be estimated that the 'white race' grew from about 22 per cent of the earth's population in

1800 to about 35 per cent in 1930.[28] In terms of wealth and power it grew by comparison with the rest infinitely more.

Of fourteen sovereign states in the Europe of 1914, excluding the Balkans, eight had – and a ninth, Spain, had until lately – considerable possessions outside. In many indirect ways the entire continent shared, as Adam Smith had pointed out long before, in the colonial contribution to trade and wealth.[29] In the realm of knowledge, too, exploration and research in a dozen fields enriched the common stock. But though retarded nations like Spain or Portugal might plume themselves on belonging to Europe and sharing in its triumphant progress, grave inequalities within Europe, as well as between Europe and the rest, were being accentuated. As a class the rich grew richer far more quickly than the poor became less poor; as a nation France drew further ahead of Spain, Germany of Russia.

Europeans of superior countries thought of inferior Europeans and non-Europeans in not very different terms. Travellers described their journeys through Spain, before the railways, as if Madrid were somewhere near Timbuctoo. Stereotypes such as the Englishman's image of Paddy the Irishman, a feckless nimble-tongued fellow at whom one felt a mixture of amusement and impatience – or of the Italian as an organ-grinder with a monkey – provided ready-made categories for Burmese or Malays to be fitted into. And if the 'native' on occasion reminded the Englishman of his familiar Paddy, Paddy might sometimes remind him of the native. Lord Salisbury, the Conservative leader, supporting coercion in Ireland, said that Irishmen were as unfit for self-government as Hottentots.[30] Ireland was subject politically and economically to England, Italy through much of the nineteenth century to Austria. Down to 1918 a large proportion of Europeans occupied a more or less colonial status, differing only in degree from that of the Asian or African countries that were annexed. There is a story of the Austrian representative saying to the Hungarian, when the Hapsburg empire was transformed into the Dual Monarchy in 1867, 'You look after your barbarians, and we'll look after ours' – meaning the Czechs, Serbs and so on. Treatment of these subject minorities was not always gentler than in colonies outside, and must have been roughened by the habits formed by Europe's ruling classes in dictating to the other continents.

It could be expected that unfree Europeans would have some fellow-feeling for the colonial peoples. Occasionally they did. Irish employees in Scotland Yard are said to have aided Indian nationalists to smuggle their literature.[31] But in general ignorance or indifference, or 'European' feeling, prevailed. Ireland took a share in the rewards by helping to conquer and manage Britain's empire. It was as a socialist, much more than an Irishman, that James Connolly denounced the empire and its war in 1914.

In the years of drift towards the catastrophe of 1914 nationalist movements against Europe were gathering up and down Asia, while others, and the socialist movement, struggled against the established order at home. At the zenith of its physical power in the world, Europe was at the nadir of its moral capacity to lead it, or even to reform itself.

Notes

(The place of publication of works cited, when not given below, may be assumed to be London.)

1 See my article on 'State and nation in Western Europe', *Past and Present*, no. 31 (July 1965).
2 The *Nakaz* or Instruction of 1767, ch. 1, para. 6, in W. F. Reddaway, *Documents of Catherine the Great* (Cambridge 1931).
3 Compte P. de Ségur, *Un Aide de Camp de Napoléon* (1873), pp. 288, 358, 360; *La Campagne de Russie* (1824). Introduction, and pp. 111, 149-50, 198-9, 250-1 (Nelson editions, Paris). Progressive Russians were sensitive to the imputation. 'We too are Europeans,' wrote S. Stepniak. 'For to be a Russian does not involve counting oneself an Asiatic . . .' (*Nihilism as it is*: pamphlets, trans. E. L. Voynich, n.d., p. 63).
4 O. Sitwell, *The Four Continents* (1955), pp. 20-3.
5 M. N. Pavlovsky, *Chinese-Russian Relations* (New York 1949), p. 102. Mongol had previously been used as the medium.
6 G. A. Lensen, *The Russian Push towards Japan* (Princeton 1959), p. 29.
7 P. Gosse, *The History of Piracy* (2nd edn 1954), pp. 200-1.
8 cf. the satirical picture of Dutch grovelling to Japan in Oliver Goldsmith, *The Citizen of the World* (1762), p. 314 (Everyman edn).
9 Jonathan Swift, *Gulliver's Travels* (1726), 'The country of the Houyhnhnms', ch. 12.
10 *The Wealth of Nations* (1776), vol. 2, p. 192 (World's Classics edn).
11 I owe this point to my friend Mr A. Jenkin, of the British Museum, who can be turned to for guidance on almost any epoch of history.
12 See Alexis de Tocqueville, *The State of Society in France before the Revolution* (2nd English edn 1873), book III, para. 2.
13 See G. F. Hudson, *Europe and China* (1931), p. 317, etc.; L. Dermigny, *La Chine et l'Occident. Le Commerce à Canton au xviiie siècle*, 1719-1833 (Paris 1964), vol. 1, ch. 1.
14 Oliver Goldsmith, *The Citizen of the World*, p. 10, and Pref.
15 Laurence Sterne, *A Sentimental Journey* (1768): opening section, on Calais.
16 W. Knight, *Lord Monboddo and some of his Contemporaries* (1900), p. 270.
17 Henry Brooke, *The Fool of Quality, or, the History of Henry Earl of Moreland* (2nd edn 1767), vol. 1, p. 157. I owe this, and the next reference, to Dr G. P. Tripathi of Patna University.
18 Robert Bage, *Hermsprong; or, Man as he is not* (1796).
19 H. Kohn, *The Idea of Nationalism*, p. 194, refers to the advocacy of a French presence in India by F. Charpentier, as early as 1664.
20 W. Reade, *The Martyrdom of Man* (1872), pp. 414-15 (Thinker's Library edn).
21 L. Anderson, *A Cruise in an Opium Clipper* (1891), ch. 33. cf. the young

Frenchman in Balzac's *Eugénie Grandet* (1833), who makes a fortune in the Indies by slave-trading and general wickedness.

22 John Ruskin, *Sesame and Lilies* (1865), p. 59 (1882 edn).

23 Boswell, *The Life of Samuel Johnson*, vol. 2, p. 111 (Dent edn 1926).

24 H. H. Prichard, *Where Black Rules White* (2nd edn 1910), p. 328.

25 A. Little, *Gleanings from Fifty Years in China* (1910), p. 52.

26 Cited by P. Shastiko, 'Russian press on 1857', in *Rebellion 1857,* ed. P. C. Joshi (Delhi 1957), p. 334.

27 ibid., Part 3. Radicals, e.g. in Russia, sometimes sympathized with the sepoys.

28 Cited by C. Cipolla, *The Economic History of World Population* (1962), pp. 102-4.

29 *The Wealth of Nations*, vol. 2, pp. 192-3.

30 J. L. Garvin, *The Life of Joseph Chamberlain*, vol. 1 (1933), p. 239.

31 D. Keer, *Veer Savarkar* (Bombay 1966), p. 49.

2 First impressions: initial English confrontations with Africans*

Winthrop D. Jordan

When the Atlantic nations of Europe began expanding overseas in the sixteenth century, Portugal led the way to Africa and to the east while Spain founded a great empire in America. It was not until the reign of Queen Elizabeth that Englishmen came to realize that overseas exploration and plantations could bring home wealth, power, glory, and fascinating information. By the early years of the seventeenth century Englishmen had developed a taste for empire and for tales of adventure and discovery. More than is usual in human affairs, one man, the great chronicler Richard Hakluyt, had roused enthusiasm for western planting and had stirred the nation with his monumental compilation, *The Principal Navigations, Voyages, Traffiques and Discoveries of the English Nation.* Here was a work to widen a people's horizons. Its exhilarating accounts of voyages to all quarters of the globe constituted a national hymn, a scientific treatise, a sermon, and an adventure story.

English voyagers did not touch upon the shores of West Africa until after 1550, nearly a century after Prince Henry the Navigator had mounted the sustained Portuguese thrust southward for a water passage to the Orient. Usually Englishmen came to Africa to trade goods *with* the natives. The earliest English descriptions of West Africa were written by adventurous traders, men who had no special interest in converting the natives or, except for the famous Hawkins voyages in the 1560s, in otherwise laying hands on them. Extensive English participation in the slave trade did not develop until well into the seventeenth century. Initially English contact with Africans did not take place primarily in a context which prejudged the Negro as a slave, at least not as a slave of Englishmen. Rather, Englishmen met Africans merely as another sort of men.

Englishmen found the peoples of Africa very different from themselves. 'Negroes' looked different to Englishmen; their religion was un-Christian; their manner of living was anything but English; they seemed to be a particularly libidinous sort of people. All these clusters of perceptions were related to each other, though they may be spread apart for inspection, and they were related also to the circumstances of contact in Africa, to previously accumulated

* Reprinted from *The White Man's Burden* (Oxford University Press 1974), pp. 3-25.

traditions concerning that strange and distant continent, and to certain special qualities of English society on the eve of its expansion into the New World.

The blackness without

For Englishmen, the most arresting characteristic of the newly discovered African was his colour. Travellers rarely failed to comment upon it; indeed when describing Africans they frequently began with complexion and then moved on to dress (or, as they saw, lack of it) and manners. At Cape Verde, 'These people are all blacke, and are called Negroes, without any apparell, saving before their privities.' Robert Baker's narrative poem recounting his two voyages to the West African coast in 1562 and 1563 introduced the people he saw with these engaging lines:

> And entering in [a river], we see
> a number of blacke soules,
> Whose likelinesse seem'd men to be,
> but all as blacke as coles.
> Their Captain comes to me
> as naked as my naile,
> Not having witte or honestie
> to cover once his taile.

Englishmen actually described Negroes as *black* — an exaggerated term which in itself suggests that the Negro's complexion had powerful impact upon their perceptions. Even the peoples of northern Africa seemed so dark that Englishmen tended to call them 'black' and let further refinements go by the board. In Shakespeare's day, the Moors, including Othello, were commonly portrayed as pitchy black and the terms *Moor* and *Negro* were used almost interchangeably. With curious inconsistency, however, Englishmen recognized that Africans south of the Sahara were not at all the same people as the much more familiar Moors. Sometimes they referred to West Africans as 'black Moors' to distinguish them from the peoples of North Africa.

The powerful impact which the Negro's colour made upon Englishmen must have been partly owing to suddenness of contact. Though the Bible as well as the arts and literature of antiquity and the Middle Ages offered some slight introduction to the 'Ethiope', England's immediate acquaintance with 'black' skinned peoples came with relative rapidity. People much darker than Englishmen were not entirely unfamiliar, but really 'black' men were virtually unknown except as vaguely referred to in the hazy literature about the sub-Sahara which had filtered down from antiquity. Native West Africans probably first appeared in London in 1554; in that year five 'Negroes,' as one trader reported, were taken to England, 'kept till they could speake the language,' and then brought back again 'to be a helpe to Englishmen' who were engaged in trade with Africans on the coast. Hakluyt's later discussion of these Africans suggests that these 'blacke Moores' were a novelty to Englishmen. In this respect the English experience was markedly different from that of the Spanish and Portuguese who for centuries had been in close contact with North Africa and had actually been invaded and subjected by people both darker and more 'highly civilized' than themselves. The impact of the Negro's colour was the more powerful upon Englishmen, moreover, because England's principal contact with Africans came in West Africa and the Congo, which meant that one of the lightest-skinned of the earth's peoples suddenly came face to face with one of the darkest.

In England perhaps more than in southern Europe, the concept of blackness was loaded with intense meaning. Long before they found that some men were black, Englishmen found in the idea of blackness a way of expressing some of their most ingrained values. No other colour except white conveyed so much emotional impact. As described by the *Oxford English Dictionary*, the meaning of *black* before the sixteenth century included, 'Deeply stained with dirt; soiled, dirty, foul. . . . Having dark or deadly purposes, malignant; pertaining to or involving death, deadly; baneful, disastrous, sinister. . . . Foul, iniquitous, atrocious, horrible, wicked. . . . Indicating disgrace, censure, liability to punishment, etc.' Black was an emotionally partisan colour, the handmaid and symbol of baseness and evil, a sign of danger and repulsion.

Embedded in the concept of blackness was its direct opposite – whiteness. No other colours so clearly implied opposition, 'beinge coloures utterlye contrary':

> Everye white will have its blacke,
> And everye sweete its sowre.

White and black connoted purity and filthiness, virginity and sin, virtue and baseness, beauty and ugliness, beneficence and evil, God and the devil. Whiteness, moreover, carried a special significance for Elizabethan Englishmen: it was, particularly when complemented by red, the colour of perfect human beauty, especially *female* beauty. This ideal was already centuries old in Elizabeth's time, and their fair Queen was its very embodiment: her cheeks were 'roses in a bed of lillies'. (Elizabeth was naturally pale but like many ladies then and since she freshened her 'lillies' at the cosmetic table.) An adoring nation knew precisely what a beautiful Queen looked like.

> Her cheeke, her chinne, her neck, her nose,
> This was a lillye, that was a rose;
> Her bosome, sleeke as Paris plaster,
> Held upp twoo bowles of Alabaster.

By contrast, the Negro was ugly, by reason of his colour and also his 'horrid Curles' and 'disfigured' lips and nose. A century later blackness still required apology: one of the earliest attempts to delineate the West African as a heroic character, the popular story *Oroonoko* (1688), presented Negroes as capable of blushing and turning pale. It was important, if incalculably so, that English discovery of black Africans came at a time when the accepted English standard of ideal beauty was a fair complexion of rose and white. Negroes seemed the very picture of perverse negation.

From the first, however, many English observers displayed a certain sophistication about the Negro's colour. Despite an ethnocentric tendency to find blackness repulsive, many writers were fully aware that Africans themselves might have different tastes. As early as 1621 one writer told of the 'Jetty coloured' Negroes, 'Who in their native beauty most delight, /And in contempt doe paint the Divell white'; this assertion became almost a commonplace. Many accounts of Africa reported explicitly that the Negro's preference in colours was inverse to the European's. Even the Negro's features were conceded to be appealing to Negroes.

The causes of complexion

Black human beings were not only startling but extremely puzzling. The complexion of Africans posed problems about its nature, especially its permanence and utility, its cause and origin, and its significance. Although these were rather separate questions, there was a pronounced tendency among Englishmen and other Europeans to formulate the problem in terms of causation alone. If the cause of human blackness could be explained, then its nature and significance would follow.

Not that the problem was completely novel. The ancient Greeks had touched upon it. The story of Phaëton's driving the chariot sun wildly through the heavens apparently served as an explanation for the Ethiopian's blackness even before written records, and traces of this ancient fable were still drifting about during the seventeenth century. Ptolemy had made the important suggestion that the Negro's blackness and woolly hair were caused by exposure to the hot sun and had pointed out that people in northern climates were white and those in temperate areas an intermediate colour. Before the sixteenth century, though, the question of the Negro's colour can hardly be said to have drawn the attention of Englishmen or indeed of Europeans generally.

The discovery of West Africa and the development of Negro slavery made the question far more urgent. The range of possible answers was rigidly restricted, however, by the virtually universal assumption, dictated by Church and Scripture, that all mankind stemmed from a single source. Indeed it is impossible fully to understand the various efforts at explaining the Negro's complexion without bearing in mind the strength of the tradition which in 1614 made the chronicler, the Reverend Samuel Purchas, proclaim vehemently, 'The tawney Moore, blacke Negro, duskie Libyan, ash-coloured Indian, olive-coloured American, should with the white European become one *sheep-fold*, under *one great Sheepheard* . . . without any more distinction of Colour, Nation, Language, Sexe, Condition, all may bee *One* in him that is One. . . .'

In general, the most satisfactory answer to the problem was some sort of reference to the action of the sun, whether the sun was assumed to have scorched the skin, drawn the bile, or blackened the blood. People living on the Line had obviously been getting too much of it; after all, even Englishmen were darkened by a little exposure. How much more, then, with the Negroes who were 'so scorched and vexed with the heat of the sunne, that in many places they curse it when it riseth'. This association of the Negro's colour with the sun became a commonplace in Elizabethan literature; as Shakespeare's Prince of Morocco apologized, 'Mislike me not for my complexion,/The shadow'd livery of the burnish'd sun,/To whom I am a neighbour and near bred.'

Unfortunately this theory ran headlong into a stubborn fact of nature which simply could not be overridden: if the equatorial inhabitants of Africa were blackened by the sun, why not the people living on the same Line in America? Logic required them to be the same colour. Yet by the middle of the sixteenth century it was becoming perfectly apparent that the Indians living in the hottest regions of the New World could by no stretch of the imagination be described as black. They were 'olive' or 'tawny,' and moreover they had long hair rather than the curious 'wool' of Negroes. Clearly the method of accounting for human complexion by latitude just did not work. The worst of it was that the formula did not seem altogether wrong, since it was apparent that in general men in hot climates tended to be darker than in cold ones.

Another difficulty with the climatic explanation of skin colour arose as lengthening experience provided more knowledge about Negroes. If the heat of the sun caused the Negro's blackness, then his removal to cold northerly countries ought to result in his losing it; even if he did not himself surrender his peculiar colour, surely his descendants must. By the mid-seventeenth century it was becoming increasingly apparent that this expectation was ill founded: Negroes in Europe and northern America were simply not whitening up very noticeably.

From the beginning, in fact, some Englishmen were certain that the Negro's blackness was permanent and innate and that no amount of cold was going to alter it. There was good authority in Jeremiah 13:23: 'Can the Ethiopian change his skin/or the leopard his spots?' Elizabethan dramatists used the stock expression 'to wash an Ethiop white' as indicating sheer impossibility. In 1578 a voyager and speculative geographer, George Best, announced that the blackness of Negroes 'proceedeth of some naturall infection of the first inhabitants of that country, and so all the whole progenie of them descended, are still polluted with the same blot of infection'. An essayist in 1695 declared firmly, 'A negroe will always be a negroe, carry him to Greenland, give him chalk, feed and manage him never so many ways.'

There was an alternative to the naturalistic explanations of the Negro's blackness. Some writers felt that God's curse on Ham (Cham), or upon his son

Canaan, and all their descendants was entirely sufficient to account for the colour of Negroes. This could be an appealing explanation, especially for men like George Best who wished to stress the 'natural infection' of blackness and for those who hoped to incorporate the Negro's complexion securely within the accepted history of mankind. The original story in Genesis 9 and 10 was that after the Flood, Ham had looked upon his father's 'nakedness' as Noah lay drunk in his tent, but the other two sons, Shem and Japheth, had covered their father without looking upon him; when Noah awoke he cursed Canaan, son of Ham, saying that he would be a 'servant of servants' unto his brothers. Given this text, the question becomes why a tale which logically implied slavery but absolutely nothing about skin colour should have become a popular explanation of the Negro's blackness. The matter is puzzling, but probably, over the very long run, the story was supported by the ancient association of heat with sensuality and by the fact that some sub-Saharan Africans had been enslaved by Europeans since ancient times. In addition, the extraordinary persistence of the tale in the face of centuries of constant refutation was probably sustained by a feeling that blackness could scarcely be anything *but* a curse and by the common need to confirm the facts of nature by specific reference to Scripture. In contrast to the climatic theory, God's curse provided a satisfying purposiveness which the sun's scorching heat could not match until the eighteenth century.

In the long run, of course, the Negro's colour attained greatest significance not as a scientific problem but as a social fact. Englishmen found blackness in human beings a peculiar and important point of difference. The African's colour set him radically *apart* from Englishmen. But then, distant Africa had been known to Christians for ages as a land of men radically different in religion.

Defective religion

While distinctive appearance set Africans apart in a novel way, their religious condition distinguished them in a more familiar manner. Englishmen and Christians everywhere were sufficiently acquainted with the concept of heathenism that they confronted its living representatives without puzzlement. Certainly the rather sudden discovery that the world was teeming with heathen people made for heightened vividness and urgency in a long-standing problem; but it was the fact that this problem was already well formulated long before contact with Africa which proved important in shaping English reaction to the Negro's defective religious condition.

In one sense heathenism was less a 'problem' for Christians than an exercise in self-definition: the heathen condition defined by negation the proper Christian life. In another sense, the presence of heathenism in the world constituted an imperative to intensification of religious commitment. From its origin Christianity was a universalist, proselytizing religion, and the sacred and secular histories of Christianity made manifest the necessity of bringing non-Christians into the fold.

For Englishmen, then, the heathenism of Negroes was at once a counter-image of their own religion and a summons to eradicate an important distinction between the two peoples. Yet the interaction of these two facets of the concept of heathenism made for a peculiar difficulty. On the one hand, to act upon the felt necessity of converting Africans would have been to eradicate the point of distinction which Englishmen found most familiar and most readily comprehensible. Yet if they did not act upon this necessity, continued heathenism among Negroes would remain an unwelcome reminder to Englishmen that they were not meeting their obligations to their own faith — nor to the benighted Negroes. Englishmen resolved this implicit dilemma by doing nothing.

Considering the strength of the Christian tradition, it is almost startling that Englishmen failed to respond to the discovery of heathenism in Africa with at least the rudiments of a campaign for conversion. Although the impulse to spread Christianity seems to have been weaker in Englishmen than, say, in the Catholic Portuguese, it cannot be said that Englishmen were indifferent to the obligation imposed upon them by the overseas discoveries of the sixteenth century. While they were badly out of practice at the business of conversion (again in contrast to the Portuguese) and while they had never been faced with the practical difficulties involved in Christianizing entire continents, they nonetheless were able to contemplate with equanimity and even eagerness the prospect of converting the heathen. Indeed they went so far as to conclude that converting the natives in America was sufficiently important to demand English settlement there. As it turned out, the well-publicized English programme for converting Indians produced very meagre results, but the avowed intentions certainly were genuine. It was in marked contrast, therefore, that Englishmen did not avow similar intentions concerning Africans until the late eighteenth century. Fully as much as with skin colour, though less consciously, Englishmen distinguished between the heathenisms of Indians and Negroes.

It is not easy to account for the distinction which Englishmen made. On the basis of the travellers' reports there was no reason for Englishmen to suppose Indians inherently superior to Negroes as candidates for conversion. But America was not Africa. Englishmen contemplated settling in America, where voyagers had established the King's claim and where supposedly the climate was temperate; in contrast, Englishmen did not envision settlement in Africa, which had quickly gained notoriety as a graveyard for Europeans and where the Portuguese had been first on the scene. Certainly these very different circumstances meant that Englishmen confronted Negroes and Indians in radically different social contexts and that Englishmen would find it far easier to contemplate converting Indians than Negroes. Yet it remains difficult to see why Negroes were not included, at least as a secondary target. The fact that English contact with Africans so frequently occurred in a context of slave dealing does not entirely explain the omission of Negroes, since in that same context the Portuguese and Spanish did sometimes attempt to minister to the souls of Africans and since Englishmen in America enslaved Indians when good occasion arose. Given these circumstances, it is hard to escape the conclusion that the distinction which Englishmen made as to conversion was, at least in some small measure, modelled after the difference they saw in skin colour.

The most important aspect of English reaction to African heathenism was that Englishmen evidently did not regard it as separable from the Negro's other attributes. Heathenism was treated not so much as a specifically religious defect but as one manifestation of a general refusal to measure up to proper standards, as a failure to be English or even civilized. There was every reason for Englishmen to fuse the various attributes they found in Africans. During the first century of English contact with Africa, Protestant Christianity was an important element in English patriotism; especially during the struggle against Spain the Elizabethan's special Christianity was interwoven into his conception of his own nationality, and he was therefore inclined to regard the Negroes' lack of true religion as part of theirs. Being a Christian was not merely a matter of subscribing to certain doctrines; it was a quality inherent in oneself and in one's society. It was interconnected with all the other attributes of normal and proper men: as one of the earliest English travellers described Africans, they were 'a people of beastly living, without a God, lawe, or common wealth' − which was to say that Negroes were not Englishmen. Far from isolating African heathenism as a separate characteristic, English travellers sometimes linked it explicitly with blackness and savagery.

Savage behaviour

The condition of savagery − the failure to be civilized − set Negroes apart from Englishmen in an ill-defined but crucial fashion. Africans were *different* from Englishmen in so many ways: in their clothing, housing, farming, warfare, language, government, morals, and (not least important) in their table manners. To judge from the comments of voyagers, Englishmen had an unquenchable thirst for the details of savage life. Englishmen were, indeed, enormously curious about their rapidly expanding world, and it is scarcely surprising that they should have taken an interest in reports about cosmetic mutilation, polygamy, infanticide, ritual murder, and the like. In addition, reports about 'savages' began arriving at a time when Englishmen very much needed to be able to translate their apprehensive interest in an uncontrollable world out of medieval religious terms. The discovery of savages overseas enabled them to make this translation easily, to move from miracles to verifiable monstrosities, from heaven to earth.

As with skin colour, English reporting of African customs was partly an exercise in self-inspection by means of comparison. The necessity of continuously measuring African practices with an English yardstick of course tended to emphasize the differences between the two groups, but it also made for heightened sensitivity to instances of similarity. Thus the Englishman's ethnocentrism tended to distort his perception of African culture in two opposite directions. While it led him to emphasize differences and to condemn deviations from the English norm, it led him also to seek out similarities. Particularly, Englishmen were inclined to see the structures of African societies as analogous to their own, complete with kings, counsellors, gentlemen, and the baser sort. Here especially they found Africans like themselves, partly because they knew no other way to describe any society and partly because there was actually good basis for such a view of the social organization of West African communities.

Despite the fascination and self-instruction Englishmen derived from discussing the savage behaviour of Africans, they never felt that savagery was as important a quality in Africans as it was in the American Indians. As was the case with heathenism, contrasting social contexts played an important role in shaping the English response to savagery in the two peoples. Inevitably, the savagery of the Indians assumed a special significance in the minds of those actively engaged in a programme of planting civilization in the American wilderness. The case with the African was different; the English errand into Africa was not a new or a perfect community but a business trip. No hope was entertained for civilizing the Negro's steaming continent, so Englishmen lacked compelling reason to develop a programme for remodelling the African natives.

From the beginning, also, the importance of the Negro's savagery was muted by the Negro's colour. Englishmen could go a long way towards expressing their sense of being different from Africans merely by calling them 'black'. By contrast, the aboriginals in America did not have the appearance of being radically distinct from Europeans except in religion and savage behaviour. English voyagers placed much less emphasis upon the Indian's colour than upon the Negro's, and they never permitted the Indian's physiognomy to distract their attention from what they regarded as his essential quality, his savagery.

It would be a mistake, however, to slight the importance of what was seen as the African's savagery, since it fascinated Englishmen from the very first. English observers in West Africa were sometimes so profoundly impressed by the Negro's behaviour that they resorted to a powerful metaphor with which to express their own sense of difference from him. They knew perfectly well that Negroes were men, yet they frequently described the Africans as 'brutish' or 'bestial' or 'beastly'. The supposed hideous tortures, cannibalism, rapacious warfare, revolting diet (and so forth, page after page) seemed somehow to place the Negro among the beasts. The eventual circumstances of the Englishman's contact with Africans served to strengthen this feeling. Slave traders in Africa necessarily handled Negroes the same way men in England handled beasts, herding and examing and buying, as with any other animals which were products of commerce.

The apes of Africa

If Negroes were likened to beasts, there was in Africa a beast which was likened to men. It was a strange and eventually tragic accident of nature that Africa was the habitat of the animal which in appearance most resembles man. The animal called 'orang-outang' by contemporaries (actually the chimpanzee) was native to those parts of western Africa where the early slave trade was heavily concentrated. Though Englishmen were acquainted (for the most part vicariously) with monkeys and baboons, they were unfamiliar with tail-less apes who walked about like men. Accordingly, it happened that Englishmen were introduced to the anthropoid apes and to Negroes at the same time and in the same place. The startlingly human appearance and movements of the 'ape' – a generic term though often used as a synonym for the 'orang-outang' – aroused some curious speculations.

In large measure these speculations derived from traditions which had been accumulating in Western culture since ancient times. Medieval books on animals contained rosters of strange creatures who in one way or another seemed disturbingly to resemble men. There were the *simia* and the *cynocephali* and the *satyri* and the others, all variously described and related to one another, all jumbled in a characteristic blend of ancient reports and medieval morality. The confusion was not easily nor rapidly dispelled, and many of the traditions established by this literature were very much alive during the seventeenth century.

The section on apes in Edward Topsell's *Historie of Foure-Footed Beastes* (1607) serves to illustrate how certain seemingly trivial traditions and associations persisted in such form that they were bound to affect the way in which Englishmen would perceive the inhabitants of Africa. Above all, according to Topsell, 'apes' were venerous. The red apes were 'so venerous that they will ravish their Women.' Baboons were 'as lustful and venerous as goats'; a baboon which had been 'brought to the French king . . . above all loved the companie of women, and young maidens; his genitall member was greater than might match the quantity of his other parts'. Pictures of two varieties of apes, a 'Satyre' and an 'Ægopithecus,' graphically emphasized the 'virile member'.

In addition to stressing the 'lustful disposition' of the ape kind, Topsell's compilation contained suggestions concerning the character of simian facial features. 'Men that have low and flat nostrils', readers were told in the section on apes, 'are Libidinous as Apes that attempt women. . . .' There also seemed to be some connection between apes and devils. In a not altogether successful attempt to distinguish the 'Satyre-apes' from the mythical creatures of that name, Topsell straightened everything out by explaining that it was 'probable, that Devils take not any dænomination or shape from Satyres, but rather the Apes themselves from Devils whome they resemble, for there are many things common to the Satyre-apes and devilish Satyres'. Association of apes and/ or satyrs with devils was common in England: the inner logic of this association derived from uneasiness concerning the ape's 'indecent likenesse and imitation of man'; it revolved around evil and sexual sin; and, rather tenuously, it connected apes with blackness.

Given this tradition and the coincidence of contact, it was virtually inevitable that Englishmen should discern similarity between the manlike beasts and the beastlike men of Africa. A few commentators went so far as to suggest that Negroes had sprung from the generation of ape-kind or that apes were themselves the offspring of Negroes and some unknown African beast. These contentions were squarely in line with the ancient tradition that Africa was a land 'bringing dailie foorth newe monsters' because, as Aristotle himself had suggested, many different species came into proximity at the scarce watering places. Jean Bodin, the famous sixteenth-century French political theorist, summarized this wisdom of the ages with the categorical remark that 'promiscuous coition of men and animals took place, wherefore the regions of Africa produce for us so many monsters'. Despite all these monsters out of Africa, the notion that Negroes stemmed from beasts in a literal sense was not widely believed. It simply floated about, available, later, for anyone who wanted it.

Far more common and persistent was the notion that there sometimes occurred 'a beastly copulation or conjuncture' between apes and Negroes, and especially that apes were inclined wantonly to attack Negro women. The very explicit idea that apes assaulted female human beings was not new; Africans were merely being asked to demonstrate what Europeans had known for centuries. As late as the 1730s a well-travelled, well-educated, and intelligent naval surgeon, John Atkins, was not at all certain that the stories were false: 'At some Places the *Negroes* have been suspected of Bestiality with them [apes and monkeys], and by the Boldness and Affection they are known under some Circumstances to express to our Females; the Ignorance and Stupidity on the other side, to guide or control Lust; but more from the near resemblance [of apes] . . . to the Human Species would tempt one to suspect the Fact.'

By the time Atkins addressed himself to this evidently fascinating problem, some of the confusion arising from the resemblance of apes to men had been dispelled. In 1699 the web of legend and unverified fact was disentangled by Edward Tyson, whose comparative study of a young 'orang-outang' was a masterwork of critical scientific investigation. Throughout his dissection of the chimpanzee, Tyson meticulously compared the animal with human beings in every anatomical detail, and he established beyond question both the close relationship and the non-identity of ape and man. Here was a step forward; the question of the ape's proper place in nature was now grounded upon much firmer knowledge of the facts. Despite their scientific importance, Tyson's conclusions did nothing to weaken the vigorous tradition which linked the Negro with the ape. The supposed affinity between apes and men had as frequently been expressed in sexual as in anatomical terms, and his findings did not effectively rule out the possibility of unnatural sexual unions. Tyson himself remarked that orangs were especially given to venery.

The sexual association of apes with Negroes had an inner logic which kept it alive: sexual union seemed to prove a certain affinity without going so far as to indicate actual identity — which was what Englishmen really thought was the case. By forging a sexual link between Negroes and apes, furthermore, Englishmen were able to give vent to their feeling that Negroes were a lewd, lascivious, and wanton people.

Libidinous men

Undertones of sexuality run throughout many English accounts of West Africa. To liken Africans – any human being – to beasts was to stress the animal within the man. Indeed the sexual connotations embodied in the terms *bestial* and *beastly* were considerably stronger in Elizabethan English than they are today, and when the Elizabethan traveller pinned these epithets upon the behaviour of Africans he was more frequently registering a sense of sexual shock than describing swinish manners.

Lecherousness among Africans was at times for Englishmen merely another attribute which one would expect to find among heathen, savage, beastlike men. One commentator's remarks made evident how closely interrelated all these attributes were in the minds of Englishmen: 'They have no knowledge of God . . . they are very greedie eaters, and no lesse drinkers, and very lecherous, and theovish, and much addicted to uncleanenesse· one man hath as many wives as hee is able to keepe and maintaine.' Sexuality was what one expected of savages.

Clearly, however, the association of Africans with potent sexuality represented more than an incidental appendage to the concept of savagery. Long before first English contact with West Africa the inhabitants of virtually the entire continent stood confirmed in European literature as lustful and venerous. About 1526 Leo Africanus (a Spanish Moroccan Moor converted to Christianity) supplied an influential description of the little-known lands of 'Barbary,' 'Libya,' 'Numedia,' and 'Land of Negroes'; and Leo was as explicit as he was imaginative. In the English translation (1600) readers were informed concerning the 'Negroes' that 'there is no Nation under Heaven more prone to Venery'. Leo disclosed that 'the Negroes . . . leade a beastly kind of life, being utterly destitute of the use of reason, of dexteritie of wit, and of all arts. Yea, they so behave themselves, as if they had continually lived in a Forest among wild beasts. They have great swarmes of Harlots among them; whereupon a man may easily conjecture their manner of living'. Nor was Leo Africanus the only scholar to elaborate upon the ancient classical sources concerning Africa. In a highly eclectic work first published in 1566, Jean Bodin sifted the writings of ancient authorities and concluded that heat and lust went hand in hand and that 'in Ethiopia . . . the race of men is very keen and lustful'. Bodin announced in a thoroughly characteristic sentence, 'Ptolemy reported that on account of southern sensuality Venus chiefly is worshiped in Africa and that the constellation of Scorpion, which pertains to the pudenda, dominates that continent.'

Depiction of the Negro as a lustful creature was not radically new, therefore, when Englishmen first met Africans face to face. Seizing upon and reconfirming these long-standing and apparently common notions, Elizabethan travellers and literati dwelt explicitly with ease upon the especial sexuality of Africans. Othello's embraces were 'the gross clasps of a lascivious Moor'. Francis Bacon's *New Atlantis* (1624) referred to 'an holy hermit' who 'desired to see the Spirit of Fornication; and there appeared to him a little foul ugly Æthiop'. Negro men, reported a seventeenth-century traveller, sported 'large Propagators.' In 1623 Richard Jobson, a sympathetic observer, reported that Mandingo men were 'furnisht with such members as are after a sort burthensome unto them'. Another commentator thought Negroes 'very lustful and impudent, especially, when they come to hide their nakedness, (for a *Negroes* hiding his Members, their extraordinary greatness) is a token of their Lust, and therefore much troubled with the Pox'. By the eighteenth century a report on the sexual aggressiveness of African women was virtually required of European commentators. By then, of course, with many Englishmen actively participating in the slave trade, there were pressures making for descriptions of 'hot constitution'd Ladies' possessed of a 'temper hot and lascivious, making no scruple to prostitute themselves to the *Europeans* for a very slender profit, so great is their inclination to white men'.

While the animus underlying these and similar remarks becomes sufficiently obvious once Englishmen began active participation in the slave trade, it is less easy to see why Englishmen should have fastened upon Negroes a pronounced sexuality virtually upon first sight. The ancient notions distilled by Bodin and Leo Africanus must have helped pattern initial English perceptions. Yet clearly there was something in English culture working in this direction. It is certain that the presumption of powerful sexuality in black men was far from being an incidental or casual association in the minds of Englishmen. How very deeply this association operated is obvious in *Othello*, a drama which loses most of its power and several of its central points if it is read with the assumption that because the black man was the hero English audiences were indifferent to his blackness. Shakespeare was writing both *about* and *to* his countrymen's feelings concerning physical distinction between peoples; the play is shot through with the language of blackness and sex. Iago goes out of his way to talk about his own motives: 'I hate the Moor,/And it is thought abroad that 'twixt my sheets/ He has done my office.' Later, he becomes more direct, 'For that I do suspect the lusty Moor hath leaped into my seat.' It was upon this so obviously absurd suspicion that Iago based his resolve to 'turn her virtue into pitch'. Such was his success, of course, that Othello finally rushes off 'to furnish me with some means of death for the fair devil'. With this contorted denomination of Desdemona, Othello unwittingly revealed how deeply Iago's promptings about Desdemona's 'own clime, complexion, and degree' had eaten into his consciousness. Othello was driven into accepting the premise that the physical distinction *matters*: 'For she had eyes,' he has to reassure himself, 'and chose me.' Then, as his suspicions give way to certainty, he equates her character with his own complexion:

> Her name, that was as fresh,
> As Dian's visage, is now begrim'd and black
> As mine own face.

This important aspect of Iago's triumph over the noble Moor was a subtly inverted reflection of the propositions which Iago, hidden in darkness, worked upon the fair lady's father. No one knew better than Iago how to play upon hidden strings of emotion. Not content with the straightforward crudity that 'your daughter and the Moor are now making the beast with two backs', Iago told the agitated Brabantio that 'an old black ram/Is tupping your white ewe' and alluded politely to 'your daughter cover'd with a Barbary horse'. This was not merely the language of (as we say) a 'dirty' mind: it was the integrated imagery of blackness and whiteness, of Africa, of the sexuality of beasts and the bestiality of sex. And of course Iago was entirely successful in persuading Brabantio, who had initially welcomed Othello into his house, that the marriage was 'against all rules of nature'. Eventually Brabantio came to demand of Othello what could have brought a girl 'so tender, fair and happy'

> To incur a general mock
> Run from her guardage to the sooty bosom
> Of such a thing as thou.

Altogether a curious way for a senator to address a successful general.

These and similar remarks in the play *Othello* suggest that Shakespeare and his audiences were not totally indifferent to the sexual union of 'black' men and 'white' women. Shakespeare did not condemn such union; rather, he played upon an inner theme of black and white sexuality, showing how the poisonous mind of a white man perverted and destroyed the noblest of loves by means of bringing to the surface (from the darkness, whence Iago spoke) the lurking shadows of animal sex to assault the whiteness of chastity. Never did 'dirty' words more dramatically 'blacken' a 'fair' name. At the play's climax, standing stunned by the realization that the wife he has murdered was innocent, Othello groans to Emilia, ' 'Twas I that killed her': and Emilia responds with a torrent of condemnation: 'O! the more angel she,/And you the blacker devil.' Of Desdemona: 'She was too fond of her filthy bargain.' To Othello: 'O gull! O dolt!/As ignorant as dirt!' Shakespeare's genius lay precisely in juxtaposing these two pairs: inner blackness and inner whiteness. The drama meant little if his audiences had felt no response to this cross-inversion and to the deeply turbulent double meaning of black *over* white.

It required a very great dramatist to expose some of the more inward bio-cultural values which led — or drove — Englishman to accept readily the notion that Negroes were peculiarly sexual men. Probably these values and the ancient reputation of Africa upon which they built were of primary importance in determining the response of Englishmen to Africans. Whatever the importance of biologic elements in these values — whatever the effects of long northern nights, of living in a cool climate, of possessing light-coloured bodies which excreted contrasting lumps of darkness — these values by Shakespeare's time were interlocked with English history and culture and, more immediately, with the circumstances of contact with Africans and the social upheaval of Tudor England.

The blackness within

The Protestant Reformation in England was a complex development, but certainly it may be said that during the sixteenth and early seventeenth centuries the content and tone of English Christianity were altered in the direction of Biblicism, personal piety, individual judgment, and more intense self-scrutiny and internalized control. Many pious Englishmen, not all of them 'Puritans', came to approach life as if conducting an examination and to approach Scripture as if peering in a mirror. As a result, their inner energies were brought unusually close to the surface, more frequently than before into the almost rational world of legend, myth, and literature. The taut Puritan and the bawdy Elizabethan were not so much enemies as partners in this adventure which we usually think of in terms of great literature — of Milton and Shakespeare — and social conflict — of Saints and Cavaliers. The age was driven by the twin spirits of adventure and control, and while 'adventurous Elizabethans' embarked upon voyages of discovery overseas, many others embarked upon inward voyages of discovery. Some men, like William Bradford and John Winthrop, were to do both. Given this charged atmosphere of (self-) discovery, it is scarcely surprising that Englishmen should have used peoples overseas as social mirrors and that they were especially inclined to discover attributes in savages which they found first, but could not speak of, in themselves.

Nowhere is the way in which certain of these cultural attributes came to bear upon Negroes more clearly illustrated than in a discourse by George Best, an Elizabethan adventurer who sailed in 1577 in search of the Northwest Passage. In the course of demonstrating the habitability of all parts of the world, George Best veered off to the problem of the colour of Negroes. The cause of their blackness, he decided, was explained in Scripture. Noah and his sons and their wives were 'white' and 'by course of nature should have begotton . . . white children. But the envie of our great and continuall enemie the wicked Spirite is such, that as hee coulde not suffer our olde father Adam to live in the felicitie and Angelike state wherein he was first created . . . so againe, finding at this flood none but a father and three sons living, hee so caused one of them to disobey his fathers commandment, that after him all his posteritie should bee accursed'. The 'fact' of this 'disobedience', Best continued, was this: Noah 'commanded' his sons and their wives to behold God 'with reverence and feare', and that 'while they remained in the Arke, they should use continencie, and abstaine from carnall copulation with their wives . . . which good instructions and exhortations notwithstanding his wicked sonne Cham disobeyed, and being perswaded that the first childe borne after the flood . . . should inherite . . . all the dominions of the earth, hee . . . used company with his wife, and craftily went about thereby to dis-inherite the off-spring of his other two brethren'. To punish this 'wicked and detestable fact', God willed that 'a sonne should bee born whose name was Chus, who not onely it selfe, but all his posteritie after him should bee so blacke and lothsome, that it might remain a spectacle of disobedience to all the worlde. And of this blacke and cursed Chus came all these blacke Moores which are in Africa'.

The inner themes running throughout this extraordinary exegesis testify eloquently to the completeness with which English perceptions could integrate sexuality with blackness, the devil, and the judgement of a God who had originally created man not only 'Angelike' but 'white'. These running equations lay embedded at a deep and almost inaccessible level of Elizabethan culture: only occasionally did they appear in complete clarity, as when evil dreams:

> . . . hale me from my sleepe like forked Devils,
> Midnight, thou Æthiope, Empresse of Black Soules, Thou general
> Bawde to the whole world.

But what is still more arresting about George Best's discourse is the shaft of light it throws upon the dark mood of strain and control in Elizabethan culture. In an important sense, Best's remarks are not about Negroes; rather they play upon a theme of external discipline exercised upon the man who fails to discipline himself. The linkages he established — 'disobedience' with 'carnell copulation' with something 'black and lothsome' — were not his alone. The term *dirt* first began to acquire its meaning of moral impurity, of smuttiness, at the very end of the sixteenth century. Perhaps the key term, though, is 'disobedience' — to God and parents — and perhaps, therefore, the passage echoes one of the central concerns of Englishmen of the sixteenth and early seventeenth century. Tudor England was undergoing social ferment, caused in large part by an increasingly commercialized economy and reflected in such legislative monuments as the Statute of Apprentices and the Elizabethan vagrancy and poor laws. Overseas mercantile expansion brought profits and adventure but also a sense, in some men, of disquietude. One commentator declared that the merchants, 'whose number is so increased in these our daies', had 'in times past' traded chiefly with European countries but 'now . . . as men not contented with these journies, they have sought out the east and west Indies, and made now and then suspicious voiages'. Literate Englishmen generally (again not merely the Puritans) were concerned with the apparent disintegration of social and moral controls at home; they fretted endlessly over the 'masterless men' who had once had a proper place in the social order but who were now wandering about, begging, robbing, raping. They fretted also about the absence of a spirit of due subordination — of children to parents and servants to masters.

They assailed what seemed a growing spirit of avariciousness, a spirit which one social critic described revealingly as 'a barbarous or slavish desire to turne the [penny]'. They denounced the labourers who demanded too high wages, the masters who squeezed their servants, and the landlord gentlemen who valued sheep more than men — in short, the spirit of George Best's Cham, who aimed to have his son 'inherite and possesse all the dominions of the earth'.

It was the case with English confrontation with Africans, then, that a society in a state of rapid flux, undergoing important changes in religious values, and comprised of men who were energetically on the make and acutely and often uncomfortably self-conscious of being so, came upon a people less technologically advanced, markedly different in appearance and culture. From the first, Englishmen tended to set Africans over against themselves, to stress what they conceived to be radically contrasting qualities of colour, religion, and style of life, as well as animality and a peculiarly potent sexuality. What Englishmen did not at first fully realize was that Africans were potentially subjects for a special kind of obedience and subordination which was to arise as adventurous Englishmen sought to possess for themselves and their children one of the most bountiful dominions of the earth. When they came to plant themselves in the New World, they were to find that they had not entirely left behind the spirit of avarice and insubordination. Nor does it appear, in light of attitudes that developed during their first two centuries in America, that they left behind all the impressions initially gathered of the *Negro* before he became pre-eminently the *slave*.

3 Black caricature: the roots of racialism*

James Walvin

Negroes were a favourite target of graphic cartoonists in the eighteenth century. The physical features, social characteristics, verbal intonations and the alleged 'natural' abilities or inabilities of the Blacks were frequently reduced to a grotesque shape by English caricaturists from Hogarth to Cruickshank. The mythology of the Blacks — as a species and as individuals — was perpetuated by cartoonists who added to and exaggerated some of the existing stereotyped images.

Another generally unconsidered type of caricature was even more influential than the graphic school in moulding a popular image of the Negro in the English mind. This was to be found in the literary tradition during the four centuries separating early travel narratives from modern racialist writing and thought. Hundreds of books, tracts, newspapers and magazines have dealt with the Negro to produce a cumulative image so absurd, so removed from reality that it belongs more to caricature, calumny and lampoon than it does to descriptive analysis. To quote the most obvious example, at the zenith of eighteenth-century graphic caricature, a flood of literature about the Negro emerged from the plantocratic writers which was the literary counterpart and complement to the work of the artists. But literary caricature, while reaching a peak during and immediately after the campaign for abolition and emancipation, had roots which went back to the pre-colonial world, and exerted an influence, in an uneven but unbroken line to the present day.

The purveyors of racialist thought in the eighteenth and early nineteenth centuries drew much of their inspiration from 'factual' material, from travel accounts dating from the sixteenth century. In their turn these accounts, as we have seen, had been profoundly influenced by speculative writing of an even earlier date. The literary caricature of the central period 1770 to 1860 in its turn influenced the emergence of more modern racialist thought. The caricatured writing of that period thus occupies a crucial role in the growth of English racialist thought, for it employed traditional and, in some cases, ancient ideas about black humanity, and put them in a more coherent form.

* Reprinted from *Black and White: The Negro and English Society 1555-1945* (Allen Lane 1973), pp. 159-766.

The Negro is possessed of passions not only strong but ungovernable; a mind dauntless, warlike and unmerciful; a temper extremely irascible; a disposition indolent, selfish and deceitful; fond of joyous sociality, riotous mirth and extravagant shew. He has certain portions of kindness for his favourites, and affections for his connections; but they are sparks which emit a glimmering light through the thick gloom that surrounds them, and which, in every ebullition of anger or revenge, instantly disappear. Furious in his love as in his hate; at best, a terrible husband, a harsh father and a precarious friend. A strong and unalterable affection for his countrymen and fellow passengers in particular seems to be the most amiable passion in the Negro breast. . . . As to all the other fine feelings of the soul, the Negro, as far as I have been able to perceive, is nearly deprived of them.[1]

This description of the Negro, in the *Gentleman's Magazine* of 1788, perhaps the most popular and influential periodical of the day, contains all the major themes. The Negro was held to be peculiarly sexual, musical, stupid, indolent, untrustworthy and violent. This view was not original or even extreme, for its basic ingredients can be found scattered through numerous publications from the mid sixteenth century. Similar sentiments were to appear until the mid nineteenth century, finding their apotheosis in the racialist writing of Carlyle and Trollope.

While the Negro became the object of particularly acute enquiry in the late eighteenth and early nineteenth centuries, he had intermittently occupied a special place in the attention of English writers and thinkers since the first European explorations in West Africa. The African's physical, social and 'natural' characteristics were described, explained and remembered. By the mid seventeenth century, as the English New World colonies underwent an economic revolution, made possible by black labour, the English literary treatment of the Negro concentrated on the relationship between the African and slavery. In order to justify both the growth of the slave trade and the development of slave societies, writers continued to focus their interests on the African and his homeland. By elaborating on, or inferring from, what was known of African life, supporters of slavery were able to present apparently convincing arguments in favour of black slavery. Much of their argument, based on anthropological or even biblical evidence, was selective, apologetic and, as often as not, totally inaccurate. Whatever its origin and degree of accuracy, the case of the slave lobby was important in keeping the African in the public-political eye. In the years after 1770 the African was subjected to even closer attention by the two powerful interest groups, the humanitarian and slave lobbies, in their respective efforts to win public support. Although emancipation finally dispelled the bitterness of political debate from the discussion about the Negro, the fate of the sugar colonies in the 1840s and 1850s maintained English interest in the role, and in the very nature, of the black African and his descendant. When Carlyle and Trollope, for example, told their armies of readers about the collapse of the

West Indies, much of their analysis took as a point of departure and as a fundamental explanation, the alleged natural and immutable features of the Negro. Trollope's visit to the West Indies took place a mere six years before the violence of the Jamaican revolt of 1865 and its bloody aftermath. The subsequent controversy about the role of Governor Eyre in the butchery of the Jamaican Negroes became a political *cause célèbre*, which sharply divided society and revived, in a particularly virulent form, many of the traditional arguments used by the slave lobby about the Negro.

Only seventeen years separated the Eyre controversy from the re-entry of the African into English domestic politics, with the invasion of Egypt in 1882.[2] Thereafter as vast tracts of land turned an imperial red, the Negro once again became a subject of intense political and intellectual debate. The need to justify and explain the new empire, coupled to the development of Social Darwinism and newer more 'scientific' approaches to the study of race, led to a far-ranging debate about the Negro and other non-white peoples. In many respects the late nineteenth century debate about race, which found a particularly acute focus in the Negro, was similar to that of the eighteenth century. While both debates were separated by a century of enormous change in racial thinking, they are none the less linked by common factors. My purpose here is to illustrate some of the prime elements of the caricature image which cut across chronological divisions and which act as links in the continuing process of misunderstanding the Negro.

Unable to understand the different and varied nature of West Indian tribal societies, Englishmen in West Africa from the sixteenth century placed great stress on the sexuality and 'immorality' of the African. Remembering too that African nakedness loomed large in the early English impressions of Africans, it can be appreciated why importance came to be attached to the concept of black sexuality. The view of the Negro as endowed with great sexual powers was later exaggerated by the developments of slave society in the West Indies, where demographic factors led to patterns of morality which seemed to fit no moral order recognized by the English.

The authoritative work of the Arab Leo Africanus, translated into English in 1600, brought home to the English the peculiar morality of West Africans. 'They have among them great swarmes of Harlots among them; whereupon a man may easily conjecture their manner of living.'[3] This view, coupled with the idea of the African as an uncivilized being, occurs time and again in early English writings on Africa. Another contemporary Englishman alleged that the Africans 'are very greedie eaters, and no less drinkers, and very lecherous, and theevish, and much addicted to uncleanliness: one man hath as many wives as hee is able to keepe and maintaine'.[4] Sexual immorality among Africans according to another English source, bordered on the perverted. They are beastly in their living for they have men in women's apparel whom they keep among their wives.'[5] English writers continually found an explanation for sexual activity among the Africans in the alleged size of the African penis. Mandingo men, wrote Richard Jobson in 1623 were 'furnisht with such members as are after a sort burthensome unto them'.[6] From that day to now, this particular belief has been commonplace and has proved influential in moulding relations between black and white. Its widespread acceptance can be seen in Shakespeare's use of black sexual imagery.

West Indian planters later added to the myths about black sexuality with stories gleaned from their partial experiences of slave society.[7] One such man, Bryan Edwards, Jamaican planter and English politician, was among the most influential and, odd as it may sound in the light of his writings of the 1790s, one of the least extreme planters when writing about the Negro. But he too dealt with the subject more in terms of caricature than reality. 'The Negroes in the West Indies, both men and women, would consider it as the great exertion of tyranny, and the most cruel of all hardships, to be compelled to confine themselves to a single connection with the other sex. Their passion', Edwards continued, 'is mere animal desire, implanted by the great Author of all things for the preservation of the species. This the Negroes, without doubt, possess in common with the rest of the animal creation, and they indulge it, as inclination prompts, in an almost promiscuous intercourse with the other sex.'[8]

Plantocratic literature tended to be infused with the paranoia which resulted from their style of life in the colonies. The fearful hate which they openly manifested towards their black property reached new heights in the late eighteenth century under pressure from the humanitarians. In the process no one expressed more fully and bitterly the plantocratic caricature of black sexuality than Edward Long, friend and associate of Bryan Edwards and himself a Jamaican planter. Long's History of Jamaica (1774) has always been viewed as a classic analysis of colonial society, but rarely has it been seen in its other equally important role, as a landmark in the evolution of English racialist thought. The Negro's 'faculties of smell', according to Long, 'are truly bestial, nor less their commerce with the other sexes; in these acts they are libidinous and shameless as monkeys, or baboons. The equally hot temperament of their women has given probability to the charge of their admitting these animals frequently to their embrace. An example of this intercourse once happened, I think, in England'.[9] Throughout his writing, Long went out of his way to equate the Negro with the animal kingdom; to show that in appearances and responses they belonged more to the animal kingdom than to humanity. As far as black sexuality is concerned Long merely added a new, more bitter twist to myths which were already widely believed in the English-speaking world.

By the early nineteenth century the English took it for granted that Negroes were promiscuous and strongly sexed. One even explained the low life expectancy among slaves by 'the premature intercourse of the sexes and the very early and excessive debauchery'.[10] In reality the causes of slave morality were rooted not in black 'immorality' but in the appalling physical conditions which dominated enslavement, transportation and life on the plantations. By this time however English writers who concerned themselves with black affairs sought an explanation for black social problems not in social terms but solely in terms of the African's individual 'characteristics'. Moreover the English tended to view these alleged characteristics as universal qualities, possessed by Negroes everywhere. This was perhaps the most damaging legacy of the process of black caricature; generations of Englishmen came to see Negroes as a species undifferentiated by time or place.

Caricatured images were largely responsible for the emergence of stereotyped roles for Negroes in white society. The English treated the Negro in such a way that he had no alternative but to behave in a way expected of him; to live up to the role imposed on him. Thus on plantations slaves rarely settled down to stable monogamous relationships, not because they were by nature promiscuous, but for the basic reason that sexual imbalance and the movement of slaves between different properties made such stable relationships virtually impossible. Similarly among Negroes in England, shifting relations with poor white women were more common than stable relations with women of their own colour. Once again, the reasons were primarily demographic. But in dealing with both situations Englishmen explained black social behaviour in terms of the Negro's alleged natural qualities, in this case his 'promiscuity'.

An equally pronounced theme has been the emphasis on black indolence. Physical conditions both in West Africa and the West Indies, so inimical to sustained work by white men, were assumed to induce an uncontrollable lethargy. Moreover Englishmen tended to believe that the natural richness of tropical soil and vegetation could be tapped with little human effort. Negroes, it was thought, had little more to do than eat what grew naturally around them. It was this particular myth which proved so tempting a proposition for would-be emigrants to Sierra Leone in 1787. [11] Geophysical conditions were equally fruitful on the other side of the Atlantic and visitors to the West Indies were staggered, as the casual visitor still is, by the luxuriant growth of fruit and vegetation. In both regions nature had evidently endowed the Negro with bountiful riches — or so it was thought. The Negro, Thomas Carlyle wrote in 1849, 'by working about half-an-hour a day . . . can supply himself, by aid of sun and soil, with as much as will suffice'.[12]

While the natural conditions of the two areas might provide a plausible setting for the myth of black indolence, its greatest strength was drawn from the need to justify slavery. Without the rigours and restraints of slavery it was felt that the Black would revert to his natural sloth. They 'do no more work, in general, than they are compelled to do by the terrors of punishment'.[13] Edward Long predictably put the point in his usual extreme fashion. 'A planter would as soon expect to hear that sugar-canes and pineapples flourish the year round, in open-air, upon Hounslow Heath, as that Negroes when freed would be brought into the like necessity or disposition to hire themselves for plantation labour. . . . Idleness, it has been observed, is the sure consequence of cheap and easy living; and none will labour, who have the means of idleness in their power'.[14] Long took as proof of his case the fate of the freed slaves in London.

The view that a 'dissolute, idle, profligate crew repose themselves here in ease and indolence'.[15] seemed to give living testimony to the belief in black indolence.

Another of Long's contemporaries commented on London's Negroes that 'not one in a hundred of them would apply steadily to labour'.[16] Once again Englishmen simply refused to look for the social origins of black behaviour but were satisfied to accept surface appearances without looking for underlying causes.

Soon after slaves had been emancipated throughout the empire the ailing West Indian sugar economy collapsed; all the worst fears and predictions of the planters seemed to have been fulfilled. Black freedom coincided with (and therefore, in the minds of Englishmen, caused) West Indian ruin. While his correlation is beguilingly simple, it ignores the complex structural economic changes already in train long before the granting of black freedom.[17] Like their eighteenth-century predecessors, nineteenth-century commentators on the West Indies looked not to the social-economic roots of the problem, but to black characteristics. Indolence among Negroes, for long used as political ammunition by the planters, was now used to explain the collapse of the sugar system. Carlyle, whose voice was heeded in a variety of circles in Victorian England, put the blame for the West Indian collapse firmly on the Black. He conjured up the vision of a 'black gentleman', 'with rum-bottle in hand . . . no breeches on his body, pumpkin at discretion, and the fruitfulest region of the earth going back to jungle around him'.[18] Even the dignified rebuttal of this view by Carlyle's former friend John Stuart Mill, was insufficient to correct the impressions left by one of the most nakedly racialist tracts to be laid before the English reading public. After the Morant Bay revolt of 1865 it was scarcely surprising that Carlyle should lead the gadarene rush of English writers who supported Governor Eyre's butchery of the former slaves.

Carlyle's racialist views were kept alive by Anthony Trollope who, after a West Indian tour for the Post Office in 1858, similarly conveyed to his white readership a view of black indolence. The West Indian Negro, he alleged, 'is idle, unambitious as to worldly position, sensual, and content with little. . . . He lies under the mango-tree, and eats the luscious fruit in the sun; he sends his black urchin up for breakfast and behold the family table is spread. He pierces a cocoa-nut and lo! there is his beverage. He lies on the grass, surrounded by oranges, bananas, and pine-apples'.[19] In the ten years between Carlyle's work and Trollope's the Negro's food had changed from pumpkin to more exotic fruits; a transmutation all the easier because it took place primarily in the author's excitable imagination.

The more grotesque assertions about black indolence will be familiar to anyone conversant with present-day West Indian middle-class society. Furthermore this myth has since travelled the Atlantic and passed into modern Britain. The belief that Negroes are basically lazy is as widely spread as the myth of potent black sexuality, despite an abundance of evidence, from both slave and free societies, to the contrary. In Brazil for example it was the skills of imported

Africans, notably in metalwork, which laid the basis for new native industries, while the pioneering bravery of escaped slaves pushed the Brazilian frontiers into the distant interior of the continent.[20] In British colonies it was the blistering work undertaken by generations of Africans which had made possible the transformation of the West Indian sugar colonies. Later, after emancipation, while West Indian black labour was no longer employed in the interests of the masters, the initiative and skills of former slaves were responsible for the emergence of a new Creole agricultural society, despite the appalling conditions which freedom entailed. Jamaican Negroes, wrote William Sewell, a visiting journalist from the *New York Times*, 'are not cared for; they perish miserably in country districts for want of medical aid; they are not instructed; they have no opportunities to improve themselves in agriculture or mechanics; every effort is made to check a spirit of independence, which in the African is counted a heinous crime, but in all other people is regarded as a lofty virtue and the germ of natural courage, enterprise and progress'.[21] Sewell's analysis was nearer to reality than was the portrayal of the Negroes as indolent beings living off the fruits of nature.

Closely related to this belief in natural indolence was the English conviction that Negroes were basically stupid; so stupid that they failed even to perceive the disastrous consequences of their own indolence. Some self-appointed 'friends' of the Negro were influenced by this view. One early humanitarian wrote, 'The dull stupidity of the Negro leaves him without any desire for instruction. Whether the Creator originally formed these black people a little lower than other men, or that they have lost their intellectual powers through disuse, I will not assume the province of determining; but certain it is that a *new Negro* (as those lately imported from Africa are called), is a complete definition of indolent stupidity.' The logical deduction from this was clear. 'The stupid obstinance of the Negroes may indeed make it always necessary to subject them to severe discipline from their masters.'[22] Thus evidence of stupidity, like evidence of indolence, was carefully used to reinforce the justice of the slave system.

Evidence for black stupidity was generally drawn from the absence of those achievements, whether in Africa, the West Indies or England, which Europeans recognized as civilized accomplishments. No less a person than David Hume seized on the dearth of black achievements as proof of the superiority of white society. 'I am apt to suspect the Negroes . . . to be naturally inferior to the Whites. There never was a civilized nation of any other complexion than white, or even any individual eminent in either action, or speculation. No ingenious manufacturers among them, no arts, no sciences. There are Negro slaves dispersed all over Europe, of which none ever discovered any symptoms of ingenuity.'[23] The Negro as a 'poor blockhead' was a recognizable figure in the English imagination even before Carlyle gave a powerful boost to the flagging dynamic of black caricature.

The myth of stupidity, like most other themes in the English misunderstanding of the Negro, found its origins on the coast of Africa, and in the West

Indian slave societies. Hostile white observers took isolated circumstances of black life and expanded them into mistaken generalizations. 'In general', wrote Edward Long, 'they are void of genius and seem almost incapable of making progress in civility or science.' The basis for this claim lay in what he had read about African society. Africans, he concluded, 'are represented by all authors as the vilest of the human kind, to which they have little more pretensions of resemblance than what arises from their exterior form'.[24] To Long and his ilk, black stupidity was self-evident. Had Negroes not been stupid they would have revealed their talents and reached the level of European accomplishments. Of the millions of Africans known to the Europeans, few had been encountered who 'comprehend any thing of mechanic arts, or manufacture; and even these, for the most part, are said to perform their work in very bungling and slovenly manner, perhaps not better than an oran-outang might'.[25]

Edward Long pushed black caricature to a new extreme, in particular giving a new twist to the old belief that Africans were more animal than human. From the first days of the exploration of West Africa Europeans had been particularly fascinated by the animal they knew as the 'oran-outang'. To use the words of Winthrop Jordan, it was a coincidence that 'Englishmen were introduced to the anthropoid apes and to Negroes at the same time and in the same place'.[26] From the sixteenth century to the late eighteenth there was a consequent European curiosity about the possibility of an evolutionary relationship between the African and the ape. At one bizarre level, it was for instance widely believed that sexual relations took place between Africans and apes.[27] English residents in West Africa were largely responsible for the dissemination of this myth. James Houston, medical officer for the African Company on the coast reported of Africans that 'their natural Temper is barbarously cruel, selfish, and deceitful, and their Government equally barborous and uncivil, and consequently the Men of greatest Eminency among them, are those who are most capable of being the greatest Rogues. . . . As for their Customs they exactly resemble their Fellow Creatures and Natives, the Monkeys'.[28]

The association between the African and the ape was a constant source of speculation in eighteenth-century literature; nowhere more clearly than in Edward Long's work which made continual and pointed reference to the physical and social features of the 'oran-outang'. Understandably, Long's argument came to the traditional conclusion — but one tinged with a bitterness peculiar to him. 'Ludicrous as it may seem I do not think that an oran-outang husband would be any dishonour to an Hottentot female.' The 'oran-outang' 'has in form a much nearer resemblance to the Negro race, than the latter bear to white men'.[29] Long undoubtedly believed his own assertions but they also had the much more useful purpose of adding an important new dimension to the slave lobby's propaganda against the abolitionists. Assertions of the animal inferiority of the Negro turned aside the abolitionist question 'Am I not a man and a brother?' In political terms however the abolitionists were able to win more and more support to their side of the argument, convincing increasing numbers of Englishmen that the Negro was indeed a man and a brother.

Yet another school of thought conceded the Negro's basic humanity but tended to regard him as an unmanageable savage who did not deserve the equality of treatment demanded for him by the abolitionists. Sixteenth-century accounts of the savagery of African life[30] were added to in the succeeding two centuries. In 1773, for example, John Norris, a slave ship captain from Liverpool, produced a 'descriptive' account of Africa, reprinted in 1789, which added to the view of the savage continent. Norris claimed that Bossa Ahadee, king of Dahomey, was 'absolute master of the life, liberty, and property, of every person in his dominion and that he sports with them, with the most savage and wanton cruelty. Piles of their heads are placed as ornaments before his palace on festival days . . . and the floors leading to his apartments are strewed with their bodies'.[31] Few slavers tried to assess their own role in contributing to whatever savagery existed in West Africa; fewer still made comparisons between black savagery and their own inhumanity towards their cargoes. Edward Long, in a vein similar to Norris's, wanted the worst of both worlds; to prove both that the Africans were animal-like and also to prove that African society was uncivilized. 'If no rules of civil polity exist among them, does it not betray an egregious want of common sense . . . ? The jurisprudence, the customs and manners of the Negroes, seem perfectly suited to the measure of their narrow intellect. Laws have justly been regarded as the masterpiece of human genius: what are we to think of those societies of men, who either have none, or such only as are irrational and ridiculous?'[32]

The centre of the argument that black society was savage depended upon a portrait of the Negro as a creature in a state of nature, without the romantic gloss of the noble savage. He was, it was alleged, so different from the European, that even his sense and sensibilities were different; 'the feelings quite natural to a Briton are not the feelings of the African'.[33] Furthermore, proponents of the slave trade argued that Africans had benefited by the slave trade, in being moved from a continent where barbarism was a common experience.

> We're the children of Cham! He his father offended
> Who gave him the curse, which to us is descended
> 'A servant of servants' alas! is our curse;
> And as bad as it is, it has saved us from worse.[14]

Both abolitionists and the slave lobby were agreed on at least one point; that slavery had made possible the conversion to Christianity of pagan Africans. Both sides agreed that African heathenism was unfortunate and sometimes abominable. 'They are said to have as many religions almost as they have deities, and these are innumerable', wrote Edward Long.[35] None the less, abolitionists were in a dilemma. While they welcomed the chance to convert the Africans, they could scarcely support the slave trade for this purpose.

Another point of contact between abolitionists and the slave lobby was their joint belief in another area of black mythology, namely that Negroes were peculiarly musical people. By an odd twist of historical progression, this view has now been adopted by the black community on both sides of the Atlantic. But its origins lie deep in the caricature image of the Negro created in the seventeenth and eighteenth centuries. Writing in 1793 Bryan Edwards noted, 'An opinion prevails in Europe that they [Negroes] possess organs peculiarly adapted to the science of music; but this I believe is an ill-founded idea.'[36] Edwards's scepticism was exceptional. Evangelicals for instance saw black musicality as an ideal opportunity for conversion to Christianity. 'The Negroes in general have an ear for music, and might without much trouble be taught to sing hymns.'[37] John Wesley too had noted the opening to religion afforded by black music. 'I cannot but observe that the Negroes above all the human species I ever knew, have the nicest ear for music. They have a kind of ecstatic delight in psalmody.'[38] Credibility seemed to be added to this myth by the testimony and behaviour of Africans themselves. Equiano told his English readers, 'We are almost a nation of dancers, musicians, and poets. Thus every great event . . . is celebrated in public dances which are accompanied with songs and music suited to the occasion.'[39] In this instance Equiano explained African love of music; it was not a natural genetic fact but a socially and culturally acquired quality through which his own people represented their history, military victories and folk-lore.

Few English commentators saw black music in these terms, preferring instead the traditional myths. They seemed to be reinforced in this by the emergence in England of black musicians both inside the black community and as entertainers trained for English enjoyment. In the mid nineteenth century Henry Mayhew calculated that fifty Ethiopian serenaders made a living on the streets of London.[40]

But the presence of black musicians in no way bore out the myth for, believing Negroes to be peculiarly suited to music, the English simply encouraged them to become musicians. In effect Negroes were fitted into a stereotyped role earmarked for them by white society. 'The fondness of the Negroes for music and the proficiency they sometimes make in it, with little or no instruction is too well known to need support.'[41] It was Thomas Carlyle who extended this element in black caricature to the extremes of racial denigration. After fulminating over the condition of the West Indies following emancipation, Carlyle continued, 'Do I then hate the Negro? No; except when the soul is killed out of him, I decidedly like poor Quashee; and find him a pretty kind of man. With a pennyworth of oil, you can make a handsome glossy thing of Quashee, when the soul is not killed in him! A swift, supple fellow; a merry-hearted, grinning, dancing, singing, affectionate kind of creature, with a great deal of melody and amenability in his composition. '[42] For all his hyperbole Carlyle was simply putting in an extreme form a belief which was already commonplace. Anthony Trollope expressed himself with less extremism but his portrait of the Negro was little less caricatured.

Only five years after Trollope's denigration of the Jamaican Negro there occurred in the island a minor black uprising followed by a savage white repression, which constitutes a turning point in the history of English attitudes towards the Negro. In the October of 1865 in the small eastern Jamaican town of Morant Bay, local disturbances triggered off wider black unrest. In the military and legal repression which followed some 500 free Jamaicans lost their lives and many more were severely punished.[43] The Royal Commission[44] which followed was extremely critical of the behaviour of the Governor, Edward Eyre, whose actions became the centre of heated political debate. After the events of 1865 English racial antagonisms crystallized more clearly than at any time since the collapse of the slave lobby.

Eyre found enormous support for his legalized savagery, notably from Ruskin, Tennyson, Kingsley, Dickens and Carlyle. Their public utterances and those from sympathetic newspapers revived the very worst English attitudes towards the Negro. Even those who expressed reservations about the handling of the Jamaican revolt often fell back on the old stereotyped views. The *Pall Mall Gazette* for example, generally sympathetic towards the Jamaicans, called the 'poor deluded Negro' 'the most inflammable and unreasoning population on earth'.[45] A missionary spoke of 'the natural tendency of the negro, when free, to sink and drag down those who try to save him'.[46] Negroes, said *The Times*, were 'careless, credulous, and dependent; easily excited, easily duped, easily frightened'.[47] To read the response to Morant Bay is to be pitched back a full century and to imagine that the efforts of the philanthropists to restore the reality of black humanity had been in vain.[48] For the Jamaicans the immediate result was the removal of the franchise from the 'ignorant and irresponsible rabble'[49] and the imposition of Crown Colonial rule.

The political consequence within the growing British empire was the abandonment of any idea of black equality and in its place there evolved a passionately held belief in separate status for colonial peoples. In the process, humanitarianism collapsed under the popular resurgence of openly racialist propaganda. Britons, alleged *The Times*, had been deceived by the humanitarians into believing that 'the world was made for Sambo, and that the sole use of sugar was to sweeten Sambo's existence'.[50] Echoes of Carlyle's earlier extremism began to creep into the public utterances of politicians and press. Once again, in English eyes, Negroes were lazy, savage, lustful and domineering and black caricature was raised to the level of acceptable political debate, thereby preventing any reasoned assessment of the black problem.

The revolt of 1865, as Christine Bolt has pointed out, was a major crisis of British liberalism. It was also the catalyst for the revival, though certainly not for the creation, of Victorian racialism. It is only partially true to claim that, by the 1860s 'the upper and middle class of the English people, especially the latter, had come to believe that Negroes were innately inferior beings'.[51] They had felt much the same way a century before, and it has seriously to be asked whether this belief had ever really died. It seems more than likely that under the pressure of philanthropy, the overt racialism of many simply submerged, until brought to the surface once again by the Indian mutiny, the Maori wars and finally the Morant Bay revolt. A similar sequence of events was to unfold again in the mid twentieth century when black and then Indian immigration tapped hidden springs of English racialism which had long remained invisible.

The racialism revived in 1865 was not absolutely identical to eighteenth-century attitudes. Similarly, to claim that the racialism of the late 1860s deeply influenced English attitudes towards the new African empire of the close of the century is not to claim perfect similarity between the two, or even to suggest that a causal link exists. But there are common denominators which make the racial responses of one generation partly explicable in terms of that generation's historical inheritance. From eighteenth-century plantocratic caricatures, to Carlyle and Trollope, through *The Times* of the 1860s to the more 'scientific' apologists for racialism late in the century, common images of the Negro were passed on.

The *Encyclopaedia Britannica* in 1810 had said of the Negro, 'Vices the most notorious seem to be the portion of this unhappy race; idleness, treachery, revenge, cruelty, impudence, stealing, lying, profanity, debauchery, nastiness, and intemperance, are said to have extinguished the principles of natural law, and to have silenced the reproofs of conscience. They are strangers to every sentiment of compassion, and are an aweful example of the corruption of man left to himself.'[52] Seventy years later, in 1884, a very different kind of *Encyclopaedia Britannica*, while less harsh, was still repeating the ancient myths. 'No full-blooded Negro has ever been distinguished as a man of science, a poet, or an artist, and the fundamental equality claimed for him by ignorant philanthropists is belied by the whole history of the race throughout the historic period.'[53] This assertion scarcely differed from that written by David Hume a century before.

Philanthropists from the 1770s to emancipation had tried to give the English reading public a corrective to plantocratic legends, but they were never able totally to expel the more grotesque and persistent themes of this caricature. In the short term, the campaign for black freedom was able to silence the racialist propaganda of the planters but it was quite unable to eradicate the more profound subconscious prejudices against the Negro. These prejudices had grown over the centuries; born of curiosity, they had been nurtured and had thrived on economic exploitation. After the development of the plantation societies, the English response to the Negro was dictated largely by economic circumstance, by the need to justify or defend slavery. Simultaneously, white reactions were stimulated and guided by the myths, which pre-dated European first-hand knowledge of Africans. These myths were often deliberately transformed by the slave lobby into pure caricature, but sometimes the caricature was simply the product of unconscious selection based on economic interest.

Thus the overtly racialist writings of Long and Carlyle were functions of quite different economic situations. But common elements can be found in the thinking of both and indeed in the wider racial consciousness of their respective generations. Similarly the reactions to the Jamaican revolt of 1865 were quite different from those which greeted the Haitian revolt of the 1790s. But similar stereotyped sentiments echo through both.

Between the English settlement of the New World and the fumbling attempts to reconstruct the colonial government of the former slave societies, successive generations had to cope with the intricate problems of colonial economics and government. Central to all these problems was the person of the imported Black. To justify his importation, his slavery, his freedom and finally his position as a free man, Englishmen conjured up a variety of stereotype images of the Negro best suited to each particular purpose. Almost without exception these images, which made such an impression on the public at large, bore little resemblance to fact. Caricature rather than truth was the hallmark of the English impression of the Negro.

Notes

1 Quoted in *Gentleman's Magazine* (1788), pp. 1093-4.
2 R. Robinson and J. Gallagher, *Africa and the Victorians* (Macmillan 1961), chs. iv, v.
3 Leo Africanus, *History and Description of Africa* (London 1896), vol. i, p. 187.
4 'A description of Guinea', *Purchas – his Pilgrimes* (Glasgow 1905-7), vol. vi, p. 251.
5 Quoted in Jordan, *White Over Black* (Penguin Books 1969), p. 13.
6 Quoted in ibid., p. 34.
7 For relationship between slaves and planters see M. J. Craton and J. Walvin, *A Jamaican Plantation* (London and Toronto 1970).
8 Bryan Edwards, *The History, Civil and Commercial of the British Colonies in the West Indies*, 2 vols. (London 1793), vol. ii, pp. 82-3.
9 Edward Long, *History of Jamaica* (London 1774), vol. ii, p. 383.
10 Jesse Foot, *Observations* (1805), p. 17.
11 H. Smeathman, *Substance of a Plan of Settlement* (London 1786), pp. 9-17.
12 Thomas Carlyle, 'Discourse on the nigger question, 1849', *Critical and Miscellaneous Essays* (London 1872), vol. vii, p. 82.
13 'A West India planter', *Consideration on the Emancipation of Negroes* (London 1788), p. 4.
14 Edward Long, *Candid Reflections* (London 1772), pp. 48, 63-4.
15 ibid., p. 48.
16 *Letter to Philo-Africanus* (London 1787), p. 17.
17 Eric Williams, *Capitalism and Slavery* (University of North Carolina Press 1944).
18 Carlyle, 'Discourse on the nigger question', p. 86.
19 Anthony Trollope, *The West Indies and the Spanish Main* (London 1859), p. 56.
20 Basil Davidson, *Black Mother* (London 1970), p. 21.

21 W. G. Sewell, *The Ordeal of Free Labour in the British West Indies* (New York 1861), p. 178.
22 William Knox, *Three Tracts* (London 1768), vol. 14, p. 38.
23 In *Gentleman's Magazine* (1771), p. 594.
24 Long, *History of Jamaica*, vol. ii, pp. 351-2.
25 ibid.
26 Jordan, *White Over Black*, p. 29.
27 ibid., pp. 28-32.
28 James Houston, *Some New and Accurate Observations* (London 1725), p.33.
29 Long, *History of Jamaica*, vol. ii, book III, ch. 1.
30 'Second Voyage of John Lok', *Hakluyt,* vol. vi, p. 167.
31 Robert Norris, *Memoirs of the Reign of Bossa Ahadee* (1789), p. 157.
32 Long, *History of Jamaica*, vol. ii, book III, ch. 1.
33 *Observations on the Bill Introduced last session* . . . (London 1816), p. 18.
34 'The negro's address to his fellows', *Instructions for the Treatment of Negroes* (1797), p. 133.
35 Long, *History of Jamaica*, vol. ii, book III, ch.1.
36 Bryan Edwards, vol. ii, ch. 1.
37 William Knox, *Three Tracts*, p. 37.
38 John Wesley, *Thoughts on Slavery* (1774).
39 Olaudah Equiano, *Interesting Narrative of the Life of Olaudah Equiano, or Gustavus Vassa, the African, written by himself*, 2 vols. (London 1789).
40 J. J. Hecht, *Continental and Colonial Servants in Eighteenth-Century England* (Northampton, Mass. 1954), p. 49; J. Walvin, *Black and White: The Negro and English Society 1555-1945* (Allen Lane 1973), ch. 4; Henry Mayhew, *London Labour and the London Poor*, 4 vols. (Dover Publications 1968), vol. iii, p. 190. But most of Mayhew's minstrels were British; an early example of the continuing, bizarre popular taste for 'nigger minstrels'.
41 William Dickson, *Letters on Slavery* (London 1789), p. 74.
42 Carlyle, 'Discourse on the nigger question', p. 86.
43 P. D. Curtin, *Two Jamaicas* (Harvard University Press 1955); M. G. Smith, *Plural Society in the West Indies* (University of California Press 1965); S. Olivier, *The Myth of Governor Eyre* (Hogarth Press 1962).
44 Parliamentary Papers (1866), vol. xxxi, p. 21.
45 Quoted in Christine Bolt, *Victorian Attitudes to Race* (Routledge & Kegan Paul 1971), p. 85.
46 ibid., p. 86.
47 *The Times*, 10 April 1866.
48 J. Walvin, *Black and White*, ch. 11.
49 The words are those of the *Saturday Review*, quoted in Bolt, *Victorian Attitudes to Race*, p. 91.
50 ibid., pp. 92-5, 98.
51 ibid., pp. 102, 105.
52 *Encyclopaedia Britannica* (Edinburgh 1810), vol. xiv, p. 750.
53 *Encyclopaedia Britannica*, vol. xvii, p. 318.

Part Two
Placing the contemporary situation in context

This section is intended to outline some of the background to the development of 'race relations' in Britain in the 1980s. The contributions will point to the importance of analysing events beyond the narrow immediate perspective of 'race', and to the necessity of maintaining an awareness of gender and class variables and their articulation with racism. Miles and Solomos provide an overview of the history of migration in Britain, and particularly focus on the role of the state in regulating these migrations and in managing the immigrants who have settled in Britain. They also provide an analysis of the political debates about the impact of migration and settlement. In drawing this together in a uniquely succinct overview they provide a context in which the subsequent contributions may be placed.

The chapter by Dummett and Dummett provides a specific case study within the time period spanned by Miles and Solomos. Their argument was stunning in its implications when first published, and remains one of the most telling analyses of the entry of party politics and Government into the legitimation of racism in Britain through the introduction of discriminatory legislation and the debate which facilitated it.

In the chapter which follows, Ben-Tovim and Gabriel review the 'Politics of race in Britain' from the 1960s to the beginning of the 1980s. They provide a review of the literature and offer an analysis of the competing perspectives which informed debate in that period. As social science if often apt to ignore or selectively remember its own development this discussion is important to an understanding of more recent developments in theory and policy. For example, their discussion of the development of Government policy, of 'race relations' pressure groups, and of extra-Parliamentary politics takes on a new significance when viewed from the perspective of the civil disorders of the early 1980s and the dramatic expansion of the 'race relations industry' in local authorities throughout Britain.

In the final chapter in this section Allen notes the failure of academics to acknowledge the significance of gender in mediating 'race relations' situations. She also examines the failure of feminist theorists to articulate 'race' into their analysis of gender inequalities. In placing both domains of neglect in a historical context she provides a foundation for an exploration of the inherent difficulties which emerge in trying to make use of empirical surveys of the position of women in contemporary Britain. In identifying the inadequacies of disciplinary or theoretical narrowness Allen is echoing a view which is increasingly evident; namely that the research on race, class and gender over the last two decades has thrown into question the viability of prioritizing any single one of these variables in accounting for contemporary 'race relations'. The Centre for Contemporary Cultural Studies text, *The Empire Strikes Back*, Hutchinson 1982, was an important landmark in launching a committed critique of old certitudes: some of the theoretical alternatives which were presented in the 1980 Unesco publication, *Sociological Theories: Race and Colonialism*, are now to be found, with additional variations, being discussed in a more combative mode, in John Rex and David Mason's edited text, *Theories of Race and Ethnic Relations*, Cambridge University Press 1986.

In following up the issues raised in this section; for an account of the earlier stages in the emergence of a racist political climate in Britain the reader should consult Paul Foot's influential *Immigration and Race in British Politics*, Penguin 1965. And for an introduction to the inhuman consequences of the legislation passed to 'curb immigration' Robert Moore's and Tina Wallace's *Slamming the Door*, Martin Robertson 1975 is invaluable. In their book *Passports and Politics*, Penguin 1974, Derek Humphry and Michael Ward identify the liberal resistance to increasing legislative racism and record its demise beneath political pragmatism and popular prejudice. The continuing illiberality in the interpretation of immigration legislation is amply illustrated in Paul Gordon's, *Deportations and Removals*, Runnymede Trust 1984, and in his *White Law*, Pluto Press 1983.

Ben-Tovin *et al.* have developed their analysis of the possibility of local political struggle in their recent text, *The Local Politics of Race*, Macmillan 1986. While changes in black participation in party politics have been examined in Muhammad Anwar's, *Race and Politics*, Tavistock 1986, and Marian Fitzgerald's, *Political Parties and Black People*, Runnymede Trust 1984. The 'extra-Parliamentary activity' of the last few years and the state's reaction to it has been a subject of a wide range of accounts among which are: Martin Kettle and Lucy Hodges, *Uprising*, Pan Books 1982; *The Scarman Report*, 1981, Penguin; and John Benyon, *Scarman and After*, Pergamon 1984.

4 Migration and the state in Britain: a historical overview

Robert Miles and John Solomos

Introduction

The development of capitalism has been accompanied by an increased spatial mobility of human beings as agricultural producers have been dispossessed and deprived of access to land, and as sellers of labour power have responded to market demand for their only commodity. Yet it has also been accompanied by the formation of the nation-state, a territorially-specific political unit within which the population is accorded citizenship. The nation-state is like a private club, of which one usually gains membership by being born within its walls, and as a result of which certain economic and political benefits accrue. But because those benefits are not usually transferable to any other club, membership induces immobility, at least international immobility. It also follows that the club must have a security system to prevent non-members from entering and sharing illegitimately in those benefits. Thus, we are confronted by a paradox (or perhaps even a contradiction) because the formation of the nation-state has effects which counter the tendency towards an increased circulation of human beings.

Within these national-political units, the state plays the central role in regulating the entry and exit of human beings. In the contemporary world, those regarded as its citizens are permitted, usually, to enter and exit freely while those who are non-citizens (or aliens) require special permission for entry and settlement. But the extent of exclusionary practice is historically variable. Thus, while the practice of exclusion is considered to be a logical concomitant of the existence of the nation-state, whether or not that 'right' is exercised, and the criteria by which exclusion is effected, depends upon historical circumstances. As we shall argue throughout this paper these circumstances involve a complex totality of economic, social, political and ideological relations.

This paper is concerned with these latter issues with reference to the example of Britain. It has four objectives. First, it offers an overview of the history of migration into Britain since the late eighteenth century, documenting the scale and determinants of different migrations. This overview is not exhaustive, and several small-scale migrations (see Holmes, 1978; Watson, 1977) are ignored. Second, it documents the role of the state in effecting or regulating these different migrations, paying particular attention to the legislation implemented by the state. The legislation covered in this paper is summarized in Table 1, which may serve as a useful point of reference in following the analysis developed below. Third, it

Table 1 *Legislation concerning the entry and settlement of migrants to Britain*

1894	Merchant Shipping Act
1905	Aliens Order
1914	Aliens Restriction Act
1919	Aliens Restriction (Amendment) Act
1920	Aliens Order
1925	Special Restrictions (Coloured Alien Seamen) Order
1947	Polish Resettlement Act
1948	British Nationality Act
1962	Commonwealth Immigrants Act
1965	Race Relations Act
1968	Commonwealth Immigrants Act
1969	Immigration Appeals Act
1971	Immigration Act
1976	Race Relations Act
1981	British Nationality Act

assesses the criteria employed by the state to effect exclusionary practices. These practices have taken many forms over the last century and have involved many branches of the state. Fourth, it analyses the role of the state in managing the immigrants legally settled in Britain and the political debates about the impact of such settlement.

Irish migration, 1790–1900

An Irish presence in Britain can be traced back over several centuries (e.g. Edwards, 1981) (as can a British presence of a different sort in Ireland) but Irish migration to Britain began to increase significantly in the late eighteenth century in response to economic circumstances in Ireland and Britain and their uneven interdependence (see Miles, 1982, pp. 121–50; also Redford, 1976; Handley, n.d., 1970). Within Ireland, a process of land consolidation was occurring in the north and east as part of the process of development of capitalist agriculture. The objective was to produce grain, meat and dairy products as commodities for exchange in Britain and the result for sections of the Irish population (including small landowners) in these regions was dispossession and ejection from the land. In the south and west, dominated by small peasant landowners or small tenant producers, a process of extensive subdivision of plots was underway, in a context where the population was increasing and the potato had been introduced as the main crop and means of subsistence. The consequent 'freeing' of sections of the population from the land coincided with attempts to establish capitalist industrial production within Ireland, especially around Belfast, where a demand for labour was developing. Following the Act of Union in 1801, and the subsequent abolition of protective tariffs in Ireland, the development of capitalist agriculture was intensified while the flow of cheap manufactured goods from British capitalist industry stemmed the rise of industrial production within Ireland.

One consequence of these processes was an acceleration from the 1790s of seasonal migration to Britain (it having begun earlier in that century), especially on the part of small peasant producers who sought a cash income to meet increasing rent demands. The potato was planted early in the year and then men of the family unit migrated to Britain to sell their labour power to British farmers, especially during harvesting. This phase of production was not widely mechanized until the 1880s, while corn acreage increased and traditional sources of temporary labour were lost as a result of a migration of British rural labourers to urban areas (Morgan, 1982, pp. 14–29). In 1841, approximately 60,000 seasonal migrants came to Britain from Ireland (Irvine, 1960, p. 239) but the numbers declined from the 1850s, although demand for their labour power remained high in certain areas (Morgan, 1982, pp. 82–3). However, seasonal migration was only a serious option for those who retained access to land in Ireland. Thus, in combination with a growing demand for semi- and unskilled wage labour in British urban areas, a second consequence was the development of an emigration from Ireland which resulted in settlement in Britain. The appearance of potato blight in 1845, and the resulting starvation, intensified a migration that was therefore already well-established (Jackson, 1963, pp. 7–9).

The 1841 Census indicated that there were more than 400,000 Irish people living in England, Wales and Scotland while the 1851 Census reflected the consequence of the famine migration, indicating an Irish population of about 727,300. The peak was evident in the 1861 Census which gave the total Irish-born population resident in Britain as 806,000, after which there was a slow decline. In 1901, the Irish-born population was 632,000 (O Tuathaigh, 1985, p. 14). As a proportion of the total population, the 1851 figures constituted 2.9 per cent for England and Wales and 7.2 per cent for Scotland (Jackson, 1963, p. 11). But Census statistics included only people born in Ireland and therefore excluded those born to Irish parents in Britain. In taking this into account, one estimate of the total population of Irish origin in Scotland in mid nineteenth century doubled that suggested by the Census statistics (Handley, n.d., p. 45). In England, the main areas of Irish settlement were London (see Lees, 1979) and Lancashire, with smaller concentrations in the West Midlands and Yorkshire (e.g. Finnegan, 1985). In Scotland, the main areas of settlement were in various parts of the west, and particularly around Glasgow. This migration and settlement led to the formation of distinct communities, identifiable by cultural differences, notably religion (e.g. Aspinall, 1982).

In purely numerical terms the number of Irish migrants to Britain has been far in excess of any other migration (for example, in 1961, there was a minimum of 1 million Irish-born people living in Britain, a statistic that does not include people of Irish descent: Jackson, 1963, p. 15), and yet there has been no state intervention to regulate this migration and settlement. The absence of legislation contrasts sharply with the response of the British state to migration from the Caribbean and the Indian sub-continent in the twentieth century, demonstrating that numbers alone are not a sufficient determinant of state intervention. The absence of state regulation of Irish migration partly reflects the facts that Ireland was the first site for colonization by English and Scottish landowners and merchants (de Paor, 1971, pp. 1–32), both actual and prospective, and that in 1800, an Act of Union incorporated Ireland into the United Kingdom. In practice, and then in law, therefore, the population of Ireland has been incorporated into a larger political unit within which it had the status of common citizenship and within which it circulated in response to economic and political circumstances, without constraints imposed by the British state. And this condition effectively remained even after the formation of the Republic of Ireland in 1922, because citizens of the Irish Republic retained the right to freely enter and settle in Britain. Even after the Irish Republic left the Commonwealth in 1947, the British Nationality Act accorded citizens of the Republic the unique status of being free to enter, settle, work and vote in Britain (Evans, 1983, p. 61).

Additionally, although there was a hostile and negative working-class response to Irish migrants to Britain which stereotyped them in terms of their Catholicism (although not all Irish migrants were adherents to the Roman Catholic religion) as well as their supposed biological inferiority (see Curtis, 1968, 1971; Gilley, 1978; Miles, 1982, pp. 135–45; O Tuathaigh, 1985, pp. 20–3), large sections of the working class did not have the vote. This limited the possibility of Irish migration becoming an electoral issue and therefore the subject of state intervention (Nugent and King, 1979, p. 31), although it might also have encouraged the widespread use of violence against Irish migrants (e.g. Handley, n.d., pp. 131–52, 232–62; Millward, 1985; Gallagher, 1985). Moreover, the migration was swelling the growing labour market at a time when capitalist development was proceeding at a fast pace and when the dominant ideology was that of *laissez-faire*, an ideology that discouraged state intervention in favour of the operation of 'market forces'.

Jewish migration, 1880–1945

In the context of the rise of industrial capitalism in Britain and the related increased mobility of population, the most significant legislative intervention by the state was a response to Jewish migration. The English (later British) state had a history of legislation to limit the entry of 'aliens' into the country but during most of the nineteenth century there were no controls on the entry of non-British subjects. Both an Act of 1836 (a product largely of earlier attempts to prevent military or political subversion during war with France) and an Aliens Bill of 1848 fell quickly into disuse and aliens were effectively freely admitted (Porter, 1979, pp. 1–3; Bevan, 1986, p. 64). In this context, the Aliens Order 1905 was a radical departure, it being a restrictive measure to limit the entry of Jewish migrants from Eastern Europe, and it formed the foundation for subsequent legislation until after the Second World War. Moreover, this legislation constituted the main feature of the legal context within which the British state responded to the emigration of Jews from Germany following the rise of fascism in the 1930s.

In the late nineteenth century, there were approximately 60,000 Jewish people living in Britain, more than half having been born in Britain. The majority of this population were shopkeepers and merchants, but a smaller proportion constituted a part of the capitalist class and another section were artisans of various kinds (Lipman, 1954, pp. 27–9, 79–81; Finestein, 1961, pp. 107–8). Between 1870 and 1914, some 120,000 Jewish people migrated to and settled in Britain (Gartner, 1973, p. 30) and by 1914 the Jewish population had grown to about 300,000 persons (Pollins, 1982, p. 130). The numerical significance of this migration is best contextualized by recalling that between 1881 and 1911, the population of Great Britain increased by ten million people. This migration changed the character of the Jewish population both economically and culturally. Most migrants originated in Eastern Europe, spoke Yiddish and had been engaged in various workshop trades or peddling (Pollins, 1982, p. 133), so that in Britain they constituted, at least initially, a culturally distinct section of the Jewish population and became concentrated in a limited range of workshop trades.

The determinants of the migration were both economic and political (Gainer, 1972, p. 1; Gartner, 1973, pp. 21–2; Pollins, 1982, p. 134). The size of the Jewish population in Eastern Europe increased from the early nineteenth century, but economic structures failed to adapt to this change, intensifying problems of poverty and famine. There was, therefore, economic pressure to migrate but this was magnified by various forms of political exclusion. The state in Eastern Europe prevented Jews from living in certain areas and from the larger cities, while pogroms led to the deaths of many thousands of Jewish people. The consequence was a large migration from Eastern to Western Europe, and thence to North America. Britain became both an intermediate transit point and a country in which to settle, not least because there were no legal restrictions to prohibit entry. In the period 1881/83, net immigration to Britain totalled 5000/6000 people per annum and, although the annual total declined during the rest of the decade, it increased to over 7000 people per annum in 1891 and to around 9000 people per annum between 1899 and 1902 (Gainer, 1972, p. 3).

This migration is best regarded as a migration of political refugees (Slatter, 1964), even though economic conditions in Eastern Europe were far from irrelevent. However, considered in relation to the British economy, this migration was not stimulated by labour demand within Britain, and this had implications for the position that these migrants were to take up in the British economy. Irish migrants already constituted a large pool of semi- and unskilled labour, and Jewish migrants did not possess the skills and experience for entry into either skilled factory work or non-manual areas of employment. They settled in the largest urbanized areas, notably in London, Birmingham, Manchester, Leeds and

Glasgow (Lipman, 1954, p. 102), where they entered a number of workshop trades, both as sellers of labour power and as petit-capitalists.

In most cases, they engaged in trades which they had practised in Eastern Europe, notably tailoring, dressmaking, boot and shoe production, furniture construction, and tobacco processing and production. These trades were undergoing a transition in Britain, being midway between workshop and factory production. There was an advanced division of labour requiring the use of an expanding semi-skilled workforce, and competition between small units of production in the context of an increasing supply of labour led to downward pressure on wages and increased productivity (Gartner, 1973, pp. 63–4; Pollins, 1982, p. 144). The result was competition with, and displacement of, indigenous labour in these sectors. In East London in particular, where a large proportion of Jewish migrants settled, many sectors of employment were undergoing structural change, and the threat of unemployment was a constant factor for sections of the working class (Gainer, 1972, p. 20).

These economic circumstances, when considered along with an extant shortage of housing, led to working-class demands for restrictions on entry (Holmes, 1979, pp. 13–16). Trade union agitation was evident in resolutions passed at Trades Union Congresses in 1892, 1894 and 1895, although that section strongly in favour of restrictions on entry was small and weak (Garrard, 1971, pp. 71, 174) because the economic consequences of Jewish migration were experienced by only certain sections of the working class. But the more significant reflection of this opposition was evident in Parliament because a small number of Conservative MPs took up the issue in order to attract working-class votes. Their support for restrictions on entry was logically and politically consistent with Conservative demands for state intervention for, for example, the protection of domestic industry (Gainer, 1972, p. 144; Pollins, 1982, p. 140). The Liberal Party, on the other hand, remained opposed to restrictive legislation because of its support for free trade and therefore the free movement of human beings as well as commodities (Garrard, 1971, p. 90).

Parliamentary support for immigration controls was linked with extra-Parliamentary action. In 1901, a Conservative MP for an East London constituency formed the British Brothers League to agitate against Jewish migration and settlement. It organized mass protest rallies and attained a membership of around 45,000 people (Gainer, 1972, pp. 60–73; Holmes, 1979, pp. 89–97). The activities of the British Brothers League gave wider public prominence to the demand for control within Parliament, and agitation within Parliament made Jewish migration a national political issue. The ideological form in which the political issue was expressed, and the motivation for some of the agitation, was explicitly racist (Gainer, 1972, p. 113) and articulated with nationalism (Garrard, 1971, p. 56).

The progress of the demand for restrictive legislation within Parliament is well documented (see Garrard, 1971; Gainer, 1972; Alderman, 1983, pp. 66–85). Demands for legislation were first raised in 1887, but could not be realized until the election of a Conservative government. But even after this happened in 1895, political circumstances obstructed their realization until 1905 when the Aliens

Order was passed. This legislation applied to the entry into Britain of all non-United Kingdom subjects, to those otherwise defined as 'aliens'. The most important provisions of the legislation were, first, that aliens could be refused permission to enter Britain if they did not have, or did not have the means to obtain, the means of subsistence in adequate sanitary condition; and, second, that an alien could be expelled from Britain without trial or appeal if he or she was found to be receiving poor relief within a year of entering Britain, if he or she was found guilty of vagrancy, or was found to be living in insanitary conditions due to overcrowding. Other provisions of the Order were that the Home Secretary was given the power to expel 'undesirable' immigrants, and that an immigrant refused permission to enter Britain could appeal to an Immigration Board. But the Order also embodied in law the provision that an immigrant could not be refused permission to enter Britain where it could be shown that he or she was the subject of political or religious persecution (Gainer, 1972, p. 190; MacDonald, 1983, p. 8; Bevan, 1986, pp. 71–2).

Soon after the Aliens Order became law, the Conservative Government was replaced by a Liberal Government which, although it failed to repeal the legislation, implemented it in a non-restrictive manner. Until 1914, approximately 4000/5000 Jews entered Britain annually (Lebzelter, 1978, p. 9). But it was the outbreak of war which initiated further legislation on immigration. The Aliens Restriction Act, 1914, passed through Parliament in a single day and gave the Government considerable powers to control immigration through Orders in Council, the justification for such powers being in terms of 'national security' in circumstances of war. The legislation applied to aliens whom the government could prohibit from entering Britain, who could be deported and who could be subject to restrictions on where they lived and travelled.

After the end of the war, the Aliens Restriction (Amendment) Act 1919 repealed the 1905 legislation and extended the 1914 Act for one year, despite the fact that the original justification for the Act no longer applied. In the following year a new Aliens Order was passed and thereafter the Acts of 1914 and 1919 were renewed annually under the Expiring Laws Continuance Acts. Under the Aliens Order 1920, immigration officers could refuse entry to an alien who was considered to be unable to provide for his or her own support and were given increased powers to deal with aliens who had evaded immigration control. Aliens had to register their residence and any change thereof. The Home Secretary gained the power to deport any alien whose presence was not considered to be 'conducive to the public good'. Finally, if an alien wished to work in Britain, he or she could only do so following the issue to an employer of a permit by the Ministry of Labour, the permit being issued only when it was shown that no British labour was available (Evans, 1983, pp. 10–12; MacDonald, 1983, pp. 8–9; Gordon, 1985, pp. 9–11; Bevan, 1986, pp. 72–4).

It was within the terms of this legislation that the British state responded to the growing numbers of Jewish and other refugees fleeing from Germany following the installation of a fascist government (Stevens, 1975; Hirschfeld, 1984). It is important to recall that the substance of that legislation was that aliens considered to be without the means to sustain themselves could be refused permission to enter Britain while poverty was not sufficient grounds to refuse entry to those claiming to be fleeing religious or political persecution. Events demonstrated that other circumstances were cited as reasons for denying entry to Britain to political refugees. Throughout the period 1933–39, the British government asserted that Britain was not a country of immigration because of its large population and high level of unemployment, and therefore the admission of Jewish (and other) refugees from Germany could only be on a limited scale (Sherman, 1973, p. 259). In this period of time, about 55,000 refugees from Germany, Austria and Czechoslovakia were admitted to Britain (Sherman, 1973, p. 271). This contrasts with the continuing and unrestricted entry of Irish citizens into Britain (Jackson, 1963, pp. 13, 194).

The main feature of state policy emerged in 1933. In the light of an initiative from the Jewish community, the Government established a principle that refugees would only be admitted if it were shown that they would not become a cost to the state. Thus, the Jewish community guaranteed to meet the costs of entry and settlement of refugees from fascism (Bentwick, 1956, p. 16). This was a highly significant condition because a requirement of exit for Jews from Germany was the confiscation by the state of most or all personal wealth and possessions. But the government also agreed that 'prominent Jews' should be admitted to Britain in order to facilitate a favourable international impression (Sherman, 1973, pp. 30–2).

During the decade, circumstances in Germany deteriorated for the Jews and the pressure to emigrate increased substantially, especially following the occupation of Austria in March 1938. The German Jewish Aid Committee in Britain announced that it could no longer undertake to guarantee that any Jewish refugee admitted to Britain would not become a charge to the state (Bentwick, 1956, pp. 45–6), while the British state considered ways of further restricting the flow of refugees into Britain. In the same month as the Nazi occupation of Austria, a visa system was introduced for aliens holding German or Austrian passports, the justification being to prevent people from beginning journeys that could not be completed. The Instructions to Passport Control Officers stated that the purpose of the visa system was to:

> . . . regulate the flow into the United Kingdom of people who, for political, racial or religious reasons, may wish to take refuge in considerable numbers. [cited in Sherman, 1973, p. 90]

The principal criterion for the issue of a visa to a refugee was 'whether or not an applicant is likely to be an asset to the United Kingdom' (cited in Sherman, 1973, p. 91). Thus, persons with an international reputation in science, medicine, art, etc., were issued immediately with visas whereas those likely to wish to seek employment were defined as unsuitable.

This new policy was justified in Parliament by asserting that although the government remained committed to the 'traditional policy' of offering asylum to those forced to leave their country, indiscriminate admission would aggravate mass unemployment and the housing shortage. Later in the same year, and probably mindful of the activities of the British Union of Fascists (Lebzelter, 1978, pp. 86–109), the Home Secretary also referred to the danger of the growth of an anti-Jewish movement in Britain if large numbers of Jewish refugees were admitted to Britain. In other words, Jews fleeing racist persecution in Germany could not be admitted to Britain because of racist agitation in Britain. What was not conceded was that mass unemployment and a housing shortage were determinants of racist agitation, as had been demonstrated in the late nineteenth century.

In late 1938, in response to the deteriorating circumstances on the Continent, there was a minor liberalization of practice. In November, it was announced that certain refugees would be allowed temporary admission to Britain, pending their migration elsewhere, and child refugees would be more easily granted entry if their maintenance was guaranteed (Bentwick, 1956, p. 65; Sherman, 1973, pp. 93, 180). But the significance of this initiative should be evaluated in the light of the fact that in the same month there were about 10,000 applications for visas awaiting action (Sherman, 1973, p. 214).

With the outbreak of war, the possibility of entering Britain diminished further. Visas previously issued were declared invalid and all immigration from Germany and territory occupied by German armed forces was prohibited. Various exceptions were made, but the numbers were small and, with the occupation of Holland, Belgium and France, they were reduced even further. It is estimated that during the war the Jewish population in Britain increased by about 10,000 people through immigration. The justification for exclusion from Britain was identical to that offered during the 1930s, added to which was a new claim about national security. Compared with the 1930s, the only significant shift in state policy was that it took over financial responsibility for the maintenance of Jewish refugees, although the overall cost declined during the war as refugee unemployment decreased (Wasserstein, 1979, pp. 81–115). Additionally, the British government continued to seek external locations where Jewish refugees might be allowed to settle.

But the public justification for the policy of exclusion from Britain appears somewhat shallow when one recalls that, following the invasion of the Low Countries, the British state made formal arrangements to admit up to 300,000 Dutch and Belgian citizens (Wasserstein, 1979, p. 132). This number was far in excess of the total number of Jewish refugees admitted to Britain between 1933 and 1945, and on the government's own logic, would have increased dramatically the housing shortage and the danger of infiltration by 'enemy agents'. Additionally, as we shall see shortly, the British state admitted 30,500 members of the Polish Government and Armed Forces in exile during the war. The motivation for this discrepancy is not explained by referring, as Wasserstein does, to the fact that German and Austrian Jews were defined as 'enemy aliens' because that, too, requires explanation in the light of what was known about Nazi policy concerning the Jews, especially after the details of the 'Final Solution' became public knowledge. It seems more likely that the government and state officials were prepared to concede to, and thereby legitimize, the widespread racism that was evident in Britain (Wasserstein, 1979, p. 116) and, at least in certain quarters, may even have been motivated by racism.

The state and British seamen, 1900–25

In the preceding section, we have been concerned with the policy of the British state towards the entry into Britain of people who were, by law, aliens, that is non-British citizens. But the legislation effected by the state was also used to deal with, and contained provisions concerning, certain categories of British subjects, specifically seamen recruited in different parts of the Empire, particularly from India and the Caribbean (although not all seamen were British subjects). Despite being British subjects, Indian seamen (widely known as Lascars) had been subject to discriminatory treatment by the state since the nineteenth century, if not before, partly in order to limit their settlement in Britain when the passage that they had worked terminated in Britain.

An Act of 1813 required the East India Company to provide subsistence for Indian sailors in Britain until they returned to India, while an Act of 1823 stipulated that Indian seamen were not British subjects and prohibited their discharge in Britain. The latter Act, however, explicitly referred to West Indian seamen as British subjects. These powers were consolidated in the Merchant Shipping Act 1894 which set out articles of agreement to be signed by Asian seamen and masters which bound the former to return to their country of origin and gave the Secretary of State the power to repatriate those who attempted to become resident in Britain (Hepple, 1968, pp. 42–4; Joshua *et al.*, 1983, pp. 14–16; Gordon, 1985, pp. 5–6). These attempts were only partially successful, as the continuous presence of Asian and Caribbean people in British seaports proved (e.g. Fryer, 1984, pp. 294–5; Visram, 1986, pp. 34–54).

After 1918, the British state reinforced discriminatory practices and made further efforts to prevent British subjects considered to be of a different 'race' settling in Britain. This occurred in the context of the ending of the First World War, during which there had been an increase in the number of British subjects from the Empire employed as seamen. Concerning discriminatory practices, Section 5(2) of the Aliens Restriction (Amendment) Act 1919 legalized different rates of pay for British subjects employed as seamen according to their 'race' (Hepple, 1968, pp. 44–5; Joshua *et al.*, 1983, p. 16). Additionally, there was a slump in employment in the shipping industry after 1918 and the relevant trade unions campaigned to restrict employment to 'white' seamen. In the resulting competition for work, Indian, Chinese and Caribbean seamen resident in Britain became the victims of racist violence in Cardiff, Liverpool and Glasgow (e.g. May and Cohen, 1974; Evans, 1980, 1985; Jenkinson, 1985). In Cardiff, the police sought to 'repatriate' these seamen (Evans, 1985, pp. 73–4). The Home Office pointed out that they were British subjects and therefore were not liable to enforced expulsion from Britain, but also made arrangements for the return of seamen who might be 'persuaded' to do so. This initiative by the state was largely unsuccessful (Joshua *et al.*, 1983, pp. 31–2).

Subsequently, a further initiative was made using Article 11 of the Aliens Order 1920. By reference to this Article, the Special Restrictions (Coloured Alien Seamen) Order 1925 was effected (Hepple, 1968, p. 45; Joshua *et al.*, 1983, pp. 32–5; Gordon, 1985, p. 7; Evans, 1985, pp. 80–1; Rich, 1986, pp. 122–30). The Order formally applied to colonial seamen, previously entitled to sign off from a ship in a British port and to seek residence there, who did not possess satisfactory documentary evidence of being British subjects. These seamen were required to obtain permission of an Immigration Officer before landing and were subject to removal from Britain. In practice, the police, Aliens Department and Immigration Officers forced 'coloured' British subjects possessing the required documentation to register under the Order, an action that deprived them of their legal status as British subjects and thereby rendered them liable to the powers of the Alien Restriction (Amendment) Act 1919 and the Aliens Order 1920, which included the requirement that they register with the police, to whom they were required to report any change of address, and made them vulnerable to the possibility of deportation. Joshua *et al.* comment that (1983, p. 32):

> . . . the Order was specifically designed to restrict the entry and settlement of black colonial British citizens. But, because the Conservative Government did not wish to undermine the notion of a British subject which was at the heart of the Empire, the Order could only achieve its ends through a series of legalistic contortions and double standards.

The concern of the state, both at the local and national level, was multi-faceted. It was responding to local racist agitation and violence against those defined as 'coloured' seamen, action that was grounded in the inability of the economic system to provide full employment. But it was also grounded in a wider, racist concern that followed from the settlement of these seamen in Britain, specifically the growth of a population that resulted from sexual relations between these seamen and indigenous women (Rich, 1986, pp. 120–44). The state attempted to resolve these conflicts and perceived problems by removing from Britain those people who were the victims of racism. In so doing, the state legitimated and perpetuated racism. In the light of these events, post-1945 developments no longer appear unique but represent a continuity in practice by the British state.

The state and European migration, 1945–51

At the end of the Second World War, the British state had legislative powers in the form of the Aliens legislation to control the entry into Britain of non-British subjects and their access to the labour market. However, the vast majority of

British subjects in the colonies and dominions retained a legal right to enter and settle in Britain. This legal right was confirmed by the British Nationality Act 1948 which, in response to the granting of independence to India, made a formal distinction between British subjects who were citizens of the United Kingdom and Colonies and those who were Commonwealth citizens, both categories of people having the right to enter, settle and work in Britain (Evans, 1983, pp. 59–62; Bevan, 1986, pp. 112–13). Additionally, citizens of the Republic of Ireland retained the right of unrestricted entry and settlement.

But, in the immediate post-war period, few migrants to Britain came from the colonies or dominions. Indeed, despite the arrival of the *SS Empire Windrush* in 1948 with some 400 British subjects from the Caribbean, there was no public conception of the possibility of a migration of British subjects from the Commonwealth and colonies while, as we shall see, privately the Government was considering the most desirable method of preventing a migration of 'coloured' British citizens from the colonies. The most important source of migrants to Britain between 1945 and 1954 was Europe. Between 1945 and 1951, 70,000–100,000 Irish people entered Britain (Jackson, 1963, p. 14) and, in addition, the state actively facilitated and encouraged two further migrations.

The first group was of Polish origin, and they joined a small Polish population in Britain (Zubrzycki, 1956, p. 37; Lunn, 1980). In 1940, the Polish Government and Armed Forces in exile (a total of 30,500 persons) were allowed to enter Britain. Additionally, the Polish Second Corps, which joined the British Command in 1942, was brought to Britain in 1946, followed by families and dependants of members of the Polish armed forces. The latter were subsequently disbanded through the Polish Resettlement Corps in the case of those who were unwilling to return to Poland (which had become part of the Soviet zone of influence) and who were given the option of settlement in Britain. It has been estimated that, in 1949, the resident Polish population in Britain consisted of 91,400 members of the Polish Resettlement Corps, 31,800 dependants of Polish ex-servicemen, 2400 distressed relatives and 2300 additional ex-members of the Polish armed forces. These groups totalled 127,900 persons, to which one can add 29,400 European Volunteers Workers of Polish origin (see below) (Zubrzycki, 1956, p. 62).

In addition to the relatively large numbers of Polish aliens who were allowed to remain in Britain, the other significant feature of this migration was the degree of state intervention in the process of settlement. In addition to the establishment of the Polish Resettlement Corps (which disbanded the Polish armed forces, assisted its members to find employment and provided English language classes), the British government initiated the Polish Resettlement Act 1947. This Act enabled various Government departments to make arrangements to meet the specific needs of the Polish population. These included the running of three Polish hospitals and the provision of educational facilities and hostel accommodation (Zubrzycki, 1956, pp. 89–92). Thus, the state made money and other resources available to settle this population in Britain, and intervened in ways which helped to maintain a distinct Polish identity and community. This was sustained by the activities of various Polish voluntary groups and the Catholic Church, the British state co-operating with the former in the process of what was officially defined as 'resettlement' rather than 'immigration'.

The central motivating forces behind this almost unique intervention of the British state to permit the entry and permanent residence of a population that was, in law, an alien population was the fact that there were significant labour shortages in the British economy. Humanitarian considerations were secondary (Stadulis, 1951/52, pp. 208–9; Vernant, 1953, p. 343). In the period 1948–50, large numbers of ex-members of the Polish Resettlement Corps were found work in agriculture, coal-mining, hotels and catering, textiles, brick-making and engineering/metal production (Zubrzycki, 1956, p. 66), and it was to these same sectors of the economy that a second group of European migrants was recruited in the late 1940s.

This group was recruited by the British state specifically to resolve labour shortages in certain sectors of the economy (notably in agriculture, coal-mining and textile production). On the European mainland, there were several camps for displaced persons or political refugees who were unable or did not wish to return to their country of birth following the redrawing of political boundaries after the defeat of Germany, and the Labour Government decided to send Ministry of Labour officials to them to recruit workers. The occupants of these camps were or had been, in law, nationals of other countries and were therefore aliens as far as the British state was concerned. But the procedures for admission under the Aliens Order 1920, concerned as they were with the admission of single persons, were not appropriate for what was to become a considerable migration. The result was, in the British context, a unique scheme, the British state undertaking to meet all the costs of recruitment, transport and repatriation on behalf of those capitalists short of labour power (ILO, 1949, pp. 438–40) and, in a number of respects, it anticipated the contract migrant labour system set up by a number of Western European states in the 1950s and 1960s (Castles and Kosack, 1973; Castles *et al.*, 1984; Miles, 1986). The total cost of the scheme up to October 1948 was £2.75 million (Tannahill, 1958, p. 56).

Those displaced persons who came to Britain were required to sign a contract, the terms of which stated that they would accept work selected by the Minister of Labour and that they could only change that employment with the permission of the Ministry of Labour. Therefore, they became European Volunteer Workers (EVWs). Following health checks, they were admitted initially for one year, an extension being dependent upon the individual complying with the conditions of the contract and behaving 'as a worthy member of the British community' (Tannahill, 1958, pp. 123–8). Many of those recruited were not initially eligible to bring their dependants with them, although most of those who eventually settled in Britain were subsequently joined by their families. The conditions of placement of EVWs in employment varied but usually included the requirements that no British labour was available, that in the event of redundancy EVWs would be the first to be made unemployed, that EVWs should join the appropriate trade union and that they should receive the same wages and conditions as British workers (Tannahill, 1958, p. 57).

EVWs were recruited during 1947 and 1948 under a number of different schemes, the most important being the Balt Cygnet and Westward Ho schemes. In total, 74,511 persons (17,422 women and 57,089 men) were recruited by these two schemes. Most originated from Estonia, Latvia, Lithuania, Poland and Yugoslavia. In addition 8397 Ukranian prisoners of war were brought to Britain for political reasons in 1947 and it was subsequently decided to treat them as EVWs. Under the North Sea and Blue Danube schemes, 12,000 German and Austrian women were recruited on a distinct temporary contract for two years, most returning to Germany and Austria on the termination of the contract. Under a similar arrangement, 5000 Italians of both sexes were also recruited (Tannahill, 1958, pp. 5–6, 30–3). Altogether, approximately 85,000 refugees were recruited as workers for employment in the late 1940s. This total was lower than that originally envisaged. For example, it was anticipated that 100,000 workers would be recruited in 1948 alone (Stadulis, 1954/52, p. 215).

Concerning the sectors of the economy to which EVWs were directed, and referring only to those recruited under the Balt Cygnet and Westward Ho schemes, 29,554 men entered agriculture, 12,216 women entered textiles, 10,968 men entered coal-mining, and 6759 women and 5156 men entered domestic service of various kinds. Other notable sectors of employment for men were brick-making, iron and steel and textiles (Vernant, 1953, p. 366; Stadulis, 1954/52, p. 213; Tannahill, 1958, p. 133). In January 1951, the state announced that once EVWs had been resident for three years, all restrictions would be lifted, freeing them from employment dictated by the Ministry of Labour. Thereafter, a large proportion of EVWs changed their employment, entering semi- or unskilled work with higher wages and/or overtime, or emigrated (Tannahill, 1958, p. 81).

Migration, colonial labour and the state 1945–62

As we have seen already, despite the fact that the vast majority of British subjects from the colonies and independent Commonwealth countries retained the right to enter and settle in the UK, the concern of the state during 1945–51 was to encourage the use of migrant labour from Europe to meet the demand for labour. Some British subjects from the colonies did arrive during this period, particularly from the West Indies, but almost as soon as they began to arrive they were perceived as a 'problem'. The relatively liberal attitude towards the arrival of European (alien) workers contrasted sharply with the fears expressed about the social and 'racial' problems which were seen as related to the arrival of 'coloured colonial workers' who were British subjects.

It was during the period from 1945–62 that the terms of political debate about 'coloured' immigration were established, leading to a close association between 'race' and immigration as a whole. Contrary to the arguments of some scholars it seems quite inadequate to see this period as an 'age of innocence' and lack of concern about black immigration into the UK (Rose *et al.*, 1969; Patterson, 1969; Deakin, 1970). Throughout this period an increasingly racialized debate about immigration took place, focusing on the supposed 'social problems' of having too many black migrants and the question of how they could be stopped from entering, given their legal rights under the 1948 British Nationality Act.

This racialization of the immigration issue took place despite the fact that when compared to the total of European workers admitted between 1945–51 the number of black workers arriving remained relatively small until the late 1950s. One estimate of black immigration between 1955 and 1962 is shown in Table 2.

Table 2 *Estimated net inward movement of West Indians, Indians, and Pakistanis, 1955–62*

Year	West Indies	India	Pakistan	Total
1955	27,550	5,800	1,850	35,200
1956	29,800	5,600	2,050	37,450
1957	23,000	6,600	5,200	34,800
1958	15,000	6,200	4,700	25,900
1959	16,400	2,950	850	27,400
1960	49,650	5,900	2,500	58,050
1961	66,300	23,750	25,100	115,150
1962	31,800	15,050	25,680	72,530
Total	259,500	75,850	67,330	402,680

Source: G. Freeman, *Immigrant Labor and Racial Conflict in Industrial Societies*, 1979, p. 23.

Although much publicity was given to the arrival of 417 Jamaicans on the *Empire Windrush* in May 1948, and subsequent arrivals by large groups of West Indian workers, the focus on 'coloured' immigration helped to obscure the fact that the majority of immigrants continued to come from the Irish Republic, from 'white' Commonwealth countries and other European countries (Patterson, 1969, chapter 1; Miles and Phizacklea, 1984, pp. 45–8). The concentration on the number of West Indian immigrants, and later on the number of immigrants from India and Pakistan, has been shown to have been an issue of debate within the Cabinet during the period 1950–5, when various measures to control black immigration and to dissuade black workers from coming to the UK were considered. On the basis of a careful analysis of Cabinet and Ministerial debates about immigration from the colonies a recent study has concluded that the period from 1948 to 1962 involved the state in a complex political and ideological racialization of immigration policy:

The period between the 1948 Nationality Act and the 1962 Commonwealth Immigrants Act is frequently characterised as one in which the principle of free entry of

British subjects to the UK was only relinquished with great reluctance and after considerable official debate. This was not the case. On the contrary, the debate was never about principle. Labour and Conservative Governments had by 1952 instituted a number of covert, and sometimes illegal, administrative measures to discourage black immigration [Carter, Harris and Joshi, forthcoming].

Additionally, throughout the 1950s the debate about immigration in Parliament and the media began to focus on the need to control black immigration. The 1958 riots in Notting Hill and Nottingham may have helped to politicize this process further, but it is clear that both before and after the riots themselves the question of control was being integrated into the policy agenda (Harris and Solomos, forthcoming).

With the growing emphasis on the control of 'coloured' immigration the terms of ideological and policy debates about the future of colonial workers in the UK turned on two themes which were to prove influential later on. First, a vigorous debate took place in and out of Parliament about the possibility of revising the 1948 Nationality Act so as to limit the number of black workers who could come and settle in the UK. The terms of this debate were by no means fixed purely by political party ideologies, and there was opposition from both Conservative and Labour politicians to the call for controls and the abandonment of the free entry principle. Second, a parallel debate developed about the problems caused by 'too many coloured immigrants' in relation to housing, employment and crime (Carter, Harris and Joshi, forthcoming). This second theme became particularly important in the period 1956–8, and in the aftermath of the 1958 riots (*Hansard* Vol 596, 1958, cols 1552–97). By linking immigration to social aspects of the 'colour problem' a theme was established which was later to influence both the immigration control legislation and the Race Relations Acts.

Controls on 'coloured' immigration had been discussed as early as 1950, and were seriously discussed again in 1955. A number of arguments were used in opposition to such controls, and it was not until 1961 that a Bill to control Commonwealth immigration was introduced by the Government. The reasons for the reluctance to introduce controls remains to some extent a matter of speculation, although the release of Government documents for the period of the early 1950s has shed some light on this non-decision making process (Carter and Joshi, 1984, pp. 55–63; Rich, 1968, chapter 7). But at least part of the reluctance to introduce controls seemed to result from a concern about whether legislation which excluded black people could be implemented without causing embarrassment to Britain's position as head of the Commonwealth and Colonies, the fear that it would divide public opinion, and a doubt about the legality of controls based on 'colour' in both British and international law (Deakin, 1968, pp. 26–30; Miles and Phizacklea, 1984, chapter 2).

By the time of the 1958 riots, however, the mobilization of opinion in and out of Parliament in favour of controls was well advanced, and it is noticeable that between these events and the introduction of the Commonwealth Immigrants Bill in 1961 important debates on immigration control took place (Patterson, 1969; Freeman, 1979, pp. 49–52; Miles, 1984). The 'riots' themselves consisted of attacks by whites on blacks, but this did not prevent them being used as examples of the dangers of unrestricted immigration. In Parliament a number of Conservative MPs, including Cyril Osborne, organized a campaign in favour of immigration controls, though they made their case against 'coloured' migrants largely through coded language. The Labour Party, along with the Liberals, generally argued against controls, though this was by no means the case for all Labour MPs and local councillors (Reeves, 1983, chapter 7; Layton-Henry, 1984, pp. 31–43).

The ambiguities in the pressure for controls became even more pronounced during 1960–1, the period leading up to the passage of the first legislative measure controlling the immigration of citizens of the United Kingdom and colonies, the 1962 Commonwealth Immigrants Act.

Immigration controls and state racism

In the previous section we argued that the racialization of the immigration issue during the 1950s laid the basis for the move towards the control of black immigration, an objective which was first implemented through the 1962 Commonwealth Immigrants Act. Part of the dilemma faced by the Conservative Government of the time was how to legitimize a policy which aimed to control black immigration as a more universal measure. William Deedes, who was a Minister without Portfolio at the time, recalls that

> The Bill's real purpose was to restrict the influx of coloured immigrants. We were reluctant to say as much openly. So the restrictions were applied to coloured and white citizens in all Commonwealth countries – though everybody recognised that immigration from Canada, Australia and New Zealand formed no part of the problem [Deedes, 1968, p. 10].

The racialization of the immigration issue along racial lines was in other words through coded language: 'commonwealth immigrants' were seen as a 'problem' only if they were black. The politicization of such terms was later to lead to a situation where, despite the continuing scale of white immigration, popular common sense perceived all immigrants as black.

Two competing explanatory models have been used to explain the move towards immigration controls. Some scholars have seen this shift as a response by the state to the pressure of popular opinion against black immigration (Foot, 1965; Rose *et al.*, 1969, chapter 16). Yet others have argued that the state was responding to the economic interests of the capitalist class, which required the adoption of a migrant labour system which undermined the right of black workers to migrate and settle freely in the UK (Sivanandan, 1982, pp. 101–26; Freeman and Spencer, 1979, pp. 63–8). Both explanations have been widely used in the extensive literature on the politics of immigration, but as we have indicated already it seems inadequate to view the role of the state as purely responsive, whether to popular opinion or to economic interests. Throughout the period 1948–62 the state was actively involved in monitoring and regulating the arrival of black workers, and helped to articulate a definition of the immigration question which was suffused with racialized categories.

The genesis of the demand for the control of black immigration during the early 1950s matured during the period 1955–8 into a concerted campaign within the Cabinet, Parliament, the media and political parties, in favour of action to 'curb the dangers of unrestricted immigration'. This in turn led to the policy debate which developed in the period leading up to the introduction of the Commonwealth Immigrants Bill in 1961 about the formulation of legislation which could exclude black labour from entry and settlement. This process can hardly be interpreted as a move from *laissez faire* to state intervention, since the state and its institutions were already heavily involved in defining the terms of the debate about the 'problems' caused by black immigration.

The acceptance of the need to extend administrative controls on black immigration into legislative action was formally announced in October 1961, when the Conservative Government announced the introduction of the Commonwealth Immigrants Bill. The controls announced under the Bill were legitimized by arguments about the need for a halt to black immigration because of the limited ability of the host society to assimilate 'coloured immigrants'. Even though some MPs and commentators were reluctant to accept that the Bill was simply a way of dealing with the immigration of 'coloured workers', the Labour Party and sections of the media identified the Bill as a response to crude racist pressures. Hugh Gaitskell, as leader of the Labour Party, led a particularly strong attack on the Bill in Parliament and its crude amalgamation of 'immigration' with 'race' (Patterson, 1969, pp. 17–20; IRR Newsletter: May 1962). But despite strong criticism from the Labour Party and sections of the press, the collective pressures against the entry of black British succeeded when the Commonwealth Immigrants Act became law in 1962.

Since it was the outcome of the sustained political campaign against black immigration the Act sought to control the entry of black Commonwealth citizens into the UK. The Act introduced a distinction between citizens of the UK and Colonies and citizens of independent Commonwealth countries. All holders of Commonwealth passports were subject to immigration control except those who were (a) born in the UK; (b) held UK passports issued by the UK Government; or (c) persons included in the passport of one of the persons excluded from immigration control under (a) or (b) (Macdonald, 1983, pp. 10–12; Gray and Lowe, 1983). Other Commonwealth citizens had to obtain a Ministry of Labour employment voucher in order to be able to enter the UK. The Act initially provided for three types of vouchers:

Category A: Commonwealth citizens who had a specific job to come to in Britain.

Category B: Applicants who had a recognized skill or qualification which was in short supply in Britain.

Category C: All other applicants, priority treatment being given to those who had served in the British forces during the war.

During the period from 1963 to 1972, when the voucher system was abolished, there was pressure to cut back the number of vouchers allocated, and this was reflected in a fall from a level of 30,130 vouchers in 1963 to 2290 in 1972. Significantly, no controls were imposed on the entry of citizens of the Irish Republic into Britain.

In terms of numbers admitted under the voucher scheme the flow of workers is indicated in Table 3. Since the Act did not exclude wives and children from entering to join parents or husbands already in the UK, the main flow of immigrants after 1962 consisted of dependants of Commonwealth citizens (Katznelson, 1976, pp. 35–6).

Table 3 *Ministry of Labour voucher holders admitted 1 July 1962 to December 1972*

Year	West Indies	India	Pakistan	Total
1962	1,600	646	391	2,637
1963	2,077	8,366	13,526	23,969
1964	2,635	3,828	3,296	9,759
1965	2,987	3,794	2,520	9,301
1966	628	2,433	721	3,782
1967	630	2,175	754	3,559
1968	240	930	374	1,544
1969	304	1,382	511	2,197
1970	322	791	381	1,494
1971	110	634	296	1,040
1972	61	225	62	348

Source: G. Freeman, *Immigrant Labor and Racial Conflict in Industrial Societies*, 1979, p. 24.

The opposition of the Labour Party to the 1962 Act was not sustained. When Harold Wilson took office as Labour Prime Minister in 1964 he announced that the Commonwealth Immigrants Act would be maintained. In 1965 the Government issued a White Paper on *Immigration from the Commonwealth* which called for controls to be maintained in an even stricter form, along with measures to promote the 'integration' of immigrants. The White Paper represented a shift in the direction of what some have called a 'Little England' policy (Rose *et al.*, p. 229), and signalled a convergence of the policies of the Conservative and Labour Parties in favour of immigration controls.

One of the features of the 1962 Act was that citizens of the United Kingdom living in independent Commonwealth countries were exempt from control provided they had a UK passport. This included a large number of European settlers as well as a sizeable number of East African Asians in Kenya and Uganda. During the period from 1965 to 1967 a steady flow of this group began to arrive in Britain and when sections of the media and MPs started to call for action to be taken to stop their arrival a heated political debate ensued in late 1967 and early 1968. As noted above the Labour Party had moved towards acceptance of the need for firm immigration controls during the period from 1963–5, and so it came as no surprise when it responded to this political campaign by introducing the second Commonwealth Immigrants Act in early 1968. This Act sought to control the flow of East African Asians by bringing them under immigration control. Under the new law any citizen of the United Kingdom or colonies, who was the holder of a passport issued by the UK Government, was now subject to immigration control unless they or at least one parent or grandparent was born, adopted, naturalized or registered as a citizen of the United Kingdom and colonies in the UK.

The political context in which the Act was passed made it difficult to argue that it was 'non-racial', as to some extent had been claimed by the Conservative Government which had passed the 1962 Act. *The Times* contrasted the behaviour of the Labour Government to the attitude of the Labour opposition in 1962 and went so far as to call the Act a 'colour bar' and 'probably the most shameful measure that Labour members have ever been asked by their whips to support' (27 February 1968). The transformation of the political climate between 1962 and 1968 was, however, clear enough for all to see in the Parliamentary debates about the 1968 Act. Given the highly politicized nature of the debate around the Act and the defensive stance taken by the Government, only a few MPs and newspaper commentators saw fit to question the racism which underlay the legislation (Freeman, 1979, p. 56 ff; Miles and Phizacklea, 1984, pp. 59–67). Indeed the period between the 1968 Act and the 1970 election, which saw the return of a Conservative Government, saw a further racialization of the immigration issue. Even though it was difficult to see how immigration could be cut even further than the controls imposed by the 1962 and 1968 Acts, it was precisely during the period 1968–70 that 'immigration' and 'race relations' became issues of partisan political debate on a larger scale than before.

During this period the Labour Government was forced on the defensive on two fronts. First, Enoch Powell's famous 'rivers of blood' speech in Birmingham in 1968 helped to popularize the common-sense racial message that even tighter controls on immigration were not enough to deal with the 'race problem'. According to Powell's argument the long-term solution to the 'immigration' issue involved the repatriation of immigrants already settled in the UK. Such a line of argument helped to push political debate beyond controls as such and established repatriation as part of the political agenda. Second, the continued arrival of the dependants of Commonwealth migrants already settled in the UK helped to keep the 'numbers game' alive, leading to increasing calls in Parliament and the media for more action to halt immigration. The combined effect of these two pressures, and the use of immigration as an electoral issue, opened up the possibility of further legislative measures.

The other major action of the Labour Government was the 1969 Immigration Appeals Act, which was officially based on the report of the Committee on Immigration Appeals headed by Sir Roy Wilson (Macdonald, 1983, p. 269). This report accepted the need for restrictions on immigration, but argued that a system of appeal ensured that the restrictions were applied fairly. Although this Act is sometimes interpreted as a positive measure, it institutionalized a process of deportation for those breaking conditions attached to entry. It also legitimized restrictions on the right of entry of those who were legally entitled to settle in the UK through the obligation that dependants seeking settlement in Britain had to be in possession of an entry certificate. Such certificates had to be applied for by an interview at the nearest British High Commission. Applicants had to prove their claimed relationship to the person legally resident in Britain, and if they were unable to do so they could be denied entry. It is under this system that many recent controversial cases have arisen (Moore and Wallace, 1975; CRE, 1985).

The marked shift of the Labour Party towards the idea of 'firm immigration controls' was part of a wider political process, which led to the introduction of the 1971 Immigration Act by the Conservative Government. During the 1970 election campaign the Conservative Party had promised that there would 'be no further large-scale permanent immigration'. When the Immigration Bill was introduced in February 1971 it was legitimized on this basis, but as a number of speakers pointed out during the debates on the Bill it was difficult to see how it would actually reduce the number of primary immigrants further. In essence the 1971 Act qualified the notion of citizenship by differentiating between citizens of the United Kingdom and colonies who were 'patrial' and therefore had the right of abode in Britain, and non-patrials who did not. The most important categories of patrials were:

(a) citizens of the United Kingdom and colonies who had that citizenship by birth, adoption, naturalization or registration in the United Kingdom or who were born of parents, one of whom had United Kingdom citizenship by birth, or one of whose grandparents had such citizenship.
(b) citizens of the United Kingdom and colonies who had at any time settled in the United Kingdom and who had been ordinarily resident in the United Kingdom for five years or more.

Under the Act all aliens and Commonwealth citizens who were not 'patrials' needed permission to enter Britain. Whilst before, Commonwealth citizens entering under the voucher system could settle in Britain, after the 1971 Act came into force they entered on the basis of work-permits. They thus became subject to control by annual work-permit, and thus to the non-renewal of the permit. This change of status has been defined by some scholars as a move towards the migrant worker system of other European countries, with Commonwealth workers who were not 'patrials' (and by definition almost certainly black) reduced to the effective status of short-term contract workers rather than settlers (Castles and Kosack, 1973; Sivanandan, 1982, pp. 108–12).

During the Parliamentary debates on the 1971 Immigration Act the amalgamation of 'immigration' with 'race' became an issue of dispute between the Conservative and Labour Parties for the first time since 1962. From 1963 the Labour Party effectively developed a 'White Britain Policy', but in 1971 it felt moved to question the treatment of Commonwealth immigrants along the same lines as aliens and the overtly racial criteria which underlay the notion of patriality. Despite the fact that it had maintained the 1962 Act and introduced the 1968 Act, Labour felt that the new Act was rightly seen as racialist because it allowed potentially millions of white Commonwealth citizens to enter under the patriality clause and settle in Britain; a right denied to almost all non-white Commonwealth citizens. Successive Immigration Rules issued by the Home Secretary to supplement the 1971 Act have emphasized the intention of the Act to keep out black Commonwealth citizens as opposed to whites (Macdonald, 1983, pp. 25–30). With the exception of the Ugandan Asians who were expelled by Idi Amin in 1972, and some of whom were allowed to settle in Britain during 1972–3, this policy has been consistently pursued ever since. Additionally such measures have emphasized the essentially sexist nature of immigration controls (WING, 1985).

The decade between 1961 and 1971 had seen the introduction of three major pieces of legislation aimed largely at excluding black immigrants. The 1971 Act eventually took away the right of black Commonwealth immigrants to settle, and thus represented an important step in the institutionalization of racist immigration controls. Perhaps the 1981 Nationality Act can be seen as the latest move in this legislative process begun in 1962. But first it is necessary to explore the other dimension of state intervention in the 'immigration/race' amalgam; namely the legislation aimed at dealing with the position of those immigrants and their dependants who had managed to settle in Britain and who enjoyed rights of citizenship.

Race relations legislation

From a very early stage of the policy response to immigration in the 1950s the question of what to do with the black workers already legally settled in Britain emerged as a major dilemma. The association of immigration with 'race' hinged upon the racialization of state responses towards migration, and the commonsense notion that 'too much' black immigration would lead to problems in relation to housing, employment and social services. Hence the emergence of a dual strategy which aimed at both the control of primary immigration and the 'integration' of those who had already entered the UK and settled.

This strategy was made particularly clear by the Labour Government's 1965 White Paper on *Immigration from the Commonwealth*, but it has its origins in the debates of the 1950s and the period leading up to the 1962 Commonwealth Immigrants Act. The notion that immigration was essentially an issue of 'race' was consistent with the view that:

(a) the growing number of black citizens actually resident in the UK was either actually or potentially the source of social problems and conflicts, and
(b) that it was necessary for the state to introduce measures to promote the 'integration' of immigrants in terms of the wider society and its fundamental institutions [Freeman and Spencer, 1979, pp. 70–4].

The linking of *immigration controls* with *integrative measures* was a significant step, since it signalled a move towards the management of domestic 'race relations' as well as legitimizing the institutionalization of firm controls at the point of entry. In the same year as the White Paper the Labour Government passed the first Race Relations Act, which enunciated the principle of ending discrimination against black immigrants, and their descendants, on the grounds of 'race'. Although fairly limited in its scope the Act was important in establishing the concern of the state with discrimination and with the broad objective of using legislative action to achieve 'good race relations' (Lustgarten, 1980).

Much has been written about the inherent contradictions involved in 'balancing' racially specific controls on immigration with measures against discriminatory practices (Freeman, 1979, chapter 5; Jenkins and Solomos, 1987). Yet at the time the two sides of state intervention were seen as inextricably linked. According to Roy Hattersley's famous formula, 'Integration without control is impossible, but control without integration is indefensible' (*Hansard*, Vol 709, Cols 378–85). The rationale of this argument was never articulated clearly, but it was at least partly based on the idea that the fewer immigrants (particularly black ones) there were, the easier it would be to integrate them into the 'English way of life' and its social and cultural values.

During the tenure of Roy Jenkins as Home Secretary in the Labour Government, this notion of 'integration' was linked to the idea that unless the political institutions helped to deal with the social problems of the immigrants and of the areas in which they lived there was the prospect of growing 'racial tension' and violence (Rose *et al.*, 1969, chapter 26). Given this perspective the Race Relations Acts of 1965 and 1968 were based on the twin assumptions of:

(a) setting up special bodies to deal with the 'problems' faced by immigrants in relation to discrimination, social adjustment and welfare;
(b) helping to educate the population as a whole about 'race relations', and hence minimizing the risk of racialized conflict developing in Britain as it had done in the United States.

The basis of these assumptions lies, as we have argued above, in the notion that it is the number of black immigrants that causes a dislocation of domestic social relations. Additionally, however, the 'numbers game' was tied to the idea that the cultural differences between the immigrants and the host population were a potential source of conflict. During the period from 1962 to 1970 both the Conservative and Labour Parties accepted the need for immigration restrictions to be balanced by measures to bring about 'integration' in the areas of housing, education, employment and the social services (Freeman, 1979; Lustgarten, 1980).

Significantly, however, the state did not seek to use the mainstream Government Departments and spending programmes to tackle this issue. While the Home Office was directly responsible for the enforcement of strict immigration controls, the responsibility for enforcing the 1965 and 1968 Race Relations Acts was given to weak quasi-governmental bodies. The 1965 Act set up the Race Relations Board, while the 1968 Act set up the Community Relations Commission and strengthened the powers of the Race Relations Board in dealing with complaints of discrimination (Abbott, 1971, chapters 9 and 10). The state itself took little action to support these bodies, and it is unclear what they achieved in terms of positive measures against discrimination. The limited nature of the actions that successive measures against discrimination have allowed is perhaps best illustrated by the political language used to legitimize the Race Relations Acts – which focused on the question of 'discrimination' and the broad objective of providing for 'equal opportunity'. The question of racism, and its structural location in British society, has remained a notable silence in policies aimed at 'improving race relations' since 1965.

During the 1960s arguments in favour of positive action against racism were perceived as idealistic, since it was argued that a 'white backlash' would follow any attempt by the state which helped immigrants and not the indigenous population. Both the Conservative and Labour Parties were keen to balance actions against discrimination with help to 'impacted areas'; which were seen literally as areas where the 'race problem' was most acute because of the 'number of immigrants'. Thus the Local Government Act of 1966 made provision for support to such areas, the Government set up the Urban Programme in 1969 in the aftermath of Powell's campaign, and passed the Local Government Grants (Social Needs) Act in 1969 (Demuth, 1977; Edwards and Batley, 1978; Higgins *et al.*, 1983). Although there was always some ambiguity about whether these programmes were simply a response to the 'impact' of immigration, they represent an important step in linking urban decline and poverty to the 'race problem', a phenomenon to which we shall return in the next section.

The preoccupation with controlling immigration which was shown by the Conservative Government after 1970 left little room for efforts to strengthen the race relations legislation. Calls for such action were beginning to be made assertively by liberal lobby groups and black organizations throughout the early seventies, but they were taken up only after the Labour Party returned to power in 1974. It published a White Paper on *Racial Discrimination* in September 1975, calling for recognition that black immigrants and their children were 'here to stay', and for specific action to deal with the second generation youngsters who were perceived as becoming increasingly frustrated by racial discrimination and a lack of equal opportunity (Home Office, 1975). The 1976 Race Relations Act followed the White Paper and came into force in 1977. Although essentially based on the model of the 1965 and 1968 Acts, the 1976 Act extended the laws against discrimination in three ways. First, it extended the law to cover not only intentional discrimination but indirect discrimination and racial disadvantage more broadly. Second, it set up a joint agency to help implement the Act, the Commission for Racial Equality. This agency replaced the Race Relations Board and the Community Relations Commission. Third, cases of discrimination in employment were to be handled by the industrial tribunal system, rather than directly by the CRE (Lustgarten, 1980).

This involved a fundamental reworking of the mechanisms for implementing anti-discrimination, but a large body of research findings since 1976 points to the limited impact of the 1976 Act on levels of discrimination (Jenkins and Solomos, 1987). The effectiveness of state action to control black immigration contrasts sharply with the largely symbolic and ineffective attempts to deal with discrimination. A study of the effect of the Race Relations Acts on racial discrimination in the labour market concludes that little if any change in levels of indirect forms of discrimination seems to have been achieved since 1968 (Brown and Gay, 1985). Even the 1976 Act seems to have resulted in ambiguous and often contradictory attempts to develop equal opportunity policies, and little attempt by central government departments to help promote the policy goal which successive administrations have espoused.

The politics of racialization and the 'enemy within'

If the main rationalization of the immigration laws and the race relations acts was the objective of producing an atmosphere for the development of 'good race relations' and integration, it needs to be said that they failed to depoliticize the question of black immigration. The racialization of British politics proceeded apace during the 1970s, and took on new forms in relation to specific issues or groups, e.g. education, the police, young blacks and urban policy (CCCS, 1982; Miles and Phizacklea, 1984; Jacobs, 1986). The restrictions imposed by the 1971 Immigration Act, and the successive Immigration Rules issued under this Act throughout the last fifteen years, have seemingly fulfilled the ostensible objective of post-1962 policies, which has been to control primary immigration and restrict secondary immigration, but the politicization of 'race' has continued during this time.

What explains this racialization of political discourses in a context of firm immigration controls? A number of issues are involved, and not all of these can be analysed in this paper, but at least two are worth noting. First, debates about 'immigration' and 'race' have taken place within a broader context of social, political and economic change which has influenced the ways in which such debates have developed. The rapid transformation of many inner city localities over the last two decades, particularly in relation to the economic and social infrastructure, has provided a fertile ground for the racialization of issues such as employment, housing, education and law and order (Hall *et al.*, 1978; Phizacklea and Miles, 1980, pp. 42–68; Solomos, 1986). This racialization process has moved public and political debate beyond the question of immigration *per se*, with the focus moving towards the identification and resolution of specific 'social problems' linked to 'race'. But the link with the immigration question is maintained at another level, because it is the size of the black population, whether in the schools or the unemployment queue which is identified as the source of the problem (Macdonald, 1983; Castles *et al.*, 1984).

Second, the continuing racialization of British politics in the context of firm immigration highlights the way in which political language is often a way of emphasizing what one wants to believe and avoiding what one does not wish to face (Edelman, 1977; Katznelson, 1986). Thus, although calls for more controls on immigration are often laced with references to the number of immigrants or to the 'large numbers' who could potentially arrive and 'swamp' British culture, such statements are not necessarily based on 'the facts' in any recognizable sense. Rather references to statistics and reports are often highly selective and emphasize symbolic fears about the present or the future. Good examples of this process are the debates which occurred during the mid 1970s about the Hawley Report on immigration from the Indian sub-continent (1976) and the Select Committee on Race Relations and Immigration report on Immigration (1978). In both cases the debates about these reports in Parliament, the media and in other contexts focused on the dangers of 'massive' numbers of immigrants arriving and the possible social and political consequences; and this despite the fact that firm controls on immigration had been implemented during the 1960s (Freeman and Spencer, 1977). Perhaps a more recent phenomenon is the case of the visa controls intro-duced in 1986 for visitors from India, Pakistan, Bangladesh, Nigeria and Ghana on the basis of controlling the number of illegal immigrants from these countries. The fact that only 222 out of 452,000 visitors from the five countries absconded as illegal immigrants in 1985, did not prevent the symbolic use of visa controls as another means of 'holding the tide' of immigration (*Guardian*, 2 September 1986).

The amalgam of 'immigration controls/race relations policies' as a solution to the 'problem' was fostered under the Labour administration between 1974–9. But in the lead-up to the 1979 election sections of the Conservative Party, including its leader Margaret Thatcher, chose to emphasize the dangers posed to British social and cultural values by the black communities already settled here. Thatcher's famous 'swamping' statement in 1978 was part of a wider campaign to use 'race' as a symbol for the neo-Conservative ideology of Thatcher's wing of the party (Barker, 1982). But even though the political language used still referred to 'immigrants', the main reference point for this campaign were the black communi-ties already settled in Britain. Immigration control remained an issue of public and policy debate, particularly in relation to dependants and the marriage partners of those settled legally (Gordon, 1985). But the period of the 1970s witnessed a shift towards the theme of the 'enemy within' which was seen as emerging through the growth in the size and composition of the black population (see Chapter 15 by Troyna in this book). The image of inner city areas becoming 'black enclaves' where British law and order could not be easily enforced, leading to the emergence of 'alien values' within these areas, was seen as a potential threat to the 'way of life' and culture of white residents (CCCS, 1982).

Extreme right-wing and fascist groups agitated around these issues throughout the 1970s, helping to mobilize political support for racist political platforms and actions against black communities. Such groupings did not succeed in becoming mass political movements themselves but they helped to popularize images of blacks as an 'enemy within' which represented a threat to 'white' culture and values.

The agitation of the extreme right-wing groups and sections of the Conservative Party in favour of 'repatriation' came to focus by the late seventies as much on the supposed dangers of this 'alien wedge' as on the question of the arrival of new immigrants. The symbolism of the language used by Enoch Powell in 1968–9 to warn of the dangers of immigration, was reworked by the late seventies around the issue of the 'enemy within'; who was in many cases no longer an immigrant but born and bred in Brixton, Handsworth, Liverpool and other urban localities. The generation and amplification of the 'mugging' issue in the early seventies, confrontations between the police and young blacks, and the identification of young blacks as an alienated group within the black communities and British society generally, helped to construct a new racialized discourse about 'black youth'. Increasingly this group was identified as drifting into either criminal activities or radical political activities which brought them into direct contact, and hence conflict, with the police. Just as in the 1950s and 1960s the 'numbers game' mobilized a conception of the 'problem' which focused on the need to keep black immigrants out, now the language of political debate seemed to shift towards the view that 'black youth' were a kind of social time-bomb which could help undermine the social fabric of the 'immigration/race relations' amalgam and possibly society as a whole.

The experience of the 1981 and 1985 riots is a case in point. During both periods one of the central themes in public and Parliamentary debates about the riots was the question of 'race'. A number of the popular papers and MPs focused on the role that young blacks played in the riots, and the linkage between the emergence of forms of violent protest and the growth of 'immigrant communities' and 'alien values' (Solomos, 1986). Indeed in the context of both the Parliamentary debates and the popular press Enoch Powell and other MPs and commentators constructed an interpretation of the riots which saw them as intimately linked to the size and concentration of the black population in certain localities. Powell proclaimed the 1981 riots as a vindication of his warnings about immigration since 1968 (*Hansard*, Vol 8, 1981, Cols 1313–14). In 1985 he repeated this assertion and linked it to a renewed call for 'repatriation' as the only effective solution to the 'problem' (*Hansard*, Vol 84, 1985, Cols 375–6). Similar arguments were made by other MPs and press commentators during both 1981 and 1985. The extreme implications of this analysis were rejected by both the Government and Opposition, along with other sections of political opinion. But there seems little doubt that the riots since 1981 represent an important watershed in the racialization of British politics. They have helped to strengthen the common-sense notion that 'black youth' are a danger to the stability of domestic 'race relations'.

The policies pursued by the Conservative Government since 1979 have helped to weaken the status of black migrants through further changes in the Immigration Rules issued under the 1971 Immigration Act, and the passage of the 1981 British Nationality Act. Debates in Parliament on both these issues give a clue to the attempt by the Government to further circumvent the rights of those black Commonwealth citizens with a legal right to enter Britain and to construct the question of 'nationality' along racial lines (*Hansard*, Vol 5, 1981, Cols 795–1193; *Hansard*, Vol 31, 1982, Cols 692–761; *Hansard*, Vol 34, 1982, Cols 355–439; *Hansard*, Vol 37, 1983, Cols 178–280; *Hansard*, Vol 83, 1985, Cols 893–989). At the same time the Government has steadfastly refused to strengthen the 1976 Race Relations Act or to adopt a more positive approach against discrimination and racism. Even after the Scarman Report of 1981 called for a co-ordinated and government led policy against racial disadvantage, a call repeated a number of times since by Lord Scarman and others, the response of the various agencies of the state has been at best limited. Rather it has continued to emphasize the need for tight immigration controls because 'of the strain that the admission of a substantial number of immigrants can place on existing resources and services' (Leon Brittan, *Hansard*, Vol 83, 1985, Col 893).

The logic of this approach is to displace conflicts and strains in 'race relations' on to the black communities as a whole or specific sections of them. This in turn has allowed the common-sense ideas which see blacks as an 'enemy within' and a threat to social stability to take further root.

Symbolic promises or structural reform?

The shift we have noted in the previous section from a preoccupation with immigration and the numbers game as such to the question of the 'enemy within' and related images of social disorder is an important development. At least in relation to the disorders experienced in 1981 and 1985 it highlights the complex processes through which racialized political discourses are working in contemporary Britain. But we should emphasize that we are far from suggesting that immigration will become less important as a political issue. Rather we see the growing usage of political symbols which depict blacks as an 'enemy within' as inextricably linked with the history of state responses which we have analysed in this paper. Indeed the post-1979 Conservative administrations have continued to mobilize the immigration question as a political symbol, and to legitimate the maintenance of racially specific controls as a necessary response to the fears of 'ordinary people' about too much immigration.

The main legislative action of the post-1979 Conservative administrations, the 1981 British Nationality Act, is a case in point. The Government argued that in introducing the Bill it was rationalizing both existing nationality and immigration legislation, in order to create a British citizenship which automatically gives the right of abode in the UK. It did this by dividing the existing category of Citizen of the United Kingdom and Commonwealth into three categories: British citizens; British Dependent Territories citizens; British Overseas citizens. Although the Government argued that the Act would make immigration control less arbitrary, public and Parliamentary responses criticized it for reinforcing racial discrimination (Layton-Henry, 1984, pp. 157–9). Indeed the category of 'British Overseas citizens' effectively excludes British citizens of (mostly) Asian origin from the right of abode in the UK. In this sense it seems correct to argue that the 1981 Act 'enshrines the existing racially discriminatory provisions of immigration law under the new clothing of British citizenship and the right of abode' (Macdonald, 1983, p. 69).

A recent Government document prepared for the OECD conference on immigration policy states the broad policy objectives in traditional terms, but links them closely to other areas of concern:

In recent decades, the basis of policy in the United Kingdom has been the need to control primary immigration – that is, new heads of household who are most likely to enter the job market. The United Kingdom is one of the most densely populated countries in Europe. In terms of housing, education, social services and, of course, jobs, the country could not support all those who would like to come here. Firm immigration control is therefore essential, in order to provide the conditions necessary for developing and maintaining good community relations. [OECD, 1986, p. 1]

In practice, therefore, the strategy pursued since 1979 has continued to legitimate the supposed link between 'firm controls' and 'good community relations'. The signs are that this amalgam will continue to guide the thinking of the mainstream of the Conservative Party.

Since 1979, however, the Labour and Alliance Parties have shown some signs of questioning the basis of this approach (Fitzgerald and Layton-Henry, 1986). The Labour Party, which was responsible for the introduction of the 1968 Commonwealth Immigrants Act, has seemingly come round to the view that current immigration laws are racist, and it aims to introduce its own legislation when in power to ensure that controls are both non-racist and non-sexist. In a Parliamentary debate on immigration in July 1985 Gerald Kaufman affirmed that the intention of a future Labour administration would be to (a) maintain firm controls on immigration and (b) ensure that such controls were applied equally to all immigrants regardless of 'race' (*Hansard*, Vol 83, 1985, Col 909–10). He accused the Conservatives of trying to identify immigration with 'race', when recent history questioned this assumption:

Viewed objectively, immigration should be neither a problem nor an issue in Britain. Substantial primary immigration ended at least a decade and a half ago, and there is no prospect of it starting again. In most years there is a net emigration from the United Kingdom. In 1983–84, 45 per cent of so-called immigrants were Britons returning to the United Kingdom. In that year only 15.5 per cent of immigrants came from the West Indies, Africa and the Indian subcontinent – the areas from which, according to the Government, there is the greatest pressure to migrate to the United Kingdom [*Idem*, Col 910].

This approach represents a marked shift from the actions of Labour Governments during 1964–70 and 1974–9, but it is difficult to say what is meant by 'non-racist' immigration controls and how a future Labour administration could effectively break away from the logic of policies since 1962 – which has been to construct black immigration into a problem. Certainly over the post-1981 period, in the aftermath of the riots, a strong black and anti-racist lobby has emerged within the Labour Party. This lobby is pressing the party into a firm commitment to implement the reforms promised (Fitzgerald and Layton-Henry, 1986, pp. 110–14).

In the context of the current political climate, however, it is hard to see how a de-politicization of the 'immigration/race' question can come about. Growing urban unrest and violence create a space for the Powellite imagery of a 'racial' civil war to take root in popular common sense, for the 'real fears' of the white population to be deflected on to the 'enemy within'. Promises of a fundamental break from its past practice by the Labour Party have to be set against the wider political background. What would be the response of Labour to a successful campaign around 'immigrant/race' by the Conservatives? Already sections of the popular press are accusing Labour of promising to open the flood gates to future primary immigration from black Commonwealth countries, and in an electoral sense such accusations may become a burden. During 1974–9 the Labour Government failed to take immigration out of politics and in the 1979 election campaign suffered from the racialized language used by the Conservatives. Its response to these pressures showed up the ambiguities in Labour thinking since the mid-1960s. Whether its responses in the future will be significantly different remains to be seen, but given the entrenched nature of racist immigration controls it is clearly going to require major structural changes to make the promises of reform a reality.

Conclusion

The central conclusion to emerge from this paper returns us to the themes set out in the introduction, namely, the role of the nation-state in the regulation of the entry and incorporation of migrant labour. The above discussion has demonstrated that it is far too simplistic to see the state as a reactive instrument of either economic forces or popular pressures in relation to the control of immigration and the management of migrant labour. Rather, we have highlighted the social, economic, political and ideological contexts which have helped to shape state legislation in this field and to bring about the present articulation between racially exclusionary practices and social policies against discrimination.

In a broad sense the state interventions described above can be seen as making a contribution to the reproduction of the dominant social relations of contemporary Britain, particularly through the regulation of migrant workers and the reinforcement of racialized and ethnically based social divisions. But such a generalization does not capture the complexity of the role of the state in relation to immigration and other important issues on the political agenda of the period we have covered. Far from the state simply responding to pressures from the outside, we have shown throughout this paper that it played a central role in defining both the form and the content of policies and wider political agendas. Indeed the state and its agencies have become the locus of struggles over the form of the political regulation of immigration and the management of domestic 'race relations'.

The histories of the various migratory movements that we have touched upon in this paper show how popular responses and state policy-making have been shaped by specific contexts and political situations. The circumstances which bring about specific types of policy response are not given but are the product of struggles and contradictions, both within and outside state institutions. During the period covered in this paper state responses to migration have by no means been uniform, although there are notable similarities, e.g. between the responses to Jewish migration and black Commonwealth migration. The treatment of Irish labour has, however, taken on different forms which are related to the historical relationships between Britain and Ireland.

We still need to know more about the dynamics and the limits of state intervention in this field, the interplay between state policies and the reproduction of capitalist social relations, and the possibilities for reform. A more adequate understanding of these processes is required if we are to understand how the interplay between immigration and the state has produced a situation whereby racist immigration controls have become institutionalized. Such an understanding would help those who are challenging the terms of the debate about immigration policy, and help us rethink the silences of the race relations legislation. In the context of virulent racism and calls for the repatriation of black citizens this is an urgent theoretical and practical task. The history we have attempted to recover in this paper should help to contextualize contemporary debates and raise questions for further analysis.

References

Abbott, S. (ed.) (1971), *The Prevention of Racial Discrimination in Britain*, London: Oxford University Press

Alderman, G. (1983), *The Jewish Community in British Politics*, Oxford: Clarendon Press

Aspinall, B. (1982), 'The Formation of the Catholic Community in the West of Scotland: Some Preliminary Outlines', *Innes Review*, **33**, 44–57

Barker, M. (1982), *The New Racism*, London: Junction Books

Bentwick, N. (1956), *They Found Refuge: An Account of Jewry's Work for Victims of Nazi Oppression*, London: Cresset Press

Bevan, V. (1986), *The Development of British Immigration Law*; London: Croom Helm

Brown, C. and Gay, P. (1985), *Racial Discrimination: 17 years After the Act*, London: Policy Studies Institute

Carter, B., Harris, C. and Joshi, S. (forthcoming) 'The 1951–55 Conservative Government and the Racialisation of Black Immigration', *Immigrants and Minorities*

Carter, B. and Joshi, S. (1984), 'The Role of Labour in the Creation of a Racist Britain', *Race and Class*, **XXV**, 3, 53–70

Castles, S. and Kosack, G. (1973), *Immigrant Workers and Class Structure in Western Europe*, London: Oxford University Press

Castles, S. *et al.* (1984), *Here for Good: Western Europe's New Ethnic Minorities*, London: Pluto Press

CCCS Race and Politics Group (1982), *The Empire Strikes Back: Race and Racism in 70s Britain*, London: Hutchinson

Commission for Racial Equality (1985), *Immigration Control Procedures: Report of a Formal Investigation*, London: Commission for Racial Equality

Curtis, L. P. (1968), *Anglo-Saxons and Celts*, Connecticut: University of Bridgeport Press

Curtis, L. P. (1971), *Apes and Angels. The Irishman in Victorian Caricature*, Washington: Smithsonian Institution Press

Daiches, D. (ed) (1981), *A Companion to Scottish Culture*, London: Edward Arnold

Deakin, N. C. (1968), 'The Politics of the Commonwealth Immigrants Bill', *Political Quarterly*, **39**, 1, 25–45

Deakin, N. (1970), *Colour, Citizenship and British Society*, London: Panther

Deedes, W. (1968), *Race Without Rancour*, London: Conservative Political Centre

Demuth, C. (1977), *Government Initiatives on Urban Deprivation*, London: Runnymede Trust

Edelman, M. (1977), *Political Language: Words that Succeed and Policies that Fail*, New York: Academic Press

Edwards, J. and Batley, R. (1978), *The Politics of Positive Action*, London: Tavistock

Edwards, O. Dudley (1981), 'The Irish in Scotland', in D. Daiches (ed.), *A Companion to Scottish Culture*

Evans, J. M. (1983), *Immigration Law*, London: Sweet and Maxwell

Evans, N. (1980), 'The South Wales Race Riots of 1919', *Llafur*, **3**(1), 5–29

Evans, N. (1985), 'Regulating the Reserve Army: Arabs, Blacks and the Local

State in Cardiff, 1911–45', in K. Lunn (ed.), *Race and Labour in Twentieth-Century Britain*, London: Frank Cass

Finestein, I. (1961), 'The New Community, 1880–1918', in V. D. Lipman (ed.), *Three Centuries of Anglo-Jewish History*

Finnegan, F. (1985), 'The Irish in York', in R. Swift and S. Gilley (eds), *The Irish in the Victorian City*

Fitzgerald, M. and Layton-Henry, Z. (1986), 'Opposition Parties and Race Policies 1979–83', in Layton-Henry, Z. and Rich, P. (eds), *Race, Government & Politics in Britain*, London: Macmillan

Foot, P. (1965), *Immigration and Race in British Politics*, Harmondsworth; Penguin

Freeman, G. (1979), *Immigrant Labor and Racial Conflict in Industrial Societies*, Princeton: Princeton University Press

Freeman, M. D. A. and Spencer, S. (1979), 'Immigration Control, Black Workers and the Economy', *British Journal of Law and Society*, **6**,1, 53–81

Fryer, P. (1984), *Staying Power: The History of Black People in Britain*, London: Pluto Press

Gainer, B. (1972), *The Aliens Invasion: the Origins of the Aliens Act of 1905*, London: Heinemann

Gallagher, T. (1985), 'A Tale of Two Cities: Communal Strife in Glasgow and Liverpool Before 1914', in R. Swift and S. Gilley (eds), *The Irish in the Victorian City*

Garrard, J. A. (1971), *The English and Immigration 1880–1910*, London: Oxford University Press

Gartner, L. P. (1973), *The Jewish Immigrant in England, 1870–1914*, London: Simon Publications

Gilley, S. (1978), 'English Attitudes to the Irish in England, 1789–1900', in C. Holmes (ed), *Immigrants and Minorities in British Society*

Gordon, P. (1985), *Policing Immigration; Britain's Internal Controls*, London: Pluto Press

Gray, S. and Lowe, A. (1983), *The Ins and Outs of Immigration and Nationality Law*, London: National Association of Citizens Advice Bureaux

Hall, S. *et al.* (1978), *Policing the Crisis*, London: Macmillan

Handley, J. E. n.d., *The Irish in Scotland*, Glasgow: John S. Burn and Sons

Handley, J. E. (1970), *The Navy in Scotland*, Cork: Cork University Press

Harris, C. and Solomos, J. (forthcoming), 'Rethinking the 1958 Riots: Immigration, "Race" and Social Change'

Hepple, B. (1968), *Race, Jobs and the Law in Britain*, London: Allen Lane

Higgins, J. *et al.* (1983), *Government and Urban Poverty*, Oxford: Basil Blackwell

Hirschfeld, G. (ed.), (1984), *Exile in Great Britain: Refugees From Hitler's Germany*, Leamington Spa: Berg Publishers

Holmes, C. (ed.) (1978), *Immigrants and Minorities in British Society*, London: George Allen and Unwin

Holmes, C. (1979), *Anti-Semitism in British Society, 1876–1939*, London: Edward Arnold

Home Office (1975), *Racial Discrimination*, London: HMSO

ILO, (1949), 'Conditions of Labour of Refugees and Displaced Persons', *International Labour Review*, **59**(4), 425–51

Irvine, H. S. (1960), 'Some Aspects of Passenger Traffic Between Britain and Ireland, 1820–1850', *Journal of Transport History*, **4**, 224–41

Jacobs, B. (1986), *Black Politics and Urban Crisis in Britain*, Cambridge: Cambridge University Press

Jackson, J. A. (1963), *The Irish in Britain*, London: Routledge and Kegan Paul

Jenkins, R. and Solomos, J. (1987), *Racism and Equal Opportunity in the 1980s*, Cambridge: Cambridge University Press

Jenkinson, J. (1985), 'The Glasgow Race Disturbances of 1919', in K. Lunn, (ed.), *Hosts, Immigrants and Minorities*

Joshua, H. *et al.* (1983), *To Ride the Storm: The 1980 Bristol 'Riot' and the State*, London: Heinemann

Katznelson, I. (1976), *Black Men, White Cities*, Chicago: University of Chicago Press

Katznelson, I. (1986), 'Rethinking the Silences of Social and Economic Policy', *Political Science Quarterly*, **101**, 2, 307–25

Layton-Henry, Z. (1984), *The Politics of Race in Britain*, London: George Allen & Unwin

Lebzelter, G. C. (1978), *Political Anti-Semitism in England, 1918–1939*, London: Macmillan

Lees, L. H. (1979), *Exiles of Erin: Irish Migrants in Victorian London*, Manchester: Manchester University Press

Lipman, V. D. (1961), *Three Centuries of Anglo-Jewish History: a Volume of Essays*, Cambridge: Heffer and Sons Ltd

Lipman, V. D. (1954), *Social History of the Jews in England, 1850–1950*, London: Watts & Co.

Lunn, K. (1980a), 'Reactions to Lithuanian and Polish Immigrants in the Lanarkshire Coalfield, 1880–1914', in K. Lunn (ed.), *Hosts, Immigrants and Minorities*

Lunn, K. (ed.) (1980b), *Hosts, Immigrants and Minorities: Historical Responses to Newcomers in British Society, 1870–1914*, Folkestone: Dawson

Lustgarten, L. (1980), *Legal Control of Racial Discrimination*, London: Macmillan

Macdonald, I. A. (1983), *Immigration Law and Practice in the United Kingdom*, London: Butterworth

May, R. and Cohen, R. (1974), 'The Interaction Between Race and Colonialism: A Case Study of the Liverpool Race Riots of 1919'; *Race and Class*, **16**(2), 111–26

Miles, R. (1982), *Racism and Migrant Labour: A Critical Text*, London: Routledge and Kegan Paul

Miles, R. (1984), 'The Riots of 1958: Notes on the Ideological Construction of

"Race Relations" as a Political Issue in Britain', *Immigrants and Minorities*, **3**, 252–75

Miles, R. (1986), 'Labour Migration, Racism and Capital Accumulation in Western Europe: An Overview', *Capital and Class*, **28**, 49–86

Miles, R. and Phizacklea, A. (eds), (1979), *Racism and Political Action in Britain*, London: Routledge and Kegan Paul

Miles, R. and Phizacklea, A. (1984), *White Man's Country*, London: Pluto Press

Millward, P. (1985), 'The Stockport Riots of 1852: A Study of Anti-Catholic and Anti-Irish Sentiment', in R. Swift and S. Gilley (eds), *The Irish in the Victorian City*

Moore, R. and Wallace, T. (1975), *Slamming the Door: The Administration of Immigration Control*, London: Martin Robertson

Morgan, D. H. (1982), *Harvester and Harvesting, 1840–1900, A Study of the Rural Proletariat*, London: Croom Helm

Nugent, N. and King, R. (1979), 'Ethnic Minorities, Scapegoating and the Extreme Right', in R. Miles and A. Phizacklea (eds), *Racism and Political Action in Britain*

OECD (1986), 'United Kingdom', National Report for OECD Conference on the Future of Migration, Paris, February 1986

O Tuathaigh, M. A. G. (1985), 'The Irish in Nineteenth-Century Britain: Problems of Integration', in R. Swift and S. Gilley (eds), *The Irish in the Victorian City*

Paor, L. de (1971), *Divided Ulster*, Harmondsworth: Penguin

Patterson, S. (1969), *Immigration and Race Relations in Britain*, London: Oxford University Press

Peach, C. (1968), *West Indian Migration to Britain*, London: Oxford University Press

Phizacklea, A. and Miles, R. (1980), *Labour and Racism*, London: Routledge and Kegan Paul

Pollins, H. (1982), *Economic History of the Jews in England*, London: Associated University Presses

Porter, B. (1979), *The Refugee Question in Mid-Victorian Politics*, Cambridge: Cambridge University Press

Redford, A. (1976), *Labour Migration in England, 1800–1850*, Manchester: Manchester University Press

Reeves, F. (1983), *British Racial Discourse*, Cambridge: Cambridge University Press

Rich, P. (1986), *Race and Empire in British Politics*, Cambridge: Cambridge University Press

Rose, E. J. B. *et al.* (1969), *Colour and Citizenship: A Report on British Race Relations*, London: Oxford University Press

Sherman, A. J. (1973), *Island Refuge: Britain and Refugees from the Third Reich, 1933–1939*, London: Paul Elek

Sivanandan, A. (1982), *A Different Hunger*, London: Pluto Press

Slatter, J. (ed.) (1984), *From the Other Shore: Russian Political Emigrants in Britain 1880–1917*, London: Frank Cass

Solomos, J. (1986), 'Political Language & Violent Protest: Ideological & Policy Responses to the 1981 and 1985 Riots', *Youth and Policy*, **18**, 12–24

Stevens, A. (1975), *The Dispossessed*, London: Barrie & Jenkins

Swift, R. and Gilley, S. (eds) (1985), *The Irish in the Victorian City*, London: Croom Helm

Tannahill, J. A. (1958), *European Volunteer Workers in Britain*, Manchester: Manchester University Press

Vernant, J. (1953), *The Refugees in the Post-War World*, London: Allen and Unwin

Visram, R. (1986), *Ayahs, Lascars and Princes: The Story of Indians in Britain 1700–1947*, London: Pluto Press

Wasserstein, B. (1979), *Britain and the Jews of Europe, 1939–1945*, Oxford: Clarendon Press

Watson, J. (ed.), (1977), *Between Two Cultures*, Oxford: Blackwell

Wing, (1985), *Worlds Apart: Women Under Immigration and Nationality Law*, London: Pluto Press

Zubrzycki, J. (1956), *Polish Immigrants in Britain: A Study of Adjustment*, The Hague: Martinus Hijhoff

5 The role of government in Britain's racial crisis*

Michael and Ann Dummett

The solution of Britain's racial problem does not depend only upon goodwill and freedom from racial prejudice — though, Heaven knows, it does depend on these, and little enough of either commodity is available: it also depends upon understanding. People who are satisfied that they have eradicated from themselves racialist assumptions and reactions suppose, very often, that they are now fully equipped to issue pronouncements about the racial situation: they are wholly mistaken. They are mistaken, not merely because they are almost certainly wrong in thinking themselves free from the infection of racialist ideas, but because they have as yet done no more than put themselves in a position from which they can begin to learn what they need to understand: to do this, they have now both to listen and to think. They have to learn to understand two kinds of things. The first is the complex reactions provoked in people who are the objects of racial prejudice and the victims of racial discrimination. Imagination — the capacity to project oneself into a wholly unfamiliar situation — is certainly needed for this, but it is hardly possible for anyone short of a genius to rely on this alone; it is for this reason that it is essential for anyone seriously concerned to listen to what black people themselves have to say, when he has established himself as a person to whom they will say it. To listen, that is, with humility; in other words, with the knowledge that he will never quite be able to know what it is like to be in that situation, rather than with the arrogant assumption that, since *he is* quite free of any colour prejudice, he has the right to condemn the attitudes of those who are its targets. As he listens, he will discover that there is no uniform reaction to this most painful experience of finding oneself rejected as a human being, that people's adjustments to the distress which is a daily accompaniment of their lives differ both according to their personalities and according to their position in society and the identity which they have been brought up to think of themselves as possessing.

The second area in which an effort is required to gain an understanding necessary for the formation of any valid views concerning possible solutions to our problems is that relating to the effects of public and social policy. The

*Reprinted from Lewis Donnelly (ed.), *Justice First* (Sheed & Ward 1969), pp, 25-78.

intricacy of the situations which arise out of the interplay between official agencies, unofficial pressure groups, the public at large and the minority groups contained within it tends to be far greater in matters touching on racial antagonisms than in any other sector of public policy, not less, as many people seem to imagine; and they therefore require to be thought about at least as deeply as any other variety of political problems. White people of a generally liberal cast of opinion are at least beginning to acknowledge, as they have been for so many years reluctant to do, that we have succeeded in creating for ourselves a racial problem of grave magnitude; but they still have hardly begun to devote any mental effort to thinking about this problem, or even to grasp that any such effort is required.

One of us was recently criticized by a speaker at the last meeting of the now defunct National Association of Voluntary Liaison Committees for overestimating the role played by Government, and by national politicians generally, in the development of Britain's racial crisis. We remain impenitent: in fact, we do not think that anyone can understand at all the character of what has happened to this country in the last eight or nine years if he fails to grasp the absolutely crucial, and almost uniformly disastrous, effects which the behaviour of both major parties, in and out of office, has had. If someone does not understand what has been happening, he will have no idea how to set about trying to prevent it from happening in the future. Perhaps the clearest way to indicate simultaneously, in capsule form, both what, in our opinion, has been happening and how remote people are, in general, from understanding what has been happening is by referring to Mr Wilson's widely reported remark to the 1969 Commonwealth Prime Ministers' Conference that he was not responsible for the 'phenomenon' of Enoch Powell. How many Commonwealth Prime Ministers were deceived by this remark, we do not know: but surely most of those who deprecate Enoch Powell's utterances will have felt some twinge of sympathy for Mr Wilson when they read this plaint. But, in our view, no one has begun to understand the course of events which has led us into our present appalling situation who does not recognize that Mr Wilson's remark, seemingly reasonable as it is, is not merely a partial untruth but an absolute untruth: the Labour Government bears the whole responsibility for the 'phenomenon' of Enoch Powell. For the existence of Enoch Powell himself, of course, God and Enoch Powell share the responsibility: but for what Mr Wilson meant by the 'phenomenon' of Enoch Powell, that, namely, with which every member of the British public now identifies him, his sustained campaign of racialist propaganda, [1] the Government bears the full responsibility. If there had not been that particular individual around, for sure some other would have appeared to undertake the nauseating task: but we can be certain that Enoch Powell personally would not have launched himself upon it, nor could anyone else have done so with success, had not both the Government and official opposition contrived so beautifully to set the stage for a performance which by then involved no risk at all for the performer.

From the beginning, just after the war, of immigration into Britain, first from the Caribbean and then from the Indian sub-continent, until about 1960, there was a steady but very slow deterioration in public attitudes towards and treatment of people with dark skins. This can be blamed on politicians only in the negative, though very real, sense that they displayed total indifference to, or unawareness of, the potential dangers inherent in the entry, among a people brought up on the traditions of imperialism, into which the myth of racial superiority had been tightly woven, of those of African and Asian descent, and in the continued failure to solve the long-standing social problems of inadequate housing and schools with which the newly awakened racialism was to become intertwined. Until the 1960s, that is, before any lead, in either direction, had been given by the country's politicians, the feelings of British people generally towards the new racial minorities in their midst were hesitant, ambiguous and confused. On the one hand, a whole mass of racialist assumption, imbibed during childhood from school textbooks, children's novels and comics, and from the cultural climate generally, lay ready in the minds of most white English men and women to be activated; and hardly a shred of actual knowledge about the Caribbean or Asian countries was present to form any barrier to these prejudices. On the other hand, several vague but quite strong traditional feelings about the rights of other human beings, about fair play and the British tradition of equality of treatment, were also present to be activated, and caused the great majority of people to feel uneasy about any direct expression of racialist ideas. Since 1960, during a decade in which both parties have actively and publicly concerned themselves with the racial situation, the deterioration in public attitudes has been spectacular. In particular, the feelings about fair play and the rights of individuals, which might, had they been properly appealed to, have stifled the latent racialism of the British, have by now been completely swamped by the mean callousness of racial prejudice. The measure of this may be taken from the public reaction to the official ill-treatment of individuals. Those of us who strove, usually unsuccessfully, during the middle 1960s, to get the press to report the treatment to which those refused entry by the Immigration Service were in practice subjected, did so in the belief, surely at that time justified, that the feelings of most people, however racially prejudiced they were, would be outraged if they could be brought to understand the things that were taking place. In one case, for example, an Indian lady living in Birmingham in the same year was widowed and had her house burnt down. Her brother in India, thinking it his duty to go to England to be with his sister, applied for a Ministry of Labour voucher. After a long delay, this was refused, so he decided instead to come as a visitor for a short period. At Birmingham airport, he was refused entry, on the ground that he had previously applied for a labour voucher and could therefore be suspected of not intending to return to India. He was held in prison, where his sister was not allowed to see him, and eventually was taken in handcuffs to the airport to be put on a plane back to India. While, by 1967, most people would have had a strong resistance to believing this (perfectly true) story, they would also have been horrified once they had been persuaded of its truth. Now, however, such stories, if they are known to concern 'coloured' people, would make no impact. Indeed, it has been possible for the Under-Secretary at the Home Office to go on television, just before Christmas, and promise the nation that he would 'get rid of' a family of children living here separated from their parents, all of them British citizens (Asians from East Africa), because he alleged that their parents had made mis-statements to the immigration officers, children whose parents saw no future for them in the country where they were living and so had been anxious to bring them to the country which had offered them its citizenship. When we consider the outcry that would have occurred in former years at the inhumanity of this decision and the coarseness of language with which it was conveyed, the references to those for whom there was no room at the inn, and contrast it with the silence with which this widely reported utterance was greeted, we gain a sharp insight into the tragic blunting of sensibilities that has occurred so far as anyone with a dark skin is concerned.

This deterioration in the general outlook has coincided with a display by politicians of great interest in the racial situation. Of course, there is an interplay: politicians imagine themselves to be responding to pressure which comes from their electorate, and in some measure this is what they are doing. Nevertheless, we believe that the activities of the politicians have not merely mirrored, but have been the primary cause of, the grave inflammation of racialist attitudes that has taken place in this decade.

In order to understand the thinking which has presumably lain behind the policies of Government and opposition, and the effects which those policies have had, we have to set these against the background of the condition of white opinion in England in these years. There is, indeed, a sense in which it can truly be said that 90 per cent of English people are racialist: that is, there had, throughout the post-war period, been a pretty steady 10 per cent minority which has been consciously anti-racialist in the sense that its members faced with equanimity, and sometimes positively welcomed, the prospect of a multi-racial society based on genuine racial equality. Many, perhaps most, of this minority have been, for most of the time, unaware of what was happening, and reluctant to believe it when they are told, perhaps out of a distaste for accepting the fact that racialism, which they had learned to think of as an attribute of certain reactionary foreign countries, needed to be fought against in their native land; but this did not affect the sincerity of their rejection of it. But it would be a great mistake to dismiss the remaining 90 per cent as a uniform mass of equally racially prejudiced people. On the contrary, it contained at the outset only a minority — perhaps as low as 15 per cent of the total population — of committed, conscious racialists. By 'conscious racialists' we mean people prepared to profess — in the right company — a straightforward undisguised belief in the inferiority of people of certain races or colours; or, to put it another way, people who could face with equanimity the prospect of a multi-racial society founded on segregation and racial discrimination against those who are not white. With the galloping deterioration in the racial climate that has marked the last few years in Britain, this minority has grown alarmingly; but still it perhaps does not represent an overall majority of the population. The majority, rather, has been composed of people whom we shall call 'crypto-racialists'. These are people who have, side by side within them, both deeply rooted racial prejudices and an awareness of the shamefulness of racial prejudice. Because of the presence of these two incompatible tendencies in their hearts, race is precisely the issue which they cannot bring themselves to face. Their prejudices make it impossible for them to treat as 'acceptable' (in Powell's word) the prospect of the one kind of multi-racial society, that founded on racial equality; the thought that They would have to be treated just like Us, that they would have to be, not tolerated or condescended to, but accorded equal dignity and the same respect for their customs and their culture, the members of this majority simply could not digest. At the same time, the awareness that was also present within them that racial prejudice was something despicable, the image that they had of themselves as liberal and fundamentally egalitarian, made it equally impossible for them to acknowledge to themselves that they found the prospect of racial equality intolerable, or to view a segregationist society as a fitting and welcome future for their country.

This frame of mind on the part of the majority of the white population made it imperative for them to disguise the issue from themselves, so as not to have to make the choice either side of which they could not bring themselves to face. Since they could not consciously accept the prospect of a multi-racial society of either of the only two kinds there are, it was necessary for them to avoid the realization of the plain fact, stated by the Labour Government itself when it was still a little naïve about the issue, in its White Paper of 1965 on *Immigration from the Commonwealth,* that Britain was already a multi-racial society. It was, instead, a necessity for them to conceal this fact from themselves: for only thus could they escape facing the agonizing divisions in their own minds.

This state of mind was from the start very well understood by various small but determined and well financed pressure groups – the Immigration Control Associations, [2] the Racial Preservation Society, the Society for Individual Freedom, the British Rights Society – and by MPs such as Peter Griffiths, Sir Cyril Osborne, Lord Elton, Sir Gerald Nabarro, Ronald Bell, Duncan Sandys. The Labour Party has been much slower to come to an understanding of it, probably because so many of their members themselves belong to this crypto-racialist majority. It is because of the understanding on the part of the racialists of the psychological condition of the majority of those they sought to influence that their propaganda has from the start represented the problem as being about immigration, rather than about race, and has made harsher restrictions on Commonwealth immigration the principal plank in their platform. So much have they neglected other aspects that, although they of course opposed and have subsequently denounced the 1968 Race Relations Act, this opposition was perfunctory and no serious attempt has so far been made to whip up public opinion about the matter.

Constant hammering away at the theme of immigration was, on the contrary, precisely the strategy to win over the crypto-racialists. On the one hand, demands for immigration control did not have to appear as nakedly racialist. The tone of the propaganda could, of course, be adjusted to suit the audience: but to those least willing to acknowledge the presence of their own prejudices, it could be represented as not racial in character at all, but merely motivated by a concern for the total population figures in this 'crowded little island'. The fact that such a concern was patently spurious did not matter at all. It made no difference that there was a net outflow of population; that in certain jobs there was a serious shortage of manpower, that firms were recruiting labour in the Caribbean, and, if the supply was cut off from there, would have to seek for it in Ireland or on the Continent; that anyone genuinely concerned about total numbers, irrespective of colour, would be bound to seek control of the largest section of immigrants, the Irish, and, when a ceiling was imposed on Commonwealth immigration, to demand a similar ceiling for European immigration. These things did not matter because what racialists were offering to the crypto-racialists was a means of deceiving themselves, to people desperately eager to be deceived. Not only could the crypto-racialists back the demands for immigration control without having to acknowledge to themselves that they were endorsing a racialist policy: but, by encouraging them to pretend to themselves that the problem consisted in that of stopping Them from coming in, they could be saved from having to recognize the central fact which otherwise would have forced on them the choice which above all they were anxious to avoid. People were, namely, being tacitly encouraged to believe that the problem was, in the notorious phrase, one of 'keeping Britain white'. By concentrating the whole time on the theme of preventing black people from coming into the country, the racialists offered a means whereby people could conceal from themselves the crucial fact that, even if not one single more black person were to arrive at London Airport or Southhampton Dock, Britain was no longer and would never be again, as such a white country; and hence that 'the problem' was not that of preventing people from coming in, but of which of the two kinds of multi-racial society we were going to become, and, if it was going to be that founded on racial equality, how the expression of racial prejudice and the practice of racial discrimination could be eliminated.

What, in short, the political parties have done is to allow the racialists to succeed in their strategy. In the process, an alarming situation has been transformed into a desperate and tragic one. With each victory it gained, racialism was able more and more to come out into the open; and, as it did so, more and more of those who were merely crypto-racialists have been converted to overt racialism. The country, which, even in 1967, was merely in danger of becoming a racialist society, is now definitely one, and is recognized as such both by the black people living in it and by the world at large. Once this happens, of course, the chance of even an eventual resolution of the racial problem becomes enormously more remote: once, that is, the racialist minorities have come to regard the society as being as such racialist, rather than as containing a certain proportion of racialist-minded individuals or groups, then the alienation between the racial groups, which is the most disastrous and the most difficult to overcome of all the effects of racialism, has begun in earnest. This is what successive Governments have managed to achieve in the short period of eight years.

The Conservative Party, in power in 1961, first decided on a policy of surrender to the clamour then being set up for the principle of free entry for Commonwealth citizens to be rescinded: the result was the Commonwealth Immigrants Act of 1962. At the time, a certain pretence was maintained that the restriction was not in any particular way aimed at those who were not white, but this was done in a curiously formalistic way: for instance, some argued that the Act ought to be made to apply to the Irish, not on the grounds that their entry required control as much as that of any other immigrant group, but that, without this, the Act would look as if it were racially discriminatory. And that, of course, is just how Hugh Gaitskell took it, and for that reason, with the rest of his party, opposed it. It was also how the country at large took it and was meant to take it. It was the first of a series of acts of appeasement of the racialists, and, of course, could not serve this purpose unless its intention and effect, of restricting 'coloured' immigration, was plainly recognizable; at the same time, precisely because the crypto-racialists could not swallow an open declaration of a racially discriminatory intent, a transparent fiction was maintained, like an elaborate piece of Chinese etiquette, that this was neither its effect nor its purpose.

During its election campaign of 1964, the Labour Party was notoriously ambiguous about immigration, leading some immigrants and liberals to believe that they intended to repeal the 1962 Act. It seems probable now that they actually were divided in opinion about it at the time: Mr Wilson's famous 'leper' reference to Peter Griffiths in the House of Commons suggests that Wilson at that time intended to follow Gaitskell's policy, and wage an all-out battle against racialism. If the Labour Government had pursued such a line, the future of this country would look very much brighter than it does now. The 1964 Labour Government's first hundred days have now faded from public memory; it is a shock to read again some of the bold speeches made in the first golden flush of victory, after twelve years of Opposition. Yet in the headlong retreat the Labour leadership has made since 1965 from its first intentions, in the whole range of political activity, there have occurred here and there uncoordinated counter-attacks. In education, financial cuts, dearer school meals, almost total inaction in the face of the 'big three' educational reports, are unexpectedly followed by a grant of a million pounds for nursery schools, and the promise of a higher school-leaving age by 1972. These two reforming measures are almost meaningless within the total running down of educational resources; do they represent an attack of conscience?—a weather eye on the next election?—or are they the result of fragmented victories and defeats, salved from cabinet wrangles and inter-departmental rivalries? Whatever the reason, this broad pattern of defeated intentions, broken up unexpectedly by measures good in themselves yet of little effect on the lines of the whole pattern, is a true picture of the Government's record in many fields. In the field of race, we have had a flight from principle and commonsense; inaction and confusion where there should have been positive policies, and, as the isolated remnant of original policy, the 1968 Race Relations Act.

The flight from principle and commonsense on racial issues can be dated from February 1965, when Gordon-Walker, already defeated by an overtly racialist campaign in Smethwick, [3] was defeated again in a by-election, this time in a supposedly safe Labour seat, Leyton. As a matter of fact, it is far from certain that Gordon-Walker's defeat owed much to his views on race. Political commentators at the time made the point that Reg Sorensen, the former Labour MP, had enjoyed enormous personal popularity in the area, and local voters strongly resented the Government's high-handed removal of Sorensen from Leyton to make room for a former minister who had no local connections. Possibly the leaders of the Government were influenced too by the sudden increase in racial awareness, after Smethwick; the national press, and television, woke up to the sensational possibilities of a 'race angle' on the most insignificant items of news, and played these up for a good deal more than they were worth. One thing is certain: very soon after their accession to power, and within days of the Leyton defeat, a volte-face was sprung upon Parliament and upon the nation by the Home Secretary, Soskice, in February 1965, when he announced, in a speech marked by numerous indications of hostility towards West Indians and Asians, [4] the tightening of immigration controls.

From then on, the Labour Government was firmly set on the course of yielding with alacrity to each fresh outburst of clamour for restricting Commonwealth immigration. It is doubtful whether, in 1965, this was yet the conscious policy that it has evidently since become. More likely, the Government was merely thoroughly frightened by the vehemence of expression of racialist feeling, and the amount of support it could attract, and was determined for the time being to appease it so drastically that they would be safe from attack by the Conservatives on this issue. If so, then, of course their calculations were awry, as the calculations of those usually are who in politics try to steal their opponents' clothes: higher and higher as the cards have been that Labour has played in this particular suit, the Conservatives have been able each time to win the trick.

The White Paper which followed a few months later, in August 1965, announced, with many other drastic new restrictions on immigration, the ceiling of 8500 labour vouchers per year for the entire Commonwealth, together with proposals of sweeping new powers for the Home Secretary (proposals never embodied in legislation, because of a belated resistance by Labour backbenchers in the House of Commons—the only successful resistance ever offered to racialist Government measures). At the same time there was heard in the White Paper the first entry of a new theme, one which was to become wearisomely familiar; the Government's positive action for integration. The combination of the two elements made the White Paper into a very remarkable document indeed, possibly the most logically incoherent Government paper ever produced. Parts 1 and 2 stated, in Soskice's severe and icy tones, the pressing necessity for a far-reaching reduction in the numbers of Commonwealth immigrants, and, like a tolling bell endlessly repeated, 'This concession will now be withdrawn', without once stopping to explain whence this neccessity arose or why the various 'concessions' were no longer found tolerable; presumably the reason was expected to be taken as obvious, though as yet still unmentionable in official statements. Part 3 was headed 'Integration', and was evidently by a different hand (presumably that of Mr Maurice Foley, the junior minister then at the Department of Economic Affairs 'with special responsibility' for Commonwealth immigrants). This section of the White Paper was remarkable for two things. It was remarkable, first, for systematically repudiating in turn every conceivable ground other than a discriminatory one that could be thought to explain the necessity alleged in Part 2 for drastically reducing the number of Commonwealth immigrants. No, immigrants did not give rise to any special health problems; no, the housing shortage was in no way due to immigration; no, immigrants did not swell the ranks of the unemployed; no, immigrants had a lower, not a higher, crime rate than the native population. Second, it was remarkable for failing to identify any problem at all connected with the presence of immigrants, save, in the section on education, the genuine, but minor one of providing teachers of English as a foreign language. Unspecified difficulties were mentioned, the need for positive action to resolve them was stressed; but, save for the negative statements already mentioned, repudiating certain misidentifications of these difficulties, nothing was said about what these problems were. Once these misidentifications were rejected, only one possibility—the true one—remained, namely, that the problem lay not in the behaviour of the immigrants, but in that of the natives—their practice of racial discrimination, and the prejudices and racialist assumptions from which this practice sprang. But the Government was not prepared at that time to publish a document thus frankly identifying the character of the most challenging problem (and that most significant for the future of the country) of all those they had to face. In the whole of Part 3, there is only one mention of racial discrimination, a passing allusion in the section on employment. A curious sort of shadow-boxing therefore went on throughout Part 3: in each area, a search was conducted for a 'solution' to a problem which remained wholly unidentified. It would be unfair to list the utter vacuity of the proposed solutions as a third remarkable feature: given the failure to mention the problem, it was inevitable. Thus, the only recommendation about employment was that Ministry of Labour Employment Exchanges should refuse to deal with employers who discriminated *as a result of their personal prejudice* (as if any employer would ever admit to being personally prejudiced, or as if it mattered whether he was discriminating in deference to his own prejudices or to the real or supposed prejudices of his employees or customers). The only proposal on education was a reiteration of the notorious Department of Education and Science recommendation of dispersing so-called immigrant children (which included children born in Britain) from schools where they numbered over 30 per cent—a policy which had earned the hostility of most immigrant parents, who saw it as a form of discrimination, there being no talk of dispersing white children who lacked the advantage of associating with black ones, but much talk of the threat to the character of the school, and to the education of white children, when the supposed 30 per cent danger mark was passed. The only proposal on housing was the application to other cities of the notorious Birmingham Corporation Act, which gave the Council the power to prohibit multi-occupation in an area in which it 'would destroy the amenities' (that is in a respectable white middle-class area), and at the same time to fine landlords of multi-occupied houses without providing anywhere else for them or their tenants to go. Thus every concrete suggestion made was either nugatory or, more often, actually discriminatory in effect.

The most substantial of the proposals made, and that which was to have by far the most significant effect on the development of the racial situation, was that which concerned 'positive work to encourage integration'. In a section dealing with this, the work of the local organizations collectively labelled by the Government 'local voluntary liaison committees' was praised—although no other kind of voluntary organization in the field was mentioned; the intention was announced to set up a National Committee for Commonwealth Immigrants, to replace a much more modest body of the same name, and to co-ordinate and assist the work of the liaison committees. Next, a promise was made that, through the New National Committee, funds would be forthcoming to these liaison committees to appoint a full-time worker ('liaison officer'). Since the problem constituted by the existence of racial prejudice and the practice of racial discrimination had not been mentioned, the eradication of these things was not listed as one of the tasks which the liaison committees, or the new National Committee, had performed and should perform; they had, instead, the more comforting task of promoting racial harmony, helping immigrants to adjust to their new environment, providing information to the native population about the immigrants, and vice versa.

The Government was thus launched upon the policy it has consistently pursued since then — the combination of an exclusionist immigration policy and a hesitant programme for integration within the country. Henceforward, when accused by white liberals or by immigrant groups of a discriminatory immigration policy, it continued to go through the motions of pretending that it was not discriminatory ('The Commonwealth Immigrants Act does not mention colour'); but the substance of its retort lay in referring to the positive work it was doing for racial harmony, by establishing the National Committee and by its encouragement of and assistance to the liaison committees. Government spokesmen reiterated that 'integration and immigration are two separate questions.'

More and more openly it came to be admitted that the whole purpose of the immigration laws was to minimize the number of people of a different colour entering the country; indeed, the Government itself began to argue that this exclusion was itself a contribution to 'racial harmony', that it was in the interests of black people themselves that their numbers be kept to a minimum, because only thus would the native population find their presence tolerable and refrain in consequence from various unnamed but undesirable acts (of which the foremost, no doubt, would be voting the Labour Party out at the next election). But according to this new line, it was perfectly consistent to couple with the positive work the Government was most earnestly doing to promote racial harmony within the country a policy of keeping as many black people out as possible: whether a man was allowed into the country, and how he was treated once he got here, were two entirely distinct questions.

It was only during 1966 that this theory came to be formulated: it was probably more a rationalization of what the Government had done than the basis on which they had acted. As we have said, the restriction announced by Soskice's speech of February 1965 and the White Paper later in the same year probably represented a panic attempt to appease the racialism the virulence of which the Government had belatedly realized by granting the principal demand of its most articulate spokesmen, rather than the outcome of any considered policy. At the same time, the Labour Party is to some small degree responsive to pressure from liberal opinion, and the inauguration in the White Paper of a 'positive policy for integration' was, again, probably more an attempt to keep this sector of opinion quiet than an application of any explicit theory. However, once formulated, the theory obviously seemed to the Government the ideal way of extricating itself from the embarrassment which the racial problem so obviously caused it. It must have seemed inspired. At one and the same time the Government could, by sticking to this theory, appease both the racialists and the liberals. Moreover, once members of the Government had grasped the psychology of the British people – the condition which we have labelled 'crypto-racialism' – the application of the theory offered the ideal way (or so it must have seemed) of keeping the issue from getting out of hand. Once the British people in general realized the nature of the choice with which the nation was presented, it would be bound, however little it might like being forced to make the choice, to divide into segregationists and integrationists, racialists and anti-racialists, and the most profound cleavage would be created within the white population at large. It was therefore essential to postpone this realization as long as possible. What better means could be found for this than the strategy already adopted by the racialists for achieving the same purpose? By resolving to yield instantly to each outbreak of clamour for restricting coloured immigration, by, indeed, making their own the propaganda of the racialists concerning the problems to which such immigrants gave rise, the same effect must surely be produced, namely that of allowing the crypto-racialist majority to continue undisturbed in their delusion that there still remained a possibility of keeping Britain white, that the problem lay in finding means of keeping the intruders out. At the same time, the efforts of promoting integration could be carried on as an alibi against any accusation of racialist policy.

In accordance with this theory, even the terms employed for describing the positive internal policy were selected to be as ambiguous as possible. Even the word 'integration', once the slogan of the American Civil Rights Movement, was degraded by Sir Alec Douglas-Home into the meaning 'inducing these people to adopt our customs and culture'. 'Racial harmony' (the favourite term of the Conservative Party) and 'good race relations' (preferred by Labour ministers) can obviously be heard as meaning either 'the eradication of prejudice and establishment of racial equality' or 'keeping the blacks in their place and stopping them causing any trouble'; anyone with an ear attuned to the American scene must recognize in the second of these two phrases an echo of the old cry of the Southern segregationalists: 'We always had good relations between the races until these outside agitators came in and started stirring up the niggers.'

It is clear that, at the same time as the White Paper was written, not only was the theory not yet formulated, but the nature of the crypto-racialism was not yet understood, and hence the use to which the theory could be put in preserving the crypto-racialists' illusions not yet spotted. This is evident from the one really good thing about Part 3 of the White Paper – the opening in which it is stated outright that 'Britain is already a multi-racial society' – just the very fact which it soon became the aim of Government policy, in unison with the racialists, to conceal from the bulk of the population.

The theory was, presumably, formulated and consciously adopted as a guide to future Government policy during 1966: and the Government has clung tenaciously to it ever since, undeterred by the disastrous consequences that have flowed from it. But this fact did not become inescapably evident until 1968. True enough, Government ministers often expounded the theory; but, of the tiny minority within the country aware how grave was the danger of Britain's becoming a racialist society, many were disposed to adopt an optimistic view of the Government's intentions. They therefore failed to see the theory as constituting the basis of future Government policy, but were inclined, instead, to regard the repeated expression of it indulgently, as a mere face-saving device on the part of a Government ashamed of its conduct during 1965. Such people did not stop to consider that there might be a further outburst of racialist demands; or, if they did, they assumed that the Government had had a change of heart, and would this time resist all pressure for further restrictions. It was not until this outburst came, initiated by Enoch Powell's speech to the 1967 Conservative Party Conference and sustained by Duncan Sandys, and the Government made its total and almost instant capitulation to it in the infamous Commonwealth Immigrants Act of 1 March 1968, that disillusion came, and the optimists discovered that the Government had in no way been merely saving its face, but had meant quite literally what it had said.

There were several reasons why, during the period 1966-7, so many of those most active in the opposition to racialism should have let themselves be so deceived. One was the personality of the new Home Secretary, Roy Jenkins. Jenkins appeared to be that rare phenomenon among British politicians, one who understood what the racial problem was about. He gave, in one speech, a classic definition of integration ('equal treatment, in an atmosphere of mutual tolerance and cultural diversity'), and, at the same time, he gave the impression of being a man resolved to work for it. It therefore seemed all the greater a betrayal when, in February 1968, he, who although no longer Home Secretary was presumably the one man in the Cabinet who could have prevented the introduction of the new Commonwealth Immigrants Act, walked through the lobby to vote in its favour.

As we shall set out later, the Government's positive policy for integration did not, in the event, prove to be very much less of a feeble mockery than might have been expected from Part 3 of the White Paper. It is undoubtedly true that, had the Government pursued its policy of promoting integration with as much vigour and resolution as it pursued the complementary policy of progressively harsher immigration restrictions, the combination of these two policies would not have been so disastrous as in fact it was. But, before we go on to examine the Government's internal racial policy in detail, it is well first to stop to consider why this dual policy could not possibly have been successful, why, in fact, the theory that 'integration has nothing to do with immigration', that 'we must try to keep them out, but see that they are fairly treated once they are here', led and was bound to lead where it has, to the catastrophic inflammation of racialist sentiment and the destruction of the bright hopes Jenkins had voiced for our society.

The foundation of the theory was, as we have seen, that, by yielding to every demand for exclusion, the Government would both appease and outflank the racialists and lull the crypto-racialists into delusions of security, while, by working for integration at home, it would satisfy the anti-racialists and the immigrants themselves, and gradually lower the level of tension and discrimination. In every one of these objectives, the policy had a drastic effect, the exact reverse of that intended. The racialists were neither appeased nor outflanked: on the contrary, each victory made them thirst more strongly for the next kill. Each successive measure, which a short time before would have seemed unthinkable, something which went beyond what even the most ardent racialists were demanding, made a further one seem possible; once a step has been taken, which at the time seems shocking, it soon comes to appear natural, and the argument begins to centre around whether or not to take the next step in the same direction. The crypto-racialists were, indeed, to a certain extent, lulled: if, in 1965, the Government had stood firmly on the principle of racial equality, it is true that a deep division would have appeared in the nation in 1965 instead of in 1968; but it would have been a division in which the opponents of racialism would have been far more numerous. For each restrictive measure had upon the crypto-racialists a far graver effect even than that of allowing them to continue to disguise the real situation from themselves: it acted as the most powerful possible *education* in racialism.

The Government had been in the difficulty that it wished to appear to different groups of people as having different motives for its immigration policy. To anyone moved by racial prejudice, it wanted to appear as taking resolute steps to prevent the country being ruined by the influx of coloured people; but, to those opposed to racialism it wished to appear as motivated solely by the desire to prevent the white backlash that would be caused by a failure to yield to pressure for restriction. Thus, after the 1968 Act, Mr David Ennals, then Under-Secretary at the Home Office and the successor to Maurice Foley as minister with special responsibility for Commonwealth immigrants, waxed extremely indignant with critics belonging to various voluntary anti-racialist bodies: could they not understand that to pass that Act was the one essential step which had to be taken for the sake of 'good race relations'? But, unfortunately, this was not the explanation which had been offered to the nation at large. Just possibly, if it had been, the worst internal effects of that monstrous piece of unjust legislation might have been averted. To have offered the same explanation to the nation at large would have been to say something like this:

These British citizens of Indian descent were guaranteed a choice of citizenship, at a time when citizenship, as it has throughout history until now, involved the right to live in the country of which one is a citizen. Now, experiencing difficulties in the country where they live, they want to exercise this right. The Government would be happy to welcome them here. They pose no threat to our culture, but would enrich it; they would create no problems in themselves, being mostly educated, skilled or professional people of just the sort any country is glad to have coming in. Unfortunately, such is the level of mindless colour prejudice which has arisen in our nation that we are afraid that, with no justification whatsoever, their unrestricted entry in the hour of their need, and in accordance with the undertaking that was freely given to them by this country, would lead to grave social tension. We are ashamed that this so, and we think that the whole nation is shamed before the world. We are resolved to eradicate this disease of racialism which has so taken hold of some of our people by every means in our power. Until then, we are forced, with the profoundest regret, to dishonour this country by introducing this Bill.

To have said this would have been to do no more than apply to that situation just the kind of thing that Jenkins had for some time been saying to carefully selected audiences of workers in race relations. But it is necessary only to spell out what the Government would have had to say if it had wanted to speak to the nation at large in the same voice in which it still tried desperately to convince anti-racialists that it was really on their side, deep down, to see how different was the impression which the Government strove to convey to the mass of the population. To achieve the effect they intended, they were driven to make their own that racialist propaganda which had dwelt for years upon the supposed 'problems' which the presence of dark-skinned people gave rise to. Instead of saying to the people of Britain, 'We cannot allow these people here because *you* do not seem capable of civilized behaviour towards them,' they said, 'We cannot allow them here because of the problems *they* would create.' The most extreme example was the speech of the Lord Chancellor in the House of Lords, which quoted figures totalling about two million for the citizens of the United Kingdom and Colonies who would be entitled to 'come to Britain tomorrow or next week or next month free of any control' *The Times,* 1 March 1968). (These figures were later shown by critics to include a very high proportion of people with dual citizenship, with no incentive or desire to come to Britain.) *The Times* reported:

> 'And all these people,' he said, 'are entitled to arrive and go, I suppose, to Huddersfield or Bradford and say: "You build the schools, and train, employ and pay the teachers to teach our children; you build the hospitals and find the doctors and nurses, we have a right to come here and you must find the houses".'

The *tone* of this speech is extraordinary enough for a Lord Chancellor; its content is stranger still, since one can hardly suppose someone of Lord Gardiner's distinction and political service to be unaware of the fact that United Kingdom citizens, whatever their colour, and however recently they arrived, pay the taxes and insurance that provide our social services, and that they form an indispensable part of the labour force in Britain that comprises doctors, nurses, teachers and builder's labourers.

Thus, to justify its immigration policy, and to endow that policy with the effect of appeasing the racialists which it intended, the Government was forced itself into producing racialist propaganda. And, of course, the effect on the nation at large was precisely what the Government, in one way, intended, to convince people that the Government too regarded black people as undesirable, as constituting 'problems' in their own persons, just as they themselves were inclined to do. When the Government itself was not saying it, people could not be expected to say to themselves, 'The Government can't let these people in because, if they did, *we* should behave so badly towards them.' What they said, of course, was, 'The Government knows all the trouble these black so-and-so's cause.' When an immigrants' protest march was staged on the Sunday before the Bill was passed, Whitehall was lined with people shouting, 'Wogs, go home!', 'We don't want you black bastards here': and what these people thought they were doing—what indeed, they *were* doing—was supporting the Government. And it has been thus with each successive act of restriction: each such act has been the most powerful influence possible—more powerful than any speech by

Powell—to educate people into adopting racialist attitudes. Each such act has proclaimed by the fact of its being carried out and explicitly by the speeches that have been made in its support that black people are undesirable and in some way their presence threatens the nation. Callaghan, indeed, in introducing the 1968 Bill spoke of the 'solemn obligations' which the Bill was violating: he could hardly have conveyed more clearly that he considered any dishonour preferable to the presence of a few thousand more people of dark skins. No amount of exhortation of employers, housing authorities and the like not to practise racial discrimination was likely to have the slightest effect in the face of that example: for, if the Government may justly keep out 'coloured' people because of the difficulties they supposedly create, or even just because of the hostility of the population towards them, why may not an employer with equal right keep them out of his firm because of the difficulties they may create for him or the hostility of his other workpeople?

The 1968 Immigration Act, like the White Paper, Soskice's February 1965 speech, and the 1962 Act before it, had in itself a more powerful effect in raising the level of prejudice and confirming the respectability of discrimination than either of Powell's two 1968 speeches. Not merely that, but they made those speeches possible. Powell was able to outmanoeuvre the Government; and put it in just the position it had tried so hard to avoid, as appearing as the sponsor and protector of black people, precisely because, during the passage of the Immigration Act, both Government and official opposition had put themselves in a position where they could not give him the lie. The Government had only just a month before been telling the nation what a danger the arrival of these people was: what had Powell done but spell out this danger more vividly? That is why Callaghan's reply to Powell amounted to no more than 'Why pick on us?—we've been trying to keep them out too.' It is also why Heath's rebuke to Powell, which many people at the time so fatuously praised for its 'courage', was so careful to avoid saying that anything that Powell had said was untrue, but, as Powell was able triumphantly to point out in his second speech on race that year, merely reprimanded him for the kind of language he had used. If either the Government or the Conservative leadership had in February adopted a position that would have allowed them with any plausibility in April to say to Powell what he deserved to have said to him, he would surely have been astute enough not to have made the speech he did. But Government and opposition had both, by their cowardice, played directly into his hands: the primary responsibility for the phenomenon of Enoch Powell lies with Wilson and Callaghan and Heath.

An outrightly racialist Government would at least have made it possible for people to see easily what was going on. Instead, the have-your-cake-and-eat-it theory of the Government inflamed racialist feeling every bit as much as an openly racialist policy would have done, while all the talk about good race relations, promoting integration, and the rest, stifled the opposition of all but a minute minority of concerned individuals who knew and understood enough about what was happening not to be deceived into discounting the danger. In 1964 the situation had become bad enough to justify asking with alarm, 'Is Britain going to go racialist?': probably, no alternative policy, good or bad, that the Government could have adopted would have made it possible to answer definitively, within the short space of four years, 'It already has'.

We now turn to analyse the character of the Government's so-called positive policy for integration at home. This falls under two principal heads, corresponding to the two statutory bodies which now exist, the Race Relations Board and the Community Relations Commission. The Board is concerned with the administration of the 1965-8 Race Relations Acts, that is, the legislation which the Government has sponsored against the practice of racial discrimination. (We should not forget that Lord Brockway, when he was Mr Fenner Brockway MP, had made several courageous and far-sighted attempts during the 1950s to bring in a private member's bill prohibiting racial discrimination. Not only was each attempt unsuccessful, he has received little publicity for them.) The commission is concerned with the supervision, encouragement and grant-aiding of voluntary work. The Race Relations Board was originally set up in the spring of 1966, under the first Race Relations Act passed in November of the preceding year. The Community Relations Commission, under Frank Cousins as Chairman, has only just come into existence, superseding the National Committee for Commonwealth Immigrants set up in December 1965, not under statute, but in accordance with the 1965 White Paper.

Legislation against racial discrimination is an indispensable minimum for any society in which that practice flourishes, if it wishes to bring about racial equality or to avoid the creation of an underprivileged and embittered racial minority. The first Race Relations Act in 1965 applied to discrimination within so narrow an area ('places of public resort', themselves quite narrowly defined) that it had no significance save as establishing in principle the desirability of such legislation. Contrary to the wishes of the then Home Secretary, Soskice, but in accordance with the advice of all race relations experts, and of most, though not quite all, the immigrant and anti-racialist pressure groups, the form adopted for this legislation followed in general principle the American and Canadian pattern, instead of a straightforward procedure of bringing offenders to trial in the courts, as Soskice wanted. This pattern consists in a machinery of voluntary conciliation by the Race Relations Board and its subordinate regional Conciliation Committees, with a resort to the civil, not the criminal, courts only in the (hopefully infrequent) cases where the conciliation procedure failed. The establishment of the Race Relations Board was, as it proved, an important step towards the introduction of more meaningful legislation, because the Board received a great many complaints in areas such as employment with which it was powerless to deal, and, in the report which it was required to present to Parliament at the end of its first year, stressed the necessity of increasing the scope of the Act. Accordingly, the Government introduced a second Race Relations Bill in April 1968.

After the passage of the original Act, the Government's reply to pressure to extend its scope was to say that it had first to be proved to be necessary. This proof was provided (though it had hardly been needed) not only by the first Annual Report of the Race Relations Board, but also by a survey carried out by PEP and sponsored jointly by the Race Relations Board and the National Committee for Commonwealth Immigrants, a survey which established conclusively the existence of widespread discrimination in employment, housing, insurance and credit facilities.

The Government duly introduced the second Bill. Had they refused to do so, their professed intention to secure 'good race relations' at home would have become transparently spurious to every observer, however lacking in understanding. After the publication of the PEP report, the Government had come even closer, in its response to pressure groups, to committing itself to introduce such a Bill; at the same time, it had insisted that such a Bill must be the last of its kind for the foreseeable future: that it would not be prepared to consider amendments to the new Act, however unsatisfactory people found it. And unsatisfactory it certainly was. The principle underlying this, for Britain, novel method of dealing with the commission of what became, under the Race Relations Acts, unlawful acts, was that as far as possible those who broke the law by discriminating on grounds of race should not be exposed to publicity, as are other offenders against the law, or even subjected to punitive measures. A public hearing should take place only when private conciliation had failed, and recourse to the law courts be resorted to only when the public hearing had in turn failed to achieve its objective. American and Canadian experience had shown that, in cases where there was enough evidence to make recourse to the courts possible, this was very rarely necessary: the case would be settled in one of the earlier stages. The fact that the legislation was passed in this form gives the lie to the propaganda against it conducted by Ronald Bell and his Society for Individual Freedom, that, by exposing offenders to publicity and punitive reprisals by the courts, racial prejudice would be inflamed: for, whatever may be thought of this in general as an argument for not making some undesirable practice illegal, this was the one area where the law had been so drawn up that the argument did not apply, and Bell's propaganda, like that of other racialists, thus flagrantly depends on misinforming the public or counting on their ignorance.

But, if such machinery is to work effectively, the conciliation procedure must itself be given some teeth. The Race Relations Board, or its subordinate investigators, needed the power to carry out their investigations without depending on the goodwill of those under suspicion of breaking the law, for instance to subpoena witnesses and documents. Under the 1968 Act, however, it was given no such power, although both it and numerous pressure groups, including the National Committee for Commonwealth Immigrants, had pointed out the importance of this. As things stand, any suspect may lawfully simply refuse to talk to the Race Relations Board or its agents, and thus in effect challenge it to go to court with such evidence as it may have been able to obtain from outside sources. Worse still, the Act furnishes the conciliation agreements arrived at in the first stage of the conciliation process with no binding force whatever. The first stage consists of an attempt by the regional Conciliation Committee to obtain an undertaking from the offender to cease the practice of discrimination in future: but, although such an agreement may contain more detailed provisions (say, for example, the posting of a notice announcing that there would be no discrimination on grounds of race), a failure to comply with it would remain no offence at all in itself: only if actual discrimination could be shown later to have occurred would the offender be liable to any action, and this would be, in the first place, simply a repetition of the same process as before. Only if the first stage of conciliation failed, and the matter was referred to the Board itself, would it be possible for the Board to make an order having any binding force. But the worst defect of all was the failure to provide any incentive for making a complaint. The individual discriminated against does not, under the Act, receive any compensation of any kind, unless, indeed, the case happens to reach the third stage of going before the courts, when he might be given a money sum in compensation. But, even in this case, there would be no question of an order compelling the person who had discriminated against him to offer him the job, accommodation, etc., he had previously denied him. This provision is contained in the corresponding American and Canadian legislation; without it, the only incentive to make a complaint is the desire that others should not suffer the injustice the complainant himself received.

The second Race Relations Act is not entirely hopeless: in particular, its scope was commendably wide. It is possible that, with a vigorous and determined Race Relations Board, the Act may be able to be used to make a significant difference to the incidence of racial discrimination. But, as a result of the ambiguity of the Government's attitude and its infirmity of purpose, it emerged as a thoroughly ill-designed and unsatisfactory piece of legislation, despite having been preceded by more and better-informed studies of the way it should be drafted than can have been the case with any other law this century. The Government statements, made before the Bill was drafted, that it would not consider amending it further once it was passed, were motivated by the desire to get what it considered unpopular legislation well out of the way before the next general election approached. There is, however, every reason why this Act should be amended as soon as possible, to remove the features which are quite capable of stultifying it altogether, and, at best, will make it a very clumsy instrument indeed for the purpose for which it is ostensibly intended.

Laws against racial discrimination, however well-designed, are unlikely by themselves to do much good if they are unaccompanied by the most vigorous work by unofficial agencies. Especially when there is a law against it, employers, landlords, etc., are unlikely to say, 'I'm refusing you because you are coloured,' but rather to deny that the vacancy still exists. The surest way to disprove this is by immediately sending a white applicant: but that requires organization. This, of course, is only one instance of the fact that the work of voluntary bodies is an essential supplement to that of an official body like the Race Relations Board, and not an alternative to it, as the opponents of the Act attempted to argue.

Direct work against racial discrimination is, however, only one function of voluntary anti-racialist organizations, which must play an important part in solving the problem of the infection of a society by racialism. Such organizations have also to help articulate the demands of those who are the targets of prejudice, to provide a means by which their voices can be heard and their grievances made known to the society. They have to exercise pressure on local and national Government, to try to educate the society to an understanding of what is taking place, to counteract the continual impact of racialist propaganda and the expression of unconsciously racialist opinion. Above all, they have to perform two functions which become the more vital the worse the situation grows: they have to provide for the member of the racial minorities a sector of his life of which he can feel that he is in control; and they have to hold open the lines of communication between majority and minority, lest alienation between the two groups becomes complete.

Whereas in the field of legislation the Government's achievement has been noticeable, though half-hearted, its policy towards voluntary organizations has been uniformly disastrous. When the formation of the National Committee for Commonwealth Immigrants was announced in the White Paper of 1965, the period of flirtation between the Government and some of the anti-racialist organizations had not yet begun. On the contrary, Soskice was still Home Secretary, and the White Paper appeared as the manifesto of an openly racialist policy inaugurated by the volte-face of Soskice's Feburary speech in the House. There was, therefore, deep dissension both between and among immigrant and inter-racial organizations over which of two opposing policies to follow in relation to the new National Committee. The National Committee had been assigned two tasks by the government: to co-ordinate the work of the voluntary liaison committees; and to advise the Government on matters relating to Commonwealth immigrants. The members of the committee itself were to be appointed directly by the Prime Minister; it was to employ a substantial permanent staff; and it was to be assisted in formulating advice to the Government by a number of advisory panels of experts in various areas, such as employment, housing, etc. Some members of the anti-racialist organizations thought it worth while to co-operate with the new National Committee, in the hope that this would prove a means of influencing in the right direction the kind of advice the Government was to receive from it. Others thought it merely a smokescreen behind which the Government could get on with the implementation of its racialist policy. On this view, the National Committee would have no effect on the policies of the Government, but would serve merely as an alibi so that the Government could deceive people into thinking that it was 'doing something for race relations': to co-operate with it was therefore merely to allow oneself to be used in a manoeuvre calculated to deceive the public. The dissension between supporters of these two strategies caused severe damage both to co-operation between different immigrant and inter-racial organizations and to the internal coherence of those organizations themselves: for instance, it can be seen clearly in retrospect that the failure of the Campaign Against Racial Discrimination to become what it had been founded to be, the focus of the whole movement against racialism, was inevitable after the defections from it of those who supported the policy of non-co-operation with the National Committee, and therefore deplored the fact that the Chairman and Vice-Chairman of CARD formed two out of the three original immigrant members of the National Committee. Thus the National Committee, simply by coming into existence, dealt a severe and almost fatal blow to the embryo British civil rights movement.

In the event, the predictions of those who advocated non-co-operation proved wholly correct. It can be argued how far this was due to a deliberate policy on the part of the Government, and how far it was due to the timidity and conformism that characterized the permanent staff at the National Committee, who in practice determined its policy to a very great extent. But there is no doubt that the practical effect was just as the pessimists had foretold. As far as the advisory function of the National Committee was concerned, it gave on the whole correct advice to the Government, but the advice was, for the most part, ignored. The final, public, gesture of contempt made by the Government towards its own creature occurred when it failed even to notify it of the Immigration Bill of 1968. The contempt was deserved, because, long after it had become apparent that the whole process of submitting carefully considered recommendations to the Government was making no difference whatever to the course of events, the National Committee simply ploughed ahead with the same time-consuming, pointless activity, without making any attempt to find a means to put pressure on the Government to accept its recommendations. Publicity was shunned as if it were the eighth deadly sin. So far from there being any mobilization of opinion behind the National Committee's policies, there was no way for even an MP to discover what advice it had given the Government and what reply the Government had returned. Some of the advisory panels discovered useful roles for themselves unconnected with advice to Government: but, in general, the whole complicated machinery degenerated into a solemn farce.

But by far the most damaging of the two kinds of activity in which the National Committee engaged was its fulfilment of its role as the friend and guide of voluntary organizations. When the National Committee came into existence, there had sprung up, in a number of localities and as a result of local initiatives, inter-racial organizations of widely differing kinds. The body of the same name which was replaced by the National Committee had devised a rough-and-ready classification of these into 'liaison committees' and 'campaign committees', a classification which was incorporated into Part 3 of the 1965 White Paper. Those which were thus classified as 'liaison committees' were in the majority, and consisted of the ones which had adopted a certain strategy, that of incorporating among their membership individuals of power and influence in the local community – city councillors, local government officials, trade unionists, the clergy and representatives of community organizations, even when these individuals might sometimes have rather ambiguous racial attitudes. The advantage of this strategy was as clear as its disadvantage: since Britain had no experience of the kind of pressure group which a civil rights organization constitutes, an unofficial organization working against discrimination stood in danger of simply not being listened to; it would overcome this initial danger by using, among its representatives, people already of standing in the community, who knew the workings of its power structure and could not be told just to go away. Those that did not choose to follow this strategy were labelled by the National Committee as 'campaign committees'. Alongside these inter-racial organizations were an even greater number and variety of local immigrant organizations, Indian, Pakistani and West Indian, some of them united in national federations. The Campaign Against Racial Discrimination sought the affiliation of all these bodies: it obtained that of some immigrant organizations, all the campaign committees, and three of the liaison committees.

There was thus a great deal of disparate resistance to the rising tide of racialism, which had yet to be welded into a movement. We have already explained how the mere foundation of the National Committee struck a grave blow at the precarious striving towards unity between these various groups. The policy which it subsequently adopted carried the damage a great deal further, and effectively ruined the liaison committees, with a very few exceptions, as a serious force. The concept of a liaison committee was something superimposed from above: no one had previously had the thought, 'Let's form a liaison committee'; rather, the concept was justified only as providing a rough-and-ready classification of heterogeneous bodies according to one feature of their mode of operation. This concept was converted by the National Committee into a rigid stereotype to which it brought great pressure to conform; and a stereotype resting on a timid, conformist ideology. This stereotype was of an organization without open membership, and not merely containing but dominated by delegates of all the community organizations; linked very tightly with the city or borough council; and eschewing any course of action capable of giving offence to powerful or influential persons. The ideology was encapsulated in the slogan, 'Our work is not race relations but community relations': it is this slogan which has provided the very name of the successor body to the National Committee. This slogan could be interpreted as conveying an important half-truth, one which has been the basis of the strategy of certain 'campaign committees' and local CARD groups: namely, that what racial minorities suffer from is identical with what the less fortunate members of the white community also suffer from — bad housing, exploitation by landlords or by employers and the like — and that prejudice is often aroused by those responsible for these social evils to provide a scapegoat for them; and hence that the remedy is not to underline the struggle for *racial* justice, but to unite the oppressed of all races in an attack on the real causes of the evils from which they all suffer. Unfortunately, this is only a half-truth, because racialism has by now acquired too much of a life of its own to be able to be dispelled, at least on the local level, by even successful attacks on genuine problems common to black and white. In any case, it was not at all what the National Committee meant when it talked about 'community relations'. It meant, not the replacement of the conflict between black and white by one between exploited and exploiters, but the avoidance of conflict altogether. The liaison committee was to be neither a pressure group for the rights of black people, nor one for the rights of all the exploited and under-privileged: it was not to be concerned for any special interests, but to be representative of the whole community at large. What in practice this meant was that it was to be controlled by those who already had power within the community. The aim of the liaison committee was to be not that of wresting from those who refused it respect for black people and for their rights: it was to be communal harmony. Conflict and confrontation were thus seen as evils in themselves; when mild suggestion would not correct an injustice, all that remained was to induce its victims to tolerate and 'understand' that injustice. This latter process was called 'helping the immigrant to adjust to his new environment'.

To those unfamiliar with the scene, it may seem incredible that, in the three years of its existence, the National Committee accomplished with almost total success the programme of thus emasculating the liaison committees. It has been possible partly because the majority of such committees now in existence are those whose formation the National Committee itself sponsored during that period, unlike the older ones which arose spontaneously; because these older ones themselves contained people not fully committed, or not resolute or self-confident enough to stand out against superior 'expert' advice; and because the National Committee had patronage in the form of Government grants for the appointment of liaison officers. The White Paper had mentioned only the liaison committees, ignoring both the campaign committees and the immigrant organizations. The National Committee followed this lead, providing virtually no service of encouragement or advice to black people's organizations or to inter-racial bodies not conforming with the liaison committee stereotype, but treating the latter, not as independent bodies to which it could offer assistance, but as companies in a regiment of which it was the headquarters staff. Not only was its treatment of them authoritarian, and the pressure it applied always in the direction of caution and conformism, most fatal of all, it usually delivered those who applied for a grant for a liaison officer — by now the majority of them — bound hand and foot into the power of a frequently hostile local authority, for the White Paper had made each grant conditional on the provision of a matching grant from the local authority, which, the more hostile it was, drove the harder bargain in terms of the right to appoint officers of the committee or even to veto proposed members.

The National Committee participated in one significant contribution to the resistance offered to the rise of racialism — its joint sponsorship, with the Race Relations Board, of the PEP Report. This apart, its practical effect was almost wholly deleterious: it was the most important single factor in the failure during this critical period to build a strong, united British civil rights movement.

It took time for this to become clear to those members of anti-racialist groups who had adopted the policy of co-operating with the National Committee. During the period when Jenkins was Home Secretary, it seemed for some time that their policy had been justified, for the impression was gained that some kind of tacit bargain had been struck. By agreeing to co-operate with the Government-sponsored structure, these people had in effect done the Government a considerable service by lending plausibility to its alibi, of taking positive steps to promote good race relations, for its racialist immigration policy, in other words of getting away with the gigantic bluff which has led us to our present unhappy state. In doing so, however, they did not realize that the Government would continue as it had begun, to promote racialism by successive surrenders over immigration, while making some feeble efforts in the right direction at home. Rather, they believed that the Government had, in return for their allowing it to escape the full censure that it deserved for its behaviour in 1965, made with them an unspoken agreement to make no more surrenders, but to make a steady, if cautious, approach to a decent policy both on immigration and at home. That was why the 1968 Immigration Act was so traumatic a disillusionment.

The National Committee, which first announced its intention of resigning en bloc over the issue, and finished by settling with the privilege of an interview with the Prime Minister (who made no concessions to them), was exposed by this crisis for the ludicrous coward it had become. Knowing that the Government already intended in the promised Race Relations Bill to overhaul the National Committee, a small group among certain of the liaison committees, headed by Rev. Wilfred Wood, produced the most imaginative and creative proposal that has yet been forthcoming in race relations in Britain. They suggested the replacement of the National Committee by a National Commission for Racial Equality which should have three new features: it should not be under direct Government control; it should be able to disburse funds to organizations of all kinds, including immigrant ones, independently of local government, for particular projects as well as for continuing expenses, and on a greatly increased scale; and, most important of all, it should contain a majority of members not nominated from above, but elected, partly by the liaison committees but preponderantly by the immigrant communities themselves through their organizations. This scheme was worked out in detail and provided a brilliant means of remedying both the desperate feeling of powerlessness on the part of the black communities to influence what most affects them or to make their voices heard, and their distrust of leaders hand-picked by Government. We believe that these proposals will continue to present the minimal conditions under which a national body of this kind could play any significant role in curing the disease of racialism, and therefore under which any Government can be taken as serious in its profession of desiring such a cure. But it is a measure of the dismal failure of our politicians to make themselves informed about what is by far the most important thing to have happened to Britain since the war, the emergence of racialism, that not one MP supported these proposals or even appeared to understand the point of them. It is also a measure of the demoralization of the liaison committees themselves that, once it became clear that Callaghan was implacably hostile to the whole spirit of the Wood proposals, the minority that had supported them dwindled to a mere half-dozen out of a total of sixty.

Instead, therefore, the National Committee has been replaced by the Community Relations Commission, headed by Frank Cousins. The membership of the commission itself is new: but it still has the old staff. Its members are not only appointed by the Home Secretary but, unlike those of the old committee, directly responsible to him. It is, of course, too soon to say how it will behave: but we venture two guesses. First, that its members will not allow themselves to be run by the permanent staff, as those of the old committee were; and, second, that they are too much habituated to command to be likely to alter the authoritarian approach of the old committee towards theoretically independent voluntary bodies.

It would be a useless exercise, now, to describe all the steps that a Government should have taken in the last ten years to ensure the establishment of a just non-racialist society in a multi-racial Britain. But a critic of Government policies must be prepared to advance suggestions for what could be done now that the present stage has been reached. Of course, the task of making practical proposals would be infinitely easier if so many serious errors had not been made: these errors have themselves created appalling difficulties which now require to be solved. Given the situation at the time of writing, these are our suggestions: making the following demands on politicians might bring results.

First in priority is the abolition of all the Aliens Acts and Commonwealth Immigration Acts: the whole jumble of measures to be repealed in a new and comprehensive Immigration Act. Our immigration policy at present is a patchwork of measures introduced in response to anti-semitism in the early 1900s, the threat of war in 1914, and anti-black prejudice in the 1960s. We suggest that a new and comprehensive law should take account of the United Nations declarations, of the provisions on migration in the Treaty of Rome (applying to Common Market countries), of economic planning within Britain, and of the need, above all, for ensuring freedom of movement, the rights of families to be together and the full equality with established citizens of newcomers from anywhere whatever. Better organization and less bureaucracy in the issuing of work vouchers, foresight about the need for housing, schools and hospitals in areas where employment is expanding, all these things need planning in such an Act. The Home Office should lose its present tight hold on the empire of immigration policy, and the responsibility should become a joint one between the ministries concerned with Housing, Employment and Productivity, Health, Social Security and Education. Great damage has been done in many instances simply because the Home Office, with a mentality attuned to the police, prisons, security and probation among its many responsibilities, has had sole responsibility for immigration. Of course, there are certain practical difficulties in bringing about such a change: Government departments are jealous of their powers and inept at co-operation, but the main priority of breaking the Home Office stranglehold must be achieved.

Second, the Race Relations Act requires amendments to bestow powers on the Race Relations Board to subpoena witnesses and examine documents. The further amendment of giving powers to the courts to order 'specific performance' (the granting of a job or of accommodation by the respondent) is, we understand, technically impossible in English law. But the use of restraining injunctions is perfectly possible. Once the essential powers of subpoena had been given to the Board, much of the machinery of the Act which now seems unlikely to be greatly used would stir into action.

Third, Government support for voluntary work in race relations, at a local level, needs to be re-thought from the ground up. The replacement of the Community Relations Commission by a National Commission for Racial Equality (as described earlier in this chapter) would be an important beginning. The grant of money to pay full-time workers in this field should not be tied to the liaison committee structure under the present conditions of one full-time worker per local authority, appointed subject to the conditions made by the local authority in providing a 'matching grant'. Far more full-time workers, working within a variety of different structures, are needed in local work. The point of all these suggestions is not only that they would achieve results in themselves. The introduction of such measures could only occur in association with a completely different attitude towards dark-coloured people from the attitude now most prevalent. Ministers could hardly introduce them in the context of black people being, by their very existence, a problem. The shifting of balance in debate would be an important part of the progress in public education and awareness that these could provide. Far more than these first steps is needed; but they are essential beginnings, and each has already had advocates, so that the ideas are not wholly unfamiliar. They need to be more widely discussed and publicized so that some action can be taken before it is too late.

Of course, the debate about realities in policy has been over-shadowed by the 'phenomenon of Enoch Powell'. No demagogue could have attempted to ride to power on the crest of the racialist wave had not the opportunity been so perfectly prepared by the combined ineptitude and cowardice of the official leadership of the two major parties; but, the opportunity created, Powell's skill and lack of scruples have enabled him to have a devastating effect. Every black person in the country not protected by some unusual environment such as a university must be able to testify not merely to the profound affront which Powell's utterances have given him, but to the shattering increase in personal abuse and expression of prejudice and hostility which each Powell speech has evoked in the white people he daily meets. The result is a situation in which the credibility of any official efforts to promote racial equality has reached vanishing point. For black and white alike, the position is now definitely established that the power structure in the country, professing to be following the will of the majority, regards the presence of black people as a threat and is going to treat them as such. No official or quasi-official agency can henceforward challenge this assumption, on pain of being accused of meddling in politics and of being repudiated by the authorities of national or local government. The National Committee for Commonwealth Immigrants, despite the inauspicious circumstances of its foundation, might have achieved much, and instead proved a fiasco; the Community Relations Commission was, in the desperately aggravated racialist climate of the time, an irrelevancy even before it came into existence.

It was not Powell, but the Government and the official opposition which created the situation which made possible the 'phenomenon of Powell'; but it would be a mistake to judge his effect as merely an intensification of the form of racialism that was already widespread when he began his campaign. Rather, the effect has been a new and significantly different stage in the development of British racialism. Previously, the demand of the racialists was for 'integration', by which they understood assimilation: if the immigrants would totally abandon their own culture and their own customs, and learn to behave like imitation white Englishmen, then perhaps they might earn the right to a patronizing tolerance. Such sanctimonious advocacy of 'integration' was customarily accompanied by complaints that 'they don't seem to want to integrate'. Powell, however, has struck quite a new note: for him, people with dark skins cannot be assimilated even if they want to be; they are just not going to be accepted for membership of the British nation, or of the English people, however humbly they apply. Just as Belloc said before the war that no one could be both Jewish and English, so Powell says expressly that no one can be black and English. 'We must be mad, literally mad', he said in April 1968, 'as a nation to be permitting the annual inflow of some 50,000 dependents, who are for the most part the material of the future growth of the immigrant-descended population. It is like watching a nation busily engaged in heaping up its own funeral pyre. . . . The word "integration" sums up a dangerous delusion suffered by those wilfully or otherwise blind to realities.' And, in June 1969 'The immigrants here are still in large numbers integral members of the communities from whence they came. Let another decade or so elapse, and this will no longer be so. The tragedy of a growing minority, *alien here* [our italics] and yet homeless elsewhere, will have been fastened on them and us forever.' No longer are conditions laid down under which people might become accepted if they conformed: they are served notice that they, and their children, and their children's children are forever intrinsically unacceptable. In November 1968 he said at Eastbourne, 'The West Indian or Asian does not, by being born in England, become an Englishman. In the law he becomes a United Kingdom citizen; in fact he is a West Indian or an Asian still.' And in June 1969 'To reduce the prospective immigrant and immigrant-descended population even to half — and that half comprising the elements most desirous and capable of becoming part of our society — would lift from the future of Britain a dark and ever more menacing shadow'. His total attitude to predominantly non-white areas in Britain is summed up in his own brief sentence, 'The people of England will not endure it.'

And, secondly, this explicit rejection of a minority now explicitly defined by racial and not cultural criteria has made it possible for Powell to bring into the open the issue which the Government, by its hypocritical policy, had hoped to be able to evade. The combined propaganda effect of Government policy and of Powell's speeches has gone so far in converting the crypto-racialists into conscious racialists that it is no longer advantageous to pretend that the issue is one of *keeping* Britain white: this slogan, so prominent in the cries of Government supporters over the 1968 Immigration Act, is heard no longer. Powell can harp on the fact that Britain is no longer white, and has given repeated notice that he (as supposedly embodying the people of this country) finds this unacceptable. So far little has been said explicitly about how, once no black person can any longer enter the country, those already here will be got rid of: the references to repatriation have deliberately equivocated over whether voluntary or involuntary removal is meant, and Powell is not going to be drawn on this until the time is ripe. What marks the beginning of a new stage, however, is that 'the problem' is no longer defined merely as that of preventing people from coming in, but as that of dealing with the intolerable fact that they are already here.

All but the wilfully blind (of whom there are many) can recognize from all this how far down the path to disaster we have travelled. By 'disaster' we do not mean the possibility of a few white people's windows getting smashed or a branch of Littlewood's burning down — what violence is to be expected, like all that there has been so far, is by white against black: we mean damage so grave to the capacity of people in this country to live together in peace with one another that our society will never recover from the resulting bitterness, guilt, resentment, and fear. Powell is set on his course; many have lined up behind him; many more will do so as soon as they think he will succeed in his bid for power. What has made all this possible is the craven policy of appeasement that the Conservative Party has followed since 1961 and the Labour Party since 1965. If our leaders do not grasp what is the effect of what they have done, and have the courage to start doing the opposite, there is not the slightest hope that Powell and his allies will not succeed in destroying, as a place where anyone, white or black, can live a decent life, the country they profess to love. Of the capacity for such courage we see very little sign.

A note on 'racialism'

The word 'racialist' has been used several times in this chapter, in connection with Enoch Powell as in other connections. It is a measure of the mental confusion and hypocrisy which now surrounds the subject of race that it may be helpful at this point to spell out the meaning of this term, and discuss its application to Powell. To give an adequate account of the variety of forms which racialism may take, and of disguises which it may assume, would require a separate chapter: here only a thumb-nail sketch, treated in a single connection only, is possible.

Racialism strictly so called consists in the belief that people are to be classified into groups according to their descent and that the groups so determined are to be treated differently and have different rights. Very often the principle of classification involves distinguishing those whose ancestry is wholly (or, as is usually and significantly said, 'purely') from one group, and those who have any ancestors from outside that group: thus the Nazis classified as non-Aryan anyone who had even one Jewish great-grandparent; and likewise the dichotomy white/coloured (used, as it in fact is, in such a way that the child of one 'white' and one 'coloured' parent is classified straightforwardly as 'coloured') involves that a 'white' person is one whose ancestors were *all* 'white', while a 'coloured' person is one *any* of whose ancestors were 'coloured'. That there should be anyone who, by virtue of mixed ancestry, escapes the classification, or that anyone's status with regard to it should not be a matter which everybody else has the right to know, is unthinkable to the racialist. Very often the racialist will deny that he assigns any rank, of superiority or inferiority, to the groups that he distinguishes: they are equal, but should be kept separate, because they are incompatible and incapable of living together in a single community. But of course it always proves that those who, on the strength of this doctrine, are to be kept out of, or expelled from, or relegated to a segregated position within, some society are the members of the group to which the racialist does *not* belong: Enoch Powell, for example, was never heard to support Tom Mboya's plea that the white man should scram out of Africa, nor to call for the repatriation of whites from Rhodesia or even Zambia.

Powell's speeches are very carefully concocted. Like all demagogues, he appreciates that he does not need to give explicit expression to all the feelings and ideas to which he is appealing. Yet, despite this awareness, it is very easy to recognize from what he has said that he is indeed a racialist in the sense defined above. Though in some passages he will use the words 'white' and 'immigrant' as though they were a pair of contrary terms, he is at pains to emphasize 'the problem' to which he proclaims the solution is that of the presence, not merely of immigrants, but of *those descended from immigrants*. These, he says will have lost one nationality without gaining another; they cannot, by being born here – and growing up here and going to school here – become English. (Sometimes he says they will remain West Indian or Asian, sometimes he says that they will have no nationality whatever.) The attack he makes is thus not merely directed at a group whose members he wants to be thought of only as representatives of that group (as when he spoke, on television, of immigrants as forming 'whole caravans, as it were'), but on a group determined by descent: the children of Italian or Polish immigrants may qualify as English, but the children of 'Afro-Asians' are in perpetuity to be denied that status, to be rejected as an 'alien' menace. But probably the feature of his speeches which most sharply betrays what is meant to be understood as underlying them is their reference to the United States, whose 'haunting tragedy' we are in danger of reproducing, the tragedy of there being 'several Washingtons in England'. What is America's haunting tragedy supposed to be? Certainly not the presence of a large number of people who are not American, and who, through generations, can never become American. Not even the most racist of American whites has ever tried to deny that black Americans are as American as apple pie. What Powell, by these references to the United States, makes plain is this: that he does not really fear an England no longer English, but an England no longer wholly white.

Of course, the most sinister part of Powell's propaganda is not those passages which reveal his racialism, in our strict sense, in its nakedness: on the contrary, it would be more effective propaganda for racialism if he had succeeded in completely eliminating such tell-tale passages. The attack on immigrants and their children as a group, the hysterical cries of alarm at the danger which is supposed to be threatening us, the absurd forecasts of sinister plots by immigrants to achieve domination over the white population, the vivid little vignettes giving an insane picture of a white population cowering under a reign of terror — these would all do their work if there were not a hint, as there is certainly no explicit statement, of the basis for all the alarmism. Despite much vague emotive talk about 'dislodgment', the threat to our identity, etc., there is not once in Powell's speeches any explanation of what he supposes the threat which his supporters praise him for his courage in exposing actually consists of. And, of course, there does not need to be. If racial prejudice were unheard of in this country, then no one would have been able to make head or tail of what Powell was talking about. But, given the extent to which racialist ideas have taken hold, there was no need for him to allow his own assumptions to become apparent: the notions which could make sense of what he said were already present in the minds of those to whom he was appealing.

One of the greatest evils which Powell has wrought has been to make it harder, rather than easier, to recognize racialism when it appears. Racialism in its pure form is so evidently despicable and irrational that the major task of racialist propaganda is to provide camouflage for those who respond to it, means by which they can pretend to themselves and to others that they are not motivated by racialism at all, but by some quite different considerations which merely happen, in the circumstances, to have the same effect. Just because Powell's appeal to racialist feelings has been so frank, it has become easier for those who with less frankness appeal to, or are motivated by, racialist ideas to disguise the fact. We have tried in this chapter to show to what an extent the conduct of the politicians of both major parties has been at once a surrender to and an encouragement of racialism. Not the least of the damage that Powell has done has consisted in the opportunity he has provided to those who diverge from him to claim that that very fact renders them innocent of racialism.

Notes

1 For further discussion of Powell, see pp 122 ff.
2 The London Immigration Control Association publishes a leaflet which states

that 'integration is a fraud and a confidence trick by which people in Britain and elsewhere are being robbed of their independence and self-government because in the multi-racial society the cause of independence and self-government is lost'. This extraordinary assertion is one of the reasons the leaflet advances for stopping immigration altogether.

3   One of the slogans which, though he subsequently denied responsibility for it, won Peter Griffiths the seat was: 'If you want a nigger neighbour, vote Labour.'

4   The *Guardian* on 5 February 1965 reported the Home Secretary as saying that at least 10,000 immigrants had 'dodged' the controls in the last two years, that henceforth people would be 'closely questioned about their intentions and planned length of stay', and that there would be 'stringent checks on dependants'. More measures might follow if these were not considered enough. The debate was conducted entirely with reference to Commonwealth immigrants. In the debate the Home Secretary was, according to *The Times* report of the same date, accused by Sir Alec Douglas Home and Mr Fletcher Cooke of 'cribbing' Conservative policy. Interestingly, he agreed to look at the question raised by some Conservative MPs of repatriating Commonwealth immigrants. He also promised new measures on deportation.

5   He has used figures and facts which investigation has several times proved false. Nobody, for instance, ever found the little old lady, the only white person left in a street, described by Powell in his April speech. His allegations that the Doyley family had terrorized Mrs Ingold in Wandsworth were denied by Mrs Ingold herself and by her daughter, who spoke warmly of the Doyleys' kindness. The forecast of 5-7 million Commonwealth immigrants and their descendants in the year 2000 has been shown by the Institute of Race Relations, using official sources and estimates, to be baseless. Powell also quoted the observation by one of his constituents that 'in this country in fifteen or twenty years the black man will have the whip hand over the white man'.

Further reading for discussion of recent legislation

Dummett, Ann and McCrudden, Christopher (1982), *Government Policy and Legislation*, Unit 7 of Open University Course E354, Open University Press
Edwards, J. and Batley, R. (1978), *The Politics of Positive Discrimination*, Tavistock
Gordon, Paul (1981), *Passport Raids and Checks: Britain's Internal Immigration Controls*, Runnymede Trust
MacDonald, I. (1977), *Race Relations: The New Law*, Butterworth
Runnymede Trust (1982), *Racial Discrimination: Developing a Legal Strategy through Individual Complaints*, Runnymede Trust

6 The politics of race in Britain, 1962–79: a review of the major trends*

Gideon Ben-Tovim and John Gabriel

Introduction

This review of the politicization of race during the recent period, and of the literature concerned with that process, is organized around a consideration of: (1) immigration legislation and administration; (2) government policies for race relations; (3) race relations pressure groups, in particular the ultra-right, anti-racist and black organizations.

Our aim is to provide a description and analysis of the overall trends and developments that have taken place during this period. We hope to examine the process, and the evaluation of that process, by which race has become the object of Government policy-formation and the basis for political action over the last seventeen years; and we hope to point to the outstanding absences in the literature which need to be filled in order to understand fully the dynamic of its own that the politics of race has assumed. Finally, we intend to provide a guide to the political reaction to racism and the racist lobby emanating from the anti-racist movement and the black communities in Britain.

Immigration legislation and administration

We have dated our review of the politics of race in Britain from 1962: this was the year in which the first Commonwealth Immigration Act was passed, and in our view this intervention marked the decisive political turning point in contemporary British race relations. For this Act constituted the first of a number of developing Government actions which have provided a legal framework for the institutionali-

*This article is a modified version of a review article reproduced in *Race Relations Abstracts,* vol. 4, p. 4 (1979). For the purposes of this article the references have been largely excised and the reader is advised to refer to the *Race Relations Abstracts* article for a much fuller bibliography. This article retains the review approach in order to provide an overview on the post-war trends and debates in the politics of race, if not an exhaustive summary of the literature.

We are very grateful for the comments on an earlier draft of this paper from Rashid Mufti, Ian Law and Kathy Stredder; and for the hospitality of the staff of the Institute of Race Relations Library.

zation of racism (Allen, 1973). This state racism has over-shadowed all subsequent discussion and action in the field. The official equation of blackness with second-class and undesirable immigrant — the principle that black people are in themselves a problem and the fewer we have of them the better — has dominated the public ideological discourse on race and has set the parameters for political action in this arena.

The dominant consensus on immigration has had catastrophic effects on the black communities in Britain, subjecting them to insecurity and harassment from state agencies (such as immigration officials, the police, the Illegal Immigration Intelligence Unit, Health and Social Security staff) and involving deportation, detention without trial, family separation, shuttlecocking, interminable delays, and all the associated personal suffering and indignities, of which the 'virginity tests' revealed publicly in *The Guardian* (1 February 1970) are only the most extreme example.

A further aspect of the insecurity engendered by the race/immigration equation of black people as a particular threat and burden has been the acts of physical violence and aggression which, as Dummett (1978, p. 11) suggests, are 'only a natural outcome' of the assumptions underlying official policy. The 'Paki-bashing' trend of the early 1970s and the more recent attacks encouraged by National Front activity on Bengalis in London's East End are, again, only the most publicized.

Much of the literature confirms that the outcome of nearly two decades of official restrictions on the presence of black people's entry to Britain has been a build-up of popular racism. Glimpses of this mass base for racist practices can be seen in the celebrated dockers' and meat porters' march in 1968 in support of Enoch Powell's 'Rivers of blood' speech, the growth of the National Front, and evidence of strongly racist attitudes from recent polls.

The outcome of Government policies in the field of immigration, then, is clear enough and one endorsed in the current literature: there has been a gradual stripping away of the rights of black Commonwealth citizens, whose enfranchised position, enshrined in the 1948 Nationality Act has now been reduced to that of an alien contract labourer, subject to a battery of administrative controls designed to make the entry of *black* ex-citizens and their families as arduous a process as possible. It is in this sense that the laws and controls have rightly been regarded as racist (see Sivanandan, 1976, 1978, Dummett, 1976).

The discussion in the literature on which we intend to focus our attention is initially over the question of how the shift from an open door, *laissez-faire* policy on New Commonwealth, that is black, immigration to the current, highly restrictive position took place.

One important strand of analysis has been to explain the changes in Government legislation on immigration in terms of a direct political expression of the changing overall economic conditions of post-war Britain. The immediate post-war period was one of labour shortage, in which black workers were actively recruited from the Commonwealth to fill Britain's serious manpower needs, after the sources of European labour had dried up. With the 'long boom' of the 1950s, the emphasis remained on the economic benefits to be gained from labour recruitment. The changing economic climate of the 1960s and the 1970s, with the gathering crisis of capitalism and mounting unemployment, provides the backcloth for the shift towards immigration controls, with the stress now placed on the economic cost rather than benefits of black immigration.

Although there are very important differences in the concepts and the analyses used by the various authors working within this framework, the dominant theme is that the changing requirements of British capitalism were the underlying reason for the shifting state policies with respect to black immigration. The shift from settler-citizen to migrant contract-worker has taken place in order to maintain, in differing economic conditions, the structurally necessary 'dual labour market', involving the maintenance of a stratum of cheap labour to carry out essential jobs that the indigenous white work force will not perform.

We have indicated elsewhere some of the problems with this analysis which, although pointing to essential structural features conditioning political developments, does not adequately deal with the process by which economic exigencies have been mediated by relatively autonomous ideological and political factors (Gabriel and Ben-Tovim, 1978). In fact there was no single, over-determining economic rationale for the shift towards restrictive controls on the black presence in Britain. Paul Foot's (1965, p. 141) remark that 'no one had the slightest idea what sort of effect the (1962) Immigration Act would have on the rate of immigration into Britain' is some indication of the area of economic indeterminacy involved in the whole issue. We have then to look at the clash of political and ideological forces at work in the early 1960s for a rounded picture of the determinants of Government policy. Attempts to interpret changes in Britain's immigration legislation in terms of the shifting economic needs and political interests of capital do not, by themselves, provide an adequate and unambiguous explanation of the eventual political outcomes.

The recent work of Professor Rex and his associates (Rex and Tomlinson, 1979), poses some of the pertinent questions frequently absent from the work of other writers: they ask how the Conservative Party could, in 1962, reconcile immigration controls with its near mystical reverence for the Commonwealth; how the liberal ethic of 'equal rights' found on both Conservative and Labour benches could be squared with unequal treatment for those immigrants who were black; and how the Labour Party's ideal of brotherhood and internationalism could be invoked in support of racial exclusiveness. What further explanations have been provided for the decision by the Conservatives to introduce controls on black immigration in 1962, which even *The Times* (27 February 1962 and 12 March 1962) considered racially discriminatory, and for the process by which the Labour Party moved from an opposition to these controls in 1962 to an enthusiastic toughening of them by 1965 when they were in office?

The Conservative Party, having made no positive provision for the integration of the new immigrants, succumbed to growing pressure for control arising from the racialism that was reaped from ten years of neglect. The restrictionist right, led by Sir Cyril Osborne, though weak in Parliament were strong in the constituencies, and it was this pressure from below, along with the public support that appeared to be mobilized by the anti-immigrant organizations for the imposition of such controls, at least in the Tory Midlands heartland, that is said to have finally won over the rest of the Parliamentary Party. R. A. Butler ultimately introduced the Commonwealth Immigration Act in 1962 in terms of the need to deal with the growing number of Commonwealth immigrants and the problems this would cause in terms of local authority services such as housing, and in terms of community integration.

On the Labour Party side, opposition to the 1962 Immigration Act was passionately spear-headed by Hugh Gaitskell, in terms of Commonwealth obligations, liberal hostility to racial discrimination and an economic realism over the responsiveness of immigration to labour market needs. The opposition to controls, used perhaps as a cause to unite a Labour Party deeply divided over clause 4 and nuclear weapons, crumbled quickly, however. By 1963, after Gaitskell's death, Harold Wilson announced at the Expiring Laws Continuance Bill debate that 'we do not contest the need for control of immigration into this country' (Foot, 1965, p. 176), although when the Tories refused the compromise of 'bilateral controls' (i.e. agreement by the Commonwealth to initiate controls at their end) Labour voted against the Bill.

But 1964 was significant for the overt use of the race card by the Conservative candidate Peter Griffiths at Smethwick ('If you want a nigger for your neighbour, vote Labour'), followed by the Labour loss at Leyton, also apparently on the race issue. Of course many of the fringe far-right candidates had also been going to the polls on a straight anti-immigrant platform, but the adoption of this crudely racist approach by the official Parliamentary candidate and its successful outcome against the national trend (though following victorious Tory anti-immigrant campaigns in 1962 and 1963 in Smethwick's local elections) helped to shift the terrain of what was politically viable; and, though Harold Wilson referred to Griffiths as a 'Parliamentary leper', none the less his victory solidified Labour's determination not to be 'soft' on the race question, as demonstrated in the heavily restrictionist 1965 Immigration Act which, 'as the *Economist* stated "pinched the Tories' white trousers" ' (Rose, 1969, p. 228) by reducing the number of work-vouchers used to control entry in the 1962 Act and by ending the issuing of vouchers to unskilled immigrants.

The widespread explanation for Labour's volte-face is essentially in terms of *ad hoc* political expediency: this bi-partisan policy on immigration, each major party 'out-trumping' the other (Crossman, 1975, p. 299) in terms of the harshness of their immigration curbs is seen then in most of the literature as a pragmatic response to popular opinion by parties concerned primarily with power.

What, then, were the pressures that operated in the early 1960s to set in motion an official state racism through immigration legislation that appeared to run, initially at least, counter to economic rationale and dominant ideological currents, though in evident harmony with popular racism?

As a measure, and partial cause, of the changing climate of popular opinion, the 1968 Notting Hill and Nottingham race riots are frequently cited (e.g. Miles and Phizacklea, 1979). The riots were used to support a growing articulation of the view that social problems of housing, health, and social services were seriously exacerbated by the presence of West Indian immigrants. Attention was focused on the rise in numbers in the late 1950s and early 1960s, which rose partly in response to the threat of controls and was about to be increased by influxes from India and Pakistan. Thus the real material conditions and problems of the working class were being connected in a simplistic causal chain with an identifiable out-group, by means, in particular, of the activities of anti-immigrant organizations such as the Birmingham Immigration Control Association, which started in October 1960 in a Birmingham housing estate. This lobby, with a degree of local press support, played a very important role within the Conservative Party, particularly through its connections with the Birmingham MPs.

We still need an explanation of how this position could have gained the ideological hegemony over contending definitions and principles within both Conservative and Labour circles. The major external constraint was the Commonwealth — the strong ties of Empire — which had caused Britain to deviate from its previous restrictionism but which was perhaps an increasing irrelevance by the post-'Wind-of-change' 1960s, or even a cause of disillusion.

The labour movement had, through its experience of employer use of immigrants as wage undercutters, and through its economistic and nationalistic tendencies, a 'negative and defensive reaction to immigration' (Miles and Phizacklea, 1977b, p. 37), as seen in their earlier hostile reaction to the mass migration of the Irish and the Jews. Thus the articulation of large scale Commonwealth immigration as a threat to working-class job security and prospects and in respect of 'its' welfare state could therefore find sympathetic reverberations amongst the working class, particularly at a time of declining prosperity.

The imperialist links of economic, political, military and cultural supremacy that had bound Britain to her former colonial subjects, now entering Britain as nominally equal co-citizens, ensured 'the existence of a reservoir of popular racism' (Hall, 1978, p. 25), a racist culture in Britain in which racial stereotypes, negative images and feelings of difference and superiority are deeply embodied (Kipling's 'Half-devil and half-child'), together with a history of legal and institutional racist practices since the senventeenth century.

Out of this analysis can be derived a pre-disposition to treat the black newcomer not simply as an equal Commonwealth citizen, but as the 'other'; as different, as inferior, as outside the British political community, as a relatively rightless object tailor-made for metropolitan capitalism's deprived industrial roles and deprived neighbourhoods whose presence in metropolitan Britain symbolized the British loss of Empire and declining world role: this black newcomer is therefore a culturally plausible scapegoat for the welfare state inadequacies, from which he actually disproportionately suffered.

This is not, however, to argue for the historically deterministic view that Britain's post-war 'indigenous' racism was the *inevitable* product of its 'imperial' racism. The point we are trying to establish is that the deterministic posing of the inevitably hostile reaction of 'public opinion' to immigrants, or black ex-colonials, or potential economic competitors, or of the labour market's inexorable creation of black under-class — the principal forms of sociological analysis made of the process — leaves no space for the ambivalence, uncertainty and confusion of British racial attitudes and policies and hence for alternative forms of political reaction and leadership, or for the intervention of political and ideological forces (with no simple class basis) which have mediated the economic exigencies and have acted to articulate and mobilize this potential racial hostility.

In other words, much of the available literature still fails to account for the concrete process of the politicization of the race issue. *Laissez-faire* discrimination could, perhaps, have been counteracted by early, positive, high-profile Government intervention; the wholesale capitulation of Labour, as of the Conservatives, to a racially defined orientation towards immigration was not inevitable but was brought about by the play of contending social forces within a unique conjuncture, which requires for an adequate explanation a very full specification of the economic, political and ideological conditions and transformations.

Here the relatively belated and ineffectual reaction by the liberal opponents of restriction has to be included in the analysis. In the face of the increasingly strident and confident 'popular' spokesmen for restriction, the liberals and left had little to offer, not being able to agree on a policy, and playing the numbers game or devoting their energies to behind the scenes lobbying for anti-discrimination legislation, though some campaigning opposition to the 1962 and the 1965 Immigration Acts was mounted, for example, by CARD and CCARD (the Co-ordinating Campaign Against Racial Discrimination).

Frequently 1968 is cited as the next significant date: this was the year of the Powell phenomenon, a period in which a leading politician espoused in apocalyptic language sentiments about 'total bans' on black immigration and 'repatriation' that were being expressed until then only by fringe right-wing forces. Powell's overt hostility to black immigration and the black presence in Britain, together with his populist articulation of antagonism to the whole establishment, brought him widespread popular support and, perhaps, the Conservative Party victory in 1970. Despite the appearance of political isolation following these speeches (sacked from the Shadow Cabinet; criticized in the leader columns) Powell was transformed overnight by the media to become its leading expert on immigration and race, which enabled the theme of the *numbers* of 'immigrants' and their 'threat' to British 'culture' to continue to dominate the agenda for subsequent discussion, and also allowed his populist appeals to reach an enormous audience.

The media, then, by their massive exposure of Powell, played an important role in helping to define and articulate the race/immigration 'problem' on Powellite terms, a process made possible and confirmed by the daily practices of the state and the earlier consensus of which, beneath the rhetoric, Powell's policies and those of the ultra-right were only the logical extension. Our overall analysis of the politicization of race must, then, stress the crucial role of the media in the *mobilization,* not simply the reflection, of public opinion.

In 1972 the admission of a mere 27,000 Asians, including children who had been expelled from Uganda, created a new 'moral panic' over immigration, as manifested in the 'red area' dispersal policy, followed by the 'mugging' scares and by fresh extremes of media sensationalism in the 1976 'Asians in four star hotel' syndrome. The themes taken up by the media and by the political right in these ways indicate the way race has been related to the other issues of welfare state 'sponging' and 'law and order' that have become the great populist themes of the late 1970s (Hall *et al.,* 1978).

The starkest political expression of this authoritarian consensus in the field of race was seen in the bi-partisan 1978 Parliamentary Select Committee Report on Immigration (Select Committee, 1978) which even the *Financial Times* acknowledged to be barely a step from Pass Laws (22 March 1978). As a demonstration of the strength of *intra*-party as well as *inter*-party consensus on black immigration, 'left-winger' Syd Bidwell defended his support for these proposals in terms of a political 'realism' which, in the 1979 General Election, enabled the Conservative Party to again take the initiative for further 'immigration curbs' in line with many of the Select Committee proposals, without any serious opposition on this issue from the Labour Party or the Liberals; this was despite the fact that the Liberal Party's manifesto included the repeal of the racist 1971 Immigration Act, and Labour called for no further restrictions on the already severely delimited black access to Britain. Presumably the other parties were hoping, out of political expediency, to 'de-politicize' (Katznelson, 1973) the issues of immigration and race by sitting tight and assuming that it would not become an electoral issue.

Once again, the latest 'immigration curbs' stemming from the Select Committee and the Conservative Party (i.e. yet further controls on black entry) like the imminent changes in the nationality laws, seem to have no definitive economic function, apart perhaps from a greater alignment with EEC practice, but are a reflection of the fact that in the field of immigration, if not elsewhere, 'racism has got out of hand' (Spencer and Freeman, 1979, p. 30).

Rather than seeing public opinion as simply forcing the reluctant hand of the liberal politician, as in some of the literature, it has been argued that popular racism, undoubtedly a significant political force, has to be seen as itself encouraged by and reflecting official state policies and practices. Perhaps it would be most accurate to see the popular articulation of racist exclusivism and the enactment of racist policies as a dialectical process, an interchange between politicians and people within structurally determinant but also very fluent conditions in which the media have played an important role as lightning-conductor of the most negative definitions and reactions from both sources.

Whichever interpretation in the literature we accept of the relationship between economic needs, ideological structures, political leadership and public opinion in the making of Government policy in the field of immigration, the definitions and practices that have been associated with the 'immigration' question have, for many writers, overshadowed all subsequent attempts at policies to combat racial discrimination and promote racial equality and justice.

Government race relations policies: 'integration', discrimination and urban deprivation

In common with most researchers and practitioners in the field, we have acknowledged the double-edged nature of Government policies on race relations. By this we mean that immigration controls on the one hand are complemented on the other by policies designed to promote 'equality of opportunity and cultural diversity in an atmosphere of mutual tolerance' (Roy Jenkins in Rose, 1969, p. 514).

The prescription then for good race relations has been viewed conventionally as entailing a good dose of immigration control, notably of would-be black immigrants, plus a less potent elixir perhaps, designed to promote equal opportunities for those already here. Indeed, as we have suggested, the former is often seen as an indispensable precondition for the latter.

'Integration' may be seen as a short-hand alternative to that formulation provided above by Roy Jenkins. It has certainly been the professed guiding principle of the liberal centre of British politics since the mid 1960s. In turn it is this dominant ideological strain (i.e. liberalism) which seems to have taken a firm hold of this area of policy and established a consensus which has been difficult to breach from left or right. Interestingly, the far right has been considerably more successful in the debate surrounding immigration control than its leading representatives (e.g. Keith Joseph, Rhodes Boyson) have been in this area of policy, though it remains to be seen whether the Thatcher Government will introduce radical departures in liberal race policies.

In the construction of policies designed to meet Jenkins' policy goal, two major problems have been regarded as significant. The first is that of *discrimination*. The second is that of *deprivation*, notably inner-area deprivation which has been related in various ways to the presence of a relatively high immigrant or black population. Discrimination has been challenged through the Race Relations Acts of 1965, 1968 and 1976. Deprivation, depending on how it has been conceived exactly, and how race problems are seen to relate to it, has been challenged in principle through the diversion of resources to inner areas (much to the consternation of some New Town planners of the post-war period).

Our task now is not only to evaluate the policies themselves and the assumptions on which they rest, but also to consider the literature which has built up around them. The precise nature of the relationship between the literature on the one hand and the policies on the other is by no means straightforward. Although the literature is clearly a response to the policies insofar as it seeks to evaluate them, it has also played some part in contributing to the analysis which now underpins certain policy statements.

Our own position should become clear on the basis of this twofold examination. For the moment it might be useful to anticipate, in summary form, our conclusions. In essence we shall argue that policies in this area, though by no means adequate to meet the requirements of the task set by Roy Jenkins, cannot be considered as merely serving to legitimate racist immigration controls and hence as subordinate to the requirements of the British economy in the mid twentieth century (see above). Nor shall we concur with the claim that all initiatives of this nature are inevitably paternalistic in character and ineffectual in consequences.

The policies themselves may well have had a limited impact and there are both economic and ideological constraints at work here. At the same time there is space for some political manoeuvrability, and national and local variations bear this out. If the latter are less startling than might be hoped, then some of the cynicism with regard to political machinery reflected in certain of the above positions must be held partially responsible. Only through a detailed consideration of the machinery itself and the use to which it might be put (or even extended and transformed) to secure certain policy objectives, can we hope to maximize its scope. Economic and ideological constraints remain, of course, but these too, it will be suggested, are not altogether immune to the effects of political intervention.

The Race Relations Acts

Despite the dominant liberal consensus referred to above which might be said to straddle the major parties on the issue of integration, the three Race Relations Acts of 1965, 1968 and 1976 have all been introduced by Labour Governments. The first of these, which had its origins in Reginald Sorenson's bill proposed initially in 1951 and subsequently taken up by Fenner Brockway, outlawed discrimination in 'places of public resort'. The Race Relations Board was set up along with local conciliation committees to act on complaints of alleged discrimination.

The National Committee for Commonwealth Immigrants had replaced the Commonwealth Immigrants' Advisory Council (set up in 1962) six months prior to the Act. Both were set up to provide information and advice to Governments with the latter co-ordinating the work of the voluntary liaison committees 'in an attempt to improve relations between the immigrants and the host community' (Heineman, 1972, p. 51). The role of CARD (Campaign

Against Racial Discrimination) was significant here both in promoting the Bill initially and in influencing its detailed provisions.

The 1968 Act to some extent responded to acknowledged deficiencies in its predecessor (PEP, 1967). Its provisions were extended to include employment and housing. It also provided for the replacement of the NCCI by the Community Relations Commission. The task of the latter was to 'promote harmonious community relations' and advise and support the local voluntary community relations councils to this end. The membership and functions of the Race Relations Board and its regional conciliation committees were increased and extended. As the title of these committees suggests, the emphasis was very much on conciliation, as CARD had wanted. Resort to the courts was at the discretion of the Board and not the complainant.

As in 1965, the 1968 Act was introduced in the same year as some measure of immigration control. In 1965 it accompanied the White Paper reducing the number of voucher holders. In 1968 it was the Commonwealth Immigration Act designed to reduce the number of potential black immigrants from Kenya via the introduction of a 'patriality' clause. The relationship between race relations legislation on the one hand and immigration control on the other is made explicit in Harold Wilson's May Day Address in Birmingham 1968. Taking his theme as the brotherhood of man he attacked racialism at home and abroad and drew attention to the 'new Race Relations Bill'. He subsequently outlined the provisions of the new Urban Programme (see below). Between these two initiatives he 'devoted some serious [sic] passages to explaining the facts of Immigration and Immigration control, the steps we were taking to prevent evasion, and "the Statistics" ' (Wilson, 1974 pp. 663-4).

The 1975 White Paper 'Racial Discrimination' (Home Office, 1975) in turn acknowledged deficiencies in the 1968 legislation. Despite the provisions of the two previous Acts, Political and Economic Planning published a series of reports (culminating in PEP, 1976; and Smith, 1977), providing further evidence of discrimination and disadvantage. The White Paper itself conceded 'the viability of legislation to deal with widespread patterns of discrimination, especially in housing and employment' (1975, para. 33). The 1976 Act in contrast to the previous two was passed by a Government which introduced no further measures to control immigration during its term of office. Nor, however, did it repeal the 1971 Immigration Act or even repeal the clause referring to patriality. Instead it introduced a Green Paper on Nationality, reinforcing this particular provision of the 1971 Act.

The new Race Relations Act extended the definition of discrimination to include indirect forms 'where unjustifiable practices and procedures which apply to everyone have the effect of putting people of a particular racial group at a disadvantage' (Race Relations Act, 1976, para. 1). The individual can now take a complaint direct to an industrial tribunal or county court and not await a decision of the Race Relations Board. The third major change is the abolition of the CRC and RRB and their replacement by the Commission for Racial Equality now invested with much wider powers (Race Relations Act, 1976, para. 7).

The above represents an attempt to overview the major provisions of each of the Race Relations Acts. By and large social science literature has been less concerned with a detailed consideration of its practical limitations and possibilities than with an analysis of the functions of the legislation and its effects. The purpose of the legislation is conceived in terms of giving the impression something is being done. It has also been seen as an attempt to deprive the black community of its most promising leaders, thus diluting the potential of a Civil Rights movement. The establishment of the NCCI is a case in point. Its effectiveness in improving immigrant/host relations has been considered minimal while at the same time, it is argued, it had a most destructive effect on CARD, the leading pressure group during this period. Local Community Relations councils, similarly, have been regarded as 'buffer institutions' heading off a direct assault on the Establishment by the black community (see for example, Katznelson, 1973; Hill and Issacheroff, 1971; Dummett and Dummett, 1969).

The arguments presented are convincing and certain effects of the legislation may well have been correctly identified here. Furthermore the impact of the legislation has been clearly undermined by the succession of Immigration Acts. What is important to challenge, however, is the view which suggests that the effects identified were those *intended*. The functionalist arguments presented here have an immediate appeal. If the legislation has been and remains largely ineffectual, then an account encapsulating these legislative initiatives within an all-embracing theory which at the same time spares us a detailed look at the particular provision of each Act is likely to prove extremely popular. If the Acts, however, were simply drawn up as a diversionary exercise, one designed to legitimate racist practices elsewhere (e.g. immigration controls), then it becomes necessary to explain the role played by progressive elements within the Labour Party as well as CARD itself in the development of those initiatives. If capitalism somehow requires this legislation, then one might expect to find its representatives and not their opponents instrumental in drawing it up.

The detailed provisions, however, are important and in the case of the 1976 Act contain considerable untapped potential: the investigative powers conferred on the CRE for example. It nevertheless contains a number of inherent weaknesses: the problems facing an individual complainant without the necessary assistance of the CRE, the problem of identifying the effects of indirect discrimination, the lack of enforcement powers to ensure that local authorities comply with the principal objective of the Act. The point is that only a detailed consideration of the Act, including an ongoing evaluation of its impact and effects and of the machinery adopted to implement it, can reveal this potential and scope. The seminar conducted at the Runnymede Trust (1979) is one form of intervention here. The problem then becomes one of taking the specific proposals made there into the political arena and incorporating them into the campaigns of various organizations and groups.

Race relations and urban deprivation policies

As we suggested above, the term 'deprivation' has come to possess a variety of meanings and its association with the race problem predictably is loose and ambiguous. For some local residents and officials, the presence of immigrants or blacks in inner-city areas is one contributory source of their decline. For others the high black population is more symptomatic of the underlying malaise of these areas.

In the former case dispersal may be considered one possible solution; compensatory social work and social education, other alternatives. Dispersal proved popular for a while with certain authorities and, within certain authorities, some departments (notably housing and education). The practice has become less common particularly since the case brought by the Race Relations Board against Birgmingham Council over its housing policy. The assumption here is clear: the groups or individuals themselves are responsible for the problem of the inner areas. In turn it encourages a casework approach to their solution.

In the case of immigrants, the problems were identified at least initially very much in terms of language and custom. The first major initiative, Section 11 of the Local Government Act 1966, reflects this. Under its provision, local authorities with new immigrant populations (i.e. settlement within the previous ten years) exceeding 2 per cent of the total could claim for grant aid from central Government 'in respect of the employment of staff' required to meet the demands of ethnic minorities. The initiative was first proposed in the White Paper of the previous year and, like the Race Relations Act of that year, might well have been prioritized in the wake of Gordon Walker's election experiences at Smethwick and Leyton and perhaps further back, the events in Notting Hill and Nottingham.

The provision has been the subject of much recent debate both from within Government departments (particularly the Home Office who have had responsibility for its administration from the beginning in 1966) and from outside pressure groups (e.g. from areas like Liverpool with a substantial black but not immigrant population, and the NUT). As a result the last Labour Government produced a Green Paper outlining proposals for its replacement (Home Office, 1978). A somewhat more flexible and equitable set of arrangements would have resulted. The swing to capital projects, moreover, might have gone some way to break with those assumptions regarding language and compensatory education referred to above. To a large extent that debate has now been pre-empted with the new Conservative Government. They will be 'reviewing the situation' (*Hansard,* 11 June 1979) but not implementing the Ethnic Needs Bill which had reached its second reading in the Commons prior to the 1979 General Election.

We noted above that Harold Wilson's announcement of the Urban Programme in May 1968 coincided with a major speech on racialism and immigration. The then Home Secretary, James Callaghan, however, insisted that the programme was designed to alleviate 'those areas of special social need' including but not exclusively aimed at those areas with a relatively high immigrant or black population. Only phase 12 was devoted exclusively to black self-help projects (e.g. Harambee), and was the result of ministerial pressure (Edwards and Batley, 1978, p. 138).

Evidence does suggest, despite this, that the programme can only be understood against the debate about Commonwealth immigration and race relations and was devised as an attempt to defuse a potentially explosive situation. In view of this, little attention was paid to the classification of what constituted social need or to establish the criteria for the selection of areas and projects. Instead, the programme seems to have been launched with a haste that militated against the development of any clear objectives or strategy. As a result the overall impact of the programme has been extremely limited. The arguments that its piecemeal, *ad hoc* nature precluded a serious attack on deprivation (which itself was never defined properly) are difficult to refute.

The Urban Programme is now being superseded by proposals outlined in the 1977 White Paper (Department of the Environment, 1977), which in turn is based primarily on the findings of the three Inner Area Studies. The problems are now identified as part institutional and structural and *not*, as with earlier initiatives, in terms of the characteristics of particular individuals or groups. Economic decline, physical decay and social disadvantage are identified as three key elements of the problem. The approach will involve relatively large cash injections and a close link-up between central and local Government in the case of Partnership Authorities and a smaller cash injection and less central control in the case of the Programme Authorities. Both will be financed (at least 75 per cent) on the basis of the submission of programmes plus project details to the Department of the Environment.

Although it was suggested in the White Paper that race problems are by no means 'co-terminous with inner area problems', it was conceded that in addition to the kinds of disadvantage experienced by all groups 'their particular needs [be] fully taken into account in the planning and implementation of policies for the inner areas' (para. 19). To what extent any of the seven Partnership Authorities and fifteen Inner Area Programme Authorities will treat this seriously in devising their programmes is questionable. Certainly para. 19 is sufficiently ambiguous to permit a variety of interpretations. The overall lack of a cohesive Government view of inner area policy and of the specific policies required to meet the needs of immigrant or black groups in the inner areas has been frequently noted (e.g. Deakin, 1978).

One final initiative worth noting here is the Community Development Project, since it underlines some of the problems we have identified both with respect to the policies themselves and their evaluation. In fact each of the twelve projects consisted of a team working with a local authority, and monitored by a local university or polytechnic. The initiative established in 1969 adopted the assumptions of the earlier measures. Poverty and deprivation were the result of individual and group characteristics and were not institutional or structural in origin. As the researchers identified this weakness in the analysis underpinning the practice, so the Government began to lose interest in the projects and eventually ceased their funding.

If the action side of the projects was misguided then to some extent so was the research, and Edwards and Batley (1978, p. 227) are understandably critical of the rhetoric which characterizes some of the later reports. Of course the CDPs were limited in scope but they offered a unique opportunity for action research projects in a local community context. There is nothing now to replace them and certainly there is no prospect of the sorts of structural changes demanded in their final reports.

Together the above initiatives must be seen as part of an overall attempt by Government to combat deprivation through the diversion of resources into areas of 'special need': a practice sometimes referred to as 'positive discrimination'. Though the initiatives have often been seen as a response to the race issue, the latter has always assumed a distinctly ambiguous role in each case. As a result there has always been considerable confusion surrounding the objectives and administration of this initiative. At the same time there is a temptation to be too dismissive. Each has offered some measure of scope and potential for involvement and accountability in local policy making. That it remains untapped is as much the responsibility of local political organizations and researchers as it is of the policy makers themselves. In a generally pessimistic review of these policies, Michael Meacher suggests that overall the 'positive discrimination mechanism is a tool with the potential for producing major social change... perhaps the best technique of social egalitarianism not yet seriously tried' (Meacher, 1974).

Mainstream policies and race relations

In addition to these *ad hoc* initiatives, and we would include the Race Relations Acts here, we should consider the impact of Roy Jenkins' remarks on the mainstream policies of central and local governments, the arena stressed in recent CRC/CRE publications as crucial for the elimination of racial disadvantage and one in which the 1976 Race Relations Act enables positive discrimination.

We can be brief here, since it is clear that they have largely fallen on deaf ears. What is more serious, perhaps, is the size of the literature in each of the major areas of home policy devoted to their discriminatory and disadvantageous effects on immigrant and black groups, that is education, employment, housing, social services and police—community relations. Indeed in the case of education, the last Labour Government was admitting these problems in its own policy statements (e.g. 'The West Indian Community', HMSO, 1978; Green Paper on 'Education in Schools', 1977).

The literature referred to above of course remains a crucial lever in influencing

Government policies or at least prodding or stirring it from its state of inertia; in addition, there is now a fair quantity of CRE material aimed at transforming local authority mainstream policies and service-delivery with respect to the black and immigrant population. The CRE's practice, however, seems to be as yet making little impact on the local authorities. It is notable that both the literature and political practice have not seriously begun to grapple with the problems of evaluating those few attempts by local authorities that have taken place to give their mainstream policies an 'ethnic dimension', or of making constructive interventions in these areas, though here the recent BBC TV series on 'Multi-Racial Britain' has begun the process of trying to record and assess instances of 'good practice'.

Conclusion

In an interesting summary of Government policies on the inner cities, McKay and Cox (1979, p. 258) write: 'Party politics and ideology and external pressure from interested groups have played minimal roles. . . instead certain ideas about poverty and urban society, together with the results of mainly internally generated research, have been of paramount influence'. The latter is quite clearly correct and we have underlined in this section the link between the analysis of deprivation on the one hand and its policy implications on the other. It is true to say that the dominant ideological character of these programmes is one which cuts across divisions between the major parties. Although much of the legislation discussed here has been initiated by Labour Governments, the Conservatives were not universally opposed to these initiatives and in the case of the 1970-4 Government made some contribution to the development of those policies (e.g. the Urban Deprivation Unit and the Inner Area Studies).

In all those initiatives reviewed above, however, there was clearly some external pressure involved. This pressure was invariably connected with the race issue. This may take the form of a riot in Notting Hill, a major speech on immigration, or an impending election. The policies then have been far less concerned with realizing some policy objective, integration or whatever, than *reacting* to a situation and feeling the need to do so quickly. The results have not only reflected the liberal consensus referred to above, but also have been imbued with a strong element of pragmatism and expedience.

There is, however, nothing inevitable about this. It is quite incorrect to write off these initiatives as part of some master plan to dilute and divide the forces of opposition. The principal problem with the literature on the subject is that it either takes this position, which can be readily accommodated within some all-embracing theory of the state and capitalist society, or it remains highly descriptive, and this effectively reproduces the ideological assumptions of the policy makers themselves.

As we have suggested earlier, a more satisfactory alternative is to assume that some manoeuvrability is possible within political practice. The policies themselves then justify careful examination. The economic and political constraints can thus be considered as the necessary framework within which variation is possible. The variations in central and local government, though not great, are nevertheless evident (see Ben-Tovim *et al.,* 1981). What is necessary is to establish the framework which provides that scope for 'good' and 'bad' practice and, in delineating its parameters, to seek to make the good, better.

Race relations pressure groups

The racist lobby: anti-immigration organizations and the National Front

We have seen how in the early 1960s, the local 'anti-immigrant' groups played an important part in persuading the Conservative Party to adopt a policy of immigration controls on Commonwealth immigrants, a campaign whose success was reflected in the large number of restrictionist motions submitted to the Conservative Party Conference in 1961 (thirty-eight out of 536): this grass-roots pressure seems to have been an important factor in finally winning the moderate Conservative leadership of Macmillan/Butler/Macleod to the control position.

Accounts of such groups are unfortunately fairly limited but it is clear that members of fascist organizations have played some part in these bodies, which have frequently ended up as 'front' organizations (Foot, 1965). The small and fractured neo-fascist movement, however, did not possess the ideological or organizational resources necessary to take full advantage of the potential of the race issue offered to them in the 1960s by the state, the major parties, the media and Enoch Powell.

A number of recent studies trace the lines of development of the extreme right from, in the inter-war period, Mosley's British Union of Fascists (later Union Movement) and Leese's Imperial Fascist League, to the post-war groups such as the League of Empire Loyalists, the British National Party, the Racial Preservation Society and later the Greater Britain Movement out of which the National Front was formed in 1967, and from which the National Party defected in 1975. (See for example, Billing, 1978).

One of the principal areas of debate has been that surrounding the apparent emergence of the National Front in the early and mid 1970s as a more or less credible political party. For instance Walker (1977) stresses the post-war Butskellite consensus which left room for a political force to the right of the Conservative party, an analysis related to the 'protest vote' theory. A number of writers suggest that the uncertain economic conditions of the 1970s provided the material cause of working-class racism and the major recruiting ground for a party intent on exploiting racial tension in terms of competition for scarce resources. The National Front's popular manipulation of the themes of crime, unemployment, urban and anti-communism in terms of a racially identifiable scapegoat has helped them build a base in some unions, schools, churches and community groups.

But for many sources, the major component of the relative success (though *only* relative) and the growth of the National Front is its explicit use of anti-immigrant, anti-black racism, which has enabled them to secure a reasonable level of political support in a climate set by the escalating capitulation to racist assumptions on immigration and a relatively weak approach to racial equality by both parties when in office. In particular, National Front support seems to grow whenever the Government of the day makes 'concessions' on immigration (as over the Ugandan and Malawian Asians).

It may be the case, as David Edgar (1975) argues in his important 'revisionist' article, that careful distinctions must be made between the official practices of racism, and the critics of this bi-partisan approach in the form of (a) Powell's combination of nationalism, populism and extreme 'liberalism', and (b) the National Front's overt national socialism with the traditional anti-semitic conspiracy theory at its core.

None the less the National Front is only mobilizing, and taking to their logical extreme (albeit opportunistically) feelings and opinions already aroused by the Powell-inspired abandonment of restraint in the public debate on immigration as well as by the daily practices of the state and by the mass media's negative reinforcement of the image of black people. In these contexts the latter are invariably treated and depicted as a problem, a threat, a category of unprincipled scroungers and muggers who are therefore an object of reasonable fear, hatred and even violence.

In terms of the National Front's electoral future, however, it may be the case that the ascendancy of the Thatcherite ultra-right, with its own successful brand of petit-bourgeois populism and authoritarianism has captured most of the potential National Front vote. This may explain the steady decline in the National Front's electoral fortunes since its 1976 peak which has perhaps forced them and other groups such as the British Movement into the articulation of their more explicitly National Socialist ideology and demands, and into a concentration on their stock-in-trade of violent extra-parliamentary activity.

The anti-racist movement

The growth of the National Front during the 1970s, with its greatly heightened scale of electoral intervention as well as increased forms of street activity, propaganda and scope of work (amongst trade unions, community groups, pensioners and school-children) led to widespread forms of anti-fascist or anti-racist organizations concerned essentially to counter the activities of the National Front (and to a lesser extent, the National Party and British Movement). This process culminated in the public launching in 1977 of the Anti-Nazi League and associated Anti-Nazi sections (Students, School Kids, Rails, Football Fans, Miners, etc.) and Rock Against Racism (see for example, Taylor, 1979).

Unfortunately there is still very little serious, as opposed to polemical, study of the anti-racist movement as a whole, of local anti-racist groups or of the

ANL and RAR: but it seems clear that these latter interventions have been successful in their strategy of moving beyond a narrow form of confrontation politics to the promotion of a counter-populist pole of attraction to the National Front. Through their imaginative use of popular music, their informal organizational structure, their high and simple propagandist profile ('Never Again'. . .'NF = No Fun' etc.), they seem to have helped win over to anti-racism, or at least neutralize, sectors of working-class youth who would otherwise be far from the progressive movement, and potentially vulnerable to the appeal of fascism.

The emergence of the ANL as a national *movement,* a catalyst for exposure and action, a symbol created almost overnight for anti-racist commitment, seems to have been a significant feature in holding back the National Front's advance, though the earlier work of the *Searchlight* and *CARF* magazines, and other anti-fascist and anti-racist groups should not be underestimated. On the other hand, some critics suggest that the anti-racists have publicized rather than weakened the National Front; and certainly the identification of the ANL with the far left, and the latter's penchant for the tactics of aggressive physical confrontation as seen in Lewisham and Ladywood in 1977, together with the ANL's early tendency to eschew the more 'official' channels of the labour movement and established progressive organizations in favour of 'spontaneous' mobilizations, has also led to the frequent equation of the anti-fascist movement with the fascists themselves as undemocratic, marginal and 'extremist'.

There seems to have been some scepticism if not hostility to the ANL/RAR development, at least initially, from sections of the black and ethnic minority organizations in terms of the high degree of energy expended on what was perhaps not deemed as serious a problem as the long-standing institutionalized racism practised by the state and in many areas of British society. Certainly it is the case that since the demise of the Campaign Against Racial Discrimination in 1966 (see Heineman, 1972) there has been no national framework from within which mass united action to promote racial equality and to oppose racism (rather than to combat the National Front) could be organized: in contrast to the increasing coherence and unification of the anti-immigrant, anti-black lobby within the mainstream of British society and on its fringes.

This is not to say that there has been a total absence of anti-racist pressure group politics other than anti-fascist work. Apart from the Campaign Against Racist Laws set up to co-ordinate national work in the field of immigration legislation, there have, as *Runnymede Trust Bulletins* and CARF bear out, been a number of regional and local anti-racist committees formed during this period, organizing a wide range of activities; there have been conferences, marches, demonstrations, a campaign was developed against the 1971 Immigration Act, lobbies over specific issues have been mounted, and several important pressure groups have been formed such as the JCWI (Joint Council for the Welfare of Immigrants), and AGIN (Action Group on Immigration and

Nationality), and also NAME (the National Association for Multi-Racial Education), each producing journals, pamphlets and propaganda, as has the Runnymede Trust and the Institute of Race Relations; several Trades Unionists Against Racism or Teachers Against Racism groups have been formed; official Labour Movement Campaigns and All-Party Committees have risen and set; the TUC has set up an Equal Rights (Race Relations) Sub-Committee. The Labour Party has a Race Relations Action Group, publishing several papers and a now defunct journal *Labour and Race*; the Liberals have produced several policy and study papers, including a 'special manifesto' for the 1979 General Election, while most of the Marxist left-wing groups have their own race relations advisory groups or special black sections, with their own publications. Apart from the Community Relations Councils (see p. 155 above) there is the National Association for CRCs which has acted mainly as an internal liaison and information body rather than a public pressure group; there has also been much anti-racist work of a sustained character carried out by Christian bodies with their specialist groups and their various publications. The NCCL has in recent years begun to play a very active role in the field of immigration campaigns and police harassment. Finally, Jewish organizations are increasing their involvement in anti-racist activities, as a result of the anti-semitic propaganda and attacks on synagogues by the ultra-right groups.

By and large though, despite these various initiatives, unfortunately as yet little documented, the struggle against racism has until recently been given relatively low priority by liberals and by the left in Britain. This has been in part related to a failure to analyse adequately the black experience in Britain: very frequently the left has economistically reduced that experience to one of simple class exploitation at the point of production, rather than seeing the class issue as over-determined by a unique form of racist oppression rooted in the slave and colonial forms of subordinate relationships into which black people have been forced, and in the post-war experiences of the domestic forms of institutional, state and popular racism.

This reduction of race to class is also manifested in the 'colour-blindness' seen in the widespread refusal of the Trade Union movement seriously to monitor the employment situation of black workers or trade union practices, or to implement special measures to combat racial discrimination and ensure racial equality, and in their ready stereotyping as 'black power' those black groups who insist on their special problems, the need for autonomous organization and the reality of racism in the working class.

This ostrich-like approach (to which there are of course exceptions) has to be seen as in part dictated by the very universalism and apparent solidarity of trade unionism and socialism, which insists on the 'equal' treatment of all irrespective of sex and colour. This apparently benevolent ideology has been used to legitimize widespread inaction with respect to racial minorities. As a result, positive action or even the acceptance of cultural pluralism may be susceptible to the cries of 'reverse racism' or 'discrimination against whites' that have been projected on behalf of the indigenous white population by the right. The leftist arguments that racism can only be opposed by the working class, by socialists or under socialism, and hence that there is no place for autonomous black politics or for broad-based anti-racist groups, suffers from a similar refusal to acknowledge the reality of racism.

This wilful colour-blindness is in fact a severe problem in most institutional fields (e.g. amongst teachers, politicians, professionals, and local authority officials). It has also to be set in the context of trade union sectionalism and economism which ensures that issues other than those of pay and working conditions are normally assigned a low priority; also that other corollary of the capitalist market, 'free collective bargaining', ensured the initial opposition of the TUC, with the CBI, to Government 'interference' in industrial relations through the employment clauses of the Race Relations Act of 1968.

The left and the labour movement, then, are frequently dismissed as racist, paternalistic, exploitative or irrelevant to the real issues and problems facing black communities in Britain; this judgement is a harsh over-generalization, but has sufficient roots in actual experience, and in the simple lack of contact between much of the labour movement/left and the black and ethnic minority organizations with their frequent base amongst the wageless black youth, to exacerbate the gap between the 'white' labour movement and black community groups.

Related to the organizational fragmentation of the anti-racist movement is the significant ideological fragmentation of the movement ensuing from the institutionalization of local racial equality activity in local Community Relations Councils by Governments that have been simultaneously fostering racism by their enthusiastic promulgation of the immigration colour bar. This has led to a division between those, both black and white, who have felt that this apparatus has been a useful arena and resource for promoting racial equality, and those who write off Government race apparatuses.

This difference in approach is similar to the 'reformist'/'revolutionary' division which led to CARD's disintegration, although the debate there also included the question of black versus multi-racial organization, national versus international arena of struggle, legal pressure versus mass action — as well as a considerable degree of personalized factional activity.

Many of these oppositions are still important sources of division and fractionalization within the anti-racist movement, but the validity of these polarizations is rarely challenged in the literature. In our view it is possible to develop an analysis of the intervention of the state in the field of race relations which accepts neither an uncritically liberal or simply pragmatic view of the state's activities, nor the totally negative position of many radical critics: and that is to see the work of the state (here as elsewhere – as *contradictory*, as double-edged, as providing points of political access and pressure, and even of democratic transformation for the ethnic minority communities, not simply as mechanisms of control and diversion. Thus the evolution of Government thinking is to call for (and finance) community self-help and the active participation of the minorities in the formulation and execution of policies in regard to their communities. In other words, legitimacy has now been won for the Community Relations movement to move from paternalism to positive action, and to ensure that the attack on racial equality is conducted through the democratization of the local state apparatuses with respect to the black communities, a process which is slowly gathering momentum in some, especially London, areas (e.g. the Lewisham CCR/Borough Council working party; the Lambeth consortium of black organizations).

Forms of black political organization

A significant aspect of that underdevelopment of the field of the political sociology of race to which we have referred is the relative paucity of studies and discussion of political organization amongst the racial and ethnic minorities. Perhaps sociologists have taken to heart Robin Jenkins's (1971) strictures on races relations research as a form of state surveillance on the black community, a view which has been spontaneously echoed in, for example, the hostility to their research encountered by the authors of the CRC's (1974) 'Unemployment and Homelessness' report, and by Rex and Tomlinson (1979) from several radical black groups. Certainly, since the publication of a number of attacks on the old race relations industry, there seemed for a considerable period to have been a reluctance by social scientists to engage in either policy-related research, or to follow up the empirical and analytical work of John (1969) on the Indian Workers' Association, Beetham (1970) on the local politicization of race or Heineman (1972) on the Campaign Against Racial Discrimination.

We have seen, however, that there is already a fairly extensive discussion of right-wing organizations, their racist ideologies, electoral successes and patterns of recruitment. This relates, in some of the literature, to the analysis of the impact of the race issue in terms of winning or losing electoral support for the major political parties amongst the white population, and the question of the voting patterns of the ethnic minority groups themselves.

The available poll evidence indicates since 1963 a wide public consensus on the need to limit black immigration, on the greater likelihood of the Conservatives keeping 'them' out and the liability of some Labour voters to switch to the Tories (if not the National Front) as a consquence. On the other hand, many studies of black voting behaviour confirm the general Labour support, very important in urban marginals, of the West Indian and Asian communities and perhaps the most solid source of Labour support in the British electorate amounting to 'three-quarters of the coloured vote' (Butler and Stokes, 1974, p. 221): this is explained by Labour's working-class appeal to a predominantly working-class black population, the Conservatives' imperialist and Powellite connections and because of Labour's more positive and interventionist (or perhaps less negative) approach to anti-discrimination and racial equality.

These dual tendencies have encouraged both Labour and Conservative parties to make some efforts to woo both the black vote and the white 'anti-immigrant' vote: the larger number of the latter, and the general contradiction involved, perhaps explain the speed with which the Labour/TUC anti-racist campaign of 1976 disappeared, the inactivity of the 1977 all-Party Joint Campaign Against Racialism, and the Conservative Party's resumption of a high profile on immigration control in 1978.

The Conservatives then appear to have abandoned the black vote to Labour, though there is evidence of a middle-class Conservative Asian vote (e.g. Anwar, 1980). But the literature also points to a current of disenchantment with Labour's restrictive approach on immigration, its inadequate performance with regard to the various problems of the black community, and its slow adoption of candidates from the minorities themselves. Thus there are no black Labour MPs, relatively few ethnic minority Labour councillors, and a weak membership base amongst the black population, particularly severely so amongst the British-born black population with no tradition of anti-colonial or Labourite solidarity.

Under these circumstances, a number of writers have pointed to regular moves towards 'floating ethnic voting' (Bentley, 1973, p. 47) in areas of high immigrant concentration, involving tactical support for candidates from other parties, for example Liberals or the far-left, or forms of independent political representation.

In considering this overall terrain of black political organization and ideology, the most fruitful source will be the material produced from within these groups themselves, such as the journals (e.g. *Race and Class, Race Today, The Black Liberator, Bradford Black, The Asian, West Indian World,* etc.) as well as manifestos, statements of aims, policy documents produced by the myriad of local ethnic minority and community groups. A growing literature of sensitive 'black testimonies' (Cottle, 1978) written from within or close to the black experience are a further vital source for understanding the ideological and cultural basis for political developments (see for example, Wilson, 1978).

A number of writers point to the major structural division between the black and white working class in Britain in terms of a labour movement concerned to protect the interests of white workers, whilst the black population is forced to rely on its own community organizations for its self-defence.

Thus, despite frequent attempts in recent debates to reduce rather than relate racial oppression to class struggle, there is something distinctive about many of the black workers' struggles that have been fought in recent years in Britain: they may be over elementary trade union rights, union recognition, up-grading, wage differentials etc., the 'normal' struggle against class exploitation and labour movement sectionalism, but they are frequently struggles for human dignity, for inclusion within the trade-union and working-class community on an equal footing: 'We will not go back like dogs. This is a fight for our dignity' (a banner in Mansfield Hosiery dispute). For the mechanism of the black workers' class super-exploitation and of the maintenance of white skilled and semi-skilled workers' differentials is racism, and open racialist attitudes and attempts at the degrading humiliation of black men and women workers on the part of management and union are frequently reported. The best known of these struggles are Mansfield Hosiery, Imperial Typewriters and Grunwicks.

As a counter-tendency to the process of racial segregation and polarization in the industrial sphere, one can point to examples of inter-racial class solidarity and unity, such as in the NUPE low-paid workers' dispute and at Fords, and also the class solidarity shown at Grunwicks by the local and national working-class movement. Though numbers of officials and stewards are low, black membership of the trade unions is high and there is no significant move to separate trade union organization.

We see then tendencies towards both 'ethnic organization' and 'class unity' (Miles and Phizacklea, 1977a) operating within the sphere of labour movement organization, particularly the former: the racist division of labour at work has forced groups of Asian or West Indian workers to develop autonomous, and frequently community-linked organizations, as a means of self-defence against managerial oppression and trade union sectionalism. But this ethnic organization process has to be seen as not necessarily operating in opposition to class unity, to which most black workers aspire; and also the impetus towards the 'black unity process' flowing from these industrial experiences should not be underestimated.

Hence the centrality of the concern of the 'ideologically oriented' black movement with questions of racial identity, consciousness, and modes of autonomous organization as a base from which to counter societal racism (Rex and Tomlinson, 1979). However, this cultural resistance has in fact, for young West Indians or British-born blacks of (part) African origin, taken on an Afro-Caribbean form. There is a widespread interest and identification with Black power, Rastafarianism and Pan-Africanism, whose distinctive themes, style, music and religion provide a 'new vocabulary and syntax of rebellion', grounded in an 'intense black cultural nationalism' (Hall *et al.*, 1978). Amongst Asian youth too, there are signs that the experience of racial exclusion is creating a 'reactive pride in their ethnic identity' (Ballard and Ballard, 1977, p. 54) which is a more over-arching consciousness, less narrowly based on caste, kinship and regional attachments than their parents' and one which is politically more radical (see the various Asian Youth Movements, for example in Bradford and Southall).

But racism is forcing the immigrant generation, too, into political awareness and action; thus common problems of racial discrimination, prejudice, harassment and violence have engendered community organizations along ethnic lines in a variety of situations. In the field of education there have developed groups of black parents opposing the ESN placement of their children or bussing, demanding Black Studies courses or a multi-cultural curriculum, or developing forms of supplementary education to compensate for the schools' teaching, atmosphere and organization which cause under-achievement by their children. There has been much activity in the areas of harassment by various aspects of the state (police, immigration, law) or in response to severe gaps in the welfare state (jobs, housing, leisure, social services) where there have sprung up numerous self-help and welfare organizations, for example, housing action groups, defence committees, local youth and community projects, nurseries, job-creation projects, hostels, advice centres, which are organized, staffed and controlled by black community groups themselves. In addition there are the many cultural organizations, for example, carnivals; and the self-defence organizations being forced on the ethnic communities by the National Front and other racist groups (see for example Moore, 1975).

These struggles and organizations have frequently been of a local and unco-ordinated character, a variety of different forms of autonomous organization in a number of different contexts rather than unified ethnic movements. Thus we find extremely significant differences of a cultural, ideological, or generational character between the many black and brown organizations in Britain: welfare and political, 'reformist' and 'revolutionary', West Indian and Asian, Pan-African and Marxist, British-born and immigrant, and further crucial sub-divisions, splits and factions within each category based on ideology, culture, language, nationality or generation.

But it seems likely that the continued experience of racism at the hands of the various state apparatuses, the fascist groups and the major British institutions themselves will foster an increase in militancy, unified political action and direct electoral involvement in terms both of ethnic organization and of black unity: thus already in the last few years we have seen the foundation of the Campaign Against Sus, which started from a number of black people's organizations; the formation of the Standing Conference of Afro-Caribbean and Asian Councillors and their production of a 'Black People's Manifesto' for the 1979 General Election; the formation and activities of the Blacks Against State harassment and Repression Groups; and in 1980 a new attempt at a National Co-ordinating Committee.

Although tactical and strategic differences as well as the other contradictions outlined above may continue to militate against the successful development of an active nation-wide and broad-based black people's organization, none the less the tendency for co-ordinated and unified actions is growing. The work of the 'Sus campaign' indicates one way in which anti-racist work may be successfully carried out in the current situation: there the black community focused on a realizable, concrete demand and has sought and gained, from a secure community base, wider research back-up and general support in a non-sectarian and non-exclusive way, winning advances in terms of both Labour and Liberal commitment decisions to 'scrap Sus' in their 1978 election manifestos, and Conservative Government repeal in 1981.

Such a strategy is concerned to combine grass-roots action with pressure for legal and institutional change, and combines a degree of autonomous black organization with inter-racial alliance and political lobbying that goes beyond the labour movement and white working class.

Conclusion: action and research

Our overall approach has been to stress that, in the field of race relations, political outcomes enjoy a level of indeterminacy in respect of their economic conditions of existence: although the material structures of racial inequality and class fragmentation are strong, there is still in our view a large area for political intervention to overcome racial injustices by liberal and left anti-racists and by the black organizations, facilitated in particular by the scope that the 1976 Race Relations Act provides for positive actions and policies by the local authority. The problem is finding ways to develop the political will and the organizational structures, with adequate strategic concreteness and flexibility, to deal both with the specific problems and complexities of racial oppression and the wider problems of class inequality that will be exacerbated over the forthcoming period.

The academic community has a responsibility to provide what assistance it can to the emergence of this process of specific demand-articulation and mobilization and positive policy-formation, by working closely with the minority groups and the anti-racist organizations to assess those points within the national and local power structures from which constructive interventions can be made and democratic advances secured to involve active black participation in the decision-making process (Gabriel and Ben-Tovim, 1979; Ben-Tovim *et al.*, 1981). It also must orient itself towards the mainstream political arena, by the provision of information, reports and evidence that can be used to educate, win over and involve key allies in the long haul of mobilizing public opinion back from racial hostility and fear engendered by imperial history, the immigration debate and Government low-profile weakness on integration, towards a commitment to taking active steps to secure racial justice and social equality.

References

Allen, S. (1973), 'The institutionalisation of racism', *Race*, vol. XV, no. 1.

Anwar, M. (1980), *Votes and Policies: Ethnic Minorities and the General Election 1979,* Commission for Racial Equality

Ballard, R. and Ballard, C. (1977), 'The Sikhs', in J. Watson (1977)

Beetham, D. (1970), *Transport and Turbans - A Comparative Study of Local Politics,* Oxford University Press/IRR

Bentley, S. (1973), 'Intergroup relations in local politics: Pakistanis and Bangladeshis', *New Community,* vol. 2, no. 1

Ben-Tovim, G. S. and Gabriel, J. (1979), 'The sociology of race — time to change course?', *The Social Science Teacher*, vol. 8, no. 4 (special edn on 'Race and education')

Ben-Tovim, G. S., Gabriel, J., Law, I. and Stredder, K. (1981), 'Race, left strategies and the state', *Politics and Power*, vol. 3, Routledge & Kegan Paul

Billing, M. (1978), *Fascists – A Social Psychological View of the National Front*, Harcourt, Brace Jovanovich

Butler, D. and Stokes, D. (1974), *Political Change in Britain*, Macmillan

Cottle, T. S. (1978), *Black Testimony – Voices of Britain's West Indians*, Wildwood House

CRC (1974), *Unemployment and Homelessness: A Report by the Reference Division*, Community Relations Commission

Crossman, R. (1975), *The Diaries of a Cabinet Minister*, Cape

Deakin, N. (1978), 'Inner areas: an ethnic dimension?', discussion paper to CES workshop

Department of the Environment (1977), *Policy for the Inner Cities*, Cmnd 6845, HMSO

Dummett, A. (1976), *Citizenship and Nationality*, Runnymede Trust

Dummett, M. (1978), *Immigration: Where the Debate Goes Wrong*, AGIN

Dummett, M. and Dummett, A. (1969), 'The role of government in Britain's racial crisis', in I. Donelly (ed.), *Justice First*, Sheed & Ward

Edgar, D. (1977), 'Racism, fascism and the politics of the National Front', *Race and Class*, vol. XIX, no. 2

Edwards, J. and Batley, R. (1978), *The Politics of Positive Discrimination*, Tavistock

Foot, P. (1965), *Immigration and Race in British Politics*, Penguin

Hall, S. (1978), 'Racism and reaction', in *Five Views of Multi-Racial Britain*, BBC/CRE

Hall, S. *et al.* (1978), *Policing the Crisis: Mugging, the State, and Law and Order*, Macmillan

Heineman, B. W. (1972), *The Politics of the Powerless*, Oxford University Press/ IRR

Hill, M. and Issacheroff, M. (1971), *Community Action and Race Relations*, Oxford University Press/IRR

Home Office (1975), *Racial Discrimination*, Cmnd 6234, HMSO

Home Office (1978), *Proposals for Replacing Section II of the Local Government Act 1966*, Home Office Consultative Document

Jenkins, R. (1971), *The Production of Knowledge at the Institute of Race Relations*, Independent Labour Party

John, D. (1969), *Indian Workers' Associations in Britain*, Oxford University Press/IRR

Katznelson, I. (1973), *Black Men, White Cities*, Oxford University Press

McKay, D. H. and Cox, A. (1979), *The Politics of Urban Change*, Croom Helm

Meacher, M. (1974), 'The politics of positive discrimination', in *Positive Discrimination and Inequality*, Fabian Research series no. 314

Miles, R. and Phizacklea, A. (1977a), 'Class, race, ethnicity and political action', *Political Studies*, vol. XXV, no. 4

Miles, R. and Phizacklea, A. (1977b), 'The TUC, black workers and new Commonwealth immigration 1954-1973', SSRC Research Unit on Ethnic Relations working paper no. 6

Miles, R. and Phizacklea, A. (eds.) (1979), *Racism and Political Action in Britain*, Routledge & Kegan Paul

Moore, R. (1975), *Racism and black resistance in Britain*, Pluto Press

PEP (1967), *A Report on racial discrimination*, no. 544, Political and Economic Planning

Rex, J. and Tomlinson, S. (1979), *Colonial Immigrants in a British City*, Routledge & Kegan Paul

Rose, E. J. B. *et al.* (1969), *Colour and Citizenship: A Report on British Race Relations*, Oxford University Press

Runnymede Trust (1979), *A Review of the Race Relations Act 1976*, Runnymede Trust

Select Committee on Race Relations and Immigration (1978), *Immigration*, First Report March 1978, HMSO

Sivanandan, A. (1976), 'Race, class and the state', *Race and Class*, vol. XVII (Spring)

Sivanandan, A. (1978), 'From immigration control to induced repatriation', *Race and Class*, vol. XX, no. 1

Smith, D. (1976), *The Facts of Racial Disadvantage:* A National Survey, no. 560, Political and Economic Planning

Smith, D. (1977), *Racial Disadvantage in Britain*, Penguin

Spencer, S. and Freeman, M. D. (1979), 'The state, law, blacks and the economy', paper to conference on 'Law and society', BSA

Taylor, S. (1979), 'Race extremism and violence in contemporary British politics', *New Community*, vol. VII, no. 1

Walker, M. (1977), *The National Front*, Fontana

Watson, J. (ed.) (1977), *Between Two Cultures*, Blackwell

Wilson, A. (1978), *Finding a voice – Asian women in Britain*, Virago

Wilson, H. (1974), *The Labour Government 1964-70*, Penguin

7 Gender, race and class in the 1980s

Sheila Allen

> There are times when class or race solidarity are much stronger than sex-gender conflict and times when relations within the family are a source of mutual resistance to class power. [Rowbotham, 1979]

This paper builds on some of the themes of the earlier one (Allen, 1980) but focuses more centrally on the issue of race and gender. It considers how the relationship between race and gender has been constructed and debated and discusses some of the more recent evidence on the similarities and differences in the social and economic position of black and white women relative to that of black and white men.

Since the late 1970s there have been many changes which require consideration if we are to understand the social relations of men and women and of black and white people in the Britain of the late 1980s. Some of these changes are to do with how people think, write about and debate issues; how they perceive their own experiences and generalize them; and how the lines are drawn between 'us' and 'them'. Other changes relate to the political, economic, demographic and legal contexts in which the thinking, acting and experience take place and in which the lines of inclusion and exclusion are drawn and redrawn. There are also continuities, or in some cases, developments of already existing relationships and experiences which have become more sharply or overtly articulated in the past decade.

The themes in *Perhaps a Seventh Person* (Allen, 1980) which remain particularly relevant are those of the continuing political and personal significance of immigration, the simple notions of culture adopted by, among others, policy makers and politicians, the invisibility of women and racial and gender stereotyping. The issue of how and to what extent class divisions are relevant to analyses of race continues to be a focus of intellectual and pragmatic concern. A significant development has been the debate around feminism and racism in the British context. This development is relevant to the class/race issue and will be considered below.

On an everyday common-sense level these divisions are not separate entities but combine together in different mixes and are experienced as a totality from an individual viewpoint. At the same time the emphasis given to one or the other may vary in different situations. For instance, the boundaries drawn between 'us' and 'them' can be based on class or gender or race or on all three together. Obviously the possibilities of where the boundaries can be drawn vary and are not simply a matter of choice. The structuring of boundaries and the processes involved in their maintenance or transformation are to be understood in a context of diversities and commonalities of experience. On a descriptive level instances can be listed endlessly, but to make sense of these an analysis of structure and process within socio-historical periods is required.

Social divisions

How are we to understand the relationship of race and gender in Britain in the late 1980s so that we can explain the processes through which racism and sexism are created and perpetuated? We have in the middle 1980s two largely discrete attempts to theorize the social divisions of race and gender. The first is monopolized by men almost exclusively white, and the other, though in the main first addressed by women, now includes numerous contributions by men. These too are with notable exceptions white. At the same time a contested terrain has developed in which black and white women engage in a critical discourse about feminist attempts to reconceptualize social divisions. On a descriptive level there is an increasing literature on and by black women in Britain to add to that produced in the United States and a number of Third World societies, all of which has relevance to the issue of social divisions.

The publisher's claim that '*The Heart of the Race* (Bryan, *et al.*, 1985) records for the first time what life is like for black women in Britain', may not be factually correct, but points to the relative newness of any recording of black women's experience in Britain by black women.[1] Here we find intertwined race, gender and class in their first-hand experiences of British society.

There are many social divisions in industrial societies including those of age, race and ethnicity, sex/gender and class/status, together with those of religion, region and nationality. In social theory class and status have taken precedence and certain homogeneities have been assumed. These are that populations are white, ethnically homogeneous and male. Any other human being, for instance, foreigner, migrant, woman, ethnic, non-white, constitutes an anomaly or a non-person. This simplification aided the development of class theories as explanatory devices or models for understanding how societies are organized, and in some cases how they change. These theories/models remain central to an understanding of social divisions in industrial societies as those attempting to incorporate or fight off the challenges of feminist scholars maintain (Lockwood, 1986). But they also remain partial or truncated explanations of the social relations of the material oppressions experienced through the divisions of race and gender. Some argue that race or gender should replace class in the theories of social organization and change. However, a more difficult but more productive way forward is to engage in exploring the ways in which these divisions are constructed together. Not only will this produce more adequate theory but it will have more practical relevance in understanding in a less partial way the relations between men and women and between black and white.[2]

It is necessary to note here that the separate social science disciplines address different sets of problems. So that, for example, the psychology which addresses individual similarities or differences pursues questions which differ from those that sociology or political science addresses. Furthermore in all of these, theoretical statements about general uniformities cannot be applied mechanically to an individual case. Nor conversely can an individual case (including individual experience) be taken as some kind of automatic proof (or falsification) of more general statements.

Although the search for explanations of why people act as they do, or why they are what they are is neither simple nor one dimensional, this does not mean that, even if we could, we stop searching for understanding and explanation. While we cannot reduce individual human action to biology, of the brain, the sex organs, skin pigmentation, hair colour or texture nor can we assume away the ways in which these have been and are used as social indicators and given social meanings. Similarly we cannot reduce human behaviour to the way in which an individual perceives the word or her/his own action apart from the social relations with others which give it meaning. These perceptions and relations are not random, haphazard or simply matters of choice. If they were then we could never predict how anyone was going to act towards us. Nevertheless the patterning of human actions cannot be explained simply as a reflection of culture or structure. When attempting to interrelate gender and race an agnostic approach to all-embracing theories is necessary. Not least because so much of macro-social theory assumes both are natural or replaces biological determinism by a cultural or social determinism. But this is not to be read as meaning that theory is redundant. Quite the contrary, in order to make sense of the interrelations of race and gender and the ways in which these articulate with other social divisions, particularly those of class, theory is unavoidable.

Race and gender: the separated discourse

It is beyond the scope of this paper to detail the divergent theories of race and ethnic relations among sociologists, leaving aside the contribution of those from several other disciplines. Equally the different attempts to theorize gender relations can only be touched on briefly. In recent times these have drawn on ideas from a very wide spectrum but in social science disciplines, such as sociology, they still occupy a marginalized position despite or perhaps because of the considerable theoretical challenge they pose. It is important to note two points however. First, that race and ethnic relations are by and large theorized as genderless. A recent collection of papers dealing with these relations had as its core Marxist, Weberian and plural society theories with in addition 'paradigms suggested by the theory of rational choice, by social anthropology, by social biology and by social psychology, as well as the micro-sociological approach of symbolic interactionism' (Rex and Mason, 1986). Whatever the differences or complementarities of these approaches and the competence with which they are discussed what is so marked is the absence from virtually all of them of any mention – let alone any serious consideration – of gender, either as it affects or is affected by race and ethnicity. This criticism is not of course peculiar to this text. On the contrary it would have been surprising if gender relations had found their way into such deliberations. Second, that when gender relations are treated as a serious social science issue race and ethnicity tend to disappear. Another collection of papers, published at the same time as the one mentioned above, deals with gender and stratification and like the first involved prominent, even eminent contributors to the debate, but ethnicity is mentioned in passing on only a few occasions and race makes no appearance at all (Crompton and Mann, 1986). Both represent positive attempts to locate race and ethnicity, or gender, within the core problematic of social sciences. Nevertheless these separate and selective theoretical discussions doubly marginalize black women and highlight how far we are from developing theory and research adequate for analysing the interrelations of class, race and gender. The increasing anger expressed by black women at this neglect is not therefore altogether misplaced.

Race and gender have been brought together in recent debates between black and white women on feminism. Since so much of the debate is couched in terms of racism and the concept of sexism is integral to much of the feminist argument I shall consider these first before turning to the debates.

Racism and sexism

In 1970 Zubaida argued against a narrow ethnocentrism and simplistic 'common-sense' interpretations of modern race relations situations and for a comparative and historical approach. He also criticized race relations research for its focus on prejudice and discrimination and its social problem perspective (Zubaida, 1970, p. 3). In part he was concerned to point out the ways in which this focus had obscured differences between groups against whom prejudice and discrimination operated and to lay claim to a means of analysing race relations which went beyond individual examples of prejudice and particular instances of racial discrimination. He saw the way forward as lying within 'A macro-sociological, theoretically guided perspective [which would have] to locate and define the groups . . . in terms of their relationship to the wider social structure and the historical development of this relationship' (ibid). The increasing prominence given in the United States to institutional racism in the late 1960s began to influence analyses in Britain (Carmichael and Hamilton, 1969; U.S. Commission on Civil Disorders, 1968). By the middle 1970s institutionalized sexism was being discussed as a much neglected aspect of the structuring of social relations. (Barker and Allen, 1976a and b).

These two terms racism and sexism entered the vocabulary not as replacements for prejudice or discrimination, nor simply as descriptions of individual action or attitudes. The analytical significance of institutionalized racism and sexism refers not to the attitudes of individuals, but to the ways in which situations are structured so that one element of complex human beings is singled out and carries inordinate weight, at times to the exclusion of all others, in influencing how they are treated. Racism and sexism relate therefore to the socially created differences between men and women and between black and white so that they are systematically used to the detriment of those who are black and those who are women.

It is important to note here the differences between the individual and institutional levels of analysis. First, individual racist or sexist beliefs undoubtedly exist and may result in actions appropriate to them. Second, racism and sexism may be pursued because of the rewards (or lack of punishments) they confer. In this case racist or sexist beliefs are not necessary to support such actions. Third, however, normally everyday routines may involve racism or sexism without those involved being aware of it. In fact they may have non-racist, non-sexist beliefs and yet not recognize the *de facto* racist and sexist consequences of normal everyday activities (Allen, 1973). An emphasis on the individual level of analysis can obscure our understanding of how racism and sexism are created and perpetuated at the institutional or societal levels.

The debates on feminism

The interrelation of race and gender have in the 1980s become the subject of discussion between black and white women in Britain. Much of this discussion has focused on the shortcomings of white feminism, sometimes also denoted as 'mainstream' or middle class, indicating that there are other kinds of feminism. In the past parallels were drawn between racial oppression and the oppression of women and at times these were extended to the poor. All have been seen as inferior, either as naturally so or through cultural deprivation. So being black or a woman have not infrequently been regarded as ascribed statuses. Though these parallels indicate widespread forms of oppression, they are conceptually inadequate and – as black women have pointed out – obscure their specific oppression. This has been described in the following way.

> It is the fact that we are women which has distinguished our experience of life from that of Black men. Our relationship with men – both Black and white – has meant that in addition to racism, Black women have had to confront a form of sexism and sexual abuse which is unique to us. But it is impossible to separate our understanding of sexism in our community from its context in a racist society because popular acceptance of racist stereotypes of Black women, Black men and Black families not only compound our sexual oppression but have also become internalised [Bryan *et al.*, 1985, p. 212].

The observation that racism alters the form and significance of sexism is important to the analysis of both. In a racially ordered society, such as Britain in the 1980s, a feminism which ignores racial divisions is open to serious criticism. Discourses which neglect the experiences of black women, deny their common interests with black men, or construct the 'ethnic' family as the major site of women's oppression have been challenged as racist (Amos and Parmar, 1984; Bhavnani and Coulson, 1986; Bourne, 1983).

The current debate owes much to the black cultural and political struggles in the United States in the 1960s and 1970s. This is particularly so in that these struggles produced a vocabulary with which to express the black experience and the aims of the movements to change black–white relations. One aspect of this change was the recognition, increasing availability and growing production of a literature by black American women.[3] Another was the influence, often unacknowledged, on the feminist movement of the late 1960s and early 1970s of ideas and ways of expressing them. In Britain there was no civil rights movement and the black power and feminist movements were far more marginalized in ideological terms. Therefore it is not only that the debate about black and white feminism had to wait until the late 1970s, but that the borrowed vocabularies do not always fit easily with the political realities of Britain's racial divisions or feminist development.

Some of the major differences in terms of race may be summarized in relation to migration, imperialism and slavery. The first two have a permanent bearing on the British situation not found in the United States. Though black people have been part of British society for a very long period, they have since the 1950s been characterized as immigrants, whatever their actual status (Allen, 1971; Fryer, 1984). So that, whereas in the United States black women's claims to full political and economic rights as citizens could less easily be denied, in Britain they could be and still are. Not least in the sense that it is frequently assumed they have somewhere, a homeland, to go back to.

Imperialism with all its cultural and material implications for the interrelations of black groups as well as white and black is of crucial importance. The divisions created by British imperialism cannot be ignored or dismissed as of no consequence within contemporary Britain. It is one of the complexities of racism in Britain, that while the black population is not a homogeneous category, it is so characterized by whites on some occasions, and on others is portrayed as highly differentiated. Both can be defined as racist, but this does not provide an analysis of the situations and circumstances which lead to such shifts. The struggle for political independence waged against British imperialism in the colonial empire became part of the political culture of Britain. The alliances between Irish and Indian politicians is but one instance of this (Visram, 1986) but there are many others where opponents and protagonists of 'colonial freedom' divided along political not racial lines. The overriding significance of slavery and its aftermath of struggles in the United States, which informed and constructed much of the background of the 1960s civil rights and black movements, enters the British situation in a different way. For most of the white population of Britain slavery was largely an American problem only tangentially connected to British history. However inaccurate or misguided this view, it constitutes the received wisdom. For sections of the black population slavery has a quite different relevance and meaning.

The development of feminism in the United States and Britain in the late 1960s and early 1970s had much in common, but there were also obvious differences. One of these was the background of racial struggles in the States, which though in large measure absent from the writings of the most prominent white feminists was already a concern of black women activists, who found themselves at the sharp end of both struggles. This led not only to the recording of black women's experience but to an exploration of race and gender as they impacted on black women. It also led some white women, notably from the South, to reassess the impact on their own lives of race and gender divisions. Angela Davis' analysis of rape, historically grounded in the manipulation of rape charges against black men, as one of the critical long-standing racist controls, was made in part in response to Brownmiller's portrayal of rape as a white feminist issue (Davis, 1982; Brownmiller, 1975). There were no such analyses of the situation in Britain where lynch mobs were not part of black–white relations and physical assaults on black women and black families lay largely in the future.

A further difference was the greater emphasis in Britain on class within feminist discussions. For at least part of the re-emergent feminist movement class was a feature distinguishing between the experience of women. Throughout this period socialist feminism, which prioritized class, engaged in a dialogue with radical feminism, which prioritized male dominance conceptualized as patriarchy, and thus from the beginning class was a contentious issue. While in the United States conceptualizations such as the feminization of poverty were adopted to deal with the statistics of women, particularly black mothers on welfare, in Britain attention was directed towards a class analysis. The male chauvinism of the labour movement was exposed in many studies of working-class struggles in which the subordination of women workers became an integral part of family wage ideology and the bourgeois conception of the domesticated woman.

In both the United States and Britain feminists had to contend with a social science which obscured the lives of women by denying the theoretical significance of gender divisions and collaborated with empirical investigations which simply ignored women or accounted for them in terms of deviations from some generally accepted male norm. In attempting to rescue women from this oblivion feminism was unable to cope with the complexities of numerous cross-cutting divisions. Therefore many feminist analyses are deficient in terms of race and class, and also in respect of age, ethnicity, nationality and religion. Many women have, however, written at different times and in different contexts, often with great insight, passion and eloquence, of the subordination and exploitation of women, through their gender, race/ethnicity and class. This literature is vast and though rarely considered by social scientists has relevance both to developing a theory of gender divisions and to practical struggles for change.[4]

The concentration of the current debate on racism within mainstream white feminism has to be put into this context, in order to provide a more comprehensive description and more clearly grounded theory.

In a discussion of 'some of the key theoretical concepts in white feminist literature and . . . their relevance or otherwise for a discussion and development of Black feminist theory' it is argued that 'The historical and cultural traditions from which they [white feminists] write are qualitatively and in essence so different that their analysis, interpretations and conclusions are of necessity going to produce "naive and perverse" accounts steeped in white chauvinism' (Amos and Parmar, 1984).

In Britain as in the United States the early discussions in the 1960s and early 1970s around feminism were frequently narrowed down to deal with what were seen as the immediate concerns. Issues close to the experience of those who became involved were taken up and others neglected. There was a focus in the main, though not exclusively, on the oppression of educated white women facing the conflicts of careers and motherhood or the politics of sexuality (Firestone, 1971; Friedan, 1963; Millet, 1971). Different positions on the issues of feminism developed, however, which crystallized in theoretical terms broadly around on the one hand the relevance of class divisions to the analysis of gender in industrial societies, deriving in the main from a socialist or marxist perspective, and on the other the primacy of male domination relative to all other divisions. Both these approaches neglected many dimensions of society relevant to the analysis of gender. The structures and processes of migration, of imperialism, of development/underdevelopment as well as of race and ethnicity were not integrated into the theories. But whatever their limitations, awareness of these dimensions was not totally absent. Sheila Rowbotham's observation in the early 1970s is an example.

> The connection between the oppression of women and the central discovery of Marxism, the class exploitation of the worker in capitalism, is still forced. . . . I believe the only way in which their combination will become living and evident is through a movement of working-class women, in conscious resistance to both, alongside black, yellow and brown women struggling against racialism and imperialism. We are far from such a movement now. But when the connection between class, colonial and sexual oppression becomes commonplace, we will understand it, not as an abstract imposed concept, but as something coming out of the experience of particular women. [Rowbotham, 1972, p. 247].

By the middle 1970s attempts were made to discuss class, race and gender together (James, 1975) and cross-cultural perspectives on women's subordination were being developed (Edholm, *et al.*, 1977; Leacock, 1975).

One of the challenges in the 1980s to 'mainstream white feminism' was that a false universalism underpinned the conceptual framework so that analyses ignored the specificities of the oppression of black women including the racism of white women as well as white men. One of the divisions within feminist scholarship as it developed in Britain was on this point of whether 'women' could be considered a meaningful category. Wallman argued for instance that ' . . . the significance of being female varies with technology, setting, class, context, task, rank, race, age, profession, kinship, wealth and economics . . . with any or all the dimensions of a situation of which it can form only a part' (1976, p. 2). On a descriptive level there can be little argument with this. One could equally state the same for men. Conceptually, however, the issue is rather different.

For example, Burja maintains that ' . . . what is required . . . is a mediating concept, to build a bridge between the biological fact of women's existence and the infinitely varied forms of her social existence'. Her suggestion is that 'in domestic labour (socially reproductive labour expended in the context of the domestic unit) we have such a concept' (Burja, 1978, p. 20). She goes on to argue that domestic labour needs to be understood not as a universal category, but in terms of its articulation with differing modes of production. She discusses such an approach not in reductionist economic terms, but in terms of the social reproduction of labour, on a day to day physical and ideological basis, within historical contexts. Her aim is to understand the bases of female solidarity or the lack of it. This kind of conceptualization, whether or not one agrees with the particulars, not only enables the bewildering diversities to be conceptualized, but directs attention to the specificities which need investigation. Delphy and Leonard on the other hand start from rather different premises. While they do not dispute the existence nor importance of social divisions other than gender, they prioritize patriarchal relations in their approach. They see the family, particularly marriage, as the core institution of gender division (and women's oppression) and in a recent discussion of social stratification argue that 'the indifference of stratification studies to the institution of the family . . . [has] weakened, sometimes to the point of non-existence, their study of the reproduction of the social structure over time'[5] (Delphy and Leonard, 1986). The long-standing and at times bitter disputes among feminists about how to conceptualize gender in relation to other divisions has frequently reflected their own materially grounded consciousness, and consequently also their blindness to ethnic and race divisions within Britain.

In a society where racial ordering is integral to the structuring of social relations, relations between women and between women and men cannot be conceptualized as though they were outside these. This still leaves open, however, how race and gender interpenetrate. While the existing shortcomings of class analyses in relation to gender are actively pursued in some intellectual debates, race is only very slowly entering into the discussions. No systematic attempts to address this issue have been made, though Barrett and McIntosh argue that the concept of patriarchy is less able to cope with the complexities of racial divisions than the approaches adopted in socialist feminism (1985). This also appears to me to be the case, but it is not only the ahistorical or universalistic aspects of patriarchy found in some versions of that approach which raise conceptual problems (Beechy, 1979); there is also the need to reconceptualize class to allow for an interactive analysis of race, gender and class. The discussions of race and class however, as was mentioned above, are as yet virtually genderless and the challenges from black feminists are ignored in this debate.[6] With these in mind it is appropriate to take up the view expressed on page 170 and briefly consider the ways in which these divisions are constructed together.

The focus on struggle

Women were involved in everyday struggles throughout the period during which these debates on race relations and feminism were being conducted. Some have sought to remind those constructing and debating theoretical approaches that everyday practice cannot be ignored if theory is to be adequate to the task of understanding and explaining social relations. For instance, Lees argues that 'The practical political realities of the relations between sex and race as active feminists encounter it (*sic*) must be the focus' (Lees, 1986). Similarly others have argued that analysis should concentrate on historically based localized struggles against racism rather than attempting to theorize race and class, where class and race are inseparable (Ben Tovim *et. al.*, 1986a, 1986b). This, however, is only a beginning.

The concepts of institutionalized racism and sexism do not relate to individual examples but seek to order innumerable cases of everyday practice and the struggle against them into a more general framework whereby forms of domination can be specified. How these relate to the class structure in Britain and its pervasive inequalities and the forms of organization developed to counter them are an essential component in specifying the impact of racism and sexism.

The concrete struggles of women workers in the late 1960s through to the present to resist poor pay and conditions have involved women from all ethnic and racial groups. Some have been headline news, but others are known only on local levels. Some have involved black and white women, while others have not. In general, women's jobs in the service industries – especially the low-paid ones – have been less racially segregated than their equivalents in manufacturing. It is not therefore surprising that the women conducting the fight for equal pay at Fords in 1968 were white, while in the Night Cleaners Campaign black and white women organized and struggled together to improve wages and conditions and fought for unionization (*Socialist Woman*, 1971, 1972; Hobbs, 1973). Black and white women, particularly in the hospital service, were involved in a number of national struggles in the 1970s. In manufacturing, in contrast, during the struggles at Imperial Typewriters and Mansfield Hosiery, black workers – men and women – fought together against racial discrimination in their pay and conditions, in which both white management and trade union officials were implicated.

The dispute at Grunwick brought together the conflicts and contradictions of class, race and gender perhaps better than any other to emerge on a national level so far in Britain. It also illustrates how a particular concrete struggle can be interpreted differently (Dromey and Taylor, 1978; Parmar, 1982; *Spare Rib*, 1977). It involved a low-waged workforce, mainly Asian and some Afro-Caribbean women, employed in poor conditions in a back street firm in West London dependent on contracts from a multi-national. When some of the women objected to their working conditions and pay and sought union help they were confronted by the full force of the law which was used unremittingly by their employer. They stood on the picket line for fifteen months and their cause was taken up by innumerable groups, students, women, trade unionists, the local Indian community and the Indian Workers Association. Mass pickets were organized, arrests and imprisonment ensued. While white male trade unionists may be castigated for sexism and racism (Parmar, 1982), trade union officials (white and male) for ignorance of immigrant workers (Dromey and Taylor, 1978), and white feminists for expressing surprise at the militancy of Asian women (Allen, 1979), the workers who stood on the picket line refused to be divided by issues of race and gender, or intimidated by personal insult or harassment from the police, the employer and his managers. While not uncritical of their union, they were keenly aware of the relevance of the right to organize as trade unionists in an attempt to settle their grievances over their working conditions. The eventual defeat of the strikers and all who supported them was not due to sexism or racism. The causes of the defeat lay in the inability of the labour movement to ensure that a law designed to protect workers seeking union recognition in unorganized firms was enforced, even under a Labour Government, and the ability of the state and the employer to use other laws against the strikers and their supporters. In other words, the defeat can only be explained by close examination of the role of the state in relation to organized labour.

In analysing industrial struggles the nature of racist and sexist oppression and resistance to them need to be clarified in terms of factors such as the composition of the workforce, the segregation of workplaces or tasks, the divisions between grades, particularly of skilled and semi-skilled workers, the degree and form of unionization and the relative power of unions and management. For these limit the grounds for unity of action particularly where they coincide with race and gender divisions.

However, when in the concrete instance we come to examine anti-racist and anti-sexist struggles in relation to the labour market and the role of the state within a particular class formation then we are thrown back into the conceptual morass we have discussed above. The data we are likely to have to hand is itself already permeated by stereotypical constructions of reality which mystify what we would examine. For, as we have seen, neither class, gender nor race is unproblematic and this extends to the measures used to collect data which could inform those who wish to ground their arguments or understanding on a quantitative basis. The criticisms of statistical records, their shortcoming as evidenced by ethnocentric or gender-blind assumptions and their limitations in indicating change over time are discussed in several texts (Irvine *et al.*, 1979; The Runnymede Trust and the Radical Statistics Race Group, 1980). Such criticisms are well founded and care is necessary in interpreting quantitative data, particularly where boundaries are crudely drawn or causes are attributed to correlations between data sets.

The definition of the black population used in a national survey carried out into the circumstances of the British black population in 1982 was justified by earlier work which showed that 'coloured' immigrants faced higher levels of discrimination than other immigrants (Smith, 1977; Brown, 1984). The black population surveyed included those from the West Indies, the sub-continent of India and Asians from Africa, and those whose family origins were in these areas (including those with only one such parent). The white population were the remainder. The Chinese, those from South-East Asian origins, and black Africans were excluded altogether. The black population surveyed was split between

> the main groups within the black population: those with family origins in the West Indies and those with family origins in the Indian sub-continent. . . . Because of further differences between the groups from the Indian sub-continent . . . those of Asian origin [are split] into groups according to country of origin India, Pakistan and Bangladesh, and African Asians are classified separately [Brown, 1984, pp. 4–5].

The white population remains undifferentiated. It may include whites from – or whose family origins were in – Africa, Ireland, Cyprus, Eastern or Southern Europe. These examples of differentiations which could be made within the white population on similar grounds to those used to differentiate the black population, point to an inconsistency in the research design. They are not meant to question the significance of the black/white divide in British society. If the purpose was to investigate this divide then the exclusion of black Africans seems hardly justified, other than on the grounds of expense, since they outnumber Bangladeshis for instance, and the breakdown into country of origin in the case of those whose origins are in the Indian sub-continent is also theoretically and methodologically questionable. No 'mixed' households, that is with white and black members (as defined) were included at all in the survey of white households. In the survey of black households such households were included, but interviews were carried out only with people of West Indian or Asian origin. These exclusions mean that not only are quantitative data lost, but so too are interviews of particular interest and possible policy relevance. These methodological and theoretical shortcomings arise not from the complexities of the divisions within Britain but from the confusion surrounding which divisions are to be investigated and how.

The data from the PSI survey and that reported in *Social Trends* (Brown, 1984; CSO, 1985, 1986) provide some quantitative guides for those interested in gender and race. In 1983 the black population of Britain, including Africans, was 3½ per cent of the total population. The Africans and Bangladeshis were 0.17 and 0.15 respectively, the Pakistanis 0.7, the West Indians 1.0 and the Indians 1.5 (CSO, 1986: Table 1.10). These differences are important only in the sense that they challenge popular stereotypes regarding the structure of the 'immigrant' population of Britain. In the PSI survey carried out in 1982 over half of those in West Indian households had been born in Britain, over 40 per cent of those in Indian and

Pakistani households and 31 per cent in Bangladeshi households, whereas just less than a quarter of Asians from East Africa were British born. These differences are a result of the varied patterns of migration which are accounted for in part by the administration of the system of migration control. It should be noted that as the majority of those born in Britain are young adults or children, the black people interviewed in the PSI survey (the head plus up to two other adults in each of the households) were overwhelmingly born outside Britain.[7] 'Only one in a hundred Asian households is presently headed by a non-white person born in this country, compared with about one in ten of West Indian households' (Brown, 1984, p. 18).

In this survey the patterns of migration from the 1950s and the demographic changes between the early 1970s and the 1980s are noted. The migration from the West Indies for both men and women took place earlier than for the other groups, with 70 per cent of the men and 54 per cent of the women arriving by June 1962 and 2 per cent and 4 per cent arriving after 1972 (Brown, 1984, Table 5). Of the groups from the Indian sub-continent: 75 per cent of Indian and 84 per cent of Pakistani and 81 per cent of the Bangladeshi men had arrived by 1972. By the same date 67 per cent of Indian women compared to 49 per cent of the Pakistani women had arrived. The figures for Bangladeshi women are unclear from the table but their entry pattern from other sources indicates that a lower percentage of them had arrived by this time. The ratios of males to females among the Pakistanis and Bangladeshis has closed over the past decade. There appeared in 1982 to be equal percentages of men and women among whites and West Indians, almost equal in the case of Indians with the other groups having an almost 60–40 split between men and women. These different patterns of migration and the effects of immigration legislation from 1962 onwards are discussed in more detail in Allen (1980). As far as women from the Indian sub-continent are concerned we still have no data on women migrating independently; the assumption remains that the men are migrants and women dependants. In the case of Asians from East Africa it has to be remembered that the vouchers for entry were issued to heads of households holding British passports and certain categories of their dependants.

> Women holding British passports had great difficulty in proving they were heads of households, widows, divorced, deserted women and those with dependant husbands came into this category. And doubly trapped were those with non-British husbands [Allen, 1980].

It would be unwise to read off too much from the statistics about sex ratios in migration before looking closely at the systems of control, which subordinate women (Lal, S. and Wilson, A., 1986; CRE, 1985).

The age structure of adults in the groups reflects past migration patterns both in the very much lower proportion of black people who are aged 65 and over compared to whites and the different peaks within the black population. White women are of course numerically a very much larger proportion of the total female population but in terms of age structure there are marked differences between them and black women. For instance, whereas 36 per cent of white women are over 55 only 7 per cent of black women are. Among young adult women (16–24) the proportions within each group are as follows: 17 per cent of white, 28 per cent of West Indian and 23 per cent of Asian women (Brown, 1984, Table 7).

The PSI survey found most concern was expressed by black people about discrimination in employment. This finding is consistent with surveys going back to the 1960s. What is clear, however, is that the differences in types of jobs and earnings found among black and white women are much less than those found among men. There are proportionately almost as many Asian women in the professional, employer or management sector (6 per cent) as white women (7 per cent) and the percentage of white women in unskilled jobs (11 per cent) is higher than either West Indian (7 per cent) or Asian women (2 per cent). The situation is very different for men where 42 per cent of white men were in the professional, employer, management sector compared to 26 per cent of the Asians and 15 per cent of the West Indians.

The position of black women in the labour market can be understood only by relating it to women more generally. I have dealt with aspects of this elsewhere and here wish only to take up one or two points highlighted in some recent discussions (Allen 1979, 1980, 1982). Briefly, the sexual division of labour segregates women into very few industrial sectors and within these they are usually in the lower segments of occupational hierarchies. They are in the main found in service industries, in jobs designated as semi-skilled, and they earn less than men. In the professions, they either constitute a very small percentage relative to men, for instance in law, medicine or university teaching, or where they are a higher percentage, such as in school-teaching, they are found disproportionately in the lower grades. As a consequence of this it has been argued that 'Black and migrant women are already so disadvantaged by their gender in employment that it is difficult to show the effects of ethnic discrimination for them' (Anthias and Yuval-Davis, 1983). But the same authors also maintain that 'black and white women may both be subordinate within a sexually differentiated labour market but black women will be subordinated to white women within this' (ibid.). If we turn to the PSI findings, as the only existing representative national data, a number of points emerge. 'There is a much larger difference between white and black men than between white and black women in terms of job levels and in terms of earnings' (Brown, 1984, p. 167). A suggested explanation of the similarity between the wages of black and white women which was reported in 1974, was 'that the enormous disparity between men and women . . . left little scope for racial disadvantage to have a further, additive effect' (ibid., p. 169). There was a trend towards closing the gap between men's and women's earnings which peaked in 1977 when women's earnings reached 75.5 per cent of men's, the result in part of the immediate effects of the Equal Pay and Sex Discrimination legislation. In 1982 the gross hourly earnings of women over 18 years old working full time (but excluding overtime) were 74.2 per cent of men's whereas in 1974 they were 67.4

per cent (EOC, 1983: Table 4.1). In 1982 the PSI survey found, not surprisingly, that women in all the groups they investigated had much lower earnings than men, and the difference between the women was within a narrow range of £7. In terms of the median earnings West Indian women earned more than white women, who earned more than Asian women, but when age was taken into account the white women earned on average £10.40 more than black women between the ages of 25–54. 'However, the most important finding in terms of earnings is that within job-level categories black women are not paid less than white women, as was the case for men (Brown, 1984, pp. 168–9). This finding is explained by the size of workplace, the differences between the public and private sector and the degree of unionization. It is argued that black women are more likely than white to be in larger workplaces, in the public sector where there is a higher level of unioniz-ation, and so their earnings overall are similar to those of white women. This is so only for West Indian women, as Asian women are more likely to be found in the private sector. The question still remains whether if we compare like with like the findings are still the same. For instance, do white and black women within the same age range and job category within the large, public, more highly unionized sector earn the same or not. Are those in the professional, management, employer category doing the same kind of job? This kind of information can only be acquired through studies which examine particular industries or services and occupations. Evidence has indicated in the past that black women in nursing are increasingly more likely to be found at lower job levels (SEN rather than SRN and within less prestigious specialisms) not only earning less but experiencing lowered career prospects (Allen, 1979; Allen and Smith, 1974; Doyal, *et al.*, 1980).

The unemployment rate of black women was twice that reported for white women in 1984 with the highest rate (40 per cent) among Pakistani and Bangladeshi women compared to just over 10 per cent for white women (Labour Force Survey, 1984). This compared to 11 per cent for white men and 34 per cent for Pakistani and Bangladeshi men. The rate of unemployment among women is much more difficult to assess than that for men. This is due to several factors, including the way unemployment is defined and recorded, and the strength of ideologies which regard women without outside jobs as housewives rather than unemployed, and stereotype Asian women further as subjected to cultures which seclude them within the home (Hurstfield, 1986; Coyle, 1984; Smith, 1981). Nevertheless, even on the official figures unemployment is a very serious problem for black women particularly since Afro-Caribbean households are more dependent on women's earnings and Asian households generally are more than twice as likely to have no wage earner as white or 'West Indian' households.

The economic activity rates for those in jobs or seeking employment are overall higher for black women than for whites. This general picture is rather different when age, part-time and full-time working and ethnic differentials are taken into account (Brown, 1984, pp. 150–1). At present, however, the empirical investi-gations of black and white have not taken account of the literature on women's work or unemployment. The portrayal of women's economic activity would be very different if all forms of women's work were taken into account (Allen and Wolkowitz, 1987; James, 1987; Pahl, 1984). Caution needs to be exercised in interpreting findings from surveys based on inadequate theoretical concepts of women's position if we are to go beyond the stereotypical presentations of both black and white women. This will only be done by addressing the structuring of racial, gender and class ordering not as separate sets of social relations but as integral parts of one system. Such an approach provides the possibility of analysing the diversities and commonalities experienced in a class-divided, gendered and multi-racial society such as Britain in the 1980s. The recognition of both the relevance of struggle for change and the integrity of personal experience is essential to developing theory. But the process is one requiring a two-way interaction between theory and practice, not one where either substitutes for the other. Everyday, pervasive sexism and racism affects in one way or another not a minority, but the lives of most of us in contemporary Britain. To struggle effectively for change requires an understanding of how and why we are divided by material or ideological constraints which circumscribe our lives, identities and imagination.

Notes

1   There are a number of accounts of individual experiences, for instance, Alexander and Dewjee (eds) 1984; Emecheta, 1972, 1974. *See also* Fryer, 1984 for brief references to individual black women e.g. pp 130–2 and Visram, 1986 where the experiences of women from the Indian sub-continent are considered in a history of Indians in Britain 1700–1947. James, 1985 includes accounts of women of different generations, from a wide range of backgrounds.

2   Black and white are discussed here because of the current British situation in which race is in the main equated with skin colour. This does not indicate that race is anything more than a social construct. In some circumstances, or at other times, divisions into races are based on factors other than skin colour (see Allen, 1971).

3   This literature has become increasingly available in Britain in the 1980s. See for instance Angelou (1978); Morrison (1981); Shange (1983, 1985); Walker (1983, 1985); Washington (1974).

4   Only a very few examples can be cited to express something of the range and complexity of women's experience (Abbott, 1983; Arnow, 1972; Barrios de Chungara, 1978; Bauman, 1985; Beale, 1986; Bernstein, 1975; CCMW, 1978; Chernin, 1985; Davis, 1971(a) and (b); Fairweather *et al.*, 1984; Namias, 1978; Stephenson, 1975). *See also* Note 3 above.

5   They are referring to studies in industrialized societies. In other types of society kinship ties in relation to status and rank have been extensively studied though not from a feminist perspective.

6   The study of sex and race has a long history, but has in general been a male preserve and concentrated on aspects such as race-mixture (Hoernle, 1934),

intermarriage (Cox, 1948), and sex and racism (Hernton, 1969) which are not part of current feminist debates. However, see Walker (1985) and Wilkinson (1975) for pertinent discussions from a black feminist perspective. In Britain there is no comparable work, but see Lewis (1985) for an autobiographical account. Barrett and McIntosh (1985) comment on the currently intense debate on fostering and adoption. This is one issue among many requiring a feminist approach to the interrelations of race, gender and class.

7   Head of household was defined as the person in whose name the house or flat was held; if held jointly the person taken to be the head was the one knowing most about housing costs and payments. This definition is an improvement on most surveys which have taken a man to be head without consideration of tenancies or house ownership, but is still likely to favour a male living in the household, for instance husband or partner or even an adult son of a widowed/deserted/single woman.

References

Abbott, Shirley (1983) *Womenfolks*, New York: Ticknor and Fields

Alexander, Z. and Dewjee, A. (eds) (1984) *Wonderful Adventures of Mrs Seacole in Many Lands*, Bristol: Falling Wall Press

Allen, Sheila (1971) *New Minorities Old Conflicts*, New York: Random House

Allen, Sheila (1973) 'The Institutionalization of Racism', *Race* XV, 1

Allen, S. and Smith, C. R. (1974) 'Race and Ethnicity in Class Formation: A Comparison of Asian and West Indian Workers', in Parkin, F. (ed.) *The Social Analysis of Class Structure*, London: Tavistock

Allen, Sheila (1979) 'A Triple Burden', paper presented at the Women's Anthropology Group Seminar, The Transnational Institute, Amsterdam mimeo

Allen, Sheila (1980) 'Perhaps a Seventh Person?', *Women's Studies International Quarterly*, vol. 3, no. 4, reprinted in Charles Husband (ed.) (1982) *Race in Britain*, Hutchinson

Allen, Sheila (1982) 'Ethnic Disadvantage in Britain', *Ethnic Minorities and Community Relations*, Block 1, Unit 4, Milton Keynes: Open University Press

Allen, S. and Wolkowitz, C. (1987) *Homeworking: Myths and Realities*, Macmillan

Amos, Valerie and Parma, Pratibha (1984) 'Challenging Imperial Feminism', *Feminist Review*, no. 17, Autumn

Angelou, Maya (1978) *I know why the Caged Bird Sings; Gather Together in My Name: Singin and swingin and gettin merry like Christmas*, New York: Bantam Books

Anthias, Floya and Yuval-Davis, Nira (1983) 'Contextualising Feminism in gender, ethnic and class divisions', *Feminist Review*, no. 15

Arnow, Harriet (1972) *The Dollmaker*, New York: Avon Books

Barker, D. L. and Allen, S. (eds) (1976a) *Sexual Divisions and Society Process and Change*, London: Tavistock Publications

Barker, D. L. and Allen, S. (eds) (1976b) *Dependence and Exploitation in Work and Marriage*, London: Longman

Barrett, Michele and McIntosh, Mary (1985) 'Ethnocentrism and Socialist-Feminist Theory', *Feminist Review*, no. 20

Barrios de Chungara, Domitila (1978) *Let Me Speak*, New York: Monthly Review Press (with Moema Viezzer)

Bauman, Jane (1985) *Winter in the Morning*, London: Virago

Beale, Jenny (1986) *Women in Ireland*, London: Macmillan

Beechey, Veronica (1979) 'On patriarchy', *Feminist Review* no. 3

Ben-Tovim, G., Gabriel, J., Law, I. and Stredder, K. (1986a) 'A political analysis of local struggles for racial equality, in Rex, John and Mason, David (eds), *Theories of Race and Ethnic Relations*

Ben-Tovim, G., Gabriel, J., Law, I. and Stredder, K. (1986b) *The Local Politics of Race*, London: Macmillan

Bernstein, Hilda (1975) *For Their Triumph and Their Tears*, London: International Defence and Aid Fund

Bhavnani, Kum-Kum and Coulson, Margaret (1986) 'Transforming Socialist-Feminism: The Challenge of Racism', *Feminist Review*, no. 23

Bourne, Jenny (1983) 'Towards an anti-racist feminism', *Race and Class*, vol. XXV, no. 1

Brownmiller, Susan (1975) *Against our will: men, women and rape*, Harmondsworth: Penguin Books

Brown, Colin (1984) *Black and White in Britain, The Third PSI Survey*, London: Policy Studies Institute, Heinemann Education Books

Bryan, Beverley, Dadzie, Stella and Scafe Suzanne (1985) *The Heart of The Race*, London: Virago

Burja, Janet (1978) 'Female Solidarity and the sexual division of labour' in Caplan, Patricia and Burja, Janet (eds) *Women United, Women Divided*, London: Tavistock Publications

Carmichael, Stokely and Hamilton, Charles V. (1969) *Black Power*, Harmondsworth: Penguin Books

Chernin, Kim (1985) *In My Mother's House*, London: Virago

Churches Committee on Migrant Workers (1978) *Migrant Women Speak*, London: Search Press

Commision for Racial Equality (1985) *Immigration Control Procedures: Report of a Formal Investigation*, London: CRE

Coyle, A. (1984) *Redundant Women*, London: The Women's Press

Cox, Oliver C. (1948) *Caste Class and Race*, New York: Doubleday

Crompton, Rosemary and Mann, Michael (eds) (1986) *Gender and Stratification*, Cambridge: Polity Press

CSO (1985) *Social Trends* **16**, London: HMSO

CSO (1986) *Social Trends* **17**, London: HMSO

Davis, Angela (1971a) 'The Black Woman's Role in the Community of Slaves', *Black Scholar*, vol. III, no. 4

Davis, Angela (1971b) *If they come in the morning*, London: Orbach and Chambers

Davis, Angela (1982) *Women Race and Class*, London: The Women's Press

Delphy, Christine and Leonard, Diana (1986) 'Class Analysis, Gender Analysis and the Family', in Crompton, Rosemary and Mann, Michael (eds) *Gender and Stratifications*, Cambridge: Polity Press

Doyal, L., Gee, F., Hunt, G., Mellor J. and Pennel, I. (1980) *Migrant Workers in The National Health Service*, Department of Sociology, Polytechnic of North London, *mimeo*

Dromey, J. and Taylor, G. (1978) *Grunwick: The Workers Story*, London: Lawrence and Wishart

Edholm, Felicity, Harris, Olivia and Young, Kate (1977) 'Conceptualising Women', *Critique of Anthropology*, nos. 9 and 10

Emecheta, Buchi (1974) *Second Class Citizen*, London: Allison and Busby

Emecheta, Buchi (1972) *In the Ditch*, London: Barrie and Jenkins

Equal Opportunities Commission (1983) *Eighth Annual Report*, London: HMSO

Fairweather, Eileen, McDonough, Roisin and McFadyean, Melanie (1984) *Only The Rivers Run Free*, London: Pluto

Firestone, Shulamith (1971) *The Dialectic of Sex*, London: Jonathan Cape

Frieden, Betty (1963) *The Feminine Mystique*, New York: Dell Publishing Company

Fryer, Peter (1984) *Staying Power, The History of Black People in Britain*, London: Pluto Press

Hernton, Calvin C. (1970) *Sex and Racism*, Aylesbury: Paladin

Hoernle, R. F. (1934) 'Race Mixture and Native Policy in South Africa', in Shapera, I. (ed.) *Western Civilisation and the Natives of South Africa*, London

Hobbs, May (1973) *Born To Struggle*, London: Quartet Books

Hurstfield, J. (1986) 'Women's Unemployment in the 1930s: Some Comparisons With The 1980s' in Allen, S. *et al.* (eds) *The Experience of Unemployment*, London: Macmillan

Irvine, John, Miles, Ian and Evans, Jeff (eds) (1979) *Demystifying Social Statistics*, London: Pluto Press

James, Selma (1975) *Sex, Race and Class*, Bristol: Falling Wall Press

James, Selma (1985) (ed.) *Strangers and Sisters, Women, Race and Immigration*, Bristol: Falling Wall Press

Lal, S. and Wilson, A. (1986) *But My Cows Arent't Going to England*, Manchester: Manchester Law Centre

Leacock, Eleanor (1975) 'Sexual Stratification: A Cross Cultural View' in Rayna Reiter (ed) *Towards an Anthropology of Women*, New York: Monthly Review Press

Lees, S. (1986) 'Sex, Race and Culture', *Feminist Review*, no. 22 Spring

Lewis, Gail (1985) 'From Deepest Kilburn', in Heron, Liz (ed.), *Truth, Dare or Promise*, London: Virago

Lockwood, David (1986) 'Class, Status and Gender' in Rosemary Crompton and Michael Mann (eds), *Gender and Stratification*, Cambridge: Polity Press

188   *Placing the contemporary situation in context*

Morrison, Toni (1981) *Tar Baby*, New York: Alfred A. Knopf
Namias, June (1978) *First Generation*, Boston: Beacon Press
Millet, Kate (1971) *Sexual Politics*, London: Sphere
Pahl, R. E. (1984) *Divisions of Labour*, Oxford: Basil Blackwell
Parmar, P. (1982) 'Gender, race and class: Asian women in resistance' in Centre for Contemporary Cultural Studies, *The Empire Strikes Back*, London: Hutchinson
Rex, John and Mason, David (eds) (1986) *Theories of Race and Ethnic Relations*, Cambridge: Cambridge University Press
Rowbotham, Sheila (1972) *Women, Resistance and Revolution*, London: Allen Lane, The Penguin Press
Rowbotham, S. (1979) 'The Trouble with Patriarchy' in Rowbotham, S. (1983) *Dreams and Dilemmas*, London: Virago
Shange, Ntozake (1983) *Sassafras, Cypress and Indigo*, London: Methuen
Shange, Ntozake (1985) *Betsey Brown*, London: Methuen
Smith, D. J. (1977) *Racial Disadvantage in Britain*, The PEP Report, Penguin Books
Smith, D. J. (1981) *Unemployment and Racial Minorities*, London: Policy Studies Institute
Socialist Woman (1971) 'Militant Women Night Cleaners: women on an 80 hour week', March-April
Socialist Woman (1972) 'Cleaners Strike Again', November–December
Spare Rib (1977) 'Risking Gossip and Disgrace – Asian women strike', no. 54, January
Stephenson, Jill (1975) *Women in Nazi Society*, London: Croom Helm
The Runnymede Trust and The Radical Statistics Race Group (1980) *Britain's Black Population*, London: Heinemann
United States (1968) Commission on Civil Disorders, Washington D.C.
Visram, Rozina (1986) *Ayahs, Lascars and Princes: Indians in Britain 1700–1947*, London: Pluto Press
Walker, Alice (1983) *The Color Purple*, London: The Women's Press
Walker, Alice (1985) *In Search of Our Mothers Gardens*, London: The Women's Press
Wallman, Sandra (1976) 'Difference, differentiation, discrimination', *New Community*, **5** (1) and (3)
Washington, M. H. (ed.) (1974) *Black-Eyed Susans*, New York: Anchor Books
Wilkinson, Doris Y. (ed.) (1975) *Black Male/White Female*, Cambridge: Schenkman Publishing Co.
Zubaida, Sami (ed.) (1970) *Race and Racialism*, London: Tavistock Publications

Part Three
Personal experiences of multi-ethnic Britain

This section has one function only: to indicate that the 'race relations' literature is dominated by secondary sources. Social scientists, like myself, or media pundits have a certain licence to offer analysis which is derived from a general, if sceptical, acceptance of our expertise or professional status. Thus even when our audience think that what we have to say is rubbish, *they* have been exposed to *our* arguments; we are shaping their debate. Thus a great deal of available literature on ethnic relations contains data that have been filtered and interpreted before they are made available to the audience. The material in this section is not representative, it is not a sample. It is illustrative of raw data – which in literature are much rarer than analysis. Yet in our daily existence we are bathed in data: conversations around us, *Yesterday in Parliament* on the radio, the press and television, writing on the wall, glances, stares and body posture, the sounds and smells of ethnicity are there. A proper study of ethnic relations must be a continuous flow between such data and analysis. Ethnic relations cannot be studied as a clinical cerebral 'problem'. A comprehension of the nature of ethnicity resides as much in the heart and bowels as in the head.

Since the first edition of this book in 1982 there has been a significant expansion in the publication of literature by members of ethnic minorities in Britain which reflects aspects of their experience here, and of their history of migration and settlement. Books such as Caryl Phillips' *The Final Passage*, Faber and Faber 1985; or Amon Saba Saakana's *Blues Dance*, Karnak 1985; are illustrative of this expanding source of insight. Publishers such as Virago and The Women's Press have done much to facilitate the voice of black women's experience being heard in Britain with such books as Beverley Bryan *et al.*'s *The Heart of the Race: Black Women's Lives in Britain*, Virago 1985; and Rhonda Cobham and Merle Collins', *Watchers and Seekers*, The Women's Press 1987.

Regrettably there will be those readers who find in this considerable literary output evidence of the oppressive nature of alien cultures, or of the pathology of the black family, or of the excessive machismo of black males. Errol Lawrence in his chapter 'In the abundance of water the fool is thirsty: sociology and black pathology', has done much to expose the construction of such received wisdoms. His chapter is one of several valuable contributions in the important text produced by the Centre for Contemporary Cultural Studies, entitled *The Empire Strikes Back*, Hutchinson 1982.

In welcoming the increased availability of black literature we should not underestimate the capacity of readers from other cultures and other statuses to selectively interpret its meaning; or to elevate it to the realm of '*literature*' where it may be celebrated as art and be evacuated of any political content. A pungent statement on black arts in Britain is to be found in Kwesi Owusu's, *The Struggle for Black Arts in Britain*, Comedia 1986.

8 A West Indian/British male

Ever since I can remember, and this is going way back, early sixties, from being very small I was always aware of being dark — black — and for a 6-year-old it wasn't very pleasant being called 'darkie' and 'monkey', not just by other kids and other people, but by your brothers and sisters as well. Because if you're dark then you're stupid — a fool — and I wasn't stupid, I wasn't a fool, but I was quiet and different. I remember wanting to be white when I grew up because being black was something bad and awful and in all my dreams I was white and I'd go round in space from planet to planet in my spaceship doing good deeds and rescuing people. Then we moved to Leeds and Leeds was a big, frightening place. I can remember the journey in the back of the van — all the way from London to Leeds and I hated every single minute of it. We moved in with some cousins and they didn't like us because we spoke differently and the house was crowded and full of tension.

I remember the first day I went to school in Leeds. I don't know why — perhaps it was because I spoke differently or looked different but this white kid came up and started to pick on me. All the resentment, all the fear and frustration of coming to Leeds just came out and I found myself attacking him. I'd never done anything before like that in my life and I haven't since, but I had to be dragged away. Since then nobody ever picked on me, which was surprising because there were kids who were stronger than me who got picked on and cowed. I still wanted to be white and most of my friends were white, I suppose, and then we moved to junior school which was just across the playground. There I had to be much more aware of black kids because we all seemed to be lumped together in the same class and I suppose because we were all black we just got on — it wasn't a question of making friendships but I still went around with my white friends. I felt I didn't belong to either group — white or black, I was in a sort of limbo of my own.

My work carried me through and everybody just left me alone. Other kids asked me to help them with their homework and it was a way of getting to know them so I did it. I was held back at school because I read fast, but I took things in and knew what I was reading about. No matter what, I had to read at the same pace as everyone else and I couldn't read the books I wanted to read out of the library. The really ridiculous thing was that we had to read as a class book 'Little Black Sambo' and the teacher used to read it and we used to follow it. So I read it on my own and put it back but I had to read it again and again and again. At that point you don't really understand things like that, you just take it for granted that you have to read it and you don't take in the images. Personally I didn't take in the images at all — as far as I was concerned I wasn't black — not like Little Black Sambo, he was a savage in the jungle. I also felt different from the other black kids because I didn't want to be in trouble all the time, be in detention and be told you were stupid — it just wasn't me, so I carried on working and I got by. The weird thing was, that although I had this attitude in me that I wasn't going to be a 'blackie' no matter what, the people I used to go round with used to come out with 'nigger' jokes. It was okay because I was supposed not to mind, 'It's all right he doesn't take offence', I was part of their group so I had to accept it. I did mind, but I didn't say, because it was something apart from me, I wasn't what they were talking about — I was almost like them. It was a really strange attitude when I look back on it now — I don't understand it — but at the same time I wasn't going to conform to what other people wanted me to be. I wasn't going to be a 'happy nigger' or an athlete, or a foot-baller, I wanted to be something that everyone else was — everyone white that is. As far as I could see there were no black guys doing 'A' levels and writing essays, they were all playing football — and I wanted to be somebody.

I worked continuously for three years, I really threw myself into it. There were still the same conflicts in my mind about my identity but they were secondary to working and proving to everybody and myself that I was worth something. I was coming top in a lot of subjects — really pushing myself, until it came to the fourth year when you choose your examination subjects for your career. I chose all the things I wanted to do — arts subjects — but I wasn't allowed to do half of them because of 'clashes' in the timetable — English Literature was my best subject. I ended up with a lot of subjects I didn't want and I was bored out of my skull — I worked at English and Art but after the first year I went 'off' and didn't work at all — couldn't be bothered any more. After all my hard work, it hadn't got me anywhere, so I switched off during lessons. But I managed to get a few reasonable grades and it was during this time I started to question my sexual identity. I was quiet and didn't go out with girls — I wasn't a batty man or bum feeler — I just didn't know. There was nobody I was close to and felt I wanted to be close to. In the fifth year I did my 'A' levels — English and Art — I dropped History because I was so apathetic by this time I couldn't get it together. My art was really freaky and I was becoming more and more and more depressed. I started to go for long walks to question my existence — I wasn't reading — I couldn't concentrate. I threw myself into my art which was disturbing and neurotic. I went to the doctor and he gave me some anti-depressants and tranquillizers. I took them for a while but they didn't make any difference so I stopped taking them. I couldn't get up in the morning as I couldn't sleep and I wandered about the streets — I once found myself at the station with £60 in my pocket and not remembering how I got there. I became worse – more schizophrenic and one day I went home from school and took an overdose. It didn't work – I woke up next day but I tried again, still without success. I wanted to kill myself because I felt I was bad and worthless – me, the dark, black evil monster from the dark dank pit. It was the beginning of a gradual breakdown.

I left school without having sorted out anything and went to Art College. It was then that I met Patti my girlfriend – she helped me a lot and we talked – I could talk to her, it just flowed. She wanted to know about me – she didn't want any of the silly personas I adopted – she wanted to know the me that was underneath, the person, not the façade. Using her as a sounding board I found out a lot about myself and I changed. I was beginning to realize what I was and who I was and where I belonged and at least I had some sense of identity, some sense of purpose, some sense of belonging. In working that out I still couldn't cope at college and develop my potential, although I completed the course. I should have gone on to do my BA but I couldn't cope with it, so I took a part-time job in a hotel. I left home, but I still felt bad and I cried a lot, something I hadn't been able to do before I met her. We went to our doctor and he gave me some psychotherapy but it didn't really help and I was admitted to hospital. I was questioning things but still didn't have any answers and being in hospital was horrible. There were two other black guys in there – one old one and a young manic one who was drugged up all of the time. It just made me worse being there and I realized I would have to work it out for myself. The environment only aggravated my state of mind, I felt I really would go mad if I stayed there. I saw a psychotherapist when I came out and she thought if I went out and had a good time it would solve my problems.

Racism doesn't exactly help you feel secure as a person. I've been followed by the police and I don't look your sort of heavy dread guy. I've had the police follow me in a car all the way up Roundhay Road at ten o'clock at night, just cruising by the side of me not saying a word. It was really eerie and I just carried on walking, because I knew that if I stopped or jumped over a wall or something they'd have got me and there'd have been no witnesses. And I've had people in the middle of town trying to run me over and other people don't believe it. Patti and I have suffered abuse from people – it happens all the time and when we tell people they're so amazed. Drivers have made U-turns to come back at me, shouting 'you wog, you bastard, you nigger' and people just walk on – I just walk on, I mean I'm so hardened to it now. I've been attacked in Safeways in Headingley and nobody did a thing – and that was when I was out with one of the children from the home where I work. You can't go into a shop without being the focus of attention because people expect you to steal something. If you go into a restaurant for a meal then you are shunted off into a corner where you won't offend the other all-white clientele.

Being a mixed couple we tend to move in racially mixed circles when we can, except where we have to move in all-white ones because of work or other reasons. This means that for a lot of the time we are with a lot of white people and we stand out. We have to fight continuously against people's stereotyped ideas about us as a racially mixed couple. When you are out you are always aware of people because they are always aware of you. They are always staring and making comments and you learn to sum people up in one go, because you have to for your own survival otherwise you could be walking straight into trouble. You learn to read body language — you immediately know if someone is being friendly or not, then you have to decide how to deal with it.

A lot of people have stereotyped attitudes about mixed couples — black as well as white. Older black women can't understand why Patti should go around with someone like me who is very dark and classed as a 'yout' and 'the yout them a' shifty an' lazy, no good'. Older black men secretly think it's all right because a lot of them go off with white women — often prostitutes. When they know that Patti is a teacher then they feel confused about this as well. Younger generation blacks who don't know us would feel that it was a promotion of the sexual stereotype — perhaps some of those who do know us as well — but most of them accept us for what we are. The same with our white friends, but for the majority of white people who see us in the streets, we just fulfil their idea of the sexual stereotype — white girls who go with black men must be of 'loose morals', just looking for sexual excitement.

I'm a lot more secure now in my black identity than I ever have been, but it took a long time getting there, through a lot of stages. I didn't go through what some would term the 'ethnic road' of, say, youth cult groups, For white kids there's always been teds, skins, mods, rockers, punks, but for black kids there's never been anything they could really identify with, that was really culturally theirs, until Rasta came along. Like, it was embarrassing to be black — for me anyway — I didn't even speak patois, I didn't want to sound like an ignorant 'wog'. It was easier to get along without any hassle by conforming to a stereotype because you were being what people expected of you, whereas it was harder and more threatening if you were something that was close to them. If you acted like the jolly buffoon or the thicko who was good at sports you were then conforming to all the stereotyped attitudes that are around, of black people being musical, good dancers etc., but not very intelligent. If you wear a woolly hat and spend your time building a sound system then you also conform to the stereotype, but if you aspire to be something else — a substitute white, an imitation white as they see it, wanting to study and do well, then you are threatening because you have the ability to take people's jobs away and be in a position of telling other people — especially white people — what to do. But in doing that you don't feel comfortable on either side of the fence because you're not black and you're not white.

A lot of people say that black people who get into the 'system' and do well are wearing a white mask, but this is just untrue. The mask is imposed by whites to make you acceptable — an honorary white, but the truth is you adapt to different situations like anyone else. I don't wear a mask. I am me, and all the ways I react in different situations are part of me, not something I assume. Black people tend to be more accepting than white people and Patti often feels a lot easier in all-black gatherings than I do in all-white ones. White people often forget that black people have to face this every day of their lives, yet if the situation was reversed they would feel a lot less confident. A white friend of mine is a good example of this — he says he feels uncomfortable if there are a lot of black people and he is the only white, yet he never expects me to mind being in all-white situations.

I've decided to become part of the 'system' to a certain extent, but in doing that I've decided I'm not going to change into being something that people will find acceptable. I'm not going to get rid of parts of myself — the black parts — that they might find threatening. I now feel comfortable speaking patois when I want to and I can switch it on and off when I like — I can see it as something good and it just flows, but it took a lot to be able to see it like that.

Most of the things I've been talking about are psychological — how people see themselves and how they see other people. Black people in Britain in my opinion are still slaves, but the chains are not on their bodies but on their minds and black kids especially need someone to help them break out of these chains, because otherwise they've got no future, they've got nothing. They've got to learn, but more important, white people have got to learn to accept them for themselves, then perhaps we can learn to accept each other.

9 A professional black West Indian/British male

The phone rings. I answer it in my usual confident manner before three European gentlemen are ushered into my office. They are brought in by my secretary. It is very strange that here am I, a black West Indian, speaking about my office and my secretary in this predominantly white society. By all accounts they are all symbols of status and reflect to some degree that I, a black man, have made it in white society. The discussion which followed is centred on a variety of things where, in today's jargon, the black expert is sought to give his advice. Invariably it is the media and they are seeking explanations as to the 'problems' which blacks are 'creating' in this society. The conversation highlights how little white society is aware of the presence of its black members. I remind my visitors that blacks have been in Britain for almost 400 years and, indeed, in sizeable quantities. A recent booklet suggested to me that in 1774 the black population in London was almost 20,000. Although the numbers of blacks have increased, the attitudes of a predominant white society have not changed since those distant days of slave ships and masters.

By all accounts, my present position would indicate a degree of success in a white man's world. I had the privilege, or more correctly, the right to attend decent schools and colleges and by many whites' standards I must be remarkable in that of the limited blacks at universities, I am currently doing post-graduate work at a second university. The passage between stepping off at Southampton into a grey, dismal-looking English south coast and now sitting in a centrally heated, beautifully furnished, artistically decorated office surrounded by symbols of the black man's world, possibly reflects to many an observer, both black and white – success. The mental torture, the psychic scars are not visible and the sleepless nights and crying days of the white man's pressure seems like a distant dream. The trappings of modern society are only symbols. The torture and pain that white society inflicts upon its black individuals can never be compensated for, in spite of those few black faces one tends to see in so-called positions of authority. White society has little room for black faces and Ellison's *The Invisible Man* and Fanon's *Black Skin, White Mask* epitomizes the frustrations and dilemma of individuals like myself.

Professional blacks are treated as rare specimens by most of their white colleagues. I am no exception. Generally speaking, racist humour is used to make simple conversation and reactions to these generally leaves us, the black individuals, feeling guilty that we have challenged them. It is a continuous process that those blacks like myself, who have moved up (in a manner of speaking) in society, have very often to contend with the labels that not only do we carry 'chips on our shoulders', but we are over-sensitive to racial issues. No one cares if after a hard day's graft the extent of my social pleasures are limited simply because blacks are not allowed; no one cares if I am a professional when I go to the shops and a white employee has no desire to serve me; no one cares if as a black professional, I wish to buy a house in a particular area of the city, when the estate agents would suggest alternatives; and no one cares when as a black professional I question the educational output that is being given to my children and to many of the young people I work with. To white society all that is irrelevant for if I have made it then everyone else can. It confirms their belief that racism is a figment of our imagination and that the benevolence of white society, indeed of British society, is so bountiful that no one should feel they are disadvantaged. To most professional colleagues, the question of colour and discrimination is a theoretical base and is expressed in the fact that society is constructed in a number of classes. It is very difficult for them to imagine that my colour and those of many black, capable individuals, is used as a weapon against us. The fact that we communicate in a common language and that we share loves for the theatre and for other middle-class orientated values, automatically gives them every right to eliminate colour in any discussion. As far as they are concerned all men are equal and so I am continuously reminded that the Bible has said this time and time again.

Today's Britain is a variety of colour and culture. These only reflect customs, rituals and skin colour and there is no resemblance to the harsh treatment that white society metes out to us. As a young boy studying in the West Indies, I recall the words of an English poet whose name escapes me:

Oh England is a pleasant place
For them that is rich and high
But England is a cruel place
For such poor folks as I.

Making it in white Britain is simply a dream for many whites let alone blacks. My colour, my cultural norms and *me* — a person — will always be viewed through white-coloured lenses with all its distortions. To those blacks who would say that they have made it, it must be at a tremendous personal sacrifice and at the end, from my own development, it really is not worth it.

My colleagues leave my office after sipping cups of tea. They are greatly impressed about both my position and knowledge and this is said quite openly. I get a sneaking impression that they are mildly shocked by my performance. This happens almost every day and thus like me, many blacks are contained in a society which sees and hears only what it wants and when it wants. I use the phone to call my secretary and life continues in the same old way.

10 A young Pakistani/British female

I was 11. Ammi-jan had told me that abba-jan didn't want me to go to Filey
on the day trip with the school. I didn't ask for an explanation, I knew it was
because I was getting older and on my way to growing up. I told the teacher
and she was surprised as I'd always gone along in previous years. I didn't explain
why. But then she didn't ask either. Maybe I couldn't have put it into words
anyway.

On the day, after the attendance call, the rest of the children got ready to go
to the coach. I came home. I understood why, ammi-jan and abba-jan weren't
being nasty. It was just the way things had to be. I reached home and began
tidying my bedroom as I did at the weekend when there was no school and
then I cried into the pillow. I had wanted to go. I didn't want to be at home
today. I didn't complain to ammi-jan, I didn't let her hear me crying. What was
there to complain about anyway? It wasn't my parents' fault. But it wasn't my
fault either that I wanted to go. Two different worlds — home and school.

When did I become aware of the two different cultures? Well, I can remember
in Lahore very vividly, when we were preparing to join my father in England.
Mother had scolded me as I was irritating her and in her way. I'd sulked and
thought, ammi-jan won't shout at me when I'm in England, they don't allow
that sort of thing there. Heaven knows where I had picked that idea up from. I
was 7 at the time. The whole atmosphere whilst packing and getting ready for
the journey was one of excitement and looking forward to something new
and different. My aunts and cousins told me we would now be leaving them and
go to live with abba-jan and uncle, who were already there. My father had left
to come to England six years previously to work. He was now settled enough for
us to join him. I looked forward to that very much.

We arrived by plane at Manchester in September 1961, and drove to Sheffield;
abba-jan was with us. We were all together, my parents, my brother and myself.
The Manchester streets were long and wide, with tall, dark buildings, the windows
looking like white rectangular eyes. The buildings, the roads appeared never-
ending. The dark buildings were large and imposing.

We arrived in Sheffield and our favourite uncle was waiting for us. All was
happiness. The sun was shining. My brother and I ran towards our uncle and held

his legs in sheer delight. My father had bought a large terrace house in which my uncle and three other male cousins were living too. They'd prepared a meal for us. It was like coming into another large family, only with different faces, minus any other females.

On waking the next morning, our uncle came into our room and taught us how to say 'Good morning'. We went to surprise our parents with the new words we'd learned, the process of integration had begun.

I can't remember feeling lonely in the early days. My cousins and uncle, all in their early 20s, used to take us to the park, into the town centre and generally gave us a lot of attention. On walking through the town centre I can remember exclaiming in awe on seeing a Negress and Sikh men with turbans on. I realized that Sikhs did not have horns sticking out of their turbans, a misconception I had developed in my own mind due to the fact that 'Singh', the surname of all Sikh men, means the word 'horn' in Punjabi.

A couple of months later, my cousins moved from our house, leaving us now as a nuclear family plus my uncle, who was my father's younger brother. We now started to make friends with other children on the street, some of whom were Polish, Italian, Ukrainian, Indian and Bangladeshi, plus one other Pakistani family. The family next door were Italian. They became a great source of friendship not only as friends for myself and my brother, but also for my mother. Ammi-jan began to form her own friendship with the mother who had a warm personality and was very hardworking, spending most of her spare time after work keeping her house clean and looking after her children. Both my mother and Maria were good cooks and would send each other any special dishes they had made. When Maria gave birth to another child she would leave the baby with my mother when she went to work. He still has a great liking for 'Mama's chapattis'.

We had arrived in England in the month of May and didn't begin school until the following September. During the months we were at home my brother and I were taught English by a Pakistani teacher, a friend of my father's who abba-jan had asked to come in a few times a week. We practised our English with the other children on the street, though our first attempts must have been trying for them. Each time they had said, 'Hello', we would reply with, 'Hello' followed by, 'I cannot speak English'. However, communication did get better with time.

On starting school we were put into the 'immigrant' class at school, along with other Asian children for the first year. We had special reading sessions with the headmaster a few times a week, for which the group was termed 'backward readers'. A few years later I can remember feeling resentment at having been called a 'backward reader'. The word has now been replaced by the word 'remedial' — a sign of changing times.

The time at primary school (up to 11 years) I can remember as one of happiness overall. As I mentioned earlier there was always a subconscious awareness of the two cultures. There were reasons for my happiness. My parents were very loving and attentive. I can remember feeling very proud when the teachers praised my father for taking so much care over our education. He would come in and talk to the teachers, more so than English parents, about our progress at school.

However, there was one aspect of school which abba-jan didn't give as much attention to — that was the social aspect. I was excluded from swimming classes and doing country dancing. The headmaster objected to this. He seemed to take on the matter as a personal battle between abba-jan and himself, using me as a go-between. Abba-jan seemed unaware of this. One particular incident comes to mind. The class had sessions of country dancing. The headmaster came up to me and said, 'Does your father know you have country dancing at school, and would he allow it?' I replied that I didn't know. He added that I must ask him and let him know abba-jan's decision tomorrow. Being aware of the negative connotations that 'dancing' has in a respectable family in Pakistan, I approached abba-jan very warily, saying, 'Are we allowed to dance?' — not explaining what type of dance I meant. He answered, 'No' without realizing, I think, that I was referring to a very innocent form of country dance in a school situation. I told the headmaster of the 'decision' and from then on I sat at the side during those classes.

There were a number of things that caused me anxiety at school which I never mentioned to my parents. There were also a number of happy events I wanted to, but was reluctant, to share. I had won the long jump at an area sports day at school which meant going on to the large stadium in my home town to take part in the inter-schools sports events. I had to have my legs uncovered and would be wearing shorts. So I took part in the event, without telling my parents, feeling inside that I was doing wrong by uncovering my legs in front of so many people. I wanted my parents to be proud of me, but asking them and getting a refusal was too big a risk to take. I can also remember that when the event was taking place at school I knew abba-jan would be coming into school for some reason. I was very anxious that he shouldn't see me in shorts and was looking out for him so that I could avoid him.

In retrospect I feel that much of my anxiety during those childhood years must have been unfounded. My parents had bought me the sports wear and therefore knew I was wearing them, so why the guilt feelings on my part? All I can say now is that at that young age I must have picked up the general social values expressed at home and applied them to myself and the school situation. I do not blame my parents as being the cause of my anxiety. I didn't commun- icate what I felt was wrong to them, so how were they to know? Because they were so loving and caring with regard to everything else, I didn't feel they were being nasty. It must have been that security at home which helped me to cope with any contradictions which arose because of cultural differences. So, there- fore, I remember my childhood as basically happily dotted here and there with a little confusion. But it must be like that for most children, Asian or not, to a greater or lesser degree.

The contradictions and conflicts over the years did increase. The adolescent years were filled with moments of having to sit back and analyse my situation *vis-à-vis* my family, my religion and the social mores of the wider society and what I would do. Now, being 23, having been through university, and being in full-time employment, away from home I feel thankful that I was exposed to two cultures at the same time. It has been a painful path to tread, at times, but it has resulted in a keen awareness and respect for the differences and more important, the similarities, between human beings regardless of colour, race or religion. I feel a special bond of love and respect for my parents who despite not understanding me during my adolescent years especially, gave me examples of human strength, love and tolerance. It can't have been an easy time for them. I was experiencing the conflict, they were watching it, not always understanding it, often not being able to help even when they wanted to.

11 A young Gujerati/British male

Ever since I came to Britain in 1964, I've always played with and have had more white friends than black. At that time (early junior school level) colour, race, prejudice, etc., were terms and experiences one was oblivious of, or were incomprehensible and thus were regarded as unimportant. In my naïveté I rationalized them by saying 'he's not a good friend', or 'he's different' etc.

My parents have never stopped me from bringing my white friends from school when I was young. In fact, they actively encouraged me in the belief that my integration with them would make it easier for me to understand the strange ways of their world and thus succeed in their society. Thus, my parents were aware of the gulf and divisions which existed with them being black, but they did not prevent me from mixing with them, because it was a crucial channel if I was to succeed. As far as I was concerned, at that time, there were no differences in colour, the visual difference to me was that they were just richer and better off materially than we were. If we were to achieve that standard, we would have to adopt their way of life, values, attitudes, etc.

Being about 5 years old when I came to England, I had few memories of India — I had not formed my Indian identity yet. Having emigrated to England, I was to form two identities alongside each other: that which my family and community socialized me into, and that which the white society wanted.

My first real encounters of racial violence was when I moved into secondary school. Gangs of white youths used to go around 'Paki-bashing'. Only when this persisted did Indians form gangs and retaliated. However, by now I had some idea of the British class structure and knew that these 'troublemakers' were from the lowest rungs. I was convinced and knew that the 'others' were not like them. Though objectively I was from the same class as they were, I differentiated myself from them and identified myself with those above me. I aspired to their good, commonsense way of life, values, attitudes, etc.

By now, I was about 15 years old and was becoming well integrated into the white culture. It was about at this age that I realized that I was leading two lives, that of an Indian at home, and the black man with a white mask outside. I realized that I was experiencing culture conflict and had difficulty in identifying with either and coming to a compromise. I now realize that in the few years before the age of 15, when I thought that I was going through the normal phase of being a rebellious teenager, that they were really acts which really manifested the internal cultural and identity crises that I was going through.

Difficulties arose when for example the norm in the white society was in the belief of 'individualism'. Youths were expected to drink, smoke, have girl-friends, etc. This was not the case in the Indian culture. The family was a tightly knit and integrated unit with the Indian community. The belief was that of 'collectivism'; life was with the people.

This presented real problems to me because on the one hand, I was expected to conform with my white friends and their culture, and on the other hand, with my family and the Indian community culture. In my confusion and torment I started questioning the medieval nature of the Indian culture, slowly coming to reject it, rationalizing it by saying that if I was to succeed in a white man's world I would have to totally behave like one etc.

Everything that I did, e.g. speaking, I would think in English and behave according to the ideology of the 'proper' English person. Even when speaking to my parents, I would hesitate and have to stop and think to interpretate meanings etc. My whole life was revolving about notions and thoughts of Western ideology, etc.

There were frequent periods of confrontation with my family when it became apparent to them, from my behaviour, that I was slipping away from them, rejecting the Indian culture and becoming totally immersed in the white culture. These confrontations often served to bring me in a state of equilibrium. From there, I would then again try the futile pursuit of trying to find a compromise between the two cultures, for this seemed the only logical way ahead. It seemed to me that my parents wanted me to succeed in the white society, yet retain my identity as an Indian; and the white society was making demands upon me to fully incorporate myself into their culture and only then would I be accepted. In a sense, they were ready and waiting with their arms to embrace me.

It was when I started to date white girls and generally go out with them that I realized that this was not so. The malicious and contemptuous looks and abuse that were received made me realize that though I wanted to be fully integrated into the white society, the white society would only let me at a superficial level. Thus, underneath the surface the divisions were to be maintained and reinforced. The purity of the Indian culture and race was insisted upon by my parents. Whereas before I felt that this was not the case for the white man, (for he could 'understand' the culture conflict and be more 'liberal' minded), I was to change my mind. Any notion that I had of being fully integrated, finding a compromise, or marrying a white girl in society, had to be rejected. I was in a situation where, should I marry a white girl, I would be excommunicated from my Indian community and be virtually in the same situation with the white society. Thus, the cost outweighs the benefits.

The emphasis which Indian parents place on educating their children, which is in accordance with white middle-class values, no doubt helps boost the child initially as he rises up the ladder. However, the wheel seems to slow down and come to halt once he reaches a certain level. He then has to decide ultimately where his true identity lies.

Being a member of the younger generation, it is we that have to bear the brunt of this identity and cultural conflict that exists and come to terms with it. To some extent I'm fortunate in that I can understand the social change etc. and have come to terms with it, but there are, no doubt, thousands of unfortunate people who are disillusioned etc. I am also fortunate in that I'm 'cushioned' from the realities of life by being a student, for the realities of racial discrimination are manifested in the work situation. This was something I experienced a couple of years ago when working in a factory for the summer. The white workers were subtle in their exploitation and discrimination of the black person.

So I set out positively to form a white identity. This resulted in a conflict and a period where I was in search for a compromise. This leaves one in a precarious and difficult situation. This leaves the vast majority of Indians, (including myself), being forced to go back and identify with their Indian culture. For I am in a situation where I cannot integrate fully into the white society and, not wanting to be rejected by both, opt for the safest and surest way by identifying with my Indian culture more.

Perhaps the majority of my generation will take this route, because to some extent we are still able to identify with the poor social and economic conditions with which they started when arriving as immigrants. So, we also suffer from a guilt complex in that we feel our parents have given their lives and suffered so that we would be better off, and yet here we are repaying them by denouncing everything they believe in and have worked for. Their blood, sweat and tears have been worthless.

However, the children of my generation will hopefully not suffer too much from the cultural and identity crises. At least my generation will have a better understanding of the acculturation processes that their children will be going through and the crisis that will confront them. Thus I hope the assimilation processes will be a little easier for them for the pressure from Indian parents will ease a little. But I doubt very much if the same will happen with regards to the white man's view on integration.

12 Extracts from *File on 4*

In which Janet Cohen interviewed residents of the East End of London*

Cohen: The older members of the Asian community are, by repute, peaceful and law-abiding. but a growing number now say moderation has failed. H. D. is a chemistry teacher and now he's trying to unite the various Asian groups to organize, and think about defence. He himself has been the victim of a white attack.

H. D. :   I was travelling in the tube and when I came out of Upton Park Station there was a group of five or six youths standing over there. One of them shouted a racist abuse at me; I looked back and the other one attacked me from the back and I fell on the footpath and they kicked me, they punched me. Fortunately there were some other people coming the other way, so when they saw them they just ran away.

Cohen: How badly hurt were you?

H. D. :   It wasn't bad, but the shock was very, very severe to me and it is still in my memory and it has affected my way of life. Nowadays, I never go out on my own in the evening, and I advise all my friends and their children not to go out on their own. In the last year it has been really very bad : these attacks are ever-increasing and they have created a sense of fear in the community. Traditionally, we have been depending upon the police and the authorities for our protection, we still believe that they have got a role to play but increasingly our youngsters feel that it's useless to go to them because they have proved ineffective, and even if you go to them they say there's no racial element in this attack; it's a violent society and attacks happen; there's no racist element at all, and our youngsters are feeling very restless and they talk about forming groups and they try to give some sort of assurance with their number and all that, that's happening.

* This is material extracted from *File on 4* first transmitted on BBC radio on 25 February 1981.

Cohen: Teachers too complain of growing racial hostility in the classrooms. J., a teacher, who is considering joining a vigilante group, says he faces a daily tide of abuse from his pupils.

J. :   Oh, it affects me all the time.

Cohen: How?

J. :   Because they call me, you know, 'Paki' and 'Paki out', and they scrawl on the door of my teaching room. I mean, I've been in the school for seven years but now things are deteriorating. They may say, well, we're doing it for a laugh or something like that, but then they are influenced by the older people you see, because in that area where I live there are, you know, lots of demonstrations organized by the British Movement.

Cohen: You know it's the British Movement, do you?

J. :   They write on my blackboard, they write BM, and then they have these Nazi signs you know under their lapel and they show it to me and they ask me to read their leaflets, they carry them around. Oh, yes, I know — the leaflets from these various movements, the New National Front, the National Front, the British Movement, kids now start saying to me, oh, you have taken our job; suddenly they have found that I have taken their job, so why don't I go back, you Paki, you see, they shout.

Cohen: Many black families don't even feel safe at home; in the heart of the East End one family claims their house has been attacked thirty-five times. White gangs, they say, have aimed bricks, bottles and air-gun pellets through their front windows. The glass is now protected by two layers of metal grilles, sheets of plywood, and then shutters. The police have advised the three adults and ten children to move into the two back rooms of the house. But the attacks continue and they aren't limited to the home. This man, who's too frightened to broadcast his name, fears for his and his brother's children; all of them have been threatened and assaulted on the streets.

Man under attack: Sometimes by, with stick, a stick, sometimes a stone.

Cohen: So they're beaten or hit with stones.

Man: Yeh, yeh, so we don't give my child out of our sight, because we are very afraid.

Cohen: Do you find they are fearful, the children, when they're at home?

Man's brother: Yes, sometimes, night time, my children is crying from their sleep, so I ask them what happened. They say, somebody broke our house, the windows; maybe it is skinhead or something. I say, no, no, no, you are sleeping and I am looking after you. Even day time, if I say, oh, my little boy or girl you open the door, somebody knocks at the door, they say no, no, no, no, no. I say, why? They say if I open the door, somebody kill us, is maybe short-haired boys kill us. I say no, no, they are your friends, like that; I just exampled them you know, becuase they are very afraid. They are, night time, they are crying, so must we tell this Parliament, or Margaret Thatcher, please you help us, because we are very afraid.

Cohen: Racial tension is no stranger to the East End of London. Traditionally, it's played host to generations of immigrants, with an uneasy mixture of hospitality and hostility. The mosque in Brick Lane, East One, came to the Muslims third-hand. First it was a Huguenot church and then a synagogue. When in the thirties the British Union of Fascists held rallies here, they found support as well as opposition. Today's violence takes place against a background of rising unemployment. In some boroughs, one person in seven is out of a job. A report published today claims that blacks are more likely than whites to lose their jobs in the economic recession, but skinheads on the streets don't see it this way. Their heads shaved, their trousers cropped six inches above the ankle, their faces pinched in the cold, they feel the blacks are stealing their jobs. As for violence against the ethnic communities:

1st skinhead: Do I condone it? Yes. They've got not right to be here.

Cohen: That families should have bricks thrown through the window, airgun pellets, that kind of thing?

1st skinhead: Well, only blacks like, and Jews, yeh. White European race, right, is the superior race and always will be.

Cohen: Is it really fair that families should be intimidated, after all, they are people?

1st skinhead: Yes, course it is. They're not people, they're parasites, they're just poncing off us.

2nd skinhead: I've just come out of prison myself, if I may say so, I just come out after doing fifteen months.

Cohen: For doing what?

2nd skinhead: Smashing a Pakistani up. I just stabbed him.

Cohen: Really?

2nd skinhead: In a pub.

Cohen: Why?

2nd skinhead: I don't know. I was just drunk and I just stabbed him through the back.

3rd skinhead: The fact is, right, ordinary people don't like 'em moving in round the East London environment round there, right, and they want 'em out.

Cohen: But is it fair to attack these families?

All skinheads: Yes, it is.

3rd skinhead: It's the only way isn't it, I mean the Government ain't doing nothing are they, nobody's doing anything, are they?

1st skinhead: It takes ten years for a bill to get through Parliament, right, and nothing happens, right, so if you give them like a good dig and all that like, it might just send a couple of them home; you know what I mean. They might think, oh, you know like, we've had enough like, we're going to get home. So we're doing our little bit.

Cohen: What's your badge, by the way?

3rd skinhead: Can't you see? (Laughter)

Cohen: I don't know what it is.

3rd skinhead: SS. Yeh. Nazi badge.

1st skinhead: Nazi sympathizer.

Cohen: What does that stand for?

3rd skinhead: That means that I like what the Nazis did.

4th skinhead: We're proud to be Nazis. We're not no party or nothing. I'm proud to be a Nazi.

3rd skinhead: We're just kids off the street, you know what I mean.

4th skinhead: We believe that the blacks are taking over our country, the Yids are taking over our country.

Cohen.   So how much violence do you think there is around here, then, towards . . .

All skinheads: There's a lot more, there's a lot more, there should be a lot anyway. There is, there is a lot going around.

Cohen: It's gangs of youths like those who are blamed for the growing number of racial assaults, but where in some boroughs immigrants make up 14 per cent of the population, members of the older generation too say they understand the powerful feelings of the young, even if they don't support violence.

1st man: Well, it's out of order, isn't it? Everyone's entitled to live, you know, you know, there's a little bit of racial in everyone, but there you go. Especially if we're sort of, we're inundated with them, ain't we, it's getting overcrowded. I mean you've got to admit, even the housing problem's enough, isn't it?

2nd man: I think, quite honestly, the economic situation today forces them into this: you get kids who are left on the streets, they haven't got any work or anything like that, they've got to take their anger out on somebody, so they take it out on the unknown. It'll certainly take years before we sort the problem out, we'll probably have to go through the sort of problems that America has suffered before we can really sort it out.

3rd man: One of them got done up in East Ham, right, they wanted to hold demos and all that lot, like. What about when people get mugged out in the street? There's no demos in East Ham for all that is there? They say the police ain't looking into all their racial things and all that; well why?

Part Four
Social identity and social structure

This section is not proposing that the analysis of 'race' and ethnic relations can ultimately be reduced to underlying psychological processes. On the contrary, its purpose is to stress the necessity of remaining sensitive to the interaction of psychological and sociological variables. Saifullah Khan challenges the dangerous simplicity of race-thinking by identifying the complex dynamics of ethnic identity and minority cultures. And echoing Bourne's (1980) attack on those who reify ethnicity as some autonomous magic property of minorities, Saifullah Khan emphasizes that ethnicity is an inter-group phenomenon which should not be abstracted from its social and economic context. From a different perspective Tajfel makes the same point. Whilst specifically identifying cognitive processes which structure the psychological realization of identity, he takes pains to indicate that the significance of such processes can only be assessed in relation to a comprehension of the specific context within which they exist. Much of the minority literature which was referred to in the introduction to the previous section addresses questions of personal identity in the context of contested ethnic, class and gender based group interests. Tajfel's chapter reminds us that there is a level of analysis which deals with psychological processes which we must attempt to incorporate into any adequate understanding of ethnicity and racism. However, in asserting this we must equally avoid the danger of psychological reductionism; of explaining social phenomena in psychological terms. Psychological processes must not be reified as being independent of the material conditions which shaped them. Michael Billig's text, *Social Psychology and Intergroup Relations* (Academic Press 1976), remains as one of the best critiques of psychologizing 'prejudice' and intergroup hostility. Equally rewarding are his *Ideology and Social Psychology*, Basil Blackwell 1982; and Julian Henriques *et al.*, *Changing the Subject*, Methuen 1984.

Troyna's chapter in describing the way in which the mass media in Britain have reported racism illustrates how 'consensus politics' has been sustained through the construction of a news framework in which attention on 'extremists' leaves the racism of the majority middle ground unexplored. His chapter provides insight into the reproduction of national values, and the construction of popular political agendas which fits well with the final chapter in this section. Miles further develops the exploration of the intermeshing of ideologies of racism and of nationalism. In the era of British politics that has come to be labelled as

Thatcherism there has been a significant exploitation and reconstruction of nationalist ideologies which makes Miles' contribution highly relevant. The links between the nationalist philosophies of the 'New Right' and the development of 'the New Racism' have been explored in a number of texts, including: Martin Barker, *The New Racism*, Junction Books 1981; Ruth Levitas, *The Ideology of the New Right*, Polity Press 1986; Paul Gordon and Franscesca Klug, *New Right New Racism*, Searchlight Publications 1986; and Paul Gilroy, *There Ain't No Black in the Union Jack*, Hutchinson 1987.

The continuing significance of the mass media in reflecting and reproducing these ideologies is touched upon in the above texts, and is also examined in: Horace Joshua *et al.*, *To Ride The Storm: The 1980 Bristol 'Riots' and the State*, Heinemann 1983; Muhammad Anwar and Anthony Shang, *Television in a Multi-Racial Society*, Commission for Racial Equality 1982; Phil Cohen and Carl Gardner, *It Ain't Half Racist Mum*, Comedia 1982; and in James Curran *et al.*, *Bending Reality*, Pluto Press 1986.

13 The role of the culture of dominance in structuring the experience of ethnic minorities

Verity Saifullah Khan

The study of ethnic relations in England is the study of a continuing inter-action between the dominant ethnic majority and the subordinate ethnic mino-rities. The culture and structures of the majority as well as those of the minorities are part of the analysis. This paper argues that there has been a notable lack of attention paid to the 'culture' of the majority ethnic system and to the ongoing relationship between it and ethnic minorities which are both integral parts of British society.

This relationship between dominant and subordinate ethnic groups is a relationship of power which is manifest in and maintained by the economic and social order. Much of the academic work on ethnic relations in England has reinforced the popular notion that it is the minorities that have 'culture' and this becomes equated with the 'problems' of ethnic relations.[1] There is little recognition of the power of the dominant 'culture' and its symbolic strategies and institutions. The language of the debate itself often reflects and reinforces the values and categories which are important features of the dominant ethnicity (Saifullah Khan, 1981a).

This paper presents a framework for the study of ethnic relations which acknowledges the power of the dominant culture in determining the future of ethnic minorities and it also emphasizes the structural determinants of the process of identity development. It starts from the assumption that 'power relations and symbolism are present in all social relations' (Cohen, 1979). Too little attention has been paid to the power of the culture of dominance in structuring the position of ethnic minorities, and too little attention has been paid to the impact of the collective action and reaction of ethnic minorities on the process of English ethnicity.[2] This framework will be developed in relation to a discussion of South Asian migration into Britain.

The dynamics of culture and ethnicity

As culture means so many different things to many (wo)men, there is a temp-tation to dispense with the notion completely (Williams, 1976; Hall, 1976). Here it will be used to refer to the system of shared meanings developed in a social and economic context which has a particular historical and political background.

Culture only has reality within the social context from which it is derived and which it helps to structure. While the nature of individual interaction and the formation of social groupings are determined by their economic base, the meanings men and women give to them depend upon, and are likely to reinforce, the social order.

A large percentage of the South Asian migrants who are the subject of this paper come from rural agricultural backgrounds which, until recent decades, have manifest a relative 'closed' system of socio-economic relations. In many such societies there is no clear distinction between the religious and the secular and between domestic 'non-productive' labour and wage-labour. In such a system, social identities are ascribed and the sense of self is strongly bound with the collective identity of the primary group of the family and kin. There is a strong sense of belonging and a security reinforced by the lack of perceived alternatives and actual options. In such a system linguistic, religious, class and caste identities are all part of sub-ethnic affiliation which is associated with a particular region of origin. The integrated nature of the cultural and the economic order provides resistance to change and strong psychological support.

When the economic base is changed or the conceptual system is undermined through alternative forms of socialization, it provides a fundamental threat to the traditional system of economic relations. The social change of urban centres in South Asia provides an example of this radical cultural change. The developing urban economy alters the composition of primary groups even when fundamental values remain strongly intact. Over time these new patterns of behaviour and the impact of the wider instituions, such as the education system, alter expectations, values and identities.

The values of a culture and the symbolic institutions which produce them have considerable power in determining the options open to individuals. It is not just the socialization of the home, or the nature of the education system which may reproduce or reinforce existing inequalities. An equally powerful determinant reaffirming the status quo is the disjunction between the 'sub-culture' of the home and the 'sub-culture' of the education system (which represents the values of the dominant ethnic group and the dominant class within it).

Every socio-cultural system is composed of sub-cultural, class or ethnic differences which reflect the different economic and social relations between them. The resultant discontinuity influences not only the flow between, but also the types of resources available to, each sub-system. Information may be unequally distributed, and interpreted, from different viewpoints produced by different relationships to the economy. Opportunities to learn particular social skills may be constrained and the values attached to them may influence self-esteem and identity development.

Culture is an information system but power defines control over communication flows. When a (dominant) sub-culture is institutionalized within the structure of a society, it not only monopolizes certain resources but it defines and symbolizes notions of relative value which are internalized by members of the different sub-cultures of that society in different ways. In England the dominant (sub) culture of the society is reproduced in the schooling of children based on middle-class values and expectations. It is not just individual teachers but, more fundamentally, the organizational and conceptual strategies of the institution, and its relationship with local working-class cultures, which produces structural disadvantage and personal rejection. The rest of this chapter will suggest additional ways in which the dominant culture institutionalizes disadvantage for members of ethnic minorities from a distinctive cultural background.[3]

An individual's meaning system is a constantly changing interpretation of the differences between his/her own perception of self and how he/she perceives others to see him/her. As a member of different collectivities, the individual negotiates a personal identity and a collective sense of belonging. While there may be logical interconnnections between different elements of a socio-cultural system there must, therefore, be no assumption of permanence or consensus. The affective link shared by those holding common values may constrain options but may also be utilized to challenge them.

The dynamic relations internal to (sub)cultural systems include two processes which are crucial to an understanding of both culture and ethnicity. Firstly, there is the relationship between ideas and action, and secondly, there is the ongoing negotiation between the symbolic and political dimensions.

At the basis of cultural processes and change there is a constant dynamic, often conflict and contradiction, between ideas and action. The link between meaning and action are evident in the dysfunction which occurs in cases of sudden incomprehensible loss. This produces an attempt to reconstruct meaning through personal relations and ritual actions. Emotional security and support involve a link with the past, and the reconstruction of the familiar through new symbolic actions provides psychological support. Economic, political and social changes within a society rarely keep in step with each other. It is the lack of fit between them which provides the source of interaction between the symbolic and the political. But there is often a hazy line between making meaning out of disorder and collectively acting to control it.

These processes are equally fundamental to the process of ethnicity, which is the interaction between two cultures in a common context (see Figure 1). While this two-way process is studied from both sides the internal dynamic between sub-cultures within both systems must also be reckoned with. The two criteria which are fundamental to an understanding of these dialectic relationships within and between socio-cultural systems are those of *political imbalance* and *cultural distinctiveness*. The objective determinants of the imbalance and difference between two systems are, however, mediated in reality by the perceptions of significant difference. These perceptions and interpretations are the product of the particular and unique historical relationship which has developed between the two (sub)systems in question.[4]

Figure 1 represents simplistically the political imbalance between two socio-

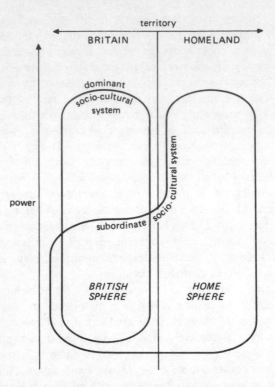

Figure 1   *Two socio-cultural systems in contact in a common context*

cultural systems. It can be used to refer to the action level of social relations; the boundary between the systems being the interface marking changes in actually what is going on. Or it can be used to discuss the identity element which refers to the significance attributed to that change by participants of the different cultural systems (Wallman, 1978). This perception of difference is partly dependent on how they define a system. What, to them, are the main components of 'culture' and how do they relate to their social environment and economy? The lack of fit between these organizational and conceptual aspects of the two systems is a fundamental determinant of the process of ethnicity. The political imbalance determines the type of economic and social exclusion or restricted participation experienced by minorities. The culturally specific interpretations of this dominance provide different mechanisms to maintain or contest the dominant construction of reality. Where there is this felt boundary and 'they' are used to define 'us' there are ethnic *relations*. And 'their' difference from 'us' is a function of our ethnicity (Wallman, 1978). 'Our' ethnicity is a product of these historically accumulated processes involving interaction with other cultures.

The nature of this interaction is, of course, determined in part by the on-going interaction of sub-cultures within the system, and their differential contact with non-members. So however it may be perceived, ethnic identity is never fixed or primordial but flexible and changing. It will be clear from later sections of this paper that the salience of its different component parts is produced by an interplay between these structural determinants and individual negotiation.

It is the movement from perception to organization, identity to action, or from consciousness to deliberate choice, which is at the heart of many debates about the nature of ethnicity. There are those scholars who have tended to study, or to focus on the individual, emotional, psychological nature of identity, and others who have chosen to look at the collective mobilizing force in the formation of interest groups. These two extremes, the identity-psychological and the action-political, are ends of a continuum which represents different mixtures of both. The main focus of inquiry should be the process along this continuum and the relationship between the 'feeling' and the 'doing' aspects. As ethnic identity is flexible and dynamic and is composed of a composite set of elements, these processes may move in different directions along this continuum at the same time for different levels of identity. We need a model which can cope with the variation and flexibilities of daily life while providing a framework that links the cultural and the political within an historical and economic perspective.

The context of change

The next step is to contextualize these relationships within a framework which allows for movement through space and over time. This involves placing the simple heuristic notions of 'two systems' in a geographical and historical framework.[5]

Taking the geographical dimension first, we should draw a distinction between a context in which indigenous ethnic groups are interacting in a common context and that in which there are non-indigenous ethnic minorities who migrated to settle in the country in the recent past.[6] In indigenous ethnic relations there is typically competition over territorial claims as well as economic and political resources. As the symbolic order is so closely tied to the socio-economic setting, there is, ideally, greater chance of ethnic mobilization and contest through existing patterns of interaction and claims to land and historically based legitimacy. Within Britain, the English have been the dominant group in relations with the Welsh and with the Scots for example. In England while the dominant English culture (and more exactly its dominant class) is fully integrated into the economic base of British society the non-indigenous minorities have been dislocated from their economic base in the homeland.

One of the main 'objective' differences between the position of the more recently arrived ex-colonial minorities and the older waves of refugee migration from Eastern Europe is the degree to which they maintain a connection with the economic base and cultural resources of the homeland. The other subjectively perceived difference, from the side of the dominant group, which also has dramatic social significance is that of colour.

Other important features of the geographical dimension are the two geographical spheres within the 'Asian' system. Just as migrants to Britain create symbolic readjustments to new economic structures, relatives in the emigration area face a similar process which feeds back into the socio-economic relations in Britain. New economic resources and sources of information from England alter social relations and expectations in the area of emigration, and the spatial separation between spheres produces differing perceptions of the other's reality in each setting (Saifullah Khan, 1977). This spatial separation and movement between these spheres may determine new emerging patterns of meaning. Migrants visiting the homeland can manipulate the different meaning and information within each setting for their own benefit. But they are also caught between the expectations of both, and the dilemmas produced are important influences on their sense of security and relationships with their children.

This geographical framework is the product of the political and economic relations established through British colonialism. Even after the colonial period the imbalance of power between the 'north' and the 'south' has ensured the continuation of economic benefit to the British system. And this same political power has enabled the halt of immigration into Britain once it proved no longer to be economically beneficial.

In the colonial period, represented in Figure 2, the dominant culture remained socially detached from, but culturally invaded, the subordinate culture. Those personnel who 'migrated' to administer British rule maintained links with their socio-economic base and ensured that the education of their children was in the homeland. Whereas, institutions of the dominant culture such as the legal and education systems had a lasting impact on the culture(s) and sub-culture(s) of the Indian sub-continent. This colonial situation involved economic, political and military backing as well as the powerful institutions of cultural imposition. Once this link had been established, a dynamic was set up directing the flow of information, the utilization of new reference models, cultural resources and conceptions of the situation (Said, 1978).

The spatial separation of the British system of social and economic relations into distinct spheres both constrained and provided advantage for communication with the homeland. Thus, the British in India controlled the content of the press reports which influenced interpretations by the rest of the population in both Britain and India. On their return to Britain, as members of the middle and upper classes, they were primarily responsible for the interpretation of this period of history. The difference between the objective situation and these subjective experiences and interpretations is particularly evident in the presentation of this information to the alternative 'sphere' of that system and in those who act as intermediaries between them.[7]

The post-colonial era was determined by the relationships established during the colonial period, Figure 3. It was these political and cultural links which encouraged migration to Britain; the main emigration areas were often those areas developed economically during colonial rule and/or those subject to disruption at Partition of the sub-continent. The economic demands for a cheap

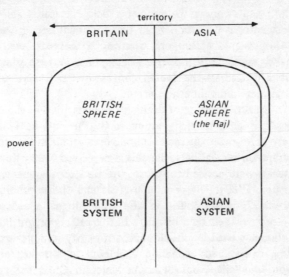

Figure 2   *The colonial period*

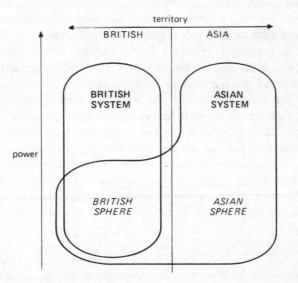

Figure 3   *The post-colonial period*

labour supply in the 1940s and 1950s drew many more workers to Britain whose particular conceptions of British life involved a view of economic success and of cultural depravity. They faced this with differing degrees of awe and feelings of inferiority.[8] The reverse migration of the post-colonial period offered potentially far greater contact between the socio-cultural systems but this was inhibited by structured exclusion from the dominant society in the fields of employment, housing, education, etc. Contrary to popular belief, however, the dominant English ethnicity was changing in response to these other socio-cultural systems as it had also in the Indian context when it was numerically the minority though the dominant ethnic group.

The two-way reactive nature of ethnicity is particularly evident in the more recent changes in English ethnicity produced by the shift in the balance of the world economy and power. As the economic opportunities for ethnic minorities have declined and an increasing social cost is perceived by the dominant system, political strategies were devised to restrict the flow of migrants and their family members (Castles, 1980). The economic crisis and the psychological readjustments faced by an English population who are no longer a leading world power has led to a threat to their own identity. In this setting one of the strategies for identity maintenance used by the dominant majority includes explanations for their prevailing social and economic problems in stronger articulations of difference from the 'alien' outsiders. As Malcolm Cross has put it, this is a classic case of blaming the victim (Cross, 1978).

Although detached from their economic base, the economic and emotional ties of South Asian migrants were supported by the age of jet travel. The mass migrations of the 1950s and 1960s produced close networks of related migrants from particular regions of origin which ensured rapid feedback to the homeland. *The dominant system, however, defined those institutions and arenas of social life where recognition and use of minority cultural resources was legitimate.* These are still essentially restricted to the private, domestic and community domains of social life and are coupled with restricted economic opportunities.

In this context the increasing numerical, economic and social base of the subordinate system in the last few decades is perceived by the dominant population to be threatening the social and economic base of their 'culture'. The two socio-cultural systems are in the common geographical setting of Britain competing for economic and cultural resources. But this perspective reminds us that the amount of physical contact between the two socio-cultural systems does not correspond to the degree of impact the one has on the other. The major determinant of the new emerging patterns of relationships and changing values in multi-ethnic regions of England is the structure and strategies of the dominant culture.

The dominant culture

Political dominance hinders the realization of the process of ethnicity by its members (Freire, 1971). By definition, it involves minimal challenge to its ideological base and/or an ongoing need to justify the social and economic structure which it upholds. But contact with subordinates provides a means and a set of resources to differentiate 'us' from 'them' in the process of differentiation. In times of strain this provides the possibility of using 'them' as justification or explanation for difficulties or contradictions in the dominant system. This may be a process of maintaining consensus within or a way of deferring criticism from without. Stressing ethnic difference from 'alien' outsiders is a means to avoid or deny class differences within the system. Similarly, social pressures created by high unemployment can be blamed on the 'out' group. Both strategies stress differences and avoid the responsibility and vested interests of the 'in' group. While it may be 'natural' to ignore or over-simplify internal divisions in the culture of the alternative system and to neglect shifts in context and meaning on *'their'* side of the boundary (Wallman, 1978), the imbalance of power allows the dominant socio-cultural system to manipulate it to their advantage.

The dominant 'culture' does not consciously consider or articulate its component elements nor expose the strategies and institutions which reinforce and maintain this dominance. Were they to be known or acknowledged they would become less efficient. One such simple strategy is to project the interest and difficulties generated by contact with another culture onto that other culture (Saifullah Khan, 1981a). By so doing, little attention is paid not only to the symbolic institutions and strategies of the dominant group, but also the structural determinants of minority ethnicity and identity. The preoccupation with minorities as 'problems' or interesting cultural exotica divert attention from the fundamental economic and political determinants of minority ethnicity and the role of the majority culture in supporting them (Saifullah Khan, 1981b).[9]

A characteristic of English ethnicity, and maybe other Western cultures of dominance, are the twin notions that culture is dispensable and that it is detachable. First, culture is not seen to have any power in its own right. For many it is an esoteric misguided system of beliefs and/or quaint behaviour held by others. This is the notion that 'they have culture: we have civilization' or that 'we base our action on rational behaviour: they have irrational beliefs'. Following from this 'if they become Westernized/English-assimilated they will become civilized/rational beings'. Therefore, culture is dispensable, serving no useful functions. It serves only to mystify or to maintain conservative tradition. Second, there is the notion that culture is detachable from the social and economic system in which it has its reality. In these perspectives culture is taken out of context and three important relationships are ignored: between meaning and action; between the social system and its economic base; and between the individual and collective representations transmitted through cultural institutions and practices across generations.

A 'culture of dominance' is characteristically then a developing process of not only an economic and political domination but also a conceptual justification and control over the situation. The former have been well analysed in terms of ethnic relations in England. *This paper seeks to stress features of*

conceptual control and colonialization which have received much less attention.
One of the reasons for this may be due to another feature of English culture and
that is its essentially 'monolingual' and 'monocultural' tradition.[10] The dominant
conceptual system, including the system of ethnic classification, is embedded in
the English language and this has developed and changed in response to the
colonial experience (Husband, 1977).

'Race' is a classification based on the belief that the perceived difference is
immutable and fixed. In England this perceived difference is based on the
criterion of colour. Although the concept of a 'race' has no scientific backing,
its salience as a social category is evident throughout British society. While
there is no dispute about the impact of racism, the adoption of concepts such
as 'race' by the media, educationalists, and academics and others, only helps
to legitimize it. 'Race' in fact means 'colour' and 'race relations' and community
relations are usually perceived to be black—white relations. Hence, the
Community Relations Councils, the laws against racial discrimination and advice
centres on immigration are all perceived to be for the 'black' members of British
society. To be 'immigrant' is to be 'black' and so this label 'immigrant' is still
used for British-born 'blacks'.[11] As there is no legitimate dual identity and as
black people cannot by definition be 'English', these members of British society
are conceptually marginalized. 'Their' identity is defined for them and the new
emerging composite identities of a new generation are seen as inevitably problematic or a threat to the 'purity' of English 'culture' (which is itself an ideal type).
The new emerging social and linguistic repertoires of the so-called 'second
generation' are not accorded value either for the individual or the society as
a whole.

These cultural categories are relevant in daily interaction and in their power
to transmit their meaning to subsequent generations of British-born members
of minority families. Two institutions in particular have institutionalized these
concepts and manifest their power through the varied and powerful meanings
they transmit. The first is the legal system, manifest especially in the introduction of immigration legislation. This legislation developed in the period after
mass migration to Britain was well underway, but also at a time when Britain
faced economic crisis and political insecurity. British identity maintenance
demanded a scapegoat and a devalued comparison to stress its sense of worth.
The immigration laws curtailed the numbers entering Britain while representing
'a practical demonstration of the strengthening of British identity' (Husband,
1977). To the English, introducing legislation symbolized action on the basis
of justice and fair play.[12] To the migrant or his children, they symbolized
insecurity and differential treatment. To both, 'immigrants' were problems
and immigration issues were the focus of 'race' relations. This process is to be
strengthened in proposed legislation which, in its blatant denial of human
rights, is likely to strengthen the hostile reaction of increasingly organized ethnic
minorities. The maintenance of a consistent justification to support these
practices is likely to stimulate further strategies of myth-making and emotive

rhetoric such as that so skilfully manipulated by Enoch Powell (Wallman, 1981).

The media is clearly another institution of great symbolic power in defining and reinforcing interpretations of reality (see Hartmann and Husband, 1974). Like the education system, it not only uses the concepts of the dominant language to convey its meaning, but, by its choice of particular linguistic codes, it introduces differential symbolic values for different (sub)cultures and languages. Success in decoding the information assumes knowledge of the relevant linguistic skills and cultural assumptions. In the education system, while the teaching of this code aims at providing full opportunities for participation in the wider society it does so at the expense of existing skills and cultural resources of bilingual and bicultural children.

Bilingualism, like biculturalism, is perceived as a problem for the individual and for the society as a whole. Unlike the criterion of 'race' (that is colour), language is underemphasized as an element of culture in England. Many children of migrants in England are thus experiencing rapid language loss and, paradoxically, it is their language which is increasingly utilized as a tool for symbolizing their ethnic solidarity.[13]

The structure of migration

The historical determinants of the South Asian migration to Britain and their impact on the development of English ethnicity are two important factors determining the personal experience affecting migrants. While the last section concentrated on aspects of English identity and ethnicity, the process of migration demands the opposite treatment. The individual and intra-ethnic process of migration and settlement have received a lot of coverage in academic studies (Anwar, 1979; Jeffery, 1976). One of the aims of the framework presented in this paper is to stress the structural determinants of ethnic identity processes. The importance of non-ethnic factors is frequently overlooked in approaches which stress individual choice and the internal logic of a cultural system. Little attention is paid to the power of the group or collectivity in maintaining and reproducing the dominant identities. With an understanding of the various structural determinants of identity formation, it is possible to make the link between individual psychological processes and those of the wider societal levels.

The South Asian migration and most mass migration to Europe in the last few decades have not been the individual movement of thousands of people but a structured movement and redistribution of human, economic, social and psychological resources. The individual migrant acts as an envoy and is an emotional and economic investment of a whole family. She/he carries their expectations and anxieties, and her/his commitment and loyalty is strengthened rather than weakened by the opportunity she/he takes with their approval and, frequently, their financial and organizational backing. Similarly, settlement in Britain is structured by arrival into an existing network of relationships and expectations (Watson, 1977). Individual choice is severely constrained by the structure and mechanics of the migration process which is determined by the underlying socio-economic-historical factors, the cultural values and patterns of organization and the migrant's own resources and skills. The migrant experience involves a physical move from one social environment to another, and a psychological adjustment involving a changing appreciation of self.[14]

Migrants leave their homeland with high motivation to succeed materially for the sake of personal prestige, the family name and material future, but also with strong warnings about the dangers of moral corruption in the West. As we have seen, the spatial separation of the two spheres of the 'Asian' system allowed a one-sided feedback from the earlier returning migrants stressing their success and achievements with minimal reference to their difficulties. By converting material and emotional resources from the British sphere of the Asian system into the homeland sphere, the migrant can support particular presentations of reality. These information and communication channels often encouraged future migration, while restricting an appreciation of its realities.

The migrant's arrival into an existing network of friends and kin perpetuated the Asian system's control over this option and frame of reference. The earlier migrant's experience of restricted access to housing, jobs and interaction with local people, their ties of loyalty and brotherhood in alien circumstances and limited social skills and material backing, contributed to concentrations of settlement in particular employment markets. Subsequent arrivals, joining kin or fellow villagers, received material and emotional support and were influenced by their perception of available material and social options. These were determined by their assessment of the actual available options, and of those seen as culturally appropriate (Saifullah Khan, 1979a).

In the short term, these traditional systems of support and introduction to a new social experience buffered the potential psychological and material difficulties. In the long term, they restricted the migrants' opportunities in terms of access to knowledge, social skills and opportunities. In areas of high population concentration the mutual support systems enabled the pooling of 'ethnic' resources, information, expertise and enterprise; enabled a greater sense of confidence and security; and facilitated communication and contact with the homeland. Such factors stress the strength of the British sphere of the Asian cultural system without underestimating the fundamental social and structural alterations demanded by the new context. One of the main consequences of the migration process for individual migrants is an increased awareness of values and behaviour previously taken for granted. In the new context their meaning and functions are altered by the readjustments caused by change in personnel, by new options and alternative explanations and the threat of the 'host' system undermining their cultural system.

While the personal reappraisal of self and ethnic identity does depend on many individual and personality factors, the actual circumstances of settlement severely limit the options and interpretations available. Access to, and the social skills for participation in, the alternative system arc especially limited in areas of high ethnic concentration. These factors in turn determine the information and perception of the dominant system, and the dimensions and strength of ethnic awareness.

While all migrants experience an increased awareness of the ethnic dimension through contact with and information received about 'non-members', the degree and reliability of their assessment of difference depends in large part on their position in the residential, employment and social structure. This is clearly illustrated in a comparison between two localities in different cities. In Bradford in the early 1970s, the concentration of Pakistanis and a high percentage of Mirpuris in certain localities and types of employment, ensured that they had minimal contact in day-to-day activities with non-Pakistanis. Due to their own perception of their (sub-ethnic) group and their appreciation of how other Pakistanis saw them, they preferred, and had the opportunity, to mix exclusively with other Mirpuris. Through migration and closer contact with non-Mirpuris there was a heightened awareness of this level of their ethnic identity.[15] But for much of the time, in most circumstances, being Pakistani as opposed to Mirpuri, was not an important level of identification. In certain settings, on certain occasions (e.g. the war with India), it became significant and only then did Mirpuris identify themselves with this larger category, accepting the role of the urban-educated spokesman with whom otherwise they would not identify (Saifullah Khan, 1976).

In South London, in contrast (and a few years later), where the South Asian population was diverse and less concentrated, villagers of similar rural background had a very different appreciation of self and the population(s) around them. By force of circumstance, many interacted with the local English, at work or in the street, and they and their wives learnt more English. Due to longer settlement in Britain, some had older children introducing them to other aspects of Western society. In this setting, women, who in Bradford would have mixed almost exclusively with fellow kin and villagers and would not work outside the home, chose to interact with other Asian women (rather than English women) across fundamental linguistic, religious and cultural boundaries. They not only knew and utilized the national-ethnic terms such as 'Pakistani' or 'Indian' more frequently, and the dominant all-embracing 'Asian' category, but in certain circumstances these categories proved a significant basis for interaction. While family visiting and marriage alliances tended to remain within the sub-ethnic level, other activities such as seeking work for the women, or socializing at work for the men, were frequently functioning at these wider, more general levels of ethnicity (Saifullah Khan, 1979c).

This brief example illustrates the importance of structural factors in determining the degree and the most salient level of ethnic identification. Ethnic identity is not fixed, constant, nor single stranded, it is flexible and shifting on different levels according to situation and context and thus it changes collectively over time.

The subordinate culture

Members of the migrant generation and their British-born children are creating and recreating meaning to fit with alterations in social relations produced by a new socio-economic setting and the experience of migration. Their structural position in British society and their background in the Indian sub-continent determine the varied and selective utilization of traditional and symbolic resources. It is the power of the dominant culture which is the major determinant of social interaction between ethnic groups. It also controls access to alternative cultural resources which includes the 'languages' through which these varied (sub)cultures are known and shared.

New experiences and new relationships forced by migration demand new systems of meaning, and over time alter patterns of behaviour and identity development. But there is also a major difference between the migrant generation and their British-born offspring. They have differential involvement in the two systems (and many sub-systems). This can be illustrated by the use of three fundamental criteria: those of *access, participation* and *identification*. *Access* to the British system depends upon opportunities perceived as available or appropriate. They are determined by the experience of structural exclusion and discrimination as well as cultural preference. The latter is based upon the interpretation of the situation which is dependent on the flow of information and resources produced by the former. *Participation*, however, implies choice. If the opportunity is there and the migrant has the 'relevant' skills the opportunity is or is not taken. But participation in institutions of the British system does not necessarily involve identification. *Identification* is the most complicated criterion and is distinguished here from internalization (used in the restricted sense of knowing, using, but not necessarily feeling attached to).

First generation migrants of South Asian origin in Britain tend to have minimal access to the British system. When they have access, for example, in the work sphere, their participation does not necessarily involve a (high) degree of identification with it. In most cases, first generation migrants identify fully with the Asian socio-cultural system, although this is increasingly the British sphere of the Asian system. Part-identifications and interactions with the British sphere tend not to involve its primary institutions and fundamental values. As the first generation was socialized in the homeland, any secondary socialization in Britain tends to be sketchy and has never been formally articulated nor systematically introduced.

Second generation British-born children, on the other hand, are socialized into the Asian socio-cultural system in the British sphere which is different in certain important respects from the socialization of their parents in the homeland, but they are then subject to a secondary socialization at school and through the media, etc. Over time they gain access to and participate in the two systems. They more or less fully internalize, and they partly identify with both. But, as we have seen, their reality is not deemed legitimate by the dominant culture nor understood by their migrant parents.

One source of conflict among minority families stems from the different assessment of the alternative system by its members. To the adult generation, with minimum contact, this is more of an unknown quantity and, with limited social skills and a feeling of security located in the Asian system, their fears are often reinforced by their reaction to their children's behaviour and attitudes. They are less aware and often less concerned with the dominant definition of their status and culture, but they interpret the unacceptable aspects of their children's behaviour as an encroachment and undermining of their system by the dominant culture.

British-born children with migrant parents or grandparents of South Asian origin are members of British society and recipients of English 'culture'. Their socialization takes place within the particular sub-culture of the British sphere of the Asian system and through the school and neighbourhood sub-cultures of the English system. The socialization of the home differs in marked respects from that in the homeland sphere of the Asian system but retains many of its distinctive features and values. The secondary socialization of the school, however, introduces a different presentation of reality. It does not reinforce the values and skills of the home, and the child's move to school presents him/her with a disjunction between two meaning systems. The education system presents a new set of relations and references, some of which have already been absorbed by the child through the media or local neighbourhood contacts. It is through the school's lack of contact with community aspirations and systems of support and education, and the lack of recognition of the child's existing social and linguistic skills that children of ethnic minorities assess the relative value placed upon their identity and affiliations. The adjustment to these competing messages and claims depends on the particular school, family and local circumstances. The lack of fit between these systems produces conflicting and flexible patterns of behaviour adapted by the individual for particular contexts or spheres of activity. These social skills of switching behaviour and linguistic codes, and the interior working through of conflicting identifications which it demands, are rarely recognized as positive, creative and psychologically strengthening processes (Weinreich, 1979).

The children of ethnic minority families belong to both systems but may internalize and/or identify with them to differing degrees. Within each they have a particular set of identities imposed by one collectivity in reaction to the other. Those of the dominant system are imposed from outside and reflect the doubly negative perception of 'coloured' children with 'different' cultures. They are perceived to be 'between' two systems and any behavioural difficulty is quickly accorded to 'cultural conflict'. But the second generation child and adolescent is 'of' two systems and creating a new one. They are participants in the ongoing dialectic between the two but they are also trapped in its ambiguities. As both their elders and the dominant majority still perceive significant boundaries between the two 'cultural' systems, they are subject to the control it produces. While their own reality counters these notions of exclusiveness they pass, in their life cycle, through periods when one acts as a dominating force over the other. But whichever is the uppermost at a particular time or place, both are seen to be moving beyond legitimate forms of behaviour.

The new generation are living in a social context which determines very different patterns of behaviour. These are typically related to distinctive spheres of activity and different categories of people. The juxtaposition of these different systems implies differential values and degrees of control due to their power imbalance. Where the socialization of the home is strong and where there is social support from minority institutions and tight social networks, the secondary socialization of the school often has less impact than majority members often assume. But in areas where children are already exposed to the language and culture of the neighbourhood or strongly influenced by the television and other media, the impact of the school is greater.

Living in both socio-cultural systems involves synthesizing patterns of identification and developing social skills which enable sudden shifts in time and space from one set of cultural resources to another. In certain settings it involves a careful manipulation of both to avoid offence to differing parties. It is these social and conceptual skills and the psychological resilience they demand which are not valued by the dominant society.[16] And the new generation's attempt to make meaning out of their particular circumstance is inevitably influenced by the dominant definition of their position. Put briefly, this reinforces the idea that 'they have the problems; their parents in particular are authoritarian and unable to understand; and that they cannot be full members of this (homogeneous white English) society, so they are bound to face psychological stress.'

The dominant culture's symbolic participation in the lives of minority members is yet another force that constrains their freedom to create their own meaning and legitimize its reality within British society. Even if the economic and political insecurities they face were reduced, it is the power of racism and these forms of cultural invasion which constrain their choices and the very concepts and languages they can utilize to express their reaction. One of the main problems of this new generation is the way the dominant society conceptualizes them. By fostering the myth of a homogeneous English culture, and using mono-cultural and mono-lingual norms to assess social skills and educational 'achievement' the dominant definition ignores the change and diversity that is part of all contemporary Western urban societies. By ignoring the dynamic and composite nature of ethnic identities and the two forms of socialization experienced by minority members, the dominant culture forces the minority identity, culture and language into illegitimate, personal, private and community spheres of life. The new generation's creative attempts to participate in and contribute to a new emerging culture is not recognized as authentic or a positive contribution to society. As these new generations are increasingly marginalized they will react more violently to resist the dominant culture and its oppressive strategies.

Conclusion

Greater emphasis on the relationships between identity and action, and culture and control, lead to an appreciation of the political dimensions of the process of ethnicity. The preponderance of reified and rigid notions of culture, and studies focusing on minority ethnicity or identity from within communities, has led to an understandable rejection of culture as mystification or simply a diversion from more important factors such as racism. If the process of ethnicity is seen to be a mutually interacting process of differentiation and organization between dominant and subordinate groups, racism can be incorporated within this framework as a, if not the *most*, fundamental element of the dominant ethnicity. If the power of culture were acknowledged in its institutional and conceptual control, we would be nearer to explaining the power of the dominant culture in structuring the experience of ethnic minorities. Similarly if we recognized the political implications of the process of ethnicity we would no longer discard culture as some backward artifact 'belonging' only to minorities. Lack of power is the inability to mobilize material and/or symbolic resources. Members of ethnic minorities are creating meaning to adjust to the reality in which they find themselves. This process shifts to collective action against powerful groups in society when their meaning is denied or degraded, by economic exploitation or cultural invasion; or both reinforcing the other.[17]

Notes

1 While the minorities have 'culture' they rarely have 'ideologies'. As this paper denies a clear distinction between the political and the symbolic, the difference between the two concepts of culture and ideology is taken to be a matter of degree. The former becomes the latter when it is attached to a concrete power interest and is defined as such by those who do not hold that definition of reality.

2 It is interesting to note, however, that attention has been paid to the impact of the dominance of middle-class values on subordinate sub-cultures in certain cultural institutions of British society, for example the education system (Bernstein, 1969; Rosen, 1972). Whereas until recently there has been little attention paid to the 'cultures' of resistance of the 'working class' or regional cultures (Willis, 1977).

3 This is an obvious case of where class and ethnic processes overlap to reinforce disadvantage for a large percentage of children of ethnic minorities. But it also suggests a situation in which there is a differential perception of that reality, which may be culturally specific.

4 The distinction between intra- and inter-cultural processes focuses around the degree of objective (sub)cultural difference and the degree of control on the economic base of that (sub)culture.

5 The naming of these two systems emerges out of this geographical dimension. They are at the highest level of abstraction. They are, however, used by their respective members to refer to their own and the other system in particular situations; and in the past in particular historical periods. It must be stressed that they are for heuristic purposes only and the systems so presented could be labelled by more specific 'ethnic' classifications such as regional Bradfordian culture and the regional Mirpuri culture of the Panjab.

6 Again there is no clear distinction between the two concepts; under a long time span non-indigenous minorities produce descendants who become incorporated into the economy of the society.

7 These intermediary individuals or institutions are particularly instructive areas for study.

8 Some sub-cultures of the different South Asian communities in Britain had already internalized their low status as perceived by the dominant sub-cultures of their society before arrival in Britain, for instance, Mirpuri and Sylheti for Panjabi and Bengali respectively.

9 The historical division between the anthropological tradition of studying other cultures and the sociological tradition of studying one's own culture without questioning that value system, has had a lot to do with this situation.

10 This is of course a myth in the sense that there is no one English culture and yet *in comparison* to many other cultural systems the English system has distinctive linguistic and cultural repertoires.

11 Similarly the 'Eurospeak', as Harold Rosen so aptly calls it, now talks about the 'problem' of second-generation migrants which is another contradiction in terms.

12 Similarly the use of Government Commissions of Enquiry symbolizes that something is being done.

13 Is this a reflection of changing criteria for cultural identification and/or a reflection of a powerlessness in which symbolic meaning is the only effective form of action (Halliday, 1978)?

14 This move involves for many South Asian migrants of rural origin the move from an out-door gregarious lifestyle to an indoor privatized urban lifestyle.

15 For many villagers who had limited mobility in the homeland, the move to England forced greater contact with other sub-ethnic groups.

16 No additional positive criteria are added to tests and other forms of evaluation which are based on an essentially mono-lingual and mono-cultural norm.

17 The model presented in this chapter is used in Saifullah Khan (1981a) and in the Open University course 'Ethnic minorities and community relations', block 3, unit 8, *Culture and Ethnicity*.

References

Anwar, M. (1979), *The Myth of Return*, Heinemann Educational
Bernstein, B. (1969), *Class, Codes and Control*, vol. 1, Routledge & Kegan Paul

Castles, S. (1980), 'The social time-bomb: education of an underclass in West Germany', *Race and Class*, vol. XXI, no. 4, pp. 369-87

Cohen, A. (1979), 'Political symbolism', *Annual Review of Anthropology*, vcl. 8, pp. 87-113

Cross, M. (1978), 'West Indians and the problem of the metropolitan majority', in M. Day and D. Marsland (eds.), *Black Kids, White Kids – What Hope?*, National Youth Bureau, Leicester

Freire, P. (1971), *Pedagogy of the Oppressed*, New York: Herder & Herder

Hall, E. T. (1976), *Beyond Culture*, Garden City, NY: Anchor Press/ Doubleday

Halliday, M. A. K. (1978), *Language as Social Semiotic*, Edward Arnold

Hartman, P. and Husband, C. (1974), *Racism and the Mass Media*, Davis-Poynter

Husband, C. (1977), 'News media, language and race relations: a case study in identity maintenance', in H. Giles (ed.), *Language, Ethnicity and Intergroup Relations*, Academic Press

Jeffery, P. (1976), *Migrants and Refugees, Muslim and Christian Pakistani Families in Bristol*, Cambridge University Press

Rosen, H. (1972), *Language and Class*, Falling Wall Press

Said, E. W. (1978), *Orientalism*, Routledge & Kegan Paul

Saifullah Khan, V. (1976), 'Perceptions of a population: Pakistanis in Britain', *New Community*, vol. 5

Saifullah Khan, V. (1977), 'The Pakistanis: Mirpuri villagers at home and in the city of Bradford', in J. Watson (ed.) (1977)

Saifullah Khan, V. (1979a), 'Housework, network, home-work: South Asian women in South London', in S. Wallman (ed.), *Ethnicity at Work*, Macmillan

Saifullah Khan, V. (1979b), 'Migration and social stress', in V. Saifullah Khan (ed.), *Minority Families in Britain: Support and Stress*, Macmillan

Saifullah Khan, V. (1979c), 'Ethnic identity among South Asians in the U.K.', in M. Gaborieau and A. Thorner (eds.), *Asie du Sud: Traditions et Changements*, Paris: CNRS

Saifullah Khan, V. (1981a), 'Some comments on the question of the second generation', *Report on Immigrant Children and Youth*, Royal Ministry of Local Government and Labour, Oslo

Saifullah Khan, V. (1981b), 'Co-operation between school, parents and the communities', *Educational Research Workshop on Education and Migrant Workers*, Dillingen

Wallman, S. (1978), 'The boundaries of "race": processes of ethnicity in England', *Man*, vol. 13, pp. 200-17

Wallman, S. (1981), 'Refractions of rhetoric: evidence for the meaning of "race" in England', in R. Paine (ed.), *Politically Speaking*, Philadelphia: ISHI

Watson, J. (1977), *Between Two Cultures: Migrants and Minorities in Britain,* Macmillan

Williams, R. (1976), *Keywords*, Glasgow: Fontana

Willis, P. (1977), *Learning to Labour*, Farnborough: Saxon House

14 The social psychology of minorities[*]

Henri Tajfel

The scope and the limits

The study of the relations between social groups within any society must first take into account the 'objective' conditions of their co-existence; that is, the economic, political, social and historical circumstances which have led to — and often still determine — the differences between the groups in their standards of living, access to opportunities such as jobs and education, or the treatment they receive from those who wield power, authority or sometimes simply brute force. But as John Rex (1970) wrote in his book on race relations, these objective conditions are always associated with widespread 'subjective definitions', stereotypes and belief systems. Our purpose here is to look at these various subjective aspects of the relations between minorities and majorities, to assess their importance in the total picture and to see how they contribute to the general pattern of the relations between the groups. Being a member of a minority presents the individuals concerned with the psychological requirements to adapt to the present situation or to do something in order to change it. The adaptations and the strategies for change which are possible are *finite* in their number and variety. We shall attempt to discuss here some of those which appear to be the most frequently used and the most important.

The 'subjective definitions' must be taken into account in the general analysis of racial or any other intergroup relations, since they are likely to contribute to the pattern of these relations and to changes in them. These subjective definitions, belief systems, identifications, cognitive structures, likes and dislikes, and the behaviour related to them, are the special province of the social psychologist. The social psychology of minorities must focus upon them, without denying in the least that the analysis of the 'objective' conditions of the development of social relations between groups must come first and foremost in our attempts to understand the nature of these relations. It is nevertheless true that human social behaviour can only be properly understood if we are able to know something about the subjective 'representations of social reality' which intervene between conditions in which social groups live and the effects of these conditions on individual and collective behaviour. This is like a spiral: the history and the

* First published as *Minority Rights Group Report* no. 38 (December 1978).

contemporary features of social, economic and other differences between social groups are reflected in the attitudes, beliefs and views of the world held by members of these groups. These 'subjective' effects of social conditions are reflected in turn in what people do, in how they behave towards their own group and towards others. The resulting forms of 'ingroup', 'outgroup' and 'intergroup' behaviour contribute, in their turn, to the present and the future of the relations between the groups; and so it goes on. Thus, although we shall be dealing here with no more than one 'frozen moment' in what is a complex and continuously changing situation, this moment often proves to be quite crucial in affecting the shape of what is to happen.

What is a minority group?

In asking this question, we are not concerned with definitions of social groups (or categories) in terms of the economic, social, cultural or other criteria by which they can be distinguished. Instead, we wish to know what are the psychological effects of these 'objective' factors on the people involved: do they or do they not feel themselves to be members of a particular social group which is clearly distinguished *by them* from other such groups? And what are the effects of these 'feelings' (of belonging or not belonging) on their social behaviour?

But before these questions can be discussed, we need to relate them to the solid realities of social differentiations. The 'feelings' of being a member of a group do not float in some sort of a social vacuum; and the corresponding belief systems cannot be properly understood if one considers them without taking into account their direct and intimate ties with the social realities of people's lives.

There are many definitions of social minorities which have been proposed by sociologists, political scientists and others. We shall retain here the set of criteria suggested by Wagley and Harris (1958), as quoted by Simpson and Yinger (1965) in their book on *Racial and cultural minorities.* According to these authors:

(1) Minorities are subordinate segments of complex state societies; (2) minorities have special physical or cultural traits which are held in low esteem by the dominant segments of the society; (3) minorities are self-conscious units bound together by the special traits which their members share and by the special disabilities which these bring; (4) membership in a minority is transmitted by a rule of descent which is capable of affiliating succeeding generations even in the absence of readily apparent special cultural or physical traits; (5) minority peoples, by choice or necessity, tend to marry within the group. [p. 17].

It is interesting and important to see that *numbers* do not play much of a part in this definition. Some numerical majorities — as, for example, in South Africa — conform to all the five criteria, while some numerical minorities — such as Afrikaaners in the same country — probably only conform to the fifth: they tend to marry within the group. Again, members of women's liberation movements in this country and elsewhere would argue that women are a 'minority' in the sense outlined above, although they would obviously not fit some of the criteria, and often are not a numerical minority. The principle guiding the definition selected by Wagley and Harris (and many other social scientists) is not to be found in numbers but in the social *position* of the groups to which they refer as minorities.

This is a sensible approach to the problem. Quite apart from the fact that certain kinds of social disabilities, shared by certain kinds of people, are more important in understanding what happens to them and what they do than are numerical considerations, it would also be very difficult to adopt a meaningful frame of reference based on numbers. The 'social' definition is more important and much more flexible. For example, the separatist movement in Quebec is a minority movement within Canada. At the same time, as the political and social changes which recently occurred in Canada gather momentum, the problems of the English-speaking minorities in Quebec (particularly of those recent immigrants whose native language was neither French nor English, and who adopted English on their arrival) are becoming more acute (see Berry, Kalin and Taylor, 1977). In some ways, the French-speaking Quebecois still conform to the Wagley and Harris description as a 'subordinate segment' in a 'complex state society'; in other ways, they constitute a majority which is beginning to create some of the usual problems for its own minorities.

The psychological criterion for referring to certain social groups as minorities is clearly stated by Wagley and Harris. They are 'self-conscious units' of people who have in common certain similarities and certain social disadvantages. But this psychological criterion is not as simple as it may appear. Some sociologists make a sharp distinction between what they call a 'social group' and a 'social category'. For example, Morris (1968) defined ethnic groups as 'a distinct category of the population in a larger society whose culture is usually different from its own'. He added that members of ethnic groups '. . . are, or feel themselves, or are thought to be, bound together by common ties of race or nationality or culture' (p. 167). This he distinguished from 'a mere category of the population, such as red-haired people, selected by a criterion that in the context is socially neutral and that does not prescribe uniform behaviour' (p. 168). By contrast, a genuine group must consist of people 'recruited on clear principles, who are bound to one another by formal, institutionalized rules and characteristic informal behaviour'. In addition, these groups must 'be organized for cohesion and persistence; that is to say, the rights and duties of membership must regulate internal order and relations with other groups'. Having already once recognized the psychological criteria that people must 'feel themselves' or must be 'thought to be' similar to each other and distinct from others in certain ways in order to be considered as an ethnic group, Morris comes back to the 'internal' characteristics of an ethnic group membership by stating that 'members usually identify themselves with a group and give it a name' (p. 168).

These clear-cut distinctions can be very useful for thinking about *some* minorities. but they may present problems if one considers many fluid and changing social situations in which men and women slowly acquire *in common* their beliefs, reactions, feelings and attitudes about their special status in a wider society. As distinct from a 'category', a social group must be, according to Morris, cohesive and long-lasting; it must also have an accepted system of internal regulations. But 'categories' and 'social groups' understood in this sense sometimes represent, respectively, the beginning and the end of a long social psychological process. There are many cases in between: a collection of people, consensually designated by a majority as somehow 'different', may begin by not accepting this difference, or by denying its interpretation. It may be a long time before this 'outside' consensus results in creating clear-cut group boundaries, formal institutionalized rules and the specific features of informal social behaviour to which Morris referred. And yet, all this time the 'feeling' of membership, of belongingness, of a common difference from others will continue to develop. The internal cohesion and structure of a minority group may sometimes come *as a result* of this development of an awareness of being considered as different. As a matter of fact, it is precisely this *development* of a special kind of awareness that some people within minorities are sometimes trying hard to achieve through social action, through initiating social and political movements.

Some years ago I had an opportunity of seeing a clear example of this kind of development. With the help of the Institute of Race Relations (as it then was), an essay competition was organized for African, Asian and West Indian students in this country on the subject of their attitudes towards the 'colour' problem before they had come here and the changes in these attitudes which occurred as a result of their experiences in Britain (cf. Tajfel and Dawson, 1965). One of the most striking common features in the essays of the students from the West Indies was their preconception at home that, on coming to Britain they would be reaching the shores of the 'mother country', that a common language, a similar education, and a social background similar to that of many indigenous British students, would ensure their immediate acceptance and an easy adaptation to their new surroundings. The 'feeling' of being different (because treated as such in many subtle and unsubtle ways) led slowly to the development of a new group identity. One of the major social categories to which they felt they had belonged underwent, for many of them, a drastic revision. As some of them wrote, their black consciousness was born here, in what they now considered a white man's country, rather than the welcoming land of their cultural heritage. 'Black skin' happens to be a socially relevant criterion for distinguishing between groups of people; red hair is not, or at least not yet. But in principle any characteristic common to a collection of people is capable of acquiring its socially relevant value connotations and thereby its power to determine social differentiations. The resulting feeling of common membership of a minority comes, in many cases, long before the individuals involved have been able to construct for themselves a cohesive and organized 'group' or even to develop special modes of 'characteristic informal behaviour' for their internal usage. Very often, of course, the process is reversed, or it progresses simultaneously in two parallel directions: a group is perceived as separate and different both from the inside and from the outside. But even here, there is no easy psychological dichotomy between a 'mere category' and a genuine 'social group'. It is usually a matter of complex interactions between the 'internal' and the 'external' criteria of group membership, of the conditions in which the 'felt' membership of a group or a category leads to various forms of social action, social conscience, systems of attitudes and beliefs, individual or collective strategies. In order to consider this variety of issues, we must turn our attention to these 'internal' and 'external' criteria of minority membership and the relationship between them.

The internal and external criteria of minority membership

As we have seen, many of the definitions of minorities include a reference to the 'subjective' characteristics of their membership, such as stereotypes, belief systems, self-consciousness, identifications, etc. In other words, for a minority to become a distinguishable social entity, there must be amongst some, many, most or all of its members an awareness that they possess in common some socially relevant characteristics, and that these characteristics distinguish them from other social entities in the midst of which they live. But, as it is clear from the sociological definitions we discussed earlier, these 'socially relevant characteristics' must be of a certain kind in order to produce the self-awareness of being a 'minority' in the sense of the term we discussed earlier. After all, in some ways all complex societies consist of nothing but minorities: professional, regional or age groups, political affiliations and any number of others. It is only when being assigned and/or assigning oneself to a particular social entity leads at the same time to certain perceived social consequences which include discriminatory treatment from others and their negative attitudes based on some *common* criteria (however vague) of membership that the awareness of being in a minority can develop.

The crucial term in all this is 'in common'. In order to understand the psychological realities of 'feeling' a member of a minority, it is important to make a clear distinction betweem *individual* differences and *group* differences. Although a lot of people may be red-haired, or obese or of small stature, they are unlikely to acquire an awareness of being 'members' of corresponding 'minorities'. These characteristics, although shared by large numbers of people, retain their *individual* significance in a person's life. It would be very difficult to think of detrimental 'group' social consequences following upon obesity, left-handedness or stammering. Obviously, any of these individual features can acquire an enormous importance in a person's life: and just as obviously, they may create for such people a number of social handicaps. And yet, we are much less likely to find in a newspaper an item which would start: 'A fat man, (or a stammerer), Mr X, is helping the police with their enquiries. . .' than 'A Pakistani, Mr X, . . .' etc. [1]

Where, then, is the difference? In order to clarify its social psychological significance, we must undertake a brief discussion of some aspects of social categorizing. To make sense of the complexity of our social environment, we tend to categorize people into groups or 'types' or 'kinds' on a large number of varying criteria. These social categorizations enable us to draw conclusions about people (rightly or wrongly), even when we know little about them apart from their category 'membership', to attribute some 'causal' meaning to their behaviour, to make predictions about their future behaviour; these categorizations also help us to find our own place in the confusing network of social relationship. In other words, to place someone in a social category often means that we can (or think we can) draw inferences about him or her on the basis of what we know (or think we know) about the general characteristics of the category to which they belong. [2]

The difference between an 'individual' attribute, such as fatness, and one which designates the membership of a minority, such as 'a Pakistani', is that the former is not a characteristic of a person from which *other* social inferences can easily be made. One type of inference which is usually *not* made from 'fat' is quite crucial for the understanding of the different social consequences of various kinds of categorization. It has to do with *other* characteristics of *other* people who are in the same category. 'Fatness' or 'stammering' or 'small stature' are not used as criteria in a social typology. Socially relevant characteristics of other people who share the same attribute are randomly related to that attribute; in other words, they have very limited implications for the social attributes of others who share the same characteristic.

The result is that fat people, or short people, or people using a certain kind of toothpaste, are collections of individuals, while Pakistanis or (at one point of time) long-haired teenagers, or ex-inmates of prisons are, or may easily become minorities. The three examples just mentioned are similar in some important ways and different in others. The similarities are that all these designations are associated with widespread negative stereotypes about the people involved; 'stereotypes' consisting of a number of *other* characteristics assigned to all, or most, of those who share the attribute. The differences are in the degree of acceptance by the people involved that they are indeed bound together in some important ways which distinguish them from people in other social categories.

This acceptance of being *together* in a low-status minority depends upon a large number of social and psychological conditions which can only be briefly discussed here. In many cases, there is a long history of social or cultural differences between the minority and other groups in the society. It is easy to find examples of categories which are definitely 'groups', in the sense that they conform to all the sociological criteria which we discussed earlier. The South Moluccans in Holland, the Arabs in Israel, the German-speaking inhabitants of Alto Adige in Italy, the racial groups in South Africa, the Kurds in Iraq, the Maronites in the Lebanon, are obvious examples. But, once again, it is important to remember that, psychologically speaking, we are dealing here with a continuum and not a simple and clear-cut distinction. The awareness of being a member of a separate minority group and the identification with it following upon this awareness depend upon the *perceived* clarity of the boundaries separating in common the members of that group from others.

In turn, the perceived clarity of these boundaries depends upon the existence and wide diffusion in the group of certain beliefs about themselves and the wider society. Three systems of belief are particularly important in this respect. The first is that the criteria of their pervasive categorization as 'separate' from and by others are such that it is impossible, or at least difficult, for a member of the minority to move out *individually* from the group and become a member of the 'majority' indistinguishable from others. In other words, it is the belief that individual social mobility (e.g. becoming a teacher, a lawyer, a doctor, a factory manager, a foreman) will not affect, in many important social situations, the identification of the individual by others as a member of the minority. The second and related belief is that this assignment by others to a certain group, largely independent as it is of the individual differences between the people so assigned as long as they share the defining criterion of the minority (e.g. colour of skin, descent, language, etc.) has certain social consequences which are common to all, or most, members of the group. The third system of beliefs concerns the minority members' *own* views about their common differences from others.

We have already discussed one way in which these views about separateness may develop. This is when they are mainly imposed from the outside, when they result from social categorizations created and consistently used by 'others'. This was the case of the West Indian students mentioned earlier: they arrived in Britain expecting that they would merge with other students, that the criterion subsequently separating them from others, the skin colour, was not relevant to their social integration in the new environment. It is only after a long period of time that they must have reached the painful conclusion that, independently of who and what they were as individuals, they could not fully 'pass' or merge because of this common defining criterion. It is only then that a new affiliation — the 'black consciousness' — has begun to develop for many of them. Once this happens, a minority enters a spiral of psychological separateness in which the 'outside' social categorizations are associated with their 'inside' acceptance by the group in a mutually reinforcing convergence.

The second case concerns a minority which already has a tradition of separateness created by its cultural, social and historical differences from others. The belief that 'passing' or leaving the group is impossible or difficult may then be determined not only by the constraints imposed by others but also powerful social pressures internal to the minority. This has often been the case with religious minorities of various kinds, with some national or ethnic minorities, with political or ideological movements.

Finally, there are some minorities which, although they are aware of their cultural, social, political or historical differences, claim at the same time the right to shed some or most of these differences as and if they wish to do so. If no continuing obstacles are laid in their path, these minorities may merge sooner or later into the surrounding society even while maintaining some of their special characteristics. The Scots living in England or the Catholics in Britain and in the United States can probably serve as examples here. In such cases, the psychological constraints, both internal and external, on leaving the group weaken with time, and the dilution of the sociological criteria of social disadvantages and discrimination is associated with the weakening of the major psychological condition for the existance of a minority: the perception of the existence of clear boundaries confining the group.

The story is very different when, for whatever reasons, the claims of the minority to merge if, when and how they wish are met by strong social and psychological resistance from the outside. We shall come back to this issue when discussing the psychological strategies employed by minorities to deal with these problems. For the present, it will be sufficient to say that this conflict between the push outwards from the minority and the creation of barriers by others may create, in time, a new consciousness of belonging, give a new strength to old affiliations, and it may finally lead to powerful internal constraints against leaving the group.

To sum up: we distinguished between three general sets of conditions which all lead to the appearance or strengthening of 'ingroup' affiliations in members of minorities. In the first of these, a common identity is thrust upon a category of people because they are at the receiving end of certain attitudes and treatment from the 'outside'. In the second case, a group already exists in the sense of wishing to preserve its separate identity, and this is further reinforced by an interaction between the 'inside' and the 'outside' attitudes and patterns of social behaviour. In the third case, an existing group might wish to dilute in a number of ways its differences and separateness from others; when this is resisted, new and intense forms of a common group identity may be expected to appear.

This group identity, made up of the affiliations with it of its members, can be considered psychologically as consisting of cognitive, evaluative and emotional components. The cognitive component is in the individual's awareness that they are members of a social group which is clearly and distinctly separate from other groups. In the case of the kind of minorities which concern us here, it is crucial — as we have seen — that this awareness be associated with the belief that — for whatever reasons — it is not easy to divest oneself of the membership of the group and to 'disappear' in the society at large. The evaluative component consists of the value connotations associated with the membership of the minority. In the case of minorities which are socially disadvantaged and/or perceived as such by their members, a complex interation between several kinds of evaluations must be taken into account. One set of value judgements results from the assessment of the minority's social position and circumstances as compared with other identifiable groups or with the 'majority' in general. The second type of evaluations consists of favourable or unfavourable judgements about the characteristics of the group. The third type has to do with the way an individual feels about his membership of the group. Therefore, an unfavourable judgement about the minority's position in the society at large can be related for an individual either to positive or to negative judgements about the characteristics of the group and about his membership of it. The simplest case would be when all these evaluations are negative and exit from the group is not particularly difficult. But when such exit is difficult or impossible – as in the case with most of the minorities which concern us here – a whole range of individual attitudes, reactions, adaptations and strategies can be expected to occur. We shall discuss in the following sections some of those which are socially the most frequent and important.

The end-results of these various networks of evaluations present some general similarities. Nevertheless, their psychological history and its possible effects on actions and attitudes may be very different, as we shall try to show later. The major similarity consists in many cases of the development of an emotional investment in one's membership of the minority. Group 'affiliations' or group 'identity' can perhaps best be understood as blanket expressions concealing the complexity of the relations between the awareness that one is a member of a group which is clearly separate from others; the diversity of the evaluation associated with this awareness; and the strength and nature of the emotional investments that derive from these evaluations and, in turn, contribute to them.

From social stability to social change: the psychological effects of minority membership

Let us begin with two truisms of general application: no social group consists of individuals who will all react in the same way to conditions in which they live; and no social group is an island – in the same sense in which 'no man is an island'. A social group can only exist as such because it is inserted into a social-system composed of many other groups. The relations – social and psychological – between minorities and other groups in society vary continuously, as a function of social conditions changing with time and of the diversity of the groups by which the minorities are surrounded. Also, each social group has its own internal structure which places different individuals in different social positions; and each group has a considerable range of individual differences in personality, abilities, social roles, family backgrounds, achievements, opportunities and luck. How, then, is it possible to talk blandly about *the* psychological effects of minority membership?

The simple answer is that this is not possible. It cannot be assumed in any discussion of these effects that facile generalizations would emerge which could be applied to all, most or even many members of one or another minority group. All the 'effects' we shall be describing apply to *some* members of *some* minorities, and a variety of patterns can be found within any one minority. All that can be achieved is to identify some patterns which appear more important than others because they are adopted by a variety of people in a variety of groups in a variety of circumstances. The generalizations of social psychology are (thankfully) limited by the creative and boundless diversity and flexibility of human social behaviour.

These reservations must be kept clearly in mind when we think about the social behaviour, attitudes, feelings and affiliations of people who belong to minorities. In a sense, a 'social psychology of minorities' has no more of a claim to a separate existence than would have a 'social psychology of majorities'. Or rather, its claims must be modest from the outset, and they need to be based on clearly stated preliminary assumptions. This is why we embarked earlier upon a lengthy discussion of what, psychologically speaking, 'is' a minority. The preliminary assumptions on which the remainder of this paper is based are quite simple, and they are closely related to our previous discussion: members of minorities, as defined earlier, have some problems in common; there is only a limited number of possible psychological solutions (or attempts at solutions) to these problems; the kind of solution adopted is closely related to the social conditions in which minorities live.

To these three assumptions can be added one wide and tentative generalization. The development of the relations between large-scale social groups (ethnic, national, cultural, social etc.) since the Second World War has been profoundly affected by two continuing processes which seem to pull in opposite directions and yet, paradoxically, complement each other. This is the simultaneous growth of interdependence and differentiation between social groups. There has never been a time before when economic and political interdependence has been so clearly present and visible in our everyday affairs, nor has there ever been before such widespread awareness that decisions taken or conditions prevailing at great distance from our own backyards are likely to affect directly and, at times, immediately the fabric of our daily lives. This growth of interdependence – and of its general awareness – has increased the complexity and created new entanglements in the forms, nature and networks of intergroup conflicts. Examples would be superfluous. It is enough to open any daily newspaper to find instances of deep and direct mutual involvements which transcend geographical distances, cultural differences, or the diversity of economic and political systems. These involvements are not mainly confined, as they often used to be, to the secret conclaves of the political decision-makers and their tortuous strategies. They affect us directly, and are *perceived as doing so* by increasing numbers of people in ever wider areas of the world.

This growing awareness of interdependence has evolved together with a world-wide push towards differentiation originating from minorities which are often at great distances from each other geographically as well as in their cultural and historical diversity. There is one crucially important element which is common to many of these movements towards differentiation: the new claims of the minorities are based on their right to decide to be different (preserve their separateness) as defined *in their own terms* and not in terms implicitly adopted or explicitly dictated by the majorities. The increasing interdependence has led to ever wider multi-national economic and political structures; it has also resulted in a backlash of demands for decentralization coming from smaller social entities which wish to preserve their right to take their own decisions and keep their own identity.

This trend towards differentiation often represents, socially and politically, a rejection of the status quo by groups which perceive themselves as separate and socially disadvantaged. This rejection also represents an important psychological development. As the French sociologist, Colette Guillaumin (1972), argued in her excellent book about racist ideologies, an important cleavage between social majorities and minorities is in the fact that, as she put it:

> a majority is a form of response to minority groups: its existence can only be conceived through the absence of clear-cut, limiting criteria as distinct from groups which are explicitly categorized and narrowly defined. Or, in other words, the membership of a majority is based on the latitude to deny that one belongs to a minority. It is conceived as a freedom in the definition of oneself, a freedom which is never granted to members of minorities and which they are not in a position to give to themselves. [p. 196, translated from the French]

Although it is doubtful that this characterization can be indiscriminately applied to *all* social minorities, Guillaumin makes an important point about the social psychological aspects of many majority-minority situations. As we have seen earlier, minorities are often defined on the basis of criteria originating from, and developed by, the majorities. They are different in certain ways which are socially important, but they are different from something which, itself, need not be clearly defined. The contemporary trend towards differentiation represents an explicit rejection of these one-sided definitions. It represents an attempt to create or preserve criteria of group definition which are not imposed from the outside. Rather than consisting of departures from the 'norm', these newly developing criteria reflect attempts to develop a positively valued identity for the group in which its 'separateness' is not compounded of various stigmas or assumed inferiorities. Social action is often closely related to these redefinitions of who, and what one is. We shall return later to the psychological 'strategies' adopted by minority groups in order to achieve these new definitions of themselves.

This powerful and world-wide push to achieve a positive differentiation represents one extreme of a social psychological continuum of the minorities' attitudes towards their position in the wider society — a continuum which moves from the total acceptance to the total rejection of that position. No doubt, most minorities are somewhere in the middle of that continuum, nearer one or the other of its extremes. The important questions are as follows: what are the psychological determinants and effects of acceptance and rejection? What are the psychological processes contributing to, and resulting from, a transition from acceptance to rejection?

The transition from acceptance to rejection

We start with the second of these two questions because, in considering it, we can already begin to discuss in a preliminary way some aspects of acceptance and rejection. An acceptance by the minority of its social and psychological inferiority must first be looked at in the framework of 'objective' social conditions — but an analysis of such conditions is a job of sociologists, economists, historians and political scientists. It is therefore beyond the scope of our discussion here. There is little doubt, however, that the prime condition for the maintenance of a status quo of inequality, formal or informal, is the unequal distribution of power — political, economic or military. Two major psychological correlates of this unequal distribution of resources help to ensure the maintenance of its stability: the perception of the system of inequalities as being *stable* or *legitimate* or both simultaneously.

It is important to stress at this point that we are concerned here with the *perceived* stability or legitimacy of the prevailing relations between groups rather than with their formal and institutional characteristics or the realities of physical or economic power. Thus, from a social psychological perspective, the perceived stability of a system of intergroup relations consists of an absence of cognitive alternatives to the existing situation. As far as the minority groups are concerned, this implies that, at the 'acceptance' extreme of our continuum, there is no *conceivable* prospect of any change in the nature and the future of the existing inferiorities. Although some exceptional individuals may be able to improve their positions and mode of life within the existing situations, and they may even be accepted and highly respected by some members of the majority, this does not affect the position of their group as a whole: as a matter of fact, such individuals are explicitly seen on 'both sides of the boundary as more or less surprising exceptions to the general rule. Their breaking through some of the barriers separating the groups has two important characteristics: they are often still regarded by the majority as remaining in some important ways specimens of the social category to which they originally belonged: and, whatever they may be or might have become is not seen as generalizing to other, more 'typical', members of the minority. Examples of these attitudes of the majority which remain unchanged, despite the outstanding achievements of some minority individuals, go far back in history. They can be found in the descriptions provided by Sherwin-White (1967) of reactions in imperial Rome to revolts by Greek and other slaves. Longinus who, as Sherwin-White wrote, was 'a severe and inhuman legalist' felt that 'you can only control the foreign scum by fear'; but:

> the kindly Pliny, famous for his humanitarian attitude towards his servants, betrays exactly the same reaction as Longinus when he relates the murder of Lucius Maredo. This man had been a master of exceptional brutality. It was no great surprise when his slaves attacked him in his bath and flung him on to the furnace to finish him off. The household was duly punished, and Pliny, like Cassius, approved. He ends the account with an interestingly irrational out-burst: 'See what dangers and insults we are exposed to. You cannot hope to secure your safety by kindliness and indulgence. They murder us indiscriminately, out of sheer criminality'. [p. 84]

Another interesting example, even if in part fictitious, is provided in William Styron's novel *The Confessions of Nat Turner.* Turner was the leader of what was 'in August 1831, in a remote region of south eastern Virginia . . . the only effective, sustained revolt in the annals of American Negro slavery'. He had outstanding personal qualities which led to relations closer than usual and, in some ways, at a more equal level than usual, with some members of his master's family. But this had no effects upon general attitudes in the family towards the master-slave relationship.

Thus, it is highly unlikely that the perceived stability of the existing relations between a majority and a minority can be seriously affected by the opportunity afforded to a few exceptional or exceptionally lucky members of the minority to escape the inflexibility of the system. Something else is needed to shake the acceptance of what appears as inevitable. The building up of 'cognitive alternatives' to what appears as unshakable social reality must depend upon the conviction, growing at least amongst some members of the minority, that some cracks are visible in the edifice of impenetrable social layers, and that therefore the time has come to push *as a group*. This pushing as a group can take a number of forms, including *unexceptional* individual social mobility encouraged by visible changes in the system. We shall return to these issues later. In today's conditions, there is very little doubt that, whatever may have been the reasons for the first appearance of visible cracks in one or another system of rigid stratifications still existing in the contemporary world, the growth of the mass media of communication has helped enormously to transplant from one social location to another the *perceived possibility* of causing new cracks. This is one of the ways in which the increasing interdependence, which we discussed earlier, has also led to increasing trends towards differentiation.

The perceived stability of the system (i.e. the absence of realistic alternative conceptions of the social order) is one important foundation of the various patterns of acceptance by the minority. The perceived legitimacy of the existing order is at least as important. Daniel Bell (1977), writing in *The Fontana Dictionary of Modern Thought*, defined legitimacy as 'the rightful rule or exercise of power, based on some principle (e.g., consent) jointly accepted by the ruler and the ruled' (p. 491). The *Concise OED* describes 'legitimate' as, amongst other things, lawful, proper, regular, logically admissible. In the case which interests us here, that of a social order based on clear-cut differences between the majority and a 'lower' minority, the perceived legitimacy would therefore imply an acceptance (or consent, in Bell's terms) of the differentiation as based on some principles acceptable to both sides and accepted by them. This was presumably the case for some of the social divisions in the feudal societies or in the Indian caste system at the time when they were still very stable. When, for whatever reasons, this consent begins to break down, an interaction between three forms of legitimacy must be taken into account: 'the legitimacy of the intergroup relationship as it is perceived by the disaffected group; the legitimacy of this relationship as it is perceived by the other groups involved; and an "objective" definition (i.e., a set of rules and regulations) of legitimacy, whenever such a thing is possible' (Tajfel, 1976, p. 298).

There is little doubt that an unstable system of social divisions between a majority and a minority is more likely to be perceived as illegitimate than a stable one, and that, conversely, a system perceived as illegitimate will contain the seeds of instability. It is interaction between the perceived instability and illegitimacy of the system of differentials which is likely to become a powerful ingredient of the transition from the minority's acceptance of the status quo to the rejection of it. It is, however, possible — at least in theory, but also probably in some concrete contexts — that perceived instability and illegitimacy need not always be inseparable to begin with (see Turner and Brown, 1978), even if it is true that, sooner or later, one is likely to lead to the other. It is, for example, conceivable that a certain kind of social or political order is so powerfully maintained by those in charge that it appears very stable, however deeply held are the convictions about its illegitimacy. In a recent television programme broadcast for the tenth anniversary of the invasion of Czechoslovakia in 1968, one of the exiled Czechs was asked in an interview whether he believed that a return of any form of the 'Prague spring' was possible, at least in the foreseeable future. His answer was negative. In this case, as in the case of the minorities which see the system as illegitimate but extremely stable, a conception of illegitimacy of the situation will continue to exert its powerful influence on actions, attitudes, beliefs and affiliations in the teeth of what appears as unshakeable. The converse can also occur: a system of differentials affecting a minority may retain, at least for a time, its perceived legitimacy even when it is seen as unstable. But although we have a good deal of evidence, both from 'real life' and from some experimental studies in social psychology (e.g. Turner and Brown 1978; Caddick, 1978; Commins and Lockwood, 1977), that a system of relations between social groups seen as illegitimate will lead to the rejection of the status quo by the disadvantaged group, there is less convincing evidence that the same would happen in a system perceived as legitimate but unstable. The psychological importance in the determination of social actions of their perception as legitimate or illegitimate is further confirmed (at least in our culture) by a very large number of social psychological studies on inter-individual aggression. Although it would be preposterous to equate a minority's rejection of its status with 'aggression', the weight of evidence from these studies is sufficiently impressive to appear relevant to a variety of large-scale social situations (see Billig, 1976, for a detailed review). It must, however, be stressed again that a theoretical separation of perceived instability and illegitimacy cannot be taken very far without losing touch with social reality. Very often they merge, either from their very inception, or because each of them can contribute to changes in the social situation in a way which causes the other to make its appearance. It is then that, as we said earlier, a rapid transition from acceptance to rejection by the minorities of their status and of their beliefs about the 'inferiority' of their group can be safely predicted to occur.

Patterns of acceptance

Social position carries with it certain experiences, attitudes, and activities not shared by people at other levels, which do modify self-evaluation and general out-look on life. . . It therefore seems valid and useful to talk of a person's social personality; meaning that part of his make-up which is contributed by the society in which he lives and moves and which he shares in large measure with all other persons living under the same conditions. This social personality is obviously different from his personal temperament or psychological individuality, which is developed by another set of factors entirely. [Warner, Junker and Adam, 1941, pp. 25-7]

This description of a 'social personality', written nearly forty years ago, is still largely valid today, although many of us would find it difficult to agree with the sharp distinction made by the authors between what 'is contributed by the society' and what is 'developed by another set of factors entirely'.

We are more likely today to conceive these different sets of factors, the 'individual' and the 'social', to be almost inseparable and interacting very closely from the beginning of an individual's life, one setting the stage for the development of the other, one creating or inhibiting the potentialities or the restrictions determined by the other (see, for example, Bruner and Garton, 1978). Be this as it may, Lloyd Warner and his colleagues were right in stressing the importance in a person's life and 'make-up' of 'what he *shares* in large measure with all other persons living under the same conditions'.

People who are members of the kind of minorities with which we are concerned here share one difficult psychological problem which can be described, in its most general terms, as a conflict between a satisfactory self-realization and the restrictions imposed upon it by the realities of membership of a minority group. 'Satisfactory self-realization' is a hopelessly vague, synthetic term which can mean so much that it is in danger of meaning very little at all. We shall therefore confine ourselves here to one of its important aspects. We shall assume, both on the basis of common experience and of an endless stream of psychological studies, that it is a fairly general human characteristic to try to achieve or preserve one's self-respect and the respect of others; that it is important for most of us to have and keep as much of a positive self-image as we can manage to scrape together; and that having to live with a contemptuous view of oneself, coming from inside or from other people, constitutes a serious psychological problem.

A person's self-image is essentially based on certain kinds of comparisons, and it consists to a large extent of the outcome of these comparisons. The comparisons may go in a number of directions such as: one's expectations, wishes or hopes as related to one's achievement, actual or subjectively assessed; a person's past as related to the present; one's characteristics (again, objectively ascertainable or subjectively assessed) as related to those of other people with whom meaningful comparisons can be made (cf. Festinger, 1954). These latter inter-individual comparisons can also have an important temporal dimension, in the sense that their outcomes may change, in a direction favourable or detrimental to oneself, as people and circumstances change with time. And finally, there are the comparisons rooted in the membership of groups to which one belongs, particularly when this membership is highly important and salient in an individual's life. These comparisons are then made with other social groups or their individual members, the choice of objects of comparison being, once again, determined by their salience, relevance or importance to an individual's life. We said earlier that 'no group is an island'. Because of the multiplicity of interdependent 'objective' relations between social groups co-existing in a complex society,

> The characteristics of one's group as a whole (such as its status, its richness or poverty, its skin colour or its ability to reach its aims) achieve most of their significance in relation to perceived differences from other groups and the value connotation of these differences. For example, economic deprivation acquires its importance in social attitudes, intentions and actions mainly when it becomes 'relative deprivation'; easy or difficult access to means of production and consumption of goods, to benefits and opportunities, becomes psychologically salient mainly in relation to comparisons with other groups; the definition of a group (national, racial or any other) makes no sense unless there are other groups around. A group becomes a group in the sense of being perceived as having common characteristics or a common fate only because other groups are present in the environment. [Tajfel, 1978]

These value-loaded comparisons with other groups or their individual members may become an important aspect of a person's self-image, particularly so when he or she belongs to a minority which is considered to be clearly separate from others and (explicitly or implicitly) 'inferior' to them in some important ways. We discussed earlier certain relationships between the 'external' and the 'internal' criteria of minority membership. As long as the external criteria and the value connotations associated with them continue to predominate, as long as the membership of a minority is defined by general consensus as a departure from some ill-defined 'norm' inherent, as Guillaumin wrote (see previous section) in the majority, the self-image and self-respect problems of minority individuals will continue to be acute.

A large number of clear examples of this has been found in many studies about the phenomenon known as 'ethnocentrism'. The term was extensively used by William Graham Sumner in his book on *Folkways* written in 1906, and has since then gained wide currency in the social sciences and elsewhere. As he wrote:

> Ethnocentrism is the technical name for this view of things in which one's own group is the centre for everything, and all others are scaled and rated with reference to it. . . Each group nourishes its own pride and vanity, boasts itself superior, exalts its own divinities, and looks with contempt on outsiders. Each group thinks its own folkways the only right ones, and if it observes that other groups have other folkways, these excite its scorn. Opprobrious epithets are derived from these differences. . . For our present purpose the most important fact is that ethnocentrism leads a people to exaggerate and intensify everything in their own folkways which is peculiar and which differentiates them from others. [pp. 12-13]

This 'universal syndrome of ethnocentrism' turned out to be considerably less universal than Sumner assumed it to be three quarters of a century ago (see Levine and Campbell, 1972, for a recent review of some of the evidence). An enormous amount of work has been done, since Sumner wrote, on the forms, conditions and development of ethnocentrism. The 'differentiation from others' to which he referred can be understood as fulfilling two main functions, one for the group as a whole and one for its individual members. For the group as a whole, it 'strengthens the folkways', that is, it contributes to the continuation of the group as an articulate social entity. For individual members of the group, positively valued differentiations from others contribute favourably to their self-image and boost their self-respect. As I wrote elsewhere, this amounts to saying to oneself, 'We are what we are because *they* are not what we are'.

One of the important exceptions to the world-wide generality of ethnocentrism has been found in the attitude towards themselves, their own group and other groups displayed, under certain conditions, by members of minorities. The conditions are usually those previously discussed: a general consensus in society about the nature of the characteristics attributed to the minority; some measure of acceptance, within the minority, of these defining criteria derived from the outside; the absence of well-established alternatives which would be based on the idea that the present situation is not legitimate and not necessarily permanent; the difficulty of 'passing' from the stigmatized group to another one; the fact that some instances of successful individual social mobility out of the minority group have not affected the nature of the generally established relations and differences between the minority and the others. But these are the 'maximum' conditions. It will be seen later that a reversal of ethnocentrism (i.e., the devaluation of themselves and of their groups by members of minorities) can also occur in social conditions which present much less of a drastic social division between the minorities and others. Social differentiations between groups, even when they take on fairly subtle forms, are reflected, as we shall see, with an amazing sensitivity in the attitude of the people who are adversely affected.

One of the extreme forms of this internalization by members of minorities of the 'outside' views about them has been well described by the eminent black American psychologist, Kenneth Clark (1965), when he wrote:

Human beings who are forced to live under ghetto conditions and whose daily experience tells them that almost nowhere in society are they respected and granted the ordinary dignity and courtesy accorded to others will, as a matter of course, begin to doubt their own worth. Since every human being depends upon his cumulative experiences with others for clues as to how he should view and value himself, children who are consistently rejected understandably begin to question and doubt whether they, their family and their group really deserve no more respect from the larger society than they receive. These doubts become the seeds of a pernicious self- and group-hatred, the Negro's complex and debilitating prejudice against himself. . . Negroes have come to believe in their own inferiority. [As quoted in Milner, 1975, p. 100]

This belief in one's own inferiority is, as Clark wrote, a complex and important issue; but it is no less crucial to understand the many and important exceptions to it and the conditions in which it is likely to disappear. We shall return to this issue in the next section of this paper, concerned with the minorities' 'patterns of rejection'. For the present, we must look in a little more detail at this acceptance of inferiority and the effects it has on the lives of those suffering from it. This is by no means confined to the social contexts in which the recognition of a minority member as such is immediate and certain (as is the case for skin colour) or in which a very large proportion of the minority are confined to *de jure* or *de facto* ghettos. For example, the phenomenon of the 'Jewish self-hatred' has been known for a long time (Karl Marx was one of its more famous victims), and contributed in important ways to Jean-Paul Sartre's *Reflections on the Jewish question,* first drafted in 1944, when the shock of the Nazi mass murders was still stunning the conscience of the world. Sartre's reflections about self-hatred are not very different from those of Clark:

> It is not the man but the *Jew* that Jews try to know in themselves through introspection: and they want to know him so that they can deny him. . . This is how can be explained the special quality of Jewish irony which is most often used against the Jew himself and which is a perpetual attempt at looking at oneself from the outside. The Jew, knowing that he is being watched, gets there first and tries to look at himself with the eyes of others. This objectivity applied to himself is yet another ruse of inauthenticity: while he contemplates himself with the detachment of someone else, he feels in effect detached from himself, he becomes someone else, a pure witness. [Translated from the 1948 French edn, pp. 117-18]

The process starts from early childhood, and evidence of its existence comes from many countries and many cultures (see Milner, 1971, for an excellent recent review). In the late thirties, the Clarks (1939) published the first of a long series of studies demonstrating that black children in the United States could be directly and objectively shown to have serious identity, identification and group preference problems already at the age of six or seven, or even earlier. The methods used by Clark and Clark, and in many subsequent studies, consisted of presenting each child 'with a variety of dolls or pictures representing the various racial groups in the child's environment', and then asking the children a number of questions about which of the dolls they looked like, which ones they would prefer to have for a friend, to play with, to be at school together, etc. It was found that the minority children (for example, the blacks in America, the Maoris in New Zealand, children of the various 'coloured' minorities in Britain) sometimes misidentified themselves in the tests (that is, they said they were 'more like' the white than the black doll) and that most of them 'preferred' in various tests the white to other dolls. Doubts have been raised, on methodological grounds, about the validity of the first of these findings – concerning misidentification of the child's own group membership. But there is a considerable weight of evidence, from several countries including Britain, supporting the findings about marked 'outgroup preference' of the minority children at ages from six or so until eleven, and sometimes well beyond. Even in a study on children of Asian origin conducted in Glasgow by Jahoda and his colleagues (1972), in which all possible care was taken to counteract such 'artifactual' effects, as, for example, the experimenter being a member of the majority (it was, in this case, 'a charming and attractive' young Indian woman), by the age of ten the children shifted their preferences towards the majority. This study is mentioned here because it probably presents a *minimum* of the effects as compared with many of the others.

In a large-scale study conducted in England, Milner was able to confirm and extend many of the previous findings, from America and elsewhere, about the development of these 'outgroup preferences' in children from racial minorities (see a detailed description in Chapter 4 of his book). In a series of studies on Maori and Pakeha (European-descended) children conducted by Graham Vaughan in New Zealand over a period of more than ten years, a similar pattern of outgroup preferences emerged for the Maori children (see, for example, Vaughan, 1978a). As Milner summarized it, the research by Vaughan has shown that the Maori children favoured other-race children when assigning desirable or undesirable attributes to members of their own and other groups; preferred other-race figures as playmates; and preferred other-race dolls to 'take home'. At the same time, recent favourable changes in the social environment of the Maori children had a drastic effect in the direction of *reducing* the disparagement of their own ethnic group in their responses to the tests (see Vaughan, 1978b). A similar effect, which can again be ascribed to variations in the social conditions, has been found by Morland (1969) who compared Chinese children in Hong Kong with the American black and white children. Hong Kong is, in Morland's words, a 'multi-racial setting in which no race is clearly dominant'. He found that preferences for their own group were displayed by 82 per cent of the white American children, 65 per cent of the Hong Kong Chinese and only 28 per cent of the black Americans.

It is, of course, difficult to establish solid links of evidence between this early rejection by children of their own group and its effects on their later development and behaviour. 'Longitudinal' studies on this subject, which could trace such a development in the same individuals over a number of years, are very difficult to organize and conduct. We can only guess, and our guesses can be helped by what we know of the deleterious effects of the 'self-hatred', about which Clark and Sartre wrote, in some adult members of minorities. Alienation from the society at large is often the result of social conditions, such as poverty, unemployment, family disintegration, overcrowding, etc.; but the search for some possibilities of regaining self-respect can also be a contributing factor to 'deviant' social behaviour. Withdrawal from the wider community's system of norms, values, prescriptions and achievements, and the creation of groups which have their own values, divergent from those which are generally approved, is one *possible* effect (not by any means confined to minorities) of what is now fashionably called a 'search for identity'. This withdrawal is rooted in the *acceptance* by the minorities of the image of themselves imposed by the society at large; and it may result in turn in the *rejection* of this image through means which are, at best, ineffective in changing the social situation, and, at worst, reinforce the existing stereotypes and divisions.

This kind of active withdrawal from the society's community of mutual respect represents one of the transitions between acceptance and rejection to which we referred earlier as the two extremes of a continuum in the behaviour and attitudes of minorities. We must now return to a description of some other forms and conditions of acceptance of 'inferiority'. The work of Vaughan on the effects of social change on the self-images of the Maori children and the comparisons made by Morland between children from different social environments provide important indications of the high sensitivity shown by minority children to the fluctuations in the prevailing social images of their group. But there is some evidence that this sensitivity goes even further and that it extends to situations in which members of the minority are not easily identifiable, and where the tensions are (at least on the surface) less acute.

The first example comes from Israel. At present, well over 60 per cent of the Israeli Jewish population consists of immigrants, or descendants of immigrants, of Middle Eastern or North African origin; most of the remainder are of European descent. The early pioneers and the founders of the state belonged overwhelmingly to the latter category. There were also some clear-cut social, cultural and educational differences between the two main waves of immigrants, those who came from Europe and those from the Arab countries who, on the whole, arrived later. By the mid sixties, most of the children from both groups, who were then ten years old or less, were born in Israel. Although serious attempts and strenuous efforts were made by the public authorities to promote social, economic and psychological integration, the cultural and socio-economic differences and the underlying intergroup tensions remained unresolved — despite the clear perception by an overwhelming majority of the population of a common danger from the outside threatening them all. It was at about that time that my colleagues and I were engaged in a research project on the development of national attitudes in children (aged about 7-11) in several European countries. One of the methods we used to test the children was exceedingly simple. Each child was shown twenty photographs of young men, presented one by one, and asked to place each of them into one of four 'posting' boxes respectively labelled: 'I like him very much'; 'I like him a little'; 'I dislike him a little'; 'I dislike him very much' (children who had reading difficulties were helped in the test). In a second session, some two or three weeks later, the same child was presented with the same photographs and two posting boxes which were labelled 'English' and 'Not English' in England (or 'Italian' and 'Not Italian' in Italy, 'Austrian' and 'Not Austrian' in Austria, etc). The same set of photographs was shown in all the countries. Nearly two thousand children were tested; half of them had the 'like-dislike' session first and the 'nationality guessing' session later; for the other half, this order was reversed. We found, in several European countries, very high correlations between the two kinds of assignments made by the children: photographs which were 'liked' tended to be placed in the own nationality box, independently of the order of the two sessions.

These findings raised a number of questions which cannot be discussed here. What is, however, of direct interest to the present discussion is a replication of the study which was made in Israel. A different set of photographs was used, half of which were of young Israelis of Oriental origin and half of European origin. Of the several hundred children who were tested, half were also from one of those two groups and half from the other. The general correlation between 'liking' and the assignment to 'Israeli' was one of the highest we found anywhere (it was not, however, significantly higher than in the data from England). However, both groups of Israeli children (the 'Oriental' and the 'European') showed a strikingly similar pattern in their reactions to the two corresponding categories of photographs: the 'Oriental' photographs were 'liked' less than the 'European' ones; they were assigned less frequently to the category 'Israeli'; and both these trends increased as a function of the age of the children. A subsequent study in Bristol on a group of adults who were not familiar with Israel showed that they were able to guess correctly, at a frequency higher than could have been expected by chance, which of the same set of photographs were 'Oriental' and which 'European'. There were, therefore, some general physiognomic differences between the two categories of photographs. But, at the same time, these differences were nowhere nearly as clear as in the studies on racial groups in Britain, America, Hong Kong or New Zealand; and, most of all, it must be remembered that a substantial majority of Israeli Jews *are* by now of 'Oriental' origin, and therefore the physiognomy of the photographs could not have been in any sense 'alien' to the children.

This preference, shown by both groups of children, for people from one ethnic category over those from another represents a striking example of the acceptance by a 'minority' of their status and image in the society. The tension between the two groups in Israel is undoubtedly not as acute as in some of the other countries in which studies were made about the minority children's preferences for the 'outgroup'; and yet, the 'Oriental' children show a high sensitivity to the social context which creates these tensions.

The subtle effects of a social or political situation on the children's attitudes towards their own and other groups can go even further. The Scots who live in England can hardly be considered a 'minority' in the sense of the term adopted in this discussion, although many of them retain their Scottish affiliations and cherish the traditional aspects of their Scottish identity. The Scots who live in Scotland are even less of a 'minority'. On the other hand, there are certainly some Scots who feel that, within the wider context of the United Kingdom, they have, *as a national group,* a number of grievances which must be redressed. Although these grievances cannot be related to any marked discrimination or prejudice against those Scots who chose to live in England, there exists in the culture of the two peoples a tradition of a historical differentiation between them which favoured the English. This tradition was reflected, in a rather unexpected way, in the studies on children's national attitudes which we discussed earlier. There was one odd exception to the general finding in several countries that the children sorting the photographs 'preferred' those which they assigned to their own national group, or that they assigned to their own national group those which they 'preferred'. The Scottish children, tested in Glasgow and asked to sort the photographs into 'Scottish' and 'Not Scottish', did not conform to the general pattern: there was no sign of a greater 'liking' for the photographs categorized as 'Scottish'. It occurred to us that the *implicit* comparisons these children may have been making when sorting the photographs was not between 'Scottish' and some undefined non-Scottish foreigners, but between 'Scottish' and 'English'. Three additional studies were conducted in order to test this possibility. A further group of children in Glasgow were asked to sort the same photographs into 'Scottish' and 'English', yet another group in Glasgow divided them into 'British' and 'Not British'; and a group of English children in Oxford also categorized them into 'Scottish' and 'English'. The results were fairly clear-cut; 'British' photographs were preferred to the 'Not British' in Glasgow; the 'English' to the 'Scottish' in Oxford; and no preference was shown in Glasgow for the 'Scottish' ones over the 'English'. As a matter of fact, there were even some indications of a preference in the opposite direction (see Tajfel *et al.*, 1972).

These studies were conducted more than ten years ago, and it is fully possible that if they were to be repeated today, when some of the attitudes in Scotland reflect the world-wide upsurge of ethnic and national affiliations, the results would be very different. But this is not the point; or rather − if these findings were *not* replicated − this would probably lend even more weight to the accumulating evidence that the social and cultural influences associated with the fluctuations of the relations between human groups have a direct and subtle impact on the sensitivities of the children.

In the case of the Scottish−English relations, there is some evidence that the impact continues with adults, or rather that it did at about the time when the studies on children were conducted. Lambert and his colleagues (1960) at McGill University in Montreal took advantage, some twenty years ago, of the fact that one of the major differences between the main ethnic minority in Canada, the Francophone population of Quebec, and the majority, was that of language. They devised for their studies a method which came to be known as the 'matched-guise technique'. Several French−English bilingual speakers were asked to read in both languages the same 'neutral' short passage of prose. The recordings of all these readings were then played to groups of French − and English-speaking Canadians who were informed that each of the passages was read by a different person. The study was presented as part of a research concerned with the ways in which personal characteristics of people are assessed from their voices alone. In this way, two interesting sets of data could be obtained simultaneously. First, it was possible to see if there were any differences in the judgements of the *same* person when he spoke French or English. And, second, the method offered the possibility of a direct comparison of these differences as seen by the groups of the Francophone and the Anglophone 'judges'.

The results of these initial studies, replicated several times in later years, were of undoubted interest from the point of view of the minority's acceptance of a general 'social image' of themselves. The English group found the English voices superior to the French in seven traits out of the total of fourteen about which they were asked to pass their judgement. These were: height, good looks, intelligence, dependability, kindness, ambition and character. They found the French superior to the English in sense of humour only. The French group found the *English* voices superior on *ten* traits out of fourteen. In addition to height, good looks, intelligence, dependability, ambition and character, these included leadership, self-confidence, sociability and likeability. They considered the French voices as superior only in religiousness and kindness. The detail of the judgements is probably not very important, nor — as in the case of the Glasgow children — is it likely that they would be the same today, at the height of the development of the Quebecois separatism. The general pattern is, however, important, since it showed the transposition of the social image of the minority, prevailing in the 1950s, onto its members' comparative assessment of their fellows' *personal* characteristics. Very similar results were obtained in subsequent studies, employing the same method, in which clear-cut differences in accents were used instead of different languages. This was the case, for example, for groups of Jews in the United States and also, in a study conducted by Cheyne in 1970 in this country, in which he used Scottish and English accents in his recordings. It is equally interesting to note that a similar study conducted some years ago in Tel Aviv and Jaffa amongst Arab and Jewish high school pupils yielded very different findings: each group judged themselves to be invariably superior to the other.

It would be a mistake, however, to exaggerate the importance of all these findings, whether concerned with children or with adults, as indicators of serious problems of *personal* identity amongst members of minorities. Their common element is that the judgements made in these studies by members of minorities about therir own groups are requested in contexts which are directly and explicitly comparative with the majority. There is, as we have seen, substantial evidence that in such conditions an unfavourable self-image has come to be internalized. But not all 'natural' social contexts include the need or the requirement for intergroup comparisions, and a person's idea about himself or herself is at least as much (and probably much more) dependent upon continuous and daily interactions with individuals from the same social group. When this group happens to have its own strongly integrated norms, traditions, values and functions, a 'negative' self-image elicited in comparisons with other groups need not by any means become the central focus of an individual's identity. This is why one can remain happy and contented inside a ghetto, as long as this ghetto has not become socially disintegrated. An excellent example of this can be found in the Jewish *shtetls* which led, at the turn of the century, their isolated lives in Russia and elsewhere in eastern Europe. The internal norms and cultural prescriptions of these small communities together with their tremendous power in guiding the lives of their members have been reflected and beautifully transmitted in the short stories of Sholem Aleichem and other writers of the period. The 'deviant' groups, to which we referred earlier, can serve as another contemporary example, providing that they can manage to create a mini-culture which is powerful enough to protect the self-respect of their members from the cold winds of disapproval blowing from the outside.

But it remains true that, fundamentally, this internal minority protection of individual self-respect is yet another facet of the minority's *acceptance* of the status quo. It is, as we have said earlier, a form of withdrawal from the society at large, a delicately poised and hard-won equilibrium which can be easily destroyed. In this kind of a situation, a community (or a deviant group) must manage to be virtually sealed off from the outside world in those aspects of their lives which really matter to them; and, in turn, those aspects of their lives which really matter are bound to be selected, in the long run, on the criterion of their safe insulation from comparability with other people who become inherently different, and thus partly irrelevant. The question is: for how long can they remain irrelevant unless the difficult achievement of social and psychological isolation is maintained? When it cannot be, the practical implications of a comparative (and negative) self-image come again to the fore. Irwin Katz, an American social psychologist, has done a good deal of work on the academic achievement of black pupils in segregated and mixed schools. Some of his earlier conclusions, based on the work done in the 1960s, may well have to be revised today; but this does not detract from their importance in suggesting what happens in situations of intergroup contact and comparison, when comparisons have to be made in terms of criteria generally accepted by the society. Here are some examples: 'where feelings of inferiority are acquired by Negro children outside the school, minority-group newcomers in integrated classrooms are likely to have a low expectancy of academic success; consequently, their achievement motivation should be low'. Or: 'Experiments on Negro male college students by the author or his associates have shown that in work teams composed of Negro and white students of similar intellectual ability, Negroes are passively compliant, rate their own performance as inferior when it is not, and express less satisfaction with the team experience than do their white companions.' Or again: 'Among Florida Negro college students, anticipated intellectual comparison with Negro peers was found to produce a higher level of verbal performance than anticipated comparison with white peers, in accordance with the assumption that the subjective probability of success was lower when the expected comparison was with whites' (Katz, 1968, pp. 283-4).

There exists, however, a half-way house between the two extremes, one of which is the psychological isolation from the surrounding society, such as was the case of a Jewish *shtetl* in Tsarist Russia or for some deviant groups in today's large cities, and the other the damaging acceptance by the minority of the majority's prevailing images. As we have seen, the first of these extremes is a psychological withdrawal from comparisons with others which is made possible by the development of separate and socially powerful criteria of personal worth: the second is the result of a social (and consequently, psychological) disintegration of a group and of its inability to create an articulate social entity with its own forms of interaction, its own values, norms and prescriptions. Needless to say, most of the minorities fall somewhere between these two extremes. Their identity is then simultaneously determined by the socially prevailing views of the majority and by the psychological effects of their own cultural and social organization. Cases of that nature are still near to the 'acceptance' end of our acceptance-rejection continuum. The continuous and daily interactions with the outside world, and the consequent *psychological* participation of a group in the system of values and the network of stereotypes of the society at large create a degree of acceptance by the minority of its deleterious image; at the same time, *some* measure of protection is offered by the social and cultural links surviving within the group. A good example of this is provided in David Milner's research in England, in which he compared the negative self-images of the West Indians and the Asian children. His description of the differences in the cultural background and the corresponding initial attitudes towards the host society is as follows:

It seemed likely that the British component of the West Indians' culture, and the 'white bias' in the racial ordering of West Indian society, would enhance their children's orientation and positive feeling towards whites in this country. In addition, the West Indians' original aspirations to integrate ensured more contact with the white community – and its hostility – than was experienced by the Asian community. Not only did the Asians' detached stance *vis-à-vis* the host community insulate them to some extent, they also had entirely separate cultural traditions which provide a strong sense of identity. In the American studies many black children internationalized the racial values that were imposed on them by the dominant white group, such that they had difficulty in identifying with their own group, and were very positively disposed towards whites. For the reasons discussed, it seemed likely that this response to racism would be more prevalent among West Indian children than among the Asian children. [pp. 117-18]

The comparisons, in Milner's work, between the two categories of children showed that 'while the Asian and the West Indian children equally reproduce white values about their groups, they do not equally accept the implications for themselves . . . the derogatory personal identity is less easily imposed on Asian children. It is as though the same pressure simply meets with more resistance' (p. 138).

And herein lies the problem. For how long can this partial resistance be maintained in succeeding generations? The cultural pressures from the surrounding society are bound to become more effective, the cultural separateness to decrease. The Asian minorities in this country, or any other minorities anywhere which live in the kind of half-way house to which we previously referred, have at their disposal a limited number of *psychological* solutions to their problems of self-respect and human dignity. Some of these solutions are, at least for the present and the foreseeable future, simply not realistic. The first is that of a *complete* assimilation, of merging in the surrounding society. This is not possible as long as the attitudes of prejudice and the realities of discrimination remain what they are. The second is that of a cultural and psychological insulation from others. This again is not possible, for two reasons at least. One is that the new generations cannot be expected to remain immune to the increasing pressures of the surrounding cultural values and social influences. At the same time, the economic and social requirements of everyday life make it both impossible and undesirable to withdraw from the network of entanglements with the outside society together with its pecking order of stereotyped images. Thus, in the last analysis, 'psychological' solutions must give precedence to social and economic changes. Minority groups cannot respond to the outside images by the creation of their own counter-images floating in a social vacuum. They must rely on the creation of social changes from which new psychological solutions can derive. Some of the 'patterns of rejection', which we shall discuss next, are relevant to this issue.

Patterns of rejection

The focus of much of the previous discussion was on the effects that the psychological status of minorities has on the ideas of personal worth and dignity, on the self-image and the self-respect of their individual members. As we have seen, these effects exist with particular clarity in situations which elicit direct comparisons between members of the minority and the majority. But there is little doubt that they do not entirely disappear even in the psychologically 'safer' social interactions confined to the minority itself and its separate cultural prescriptions.

Underlying this centrality of a positive self-image and of its erosion was the conception that *social comparisons* are crucial in the development of our image of ourselves. In the relations between minorities and majorities (or between any other distinct social groups), the comparisons between the groups, or between individuals clearly identified as belonging to one group or another, make an important contribution to this image of oneself. In situations of considerable intergroup tension or conflict this can become, for a time, one of the most important facets of this image. This is one of the reasons why comparisons which are made in such situations are often associated with powerful emotions. Even differences between groups which might be emotionally neutral to begin with may then acquire strong value connotations and a powerful emotional charge. This is often the case with nationalism. Almost anything can be thrown into this boiling stew: differences 'between languages, landscapes, flags, anthems, postage stamps, football teams . . . become endowed with emotional significance because they relate to a superordinate value' (Tajfel, 1974, p. 75). The importance of these intergroup comparisons is also well exemplified in the large number of industrial conflicts which have to do with differentials. As Elliot Jaques exclaimed in desperation in a letter to *The Times* (29 October 1974): 'Is it not apparent to all that the present wave of disputes has to do with relativities, relativities and nothing but relativities?' We found in some laboratory experiments (e.g. Tajfel, 1970) that the establishment of a *difference* between two groups in favour of their own was often more important to the schoolboys with whom we worked than the absolute amounts of monetary rewards that they could get.

Starting from the results of these studies, Brown (1978) found a similar pattern when doing research in a large factory with shop stewards belonging to different unions. As we know from common experience and from many sociological and psychological studies, 'relative deprivation' can be, within limits, a more important determinant of attitudes and social behaviour than are the 'absolute' levels of deprivation (see Runciman, 1972; Tajfel, 1978 for more extensive discussions of this issue).

As we have seen in the previous section, the 'comparative' self-image of members of minorities is often derogatory. The question is: what can they do about it? This is by no means a 'theoretical' or an 'academic' issue. In the preface to his book on *Ethos and Identity*, Epstein (1978) recently wrote:

> I found myself asking how such groups manage to survive as groups at all, and why they should strive so consciously to retain their sense of group identity. At the same time, I am keenly aware that if I achieved any insight into these situations it was because they touched some chord of response that echoed my own ethnic experience as a Jew of the Diaspora. Reflecting on all this, the one major conviction that emerged was the powerful emotional charge that appears to surround or underlie so much of ethnic behaviour . . . . [p. XI]

There is little doubt that personal problems of worth, dignity and self-respect involved in being a member of a minority, and shared with others who are in the same situation, are an important ingredient of this high 'emotional charge'. I have defined elsewhere the 'social identity' of individuals as consisting of those aspects of their self-image and its evaluation which derive from membership of social groups that are salient to them; and, in turn, much of that self-image and of the values attached to it derive from comparisons with other groups which are present in the social environment. These comparisons are rarely 'neutral'. They touch a 'chord of response' which echoes the past, the present and a possible future of 'inferiority'. It is therefore not surprising that emotions and passions will rise in the defence of one's right to have and keep as much self-respect as has the next man or woman.

As we asked earlier: what can the minorities do about it? One obvious answer for some of their members is assimilation to the majority, whenever this is possible. Assimilation, as Simpson (1968) wrote,

> is a process in which persons of diverse ethnic and racial backgrounds come to interact, free of these constraints, in the life of the larger community. Wherever representatives of different racial and cultural groups live together, some individuals of subordinate status (whether or not they constitute a numerical minority) become assimilated. Complete assimilation would mean that no separate social structures based on racial or ethnic concepts remained. [p. 438]

There are many variants of this process, psychologically as well as socially. From the psychological point of view, a distinction can be made between at least four kinds of assimilation. The first, which would present no particular problems to the assimilating individuals, is when there are no constraints to social mobility imposed by either of the two groups involved. But whenever this happens (as has been the case, for example, for some immigrant ethnic groups in the United States), the minority ceases to exist as such, sooner or later. There is a psychological merging in which, even when the defining label is maintained and invoked from time to time, it has lost most of the characteristics which define a 'minority', both psychologically and socially. Individual assimilation has then become the assimilation of a social group as a whole, the case to which Simpson referred as the disappearance of 'separate social structures based on racial or ethnic concepts'.

The second kind of assimilation presents more difficulties to the assimilating individual. This is when, although the people who moved from one group to another may well interact in their new setting in many ways which are 'free of constraints', they have not been fully accepted by the majority. Paradoxically, they are regarded as still typifying in some important ways the unpleasant characteristics attributed to their group and at the same time as 'exceptions' to the general rule. A classic example of this kind of situation was provided between the late eighteenth century and very recent times in some European countries with a strong tradition of anti-semitism. Despite this, a number of Jews managed to break through the barriers of prejudice and discrimination, and some even achieved very high positions in the 'outside' society. But the breaking of the barriers by some did not succeed in breaking them for the group as a whole nor did it eliminate the widespread prejudice. At the turn of the century, the Dreyfus affair in France provided a dramatic case history of this inherent ambiguity. This was one of the turning points for the Viennese journalist Herzl, one of the founders of Zionism, in his search for alternative solutions for the Jewish minorities in Europe.

Dreyfus was probably a good example of the psychological problems encountered in this kind of assimilation. His identification with the majority, as a Frenchman and an officer in the army, not different from any other Frenchman, was total. A little later, the German-Jewish industrialist and statesman Rathenau, who was assassinated by right wing nationalists in 1922, when he was minister for foreign affairs, was able to write, no more than twenty years before Hitler's accession to power:

> what made the conquerors the masters, what made the few capable of subduing the many was fearlessness, toughness and a purer spirit; and there is no way of preserving these advantages during a period of tedious inaction or of protecting the nobler blood against interbreeding . . . Thus has the earth squandered its noblest racial stocks . . . . [as quoted by James Joll in the *TLS*, 25 August 1978]

We cannot speculate here about Dreyfus' or Rathenau's possible emotional problems caused by their total adherence to their identity as members of the majority. It is, however, a fair assumption that, as long as the subordinate minority is conceived by others (and sometimes also from the inside) as inherently different and separate, assimilation, even when free of many constraints, is likely to create personal conflicts and difficulties. One of its well-known effects is the leaning-over backwards in the acceptance of the majority's derogatory views about the minority; and this is probably another determinant of some of the Jewish 'self-hatred' to which we referred in the preceding section of this paper. A more drastic example can be found in the acceptance by some inmates of concentration camps during the Second World War, who belonged to many ethnic or national groups, of the attitudes, values and behaviour of their jailers.

What is more important from the point of view of wider generalizations about the social psychology of minorities is that, in conditions of marked prejudice and discrimination, the assimilation of the few does not solve the problems of the many. It is an uneasy compromise, in those who have succeeded in assimilating, between the acceptance and the rejection of their inferior status as members of the minority. Rejection, because they have attempted to leave behind them some at least of the distinguishing marks of their 'inferiority'; acceptance, because they must often do this by achieving and emphasizing a psychological distance between themselves and other members of their previous group. It needs to be stressed once again that this kind of compromise remains uneasy and full of potential personal conflicts only when no more than a small back door is open for a passage from one group to another, when most of the members of the subordinate groups are firmly kept in their place, and when the existing prejudice and discrimination are not markedly affected by the presence of a few 'exceptions' who are often considered to 'prove the rule' in one way or another. It is because of these personal conflicts that the French colonial policies of selective cultural assimilation, based on stringent criteria for deciding which members of the native populations could be considered as more or less French, proved to be a breeding ground for discontent and revolt amongst some of those who passed the tests. Frantz Fanon was one of the more famous examples; so were Aimé Césaire, a poet from Martinque, and Léopold Senghor, also a poet and later the President of Senegal, who both developed the idea of *négritude*, a positive conception of Negro identity.

The third kind of assimilation presents problems similar to the previous one but made more acute by the fact that it is 'illegitimate'. In the case of Dreyfus, Rathenau, Fanon, Césaire or Senghor, everyone knew that they were Jews or Negroes. Hiding one's origins in order to 'pass' is a different matter altogether. The innocuous forms of it are quite frequent in countries such as Britain or the United States where changing one's name does not present much of a legal difficulty and can often let one off the hook of being foreign-born or of foreign descent. There was a time in England when a physician called Goldsmith could get more easily his first job in a hospital than one called Goldschmidt. The same was true in, for example, some banks and some of the more 'exclusive' large commerical emporia. It is, however, a very different matter when 'passing' is illegal, as it is in South Africa or was in Nazi Germany, or when it must imply a total and very careful hiding of one's origins, as in the case of light-skinned Negroes in the United States.

The 'illegitimate' forms of assimilation lead to an identification with the new group and a rejection of the old one which are sometimes even stronger than in many cases of 'legitimate' assimilation. Paradoxically, this might occur even when assimilation is in the opposite direction – from the majority to the minority. Arthur Miller, in his novel *Focus* written in the early 1940s, provided a beautifully analysed fictitious account, and the American journalist J. H. Griffin supplemented it with a counterpart of real experiences in his book *Black Like Me* (1962). The hero of Miller's story is a fairly anti-semitic 'average' American who must start wearing spectacles because of his declining sight. This makes him look like a Jew. He finds it impossible to persuade anyone around him that he has not been until now a wolf in sheep's clothing, a Jew who successfully 'passed'. His whole life is changed as a result, he encounters discrimination in many of his basic daily activities, and for a time struggles vainly proclaiming his innocence. He finally gives up and makes a conscious choice of a strong Jewish identification. Poetic licence allowed Miller to use a few initial improbabilities to set his stage. But his subsequent analysis rings true and it is confirmed by the account of Griffin who chemically darkened his skin in order to see, from the other side of the fence, what it was like, in the late 1950s, to *feel* a black in a Southern state. His subsequent attitudes were not very different from those described by Miller.

To sum up in returning to the more usual forms of 'illegitimate' assimilation: the threats and insecurities of their new lives undoubtedly contribute to the attitudes of those who managed to 'pass' and constantly face the danger of being unmasked. One of the precautions they can take is to proclaim their dislike of the 'inferior' minority. It does not take much to set this pattern into motion. In a recent experimental study (soon to be published) conducted in a classroom with schoolgirls, Glynis Breakwell managed to create two groups of different status, the assignment to higher or lower status being based on the level of performance in a fairly trivial task. At the same time, it was possible to cheat in order to find oneself in the 'higher' group. The 'illegitimate' members of the higher group showed, in some of the subsequent tests, a more marked differentiation in favour of that group than did its legitimate members. It must be hoped that the study also served as a useful educational experience for its participants: complete anonymity was preserved, but in a subsequent 'debriefing' session the purpose and implications of the study were carefully explained to them.

The fourth kind of assimilation is so different from those previously discussed that it is probably inappropriate to use the same term in referring to it. Some sociologists call it 'accommodation', and John Turner (1975) discussed its social psychological aspects in terms of what he called 'social competition'. The ambiguities and conflicts of the simultaneous acceptance and rejection of minority status, present in the second and third forms of assimilation which we have just discussed, do not usually make their appearance here. 'Accommodation' or 'social competition' consist of the minority's attempts to retain their own identity and separateness while at the same time becoming more like the majority in their opportunities of achieving goals and marks of respect which are generally valued by the society at large. There are usually two important pre-liminary conditions, one or both of which are necessary for this 'social com-petition' to occur. The first is that the previous successful assimilation by *some* individual members of the minority has not affected, or has not appeared to affect, the *general* inferior status of the minority and the prevailing negative attitudes towards it. The second consists of the existence of strong separate cultural norms and traditions in the minority which many or most of its members are not willing to give up. The first of these conditions cannot remain for long unrelated to the attempts, within the minority, of creating the second; we shall return later to a discussion of some forms of this relationship. From the psychological point of view, their common elements are, once again, in the attempts to create or preserve a self-respect associated with being a member of a social group which does not get its due share of respect from others; and in trying to achieve this, *in part*, through establishing comparisons with others which will not remain unfavourable on the criteria which are commonly valued by all groups in the society.

The development of black social movements in the United States since the Second World War provides an example of several of these processes simul-taneously at work. Some of the earlier leaders of the National Association for the Advancement of Coloured People (NAACP) believed that the way ahead was in the assimilation in the wider society of as many blacks as possible and that this would finally lead to the label 'black' becoming more or less irrelevant to a person's status or social image. Although there is no doubt that this kind of integration has made great strides in the last thirty years or so, both socially and psychologically, it is also true that prejudice, discrimination and the differences in status and opportunities have by no means disappeared. An important aspect of the militant black movements of the 1960s has been a new affirmation of black identity best reflected in the famous slogan: 'Black is beautiful'. There is the affirmation here that the black minority does not have to become like the others in order to 'merit' the granting to it of equal economic and social chances and opportunities.

On the contrary, there is a stress on a separate cultural identity, traditions and roots which found its most popular expression in the novel of Alex Haley and the television film based on it. There is also the rejection of certain value judgements which have hitherto been implicitly accepted inside the minority. This is the case with the negative cultural connotations of blackness. It is not only that having black skin does not matter and should be forgotten in a gen-uinely free human interaction. The declared aim is not to neutralize these traditional and deeply implanted value judgements but to reverse them.

In other words, this is a movement towards 'equal but different'; though it would be highly misleading, for a number of obvious reasons, to equate it with the similar slogan of the South African apartheid. Underlying this kind of social movement (of which there are by now many examples amongst minorities all over the world) are certain psychological issues which need further discussion.

We have previously characterized 'social competition' as based on the minority's aims to achieve parity with the majority; but in other ways, the minority aims to remain different. As we have seen, in some cases, such as for the black Americans, this kind of movement develops after the attempts to obtain a straightforward integration into the wider society have been perceived by some as a failure. This means that, in the eyes of some people, the expectation or the hope that there is a chance to integrate *as individuals* and on the basis of individual actions alone has more or less vanished. The remaining alternative, both for changing the present 'objective' social situation of the group and for preserving or regaining its self-respect, is in acting in certain directions not as individuals but as members of a separate and distinct group. In conditions of rigid social stratification this can reach very deeply. Beryl Geber conducted, some years ago, research on the attitudes of African school children in Soweto, the African township near Johannesburg, in which very serious riots occurred in recent times. One of the tasks the children were asked to complete was to write their 'future autobiography'.

As Geber reported, in many of these autobiographies the *personal* future was tightly bound up with the future of the Africans as a whole, with future personal decision and actions which aimed not so much at the achievements of individual success as at doing something, as a member of the group, for the group as a whole.

These attitudes towards the present and the future, based on group membership rather than on individual motives and aspirations, are diametrically different from those which underlie the attempts at individual assimilation. They imply that, in addition to obtaining some forms of parity, efforts must also be made to delete, modify or reverse the traditional negative value connotations of the minority's special characteristics. In social competition for parity, the attempt is to shift the position of the *group* on certain value dimensions which are generally accepted by the society at large. In the simultaneous attempts to achieve an honourable and acceptable form of separateness or differentiation, the problem is not to shift the group's position within a system of values which is already accepted, but to change the *values* themselves. We must now turn to a discussion of this second aspect of 'equal but different'.

There is now a good deal of evidence (cf., for example, Lemaine, 1974, 1978) that the achievement of some forms of clear differentiation from others is an important ingredient of people's ideas about their personal worth and self-respect. This is true in many walks of life, and – predictably – it becomes particularly marked when individuals or small groups of people are engaged in creating new forms of human endeavour — for example, in art or in science. The race amongst scientists to be the 'first' with a discovery (see, for example, the account by Watson in *The Double Helix*, 1968) is not only explicable in terms of a hope to reap the rewards and honours which may be awaiting the winner. To be creative is to be different, and there have been many painters and composers who endured long years of hardship, derision, hostility or public indifference in defence of their right or compulsion to break out of the accepted moulds. At the same time, differentiation from others is, *by definition*, a comparison with others. The creation of something *new* is not possible unless there is something *old* which serves as a criterion for the establishment of a difference from it. No doubt, this powerful tendency to differentiate has sometimes led, in science and also in the 'mass' culture, to the creation of worthless fads whose only notable characteristic is their 'shock value', their capacity to appear as clearly different from what went on before. It is this same tendency which also sometimes results in the attempts by the aspiring innovators to magnify and exaggerate small or trivial differences between what they are doing and what has been done by others.

Whether genuinely creative or not, these are some of the examples of the process of social comparison upon which, as we have said earlier, must be based most of the attempts to create, achieve, preserve or defend a positive conception of oneself, a satisfactory self-image. This is true of social groups as well as of individuals. In the case of minorities, this 'social creativity' may take a number of forms. For groups who wish to remain (or become) separate, and yet obtain equality, this creation of *new* forms of comparison with the majority will be closely associated with social competition which we have previously discussed. Sometimes, when direct social competition is impossible or very difficult, social creativity of this kind may become, for a time, a compensatory activity, an attempt to maintain some kind of integrity through the only channels which remain available.

In principle, there are two major forms of the minorities' social creativity, and although they often appear together in 'real life', it is still useful, for purposes of our discussion, to distinguish between them. The first is to attempt a re-evaluation of the *existing* group of characteristics which carry an unfavourable connotation, often both inside and outside the group. We have already seen an example of this with 'Black is beautiful'. The second is to search in the past of the group for some of its old traditions or separate attributes, to re-vitalize them and to give them a new and positive significance. A version of this can also be the *creation* of some new group characteristics which will be endowed with positive values through social action and/or through an attempt to construct new attitudes.

There are many examples of each of these forms of attempting to achieve a new group distinctiveness. A strong emotional charge often accompanies movements towards a re-establishment of equal or high status for the separate language of an ethnic minority. The national language easily becomes one of the major symbols of separateness with dignity, of a positive self-definition (see Giles, 1977 and 1978 for extensive discussion). This has been the case in Belgium, in Quebec, in the Basque country, in a predominantly Swiss-German *canton* containing a French-speaking minority which fought for secession; it was also an important ingredient of several nationalist movements which were faced, in the central and eastern Europe of the nineteenth century, with attempts at cultural Russification or Germanization by the governing authorities from Petersburg, Vienna or Berlin. In cases when this leads to a general acceptance of bilingualism, both official and public, the results can be sometimes a little paradoxical. In the Friesian region of The Netherlands one can see, on entering some villages, *two* identical signposts offering information about the name of the village; this is so because it happens that the name is the same in Dutch and in Friesian. Some years ago, at the time of the intense battle in Belgium for establishing the social and cultural parity of Flemish with French, it was sometimes easier in Antwerp to obtain information when asking for it in English than in French, although it was quite obvious that the respondent's French was much better than his or her English. These anecdotal examples reflect a deeper and more serious psychological reality: if one considered no more than the possible 'objective' advantages, social, political or economic, which may flow from the re-establishment of a high or equal status for an ethnic minority's language, one would miss the crucial part that it plays as one of the most evident and powerful symbols of distinctive identity. The increasing predominance of French in Quebec (which, in some cases, even blots out the official policy of bilingualism) may well create some new 'objective' difficulties in a continent so overwhelmingly dominated by another language; and yet, the separatist linguistic pressure remains steady in the Province.

It may be useful to return briefly from these linguistic considerations to 'Black is beautiful'. As I wrote some time ago:

The very use of the term 'blacks' in this text, which would have had very different connotations only a few years ago already testifies to these changes. The old interpretations of distinctiveness are rejected; the old characteristics are given a new meaning of different but equal or superior. Examples abound: the beauty of blackness, the African hair-do, the African cultural past and traditions, the reinterpretation of Negro music from 'entertainment' to a form of art which has deep roots in a *separate* cultural tradition. . . At the same time, the old attempts to be a little more like the other people are often rejected: no more straightening of hair for beautiful black girls or using of various procedures for lightening the skin. The accents, dialects, sway of the body, rhythms of dancing, texture of the details of interpersonal communication – all this is preserved, enhanced and re-evaluated. [1974, pp. 83-4]

The interesting aspect of this list of newly evaluated attributes is that some of them have not been, by any means, negatively evaluated in the past. Negro music and dance, or Negro prowess in athletics have long been a part of the general stereotype, used both inside and outside the group. But they were perceived as largely irrelevant to the *rest* of the Negro image; in some subtle ways they probably contributed to the general stigma of inferiority. A similar phenomenon appears in anti-semitism. As Billig (1978) recently pointed out, there are many examples in the publications of the National Front of Jews being referred to as impressive in their achievements, 'intelligent', capable of great solidarity and self-sacrifice, etc. This only serves to enhance the dire warnings about their plot to take over the world. The evaluations attached to any presumed attributes of a minority cannot be properly understood when they are considered in isolation. Their social and psychological significance only appears when they are placed in the context of the general conceptual and social category of which they are a part. Their meaning changes with the context. This is why some of the well-intentioned efforts to present minority groups as having various 'nice' attributes have often failed to produce a decrease in prejudice.

The second major form of the search for a positive distinctiveness finds again some of its striking examples in the domain of language. The attempts to revitalize the use of Welsh are a crucial part of Welsh nationalism. But perhaps the most dramatic example known in history is Hebrew becoming, in a period of no more than about thirty years, the undisputed first (and often the only) language of well over two million people. Once again, it is easy to point to the concrete need for having a common language in a country to which people came, in the span of one or two generations, from all over the world and from many cultures. And yet, there have been some controversies in the early years as to whether modern Hebrew should continue to be written in its own alphabet or whether Latin alphabet should be adopted. The latter solution would have been an easier one for a number of reasons. The first alternative, backed by cultural tradition and, at the same time, strengthening the distinctive new identity, was finally chosen.

Ethnic minorities in which national movements develop usually have at their disposal the possibility of backing their claims by returning to the past. Language is only one of these distinctive traditions emerging from recent or remote history. The claim for a new separate unity *now* can be made much more effective in the minds of people if it is supported by ideas about the existence of a separate unity in the distant past. And thus, each of these movements must rely on a combination of myths, symbols and historical realities which all help to stress the *distinctive* nature of the group and its right to continue its distinctiveness. In his book on *The Nationalization of the Masses*, the historian George Mosse (1975) discussed what he called the 'aesthetics of politics'. Taking the example of the development of mass nationalism in Germany in the nineteenth and twentieth centuries, to which he referred as 'the growth of a secular religion', he also wrote: 'As in any religion, the theology expressed itself through liturgy: festivals, rites and symbols which remained constant in an ever-changing world' (p. 16). In all this, the internal unity of a national 'group' can become indissolubly linked to its *inherent* and *immutable* differences from others. At this point, nationalism is capable of shading into racism. But, in the case of many national movements growing inside ethnic minorities, this need not be the case, and very often it is not. With the creation and revival of distinct symbols, of cultural traditions, of modes of social behaviour sanctified by a real or a mythical past, and of new stereotypes stressing the differences between the 'ingroup' and the 'outgroup', the enhanced separate identity of the group can become powerfully reflected in the feelings and attitudes of its members. As we have already seen, this is closely linked to the image they have of their *personal* integrity, dignity and worth.

There are, however, minority groups which cannot find very much in the past in the way of symbols and traditions of a separate identity. The differences from others must then be created or enhanced, and re-evaluated in the present, as soon as possible. Women's liberation movements went through some developments, whose nature can be attributed to the overriding need for creating a conception of *different* but equal. In the early times, when the suffragettes made the headlines, the main idea in relation to men seems to have been that 'whatever you can do, I can do better' (or at least as well). This was therefore a fairly pure form of John Turner's 'social competition' in which two groups aim to achieve the same goals by the same means. The increasing sophistication of the movement, particularly as it developed in the last ten years or so, shifted the stress to a synthesis of social competition with the conception of a differentiation *in* equality (see, for example, Williams and Giles, 1978). In these more recent developments, there is still a continuing insistence that there are many jobs which women can do as well as men, although they are often debarred from them by the past and present sex discrimination and the corresponding dominant public attitudes partly determined by the way we socialize our children.[3]

There is, however, also the insistence that many of the things women traditionally do, or are uniquely capable of doing, have been debased and devalued in society. This is, therefore, once again, an attempt to re-evaluate the differences rather than to become more like the 'superior' group. This strategy is justified by some evidence (see Williams and Giles, 1978) of a psychological connection between an increase in the number of women taking a particular job and a decrease in the social status or prestige of the job.

An interesting parallel of this search for new dimensions of equal comparisons can be found in a semi-experimental study conducted by the French social psychologist, Gérard Lemaine (see Lemaine *et al*, 1978, for a recent account in English). A competition to build huts was arranged between two groups of boys at a summer camp, but one group was given less adequate building materials than the other. Both groups were aware of the discrepancy which was based on an explicitly random distribution of resources between them. Consequently, the 'inferior' group did two things: first, they built an inferior *hut*, but they surrounded it with a small garden. Then, they:

engaged in sharp discussion with the children from the other group and the adult judges to obtain an acknowledgement of the legitimacy of their work. Their arguments were approximately as follows: we are willing to admit that the others have built a hut and that their hut is better than ours; but it must equally be admitted that our small garden with its fence surrounding the hut is also a part of the hut and that we are clearly superior on this criterion of comparison. [Translated from the French]

This example contains at least three implications for our discussion. The first is that certain social conditions resulting in the 'inferiority' of a group lead to genuine social creativity, to a search for new constructive dimensions of social comparison. The second is that one of the major problems likely to be encountered by minority groups engaging in this kind of creativity is in gaining a *legitimization* of their efforts. This legitimization has two sides to it. First, the newly created or newly evaluated attributes of the minority must gain a wide and positive acceptance inside the group itself. This may often prove difficult, as it can only be done if and when the patterns of acceptance by the minority of their 'inferiority', which we discussed earlier, can be broken down. What is likely to prove even more difficult is obtaining from other groups the legiti- mization of the new forms of parity. In addition to the conflicts of objective interests, which are often bound to be involved, the positively valued 'social identity' of the majority and of its individual members depends no less on the outcomes of certain social comparisons than do the corresponding con- ceptions in the minority. One is back to 'we are what we are *because* they are not what we are', or as good as we are. Some of the cyclical changes in fashions used to reflect this need of 'superior' groups for marking their continuing differentiation from others. If a certain style or details of dress, clearly pointing to the 'superior' status of the wearer, began to be imitated by those 'from below', appropriate changes were made (see Laver, 1964). Unfortunately, social changes of more profound impact are not as easy to invent as changes in fashion; and therefore, some of the new 'creations' by minorities must be stopped or denied their validity rather than walked away from.

Finally, our discussion implies a possible *inevitability* of certain forms of competitive or conflicting intergroup social comparisons and actions if and when minorities are ready to reject their inferior status and the ideas about their 'inferior' attributes. As long as complex societies exist, distinct social groups will continue to exist. As we have seen, intergroup differences easily acquire value connotations which may be of profound personal importance to those who are adversely affected; but the preservation and defence of certain outcomes of these comparisons are also important to those who benefit from them in the 'social image' they can create for themselves. This is not quite like an irresistible force encountering an immovable object, because neither is the force irresistible nor is the object immovable; social situations rarely, if ever, end up in this kind of suspended animation. But the seeds of conflict and tension are always there, although it is scientifically superficial as well as dubious to attribute them to some vaguely conceived, inherent human tendencies of social 'aggression'. We are not dealing in this field with haphazard and unorganized collections of individual aggressions.

There are no easy solutions in sight. It is true that different social groups may be able to derive their self-respect and integrity from excelling in different directions which are not directly competitive. But, in the first place, these different directions are also very often socially ranked according to their prestige; and, secondly, the self-respect of any group *must* be based, in many important ways, on comparisons with other groups from which a favourable distance must therefore be achieved or maintained.

These fairly pessimistic conclusions have not taken into account the unavoidable persistence of conflicts of objective interests between social groups. But perhaps it is here that, paradoxically, we can place some of our hopes for the future. The present conditions of interdependence also imply that few social conflicts between groups can be of a 'zero-sum' variety, all gain to one of the parties, all loss to the other. In the present conditions, there is always bound to be some distribution of gains and losses across the line. This being the case, it may be useful to see in each intergroup situation whether and how it might be possible for each group to achieve, preserve or defend its vital interests, or the interests which are perceived as vital, in such a way that the self-respect of other groups is not adversely affected at the same time. We must hope that the increasing complexity and interweaving of conflicts between groups will lead to a progressive rejection of simple 'all-or-none' solutions, of the crude divisions of mankind into 'us' and 'them'. To achieve this we need less hindsight and more planning. There is no doubt that the planning must involve two crucial areas of human endeavour: education, and social change which must be achieved through genuinely effective legislative, political, social and economic programmes. This will not be easy and starry-eyed optimism will not help; nor will good intentions alone, however sincere they may be. But there is no doubt that the solution of the social and psychological problems which concerned us here is one of the most urgent and fundamental issues which will have to be directly confronted in a very large number of countries (of whatever 'colour' or political system) before the century is over.

Notes

1   The following item (by no means exceptional) appeared in *The Times*, 6 September 1978:

> A young British hitch-hiker was charged with murder by the police at Katerini, south of Salonika, today. . . .Mr X, aged 20, a British passport-holder of Sinhalese extraction, whose home is in Birmingham, was remanded in custody pending trial. He is accused of killing one of two

gypsies who attacked his girl companion . . . he and Miss Y, aged 20, of Solihull, Birmingham, had been hiking to Salonika. They were picked-up by two gypsies driving a small pick-up van . . . The Britons were forced out of the car by one gypsy holding a double-barrelled shot-gun, while the other attacked the girl.

The Sinhalese and the two gypsies are identified as such. For Miss Y, who, judging from her name, is a member of the 'majority', no other identi-fication, apart from her provenance from Birmingham, seems necessary. In the case of Mr X, also from Birmingham, we are additionally informed of his 'extraction'. We do not know whether the two gypsies are Greek (or any other) 'passport-holders'. It is apparently enough to know that they are gypsies. (See Husband 1977, for a review of evidence and a dis-cussion about newspaper reports of this kind.)

2   A good example of the use of social categorizations for reducing the cognitive complexity of the social environment is provided in the field work of the social anthropologist Clyde Mitchell (1970) as reported in A. L. Epstein's book on *Ethos and identity* (1978).

> Categorization . . . is a common reaction in a situation where social relationships are of necessity transitory and superficial but at the same time multitudinous and extensive. In such circumstances people seek means of reducing the complexity of social relations with which they are confronted. They achieve this by classifying those around them into a restricted number of categories . . . Mitchell . . . was able . . . to show how Africans on the Copperbelt were able to reduce the hundred or so ethnic groups represented in the urban population to a mere handful of categories. In this way we are presented with a model of social relations among urban Africans in one of its aspects, a kind of overall 'cognitive map' by reference to which the African in town charts his way through the maze created by the fact that so many of those with whom he is in contact, direct or indirect, are total strangers to him. [pp. 10-11]

For a more extensive discussion of social categorizing see Tajfel, 1969, 1978.

3   That this direct social competition is still fully justified is clearly shown in a recent research report from the United States (summarized in the *News-letter of the Institute for Social Research*, University of Michigan, Spring 1978):

> In 1975 the average hourly earnings of white men were 35 per cent higher than for white women, and 78 per cent higher than for black women. . . . But findings from the Survey Research Center's Panel Study of Income Dynamics clearly shows that . . . average differences in . . . qualifications account for less than one-third of the wage gap between

white men and black women, less than half of the gap between white men and white women, and less than two-thirds of the gap between white men and black men.

In addition:

differences in what economists call 'attachment to the labour force' explain virtually none of the differences in earnings between men and women. . . . [p. 7]

References

Berry, J. W., Kalin, R. and Taylor, D. M. (1977), *Multiculturalism and Ethnic Attitudes in Canada*, Ottawa, Minister of Supply and Services

Billig, M. (1976), *Social psychology and intergroup relations*, Academic Press (European Monographs in Social Psychology)

Billig, M. (1978), *Fascists: A Social Psychological View of the National Front*, Academic Press (European Monographs in Social Psychology)

Breakwell, G. (forthcoming), 'Illegitimate group membership and intergroup differentiation', *British Journal of Social and Clinical Psychology*

Brown, R. (1978), 'Divided we fall: an analysis of relations between sections of a factory workforce', in H. Tajfel (ed.) (1978)

Bruner, J. and Garton, A. (eds.) (1978), *Human Growth and Development*, Oxford: Clarendon Press

Caddick, B. (1978), 'Status, legitimacy and the social identity concept in intergroup relations', Ph.D thesis, University of Bristol

Cheyne, W. M. (1970), 'Stereotyped reactions to speakers with Scottish and English regional accents', *British Journal of Social and Clinical Psychology*, vol. 9, pp. 77-9

Clark, K. B. (1965), *Dark Ghetto*, New York: Gollancz

Clark, K. B. and Clark, M. P. (1939), 'The development of consciousness of self and the emergence of racial identification in Negro pre-school children', *Journal of Social Psychology*, vol. 10, pp. 591-9

Commins, B. and Lockwood J. (1977), 'The effects on intergroup behaviour of legitimate and illegitimate social inequalities: a social comparison approach', unpubl. ms., Northern Ireland Polytechnic

Epstein, A. L. (1978), *Ethos and Identity*, Tavistock

Festinger, L. (1954), 'A theory of social comparison processes', *Human Relations*, vol. 7, pp. 117-40

Geber, B. (forthcoming), *Soweto's Children: The Development of Attitudes*, Academic Press (European Monographs in Social Psychology)

Giles, H. (ed.) (1977), *Language, Ethnicity and Intergroup Relations*, Academic Press (European Monographs in Social Psychology)

Giles, H. (1978), 'Linguistic differentiation in ethnic groups', in H. Tajfel (ed.) (1978)

Griffin, J. H. (1962), *Black Like Me*, Collins

Guillaumin, C. (1972), *L'idéologie raciste: genèse et langage actuel*, Paris: Mouton

Husband, C. (1977), 'News media, language and race relations: a case study in identity maintenance', in H. Giles (ed.) (1977)

Jahoda, G., Thomson, S. S. and Bhatt, S. (1972), 'Ethnic identity and preferences among Asian immigrant children in Glasgow: a replicated study', *European Journal of Social Psychology*, vol. 2, pp. 19-32

Katz, I. (1968), 'Factors influencing Negro performance in the desegregated school', in M. Deutsch, I. Katz and H. R. Jensen (eds.), *Social Class, Race and Psychological Development*, New York: Holt, Rinehart & Winston

Lambert, W. E., Hodgson, R. C., Gardner, R. C. and Fillenbaum, S. (1960), 'Evaluational reactions to spoken languages', *Journal of Abnormal and Social Psychology*, vol. 60, pp. 44-52

Laver, J. (1964), 'Costume as a means of social aggression', in J. D. Carthy and F. J. Ebling (eds), *The Natural History of Aggression*, Academic Press

Lemaine, G. (1974), 'Social differentiation and social originality', *European Journal of Social Psychology*, vol. 4, pp. 17-52

Lemaine, G., Kastersztein, J. and Personnaz, B. (1978), 'Social differentiation', in H. Tajfel (ed). (1978)

Levine, R. A. and Campbell, D. T. (1972), *Ethnocentrism: Theories of Conflict, Ethnic Attitudes and Group Behaviour*, New York: Wiley

Milner, D. (1975), *Children and Race*, Penguin

Mitchell, J. C. (1970), 'Tribe and social change in South Central Africa: a situational approach', *Journal of Asian and African Studies*, vol. 5, pp. 83-101

Morland, J. K. (1969), 'Race awareness among American and Hong Kong Chinese children', *American Journal of Sociology*, vol. 75, pp. 360-74

Morris, H. S. (1968), 'Ethnic groups', in *International Encyclopedia of the Social Sciences*, vol. 5, New York: Macmillan/Free Press

Mosse, G. L. (1975), *The Nationalization of the Masses*, New York: Meridian

Rex, J. (1970), *Race Relations in Sociological Theory*, Weidenfeld & Nicolson

Runciman, W. G. (1972), *Relative Deprivation and Social Justice*, Penguin

Sartre, J. P. (1948), *Réflexions sur la question juive*, Paris: Gallimard

Sherwin-White, A. N. (1967), *Racial Prejudice in Imperial Rome*, Cambridge University Press

Simpson, G. E. (1968), 'Assimilation', in *International Encyclopedia of the Social Sciences*, vol. 1, New York: Macmillan

Simpson, G. E. and Yinger, J. M. (1965), *Racial and Cultural Minorities*, New York: Harper & Row

Styron, W. (1966), *The Confessions of Nat Turner*, Cape

Sumner, W. G. (1906), *Folkways*, New York: Ginn

Tajfel, H. (1969), 'Cognitive aspects of prejudice', *Journal of Biosocial Science*, Supplement no. 1, reprinted in P. Watson (ed.), *Psychology and Race*, (Penguin 1973)

Tajfel, H. (1970), 'Experiments in intergroup discrimination', *Scientific American*, vol. 223, no. 5, pp. 96-102

Tajfel, H. (1974), 'Social identity and intergroup behaviour', *Social Science Information*, vol. 13, no. 2, pp. 65-93

Tajfel, H. (1976), 'Exit, voice and intergroup relations', in L. H. Strickland, F. E. Aboud and K. J. Gergen (eds.) *Social psychology in transition*, New York: Plenum Press

Tajfel, H. (ed.) (1978), *Differentiation between Social Groups: Studies in the Social Psychology of Intergroup Relations*, Academic Press (European Monographs in Social Psychology)

Tajfel, H. and Dawson, J. (eds.) (1965), *Disappointed Guests*, Oxford University Press

Tajfel, H. *et al.* (1972), 'The devaluation by children of their own national and ethnic groups: two case studies', *British Journal of Social and Clinical Psychology*, vol. 11, pp. 235-43

Turner, J. (1975), 'Social comparison and social identity: some prospects for intergroup behaviour', *European Journal of Social Psychology*, vol. 5, pp. 5-34

Turner, J. and Brown, R. (1978), 'Social status, cognitive alternatives and intergroup relations', in H. Tajfel (ed.) (1978)

Vaughan, G. M. (1978a), 'Social change and intergroup preferences in New Zealand', *European Journal of Social Psychology*, vol. 8, pp. 297-314

Vaughan, G. M. (1978b), 'Social categorization and intergroup behaviour in children', in H. Tajfel (ed.) (1978)

Wagley, C. and Harris, M. (1958), *Minorities in the New World*, New York: Columbia University Press

Warner, W. L., Junker, B. H. and Adams, W. A. (1941), *Colour and Human Nature: Negro Personality Development in a Northern City*, ACE

Watson, J. B. (1968), *The Double Helix*, New York: Atheneum

Williams, J. and Giles, H. (1978), 'The changing status of women in society: an intergroup perspective', in H. Tajfel (ed.) (1978)

Further reading

Hall, S. and Jefferson, T. (eds.) (1976), *Resistance Through Rituals*, Hutchinson

Stone, M. (1981), *Education of the Black Child in Britain*, Fontana

15 Reporting racism: the 'British way of life' observed

Barry Troyna

Introduction

It is almost platitudinous nowadays to make the point that public knowledge about a range of national and international events is often founded upon images, definitions and explanations provided by the media. But it is important, nevertheless, not to underestimate the media's efficacy in structuring peoples' attitudes, beliefs and assumptions as well as enhancing their knowledge about certain issues and themes. It is in this context that we need to ensure that both the press and broadcasting media are carefully, consistently and critically scrutinized. We need to be aware of the images of the world they routinely present; how and by whom these images are constructed and signified; and their impact upon their audiences' perceptions and conceptions of reality. At a broader level of social and political analysis we need to interrogate the ideological functions of the media: to which forms of political and social systems they declare an allegiance and to which systems, modes of action and political ideologies they are inimical. It is only from this broader perspective that we can begin to comprehend fully the major interpretive frames through which the media report events.

In that sphere of social relationships commonly termed 'race relations' the influence of the media's representations of reality assumes particular significance for a number of reasons. To begin with, it is self-evidently the case that for those white people living in areas where contact with black communities is at most partial and indirect there is likely to be a heavy reliance on the media for information about the size and nature of the black communities and for interpretations of the relationship between those communities, the white majority and state agencies. On the basis of media-derived understandings, opinions, attitudes, maybe even actions might be affected. Second, in a society which increasingly deserves the epithet, multi-racist Britain, where individualized and institutionalized racism is the norm, the role of the media as part of this scenario compels our attention. Of course, given that the media are more effective in reinforcing rather than completely shaping attitudes – despite what conventional wisdom might suggest – it may well be true that the adoption of anti-racist postures by those in the press and broadcasting would not, in themselves, be sufficient to weaken the tenacity of racism in Britain. At the same time, this does not absolve media practitioners from challenging this state of affairs. The fact remains, however, that during the 1960s and 1970s news and current affairs reporters did little to question, let alone challenge explicitly, racist stereotypes, assumptions or ideologies. In fact, they played a prominent part in sustaining and legitimating them (Cohen and Gardner, 1982; Evans, 1976; Hartmann and Husband, 1974; Seymour-Ure, 1974; Troyna, 1981). A brief glimpse at the findings of two major research surveys into the nature and impact of news which was 'race-related' in this period should be sufficient to demonstrate this point.

Paul Hartmann and Charles Husband analysed the way four national newspapers reported 'race-related' news between 1963 and 1970 and found that throughout the period: 'the press has continued to project an image of Britain as a *white* society in which the coloured population is seen as some kind of aberration, a problem or just an oddity' (1974, p. 145). My own research into local and national press coverage of this and associated themes in the late 1970s showed that there had been little qualitative change in emphasis or orientation in the intervening years. Hartmann and Husband had identified the portrayal of Blacks as 'an external threat' to UK society as the most salient feature of press reporting in the 1960s. By the late 1970s this image had simply been transmuted into a picture of Blacks as 'the outsider within'. The press continued to assign them conditional citizenship, disparaged consistently their cultural differences and presented them, above all, as 'a problem to and essentially different from the mainstream of the society' (1981, p. 80). In their different ways the two research studies showed how the media help to 'rationalize' and exemplify racist attitudes amongst white communities in the UK.

So how do we account for the consistencies in this pattern of reporting? Well, at one level we might look for explanations within the profession itself; that is, its personnel and their habitual professional practices. On the first of these it is important to note that journalism has been and, to a lesser extent, continues to be dominated by white reporters. Roughly at the time of the two research studies mentioned earlier it was estimated that: 'Of the 28,000 journalists working on British newspapers and magazines, less than 2 dozen (or 0.1 per cent) are black' (Morrison, 1975, p. 167). One might infer, then, that the racist values which suffuse UK society are likely to inform, directly or indirectly, the way a white-dominated profession understands and presents news about 'race'. Indeed, the chances of taken-for-granted assumptions about white superiority being challenged are minimized even further by the fact that these professionals are united not only by a common ethnic identity but also by similar educational careers and class background. As one journalist put it to me: 'We're like clones, with all very similar backgrounds, the majority Oxbridge graduates.' This uniformity of assumptions and perspectives was highlighted by John Clare, the BBC's community affairs correspondent, in his paper to the post-Scarman conference at Leicester in 1982. There he informed his audience that:

A few weeks after the riots in Brixton, my teenage daughter presented me with a cartoon which she had cut out of one of the pop music papers which she reads. It shows a riot at full swing – crowds, bricks, bottles, smoke – and there, standing amid the smouldering ruins, are a reporter and a television crew. The caption reads: 'Now over to our community relations correspondent, for a gullible, white, middle-class, university-educated, nonentity's views of today's events.' It is in that spirit that I would like you to consider what follows . . . [1984, p. 46].

We might also wish to consider the impact of news values, those unwritten guidelines which inform journalists' habitual professional practices, as an explanation for the content, nature and thrust of 'race-reporting'. News values are intended to distinguish newsworthy events and issues from the plethora of everyday occurrences which, according to professional judgements, would not attract the public's interest. News values, with their emphasis on the sensational, the extraordinary and the negative, orient journalists towards topics in which black people, if they are present at all, are likely to appear for negative reasons. That is to say, the media are likely to confer upon them the status of 'illegal immigrants', social security 'scroungers', 'muggers' or 'rioters'. For some media researchers it is the immutable and sacrosanct status of news values which explains primarily the orientation and focus of 'race-related' news. To change them would be to undermine the legitimacy of those professional assumptions about what constitutes 'good news'. As James Halloran has argued;

> There can be no doubt that, from time to time and from place to place, the treatment by the media of racial and ethnic issues has certain idiosyncratic and unfortunate features, but the treatment is best seen as stemming from *normal journalistic practices* rather than as something unique or special to race [1981, p. 8. Emphasis added].

The hostile reception of certain sections of the press to the argument that journalists should be more aware of the implications of sensational reporting of 'race' matters and the stubborn refusal of many journalists to re-appraise their practices in the light of the NUJ's guidelines on 'race' reporting suggest that we must treat Halloran's comments seriously. But it seems to me over-simplistic to invest news values and the 'normal journalistic practices' they impel, with complete explanatory power. The media, after all, are not immune from the racist commonsense which pervades UK society. What Martin Barker has called the 'new racism', that is, 'theories which result in justifications for keeping ourselves separate' and a defence of our (superior) 'way of life' (1981) constitutes an important part of the media's ideology. Put simply, the 'new racism' helps comprise those images, concepts and premises which together provide the framework through which the media represent and interpret news about 'race-related' matters. Of course, the 'new racism' does not operate in isolation from other components of media ideology. As Stuart Hall has made clear: 'ideologies do not consist of isolated and separate concepts, but in the articulation of different elements into a distinctive set or chain of meanings' (1981, p. 31). In this chapter I am concerned with the way the 'new racism', as part of the media's ideological baggage helps to legitimate and reproduce the existing social order in which racist assumptions are firmly embedded and taken-for-granted. As Ralph Miliband, among others, has argued, the media 'fulfil a conservative function' (1973, p. 211) in western capitalist societies and reflect an unswerving commitment to the values and institutions of liberal-democracy. I want to show that the media's pre-eminent concern with those values and institutions (which, in part, comprise the 'British way of life') helps to sanctify a racist image and valuation of society. To sustain empirically this argument I want to focus primarily on the way the media presented the policies and activities of a contemporary fascist group, the National Front (NF), in the 1970s. I then want to look more briefly at media coverage of the 'race row' involving the Bradford headteacher, Raymond Honeyford. In both case studies we shall see how the presence of black citizens in the UK is constructed in such a way that it is seen as a threat to the body politic and the political and social attributes of a society which, despite substantial contrary evidence, continues to see itself as a 'tolerant' society.

To set the scene for this focused examination I want to elaborate more fully on how the commitment to a consensus definition of politics is articulated and secured in media discourse.

The parameters of legitimacy

According to Stuart Hall, 'consensual' views of society represent 'The National Interest' 'transcending all other collective interests' (1974, p. 272). As I have already noted those modes of behaviour, beliefs and opinions which fall outside the parameters of the 'consensus' are routinely ascribed illegitimate status in the media. This, of course, challenges the axiom that the media are 'balanced', 'impartial' and 'objective' but it is a concession which even media practitioners are willing to admit: 'Yes we are biased – biased in favour of parliamentary democracy', is how one senior editor typified the BBC's stance on politics (quoted in Curran, 1974, p. 782). It is from this preference for reporting within the framework of parliamentary democracy that we can understand why, as Howard Davis and Paul Walton argue, 'subjects like political violence, criminal deviance, international sporting competitions or the royal family are not approached from a neutral stance . . .' (1983, p. 9). As they go on to show with regard to the media's handling of 'terrorist' groups, the ' "need for closure" . . . overrides the "need for balance" ' so that certain linguistic techniques are deployed 'to demonstrate their divergence from the core values of society and the self-exclusion of terrorist groups from normal life' (1983, p. 15). These linguistic (and graphic) ploys facilitate the media's designation of 'terrorist' activities as illegitimate and criminal, above all else. In other words, media coverage is geared towards the disengagement of these activities from the political context which have prompted them and a reconstitution of those activities into an inferential framework which takes 'the violent society' as its main unifying theme. As Philip Schlesinger and his colleagues note:

> mugging, the Angry Brigade bombings, IRA campaigns, criminal shootings of the police, football hooliganism, violence during picketing, rioting and political demonstrations, are all represented as symptoms of an underlying social malaise – an eruption of unprecedented criminality and lawlessness which poses a fundamental threat to law and order [1983, p. 3].

Media coverage of the IRA in Northern Ireland exemplifies this process. Because its members have tended to violate the ideology of the 'consensus' and undermined the rule of law, they have been signified routinely as illegitimate by the media and, as Schlesinger and his colleagues suggest, placed in the 'twilight zone' of thugs, anarchists and subverters of the social order. The point I want to stress is that the political *raison d'etre* of the IRA and the grievances which prompt their actions are, at best, cursorily acknowledged in the media's routine reporting. One example should be sufficient to demonstrate this point. In July 1982 the IRA bombed the Household Cavalry and a bandstand in Regent's Park, London. This was unanimously condemned in the editorial pages of Fleet Street where the *Daily Mirror*'s comments typified the general reaction. Under the heading, 'Evil, Pitiless', the *Mirror* characterized the IRA as 'the most consistently wicked gang of killers in the Western world'. It went on to insist (and this is the crucial element of the coverage) that: 'They claim to fight for a cause. But no cause could justify such evil' (21 July 1982). Violence, then, whatever its premise, is presented in media discourse as *prima facie* evidence of an illegitimate threat to the social order. It is defined as anathema to 'The National Interest' and a challenge to the 'consensus'. In the words of Terry Ann Knopf:

> Both the general public and the media share the same dislike of protestors: both are unable to understand violence as an expression of protest against oppressive conditions: both prefer the myth of orderly, peaceful change, extolling the virtues of private property and peaceful decorum. People are expected to behave in a certain way; they just don't go around yelling or cursing or throwing rocks [1970, p. 858].

What I have outlined so far has stressed the range of behaviours permissible within 'consensus politics'; that is, I have suggested that the actions of political groups, and the extent to which these accord with the conventions of parliamentary democracy, help determine whether or not they will be signified as legitimate by the media. In simple terms, while certain sections of the media may not agree with, say, the view of CND or civil rights demonstrators they respect the rights of those marchers as long as they, themselves, defer to the conventional modes of protest in a liberal-democracy. But part of the ideological consistency of 'consensus politics' is also differentially to ascribe legitimate status to political beliefs and opinions. There are, after all, certain political beliefs and ideologies such as fascism and communism which fall outside the range of views which are acceptable to the media. These are discredited ideologies which will be characterized as illegitimate and negative in media representations. Now in some cases political groups and organizations may embrace what are defined by the media as illegitimate forms of action and political ideologies. The result: journalists and broadcasters will invoke the 'need for closure', to use Davis and Walton's phrase, and portray them in unambiguously hostile terms. But a more equivocal response from the media is generated by groups or organizations which violate only one or other of the ideological dimensions of 'consensus politics'. An organization or group which, say, adheres to the rules of parliamentary democracy but which also propagates 'unacceptable' beliefs and political programmes arouses considerable tension for its representation in the media. (This has been an enduring problem for the media in their relationship with Sinn Fein whose members comprise the legal, political face of the IRA, itself a proscribed organization.) On the face of it, similar tensions are aroused in media representations of a group or organization, however loosely defined, which has a legitimate cause to protest but which seeks to ignore conventional political channels to communicate that protest. What interests me in the next section of this chapter is how that tension is managed and the implications of this for the media's stance on race relations in the UK.

Beyond the pale? Reporting racism

From the foregoing discussion it should be clear why the relationship between the National Front and the media is worthy of attention, despite the party's recent decline in electoral fortunes and impact on public consciousness.[1] The NF's political programme derives from fascist origins and its most prominent spokespersons have been especially influenced by the theories of 'racial fascism' associated originally in Britain with Arnold Leese and the Imperial Fascist League, formed in 1929. The accompanying diagram (Figure 4) shows this intellectual lineage quite clearly and reinforces John Morell's claim that: 'Modern racialists have been able to draw on Leese's theories and use them with only minor modifications for the more topical problem of black immigration' (1980, p. 71). This is not the place to analyse in depth the ideological foundations of the NF's policies, which has been dealt with fully elsewhere (Billig, 1979; Husbands, 1983; Taylor, 1982). But it is important to emphasize the centrality of racism in this ideology and to point out that it is racism, pre-eminently, which is 'the great common tie' which binds supporters and sympathizers of the party together (Fielding, 1981, p. 92). It is also pertinent to draw attention to the fact that the leitmotif of the NF's recruitment campaign has been the threat – cultural, physical and economic – which the presence of black people in Britain allegedly pose to white communities. As Martin Webster, then the party's National Activities organizer, admitted in the party's main theoretical organ, *Spearhead*, in the mid 1970s:

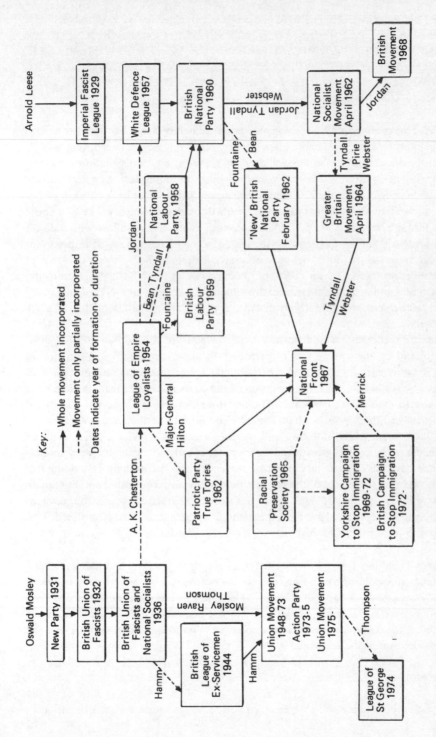

Figure 4 *Fascist groups and the origins of the National Front*

IF THE BRITISH PEOPLE ARE DESTROYED THROUGH RACIAL INTER-BREEDING, THEN THE BRITISH NATION WILL CEASE TO EXIST. IF WE CANNOT GET THAT MESSAGE THROUGH TO THE BRITISH PEOPLE, THEN ALL OTHER POLICIES, NO MATTER HOW IMPORTANT THEY ARE IN THEMSELVES, WILL BE UTTERLY MEANINGLESS AND IRRELEVANT [July 1975, p. 17. Original emphasis].

The racist premises of NF ideology are underpinned by a much broader conspiratorial interpretation of Jewish plans to dominate the world. According to this view, Jewish domination will be achieved by encouraging miscegenation – thereby destroying the 'purity' of all other 'races' – whilst forbidding Jews to marry outside their own religious group. The conspiracy theory is the organizing concept of NF ideology and, as David Edgar suggests, it runs through the ideology 'like Blackpool runs through rock' (1977, p. 116). Here, too, there are parallels with Leese's 'racial fascism' and his fixation with the idea of a Jewish conspiracy. It is important for our purposes to note that this obsessive belief in the 'ubiquitous hand of (Jewish) conspiracy' (Taylor, 1978, p. 7) characterizes the NF's conception of the mass media and provides the context in which the allegedly anti-Nationalist, anti-racist, anti-fascist and anti-NF images in the media are made intelligible to party followers.

The NF's conception and portrayal of the mass media as vassals of Zionist control and as 'the enemy within' performs an important ideological function in that it helps sustain and reinforce the party's conspiratorial interpretation of events. Nevertheless, since the inception of the party in 1967 its leaders have been sensitive to the media's consensual stance on politics and the legitimacy accorded particularly to those groups which abide by the rules of parliamentary democracy. For this reason, party literature and public statements stress the importance of the media to the party's growth and development (Troyna, 1980) and party spokespersons encourage supporters to pursue their activities accordingly.[2] By doing this it is hoped that the image of the NF as a democratically constituted and legitimate party will be highlighted and diffused through NF-related news. 'Impression-management', therefore, has been the name of the game, a strategy outlined from the beginning by the NF's first chairman, A. K. Chesterton:

There is one fact I would ask you to look squarely in the face, and that is, being a movement espousing a cause which is not considered fashionable, we get a bad press and consequently a bad public image. That is just one of the facts of life which we have to take in our stride, but we can see to it that *we* do not give *ourselves* a bad public image, and this would only be too easy to do if the leadership tolerated bad behaviour on public occasions.

He continued:

A nation once noble and very great cannot be rescued from the mire by jackasses who play straight into the enemy's hands by giving the public the image of us that the enemy most dearly wants to be given [*Spearhead*, November/December, 1967, pp. 6–7].

The need for exemplary behaviour has since been underlined repeatedly by party leaders. Fielding, for example, reported that on a demonstration in Leicester, Webster urged supporters to 'just ignore' the anti-fascist opposition in the hope that if violence did ensue it would be the protestors not the NF who would be blamed for starting it (1981, p. 158). Similarly, after the violent confrontation in Red Lion Square in 1974 *Spearhead* praised supporters for their restraint and reported how 'the orderly and dignified NF ranks composed of decent looking British people' contrasted in media coverage of the event with the 'hate-crazed, contorted, hideous and largely alien faces of the Left'. Party leaders were clearly satisfied with the day's events and reported that 'nearly all of (the publicity) reflected creditably on the NF' (*Spearhead*, July 1974, p. 18).

The party's volatile public demonstrations represent a strategy which has been vigorously pursued since 1974. The imperative is clear: to ensure that public attention remains focused on the party. Equally important, however, has been for the party to contest council, general and by-elections. The decision, for instance, to field over fifty candidates in the most recent General Elections (1974, 1979 and 1983) was taken on the understanding that this would give the party a 'statutory' right to a Party Political Broadcast (but see Robertson, 1979 and Tracey and Troyna, 1979 for discussion). It is for this reason that Webster was not unduly distressed at the loss of all ninety deposits at the October 1974 General Election. He told reporters: 'We are laughing all the way to the bank. Where else can you get simultaneous five minute broadcasts on the BBC and ITV for thirteen and a half grand?' (*Guardian*, 12 October 1974). Webster's reply is highly illuminating because it hinged on the assumption that the media adopt a pragmatic, and pre-eminently behaviouristic view of which groups fall within the parameters of the 'consensus'. By fielding over fifty candidates at General Elections the NF has been able to exploit that view. The veracity of Webster's reply was demonstrated in September 1978 when Peter Hain of the Anti-Nazi League (ANL) wrote to the Director Generals of the BBC and IBA, then Ian Trethowan and Brian Young, respectively, calling for a ban on NF Party Political Broadcasts and coverage of their electoral activities. Hain's argument rested on the ANL's insistence that: 'The factor that could . . . and should exclude (the NF) from uncritical TV coverage is a form of racial ideology that threatens the freedom of biologically defined groups not only to speak, but also to be' (Edgar, 1978, p. 15). However, these objections were summarily dismissed by Trethowan who, in his reply to Hain maintained that: 'The National Front should be given the coverage in our Election reporting which their position in the Election calls for, no more and no less'. His assertion that 'at the end of the day we must give fair treatment to all legally constituted political parties seeking the votes of the electorate in a legal way' (quoted in Tracey and Troyna, 1979, p. 13) echoed the BBC's commitment to 'consensus politics' articulated some months earlier by the then Chair of the Corporation, Sir Michael Swann:

> It would be a very troubling constitutional situation if we ever failed to put out an Election Broadcast for a legitimate party. But it would be hardly less troubling if we were to suppress the National Front in any other way. It would, after all, be a negation of those principles of freedom of speech that we have fought for so long . . . . Freedom of speech must be indivisible [1978, p. 6].

In the context of a General Election then, the media's management of the NF is achieved in an unproblematic fashion. Of pre-eminent concern is adherence to the rules and conventions of parliamentary democracy; an insistence that freedom of speech must be upheld. Of subordinate concern is the effect which the mass dissemination of racist politics has on the welfare and security of black citizens in the UK. How far does this orientation apply to the coverage of the NF by other media and in other contexts?

I mentioned earlier how much importance NF spokespersons attached to demonstrations in attracting public attention to the party. Again this reflects their awareness of how 'news values' operate in everyday journalistic practices. It is undoubtedly the case that the bulk of NF-related news derives from the party's recurrent and provocative intrusions into areas of black and Jewish settlement. The disorders which ensued NF demonstrations and meetings in Red Lion Square in 1974, Lewisham and Ladywood in 1977 and Leicester and Southall in 1979 attracted saturated coverage in the daily national press and it is from the way these events were reported that we can explicate most clearly the media's stance on the NF.[3]

Even the most cursory perusal of the way the media have reported these and other NF-related disturbances would reveal that the politics of the party are unanimously condemned in news and leader articles. This is a predictable response to an ideology which, in its most blatant form, lies beyond the parameters of press definitions of legitimate and acceptable political beliefs. The press characterization of the NF after the violent clashes in Red Lion Square in 1974, during which Kevin Gately, a student from Warwick University, was killed, illustrates vividly press opposition to NF ideology and set a pattern of reporting which has been closely adhered to ever since. The *Daily Mail*, for instance, claimed to 'deplore the politics' of the NF and the *Daily Telegraph* insisted that the party was 'extreme and deservedly unpopular'. The *Sun* was more virulent in its denunciation of the NF, describing it as an 'odious movement' and asserting that:

> National, it certainly is not. And what it is a front for may be judged by the fact that its Chairman is Mr John Tyndall who has been in jail for trying to set up a Nazi-style organization [*Sun*, 17 June 1974].

What is significant is that condemnation or even discussion of the NF's racist politics constitutes only a subordinate theme in these reports. That is to say, the press consistently underplays the question of why the NF decides to hold its demonstrations in areas where local residents are likely to feel threatened by its presence, and focuses its attention instead on the manifest consequences of those decisions: namely, violence between what are seen as two opposing, extremist groups. The following headlines exemplify the degree to which other aspects to these events – including, most importantly, the racist ideology and motivations of the NF – are subordinated to an overwhelming, some might say exclusive concern with disorder and the outbreak of violence.

'Violence in the Streets'   (*Sun*, 17 June 1974)
'Storm over Battle in Red Lion Square'   (*Daily Express*, 17 June 1974)
'Police Besieged in Clash over "Front" '   (*Sunday Telegraph*, 14 August 1977)
'104 Hurt in Bloody Race Riot'   (*Observer*, 14 August 1977)
'Thug Law'   (*Daily Express*, 15 August 1977)
'Hate Mob Runs Riot in Brum'   (*Daily Mirror*, 16 August 1977)
'300 Arrested in Rioting'   (*Daily Telegraph*, 24 April 1979)
'Battle of Hate'   (*Daily Express*, 24 April 1979)

The media's deployment of these themes is a characteristic not only of its coverage of NF-related disorders but also of political demonstrations generally (Gittin, 1977; Halloran *et al.*, 1970). It is explicable largely in terms of journalists' tendency to prioritize 'violence' as the most important 'news value'.[4] The use of 'violence' as the lens through which NF-related disorders were seen and interpreted by the media demonstrates the truth of John Whale's claim that 'journalists are better at reporting the fact than the matter of protest' (1971, p. 48). Because attention is selectively focused on *what* happens (i.e. violence) rather than *why* it happens (i.e. because the NF has decided to propagate its racist views in areas containing significant black communities) the press consistently attributes the cause of the disturbances to the 'orchestrated' attempts of anti-NF demonstrators to halt the party's marches or meetings. Commenting on the Lewisham disorders of August 1977, for instance, the *Daily Telegraph* drew its readers' attention to 'the looks of sadistic pleasure of the extremists as they put the boot in' (15 August 1977). Two years later the same paper reproduced uncritically Sir David McNee's interpretation that: 'The disturbances that took place in the strets of Southall this afternoon were unprovoked acts of violence against police and property by groups of people determined to create an atmosphere of tension and hostility.' The *Telegraph* then went on to say that these demonstrators included 'members of the Indian Workers' Association, the Ealing Community Relations Council and the Socialist Workers' Party' (24 April 1979). Significantly, the *Telegraph* did *not* consider NF followers to be amongst the 'group of people determined to create an atmosphere of tension and hostility'. In short, the aggressive resistance of anti-NF demonstrators to the provocative actions of that racist party are routinely juxtaposed in media presentations against the NF's 'legitimate' mode of action. As a result, it is the protestors rather than the cause of the protest, the NF, which is defined as the more immediate threat to the political stability of the nation. We can see this same frame of reference in the *Daily Mail* after the Lewisham disorders of 1977. There, Lord Hailsham described the NF as 'a thoroughly detestable organization' but insisted that the 'still nastier Socialist Workers Party' had assembled at Lewisham 'not so much (from) a love of coloured people or a mere hatred of fascism' but 'to dictate by means of their strong arm tactics who should and who should not be allowed to organize and demonstrate in this supposedly free country' (15 August 1977).

These reports clearly show that the vehement denunciation of the NF's racist belief system is consistently subordinated to an emphasis on its political behaviour. They also help to explain why the NF repeatedly emerged from these disturbances with 'spurious virtue', to use the *Guardian's* phrase, compared to its opposition. Thus in contrast to what George Gale of the *Daily Express* termed 'the left wing fascists', the NF 'is not committed to violence or to the overthrow of parliamentary institutions'. For Gale, 'The threat to law and order comes entirely from the fascist left' whereas 'The country faces no such threat from any Right wing group which nowadays indeed make passionate noises about liberty and the need to defend Parliament and the rule of law' (15 August 1977).[5] But for whom is that 'liberty' available? Along with the *Daily Telegraph* which, after the 1977 Lewisham disorders, proclaimed: 'Nor can native-born Englishmen properly be denied the right to march through a part of *their* capital city *merely because* it is settled by immigrants (15 August, emphasis added), Gale's comments exemplify the insidious though pervasive nature of the 'new racism'. The mere existence of the NF, its ability to contest elections, hold meetings and marches is shown to exemplify the 'superior way of life' in Britain which must be defended at all costs. This liberty must be upheld even if, in the process, it constrains the freedoms enjoyed by black citizens who are, it would seem, contrasted with 'native-born Englishmen'. Put simply, press reporting of the NF, with its emphasis on modes of political action resonates closely with the ideology of the 'new racism'. More than this, the 'new racism' allows the orientation of these reports to appear more intelligible and reasonable to readers. As the *Observer* put it after the Red Lion Square disturbances: 'However detestable in a multi-racial society the views of some extreme right wing organizations might be, they are still entitled to the same freedoms as the rest of us' (23 June 1974). But 'the rest of us' is an exclusive rather than inclusive term; it can only refer to those people whose existence in the UK is not threatened explicitly by the freedoms accorded the NF; that is, white people. A clear-cut case of common-sense racism infused into news reporting.

British values observed

We have now seen those British values which journalists and broadcasters cherish particularly; we have also noted how they tend to assess modes of behaviour largely by the extent to which they approximate to those values. Above all else, the analysis has shown how this ideological imperative towards defending the sanctity of those values impelled a less committed concern in the media for the welfare and civil liberties of black citizens. Thus a racist definition of citizenship rights for Blacks has been infused, almost imperceptibly into NF-related views; the 'new racism' with its emphasis on the superiority and inviolability of the 'British way of life' becomes an integral part of the framework within which the media attend to and interpret the activities of the NF. Indeed, one can go further than this. Because of the media's overwhelming commitment to the traditions of the 'British way of life' and the attention paid to the NF's apparent allegiance to these traditions it is the presence of black people, *per se*, which is seen as problematic because of its potentially inhibiting effect on some of those traditions; namely freedom of speech, freedom to march, to hold meetings and so on. This has been a recurrent theme during the 1980s in relation, for example, to the presence of Patrick Harrington, a prominent NF member, at the Polytechnic of North London and, even more the case, to the controversy surrounding the Bradford headteacher, Raymond Honeyford. This is not the place to elaborate the details of the Honeyford case (but see Foster-Carter, 1985); suffice it to say here that between Summer 1983 and Spring 1985 he published a series of articles in the right-wing, conservative magazine, *The Salisbury Review*, criticizing the orthodoxy of multiracial education. This brought him into direct conflict with his Local Education Authority's (LEA) published commitment to this educational philosophy and set of practices. The result: Honeyford's suspension from his headship and a subsequent reinstatement in September 1985. The point I want to draw attention to is the media's insistence that Honeyford should be allowed to publish freely his views on 'racial matters'. Editorial and feature article headlines such as *No taboo* (*Bradford Telegraph and Argus*, 20 March 1984), *Hunt the Hersey* (*Times*, 26 March 1984) and *Pilloried for Speaking Out* (*Daily Telegraph*, 1 April 1985) help confirm the impression, cultivated in 'race-related' views of the 1960s and 1970s, that the freedoms enshrined in the 'British way of life' – in this instance, freedom of speech – are undermined by the settlement of black people in this country. In blunt terms, media discourse crystallizes, to a greater or lesser extent, around the proposition that the development of a multiracial society is anathema to the 'British way of life'. It is a proposition exemplified in Lynda Lee-Potter's article on Honeyford in the *Daily Mail* (18 September 1985). The article is entitled 'The Courage a Mob Can't Forgive' but more revealing is the sub-heading: 'WHY RAY HONEYFORD'S FIGHT IS *OUR* FIGHT, TOO' (Emphasis added). Once again, then, we witness the subtle deployment of an exclusive category to differentiate white from black citizens, for it is the fight 'to openly voice his fears in racial matters' that Lee-Potter refers. What is omitted from the scenario painted by the journalist is that, to begin with, Honeyford published his critique in a magazine where the enforced repatriation of black citizens has been advocated as a legitimate policy proposal. Secondly, that Honeyford's articles are regularly suffused with common-sense assumptions about the differential value of black and white cultures and by simplistic race thinking (see p. 18) (Honeyford, 1984). Thirdly, that his apparently 'incontrovertible' remarks about how the educational attainment levels of white students will be depressed in classes containing a significant number of students for whom English is not their first language cannot be fully sustained by empirical evidence. Finally, what is ignored from this and other articles is the negative impact of Honeyford's assertions on the self-image and group identity of the school's students (most of whom are of South Asian origin); on the relationship between black and white students, and their parents; and on the confidence which parents have in Honeyford's willingness to organize the school along the anti-racist lines prescribed by his employers, the LEA (Troyna, 1986).

Contrary to the impression cultivated by Lynda Lee-Potter, constraining racist rhetoric is not to undermine the principle of freedom of speech. It is to ensure that the principle is not abused. Put differently, it is an emancipatory doctrine which is designed to ensure that all citizens should be allowed civil liberties, irrespective of their ethnic, gender or class backgrounds. Lee-Potter's article is both ethnocentric and consistent with the discourse of 'the new racism': it focuses on the freedoms allegedly denied white citizens in a multiracial society and deni-grates the right of black citizens to be treated equally, protected from abuse and with full citizenship rights. To say that Honeyford has been 'condemned for telling the truth' is factually wrong. More important, it helps to locate Blacks as separate from and a threat to the political and social attributes of the 'British way of life'.

Media coverage of the NF in the 1970s and the Honeyford affair in the 1980s reveal not only important ideological consistencies but, more broadly, strong resonances with the media's commitment to the ideology of the 'consensus'. What is embraced in the media's reporting of both case-studies is a passionate commit-ment to the 'British way of life', an image of black settlement in the UK as a threat to this way of life and an implicit, sometimes explicit, defence of the theory that the multiracial society, and its peaceful development, is 'naturally' impossible. This is, as we are constantly reminded in the media, 'a remarkably tolerant society' (*Daily Telegraph*, 11 September 1985); what threatens it, according to Paul Johnson in the *Daily Mail* is 'the kinds of dilemmas (which) arise' when 'different races live together' (14 September 1985). Here we see the 'new racism' in its most blatant form, the reliance on theories and arguments against other cultures 'not because they are inferior, but because they are part of different cultures' (Barker, 1981, p. 24). In attempts to explain the civil disorders of 1980, 1981 and 1985 journalists drew attention to the alleged failure of black youth to respect the traditions of the 'British way of life' in accounting for their predilection towards violent protest. In the words of Keith Waterhouse then, the youth of Handsworth 'rioted' because 'they haven't any values' (the *Mirror*, 12 September 1985). It is an argument which coincides well with the media's commitment to the rules and procedures of parliamentary democracy and is used to account for why these rules have been eschewed by the youths.[6]

In the absence of a detailed interrogation of how and why racism constitutes such a divisive effect in contemporary UK society, the media present a naturalized version of reality which deflects concern away from those hostile and insidious assumptions, practices and arrangements which inhibit the growth of a peaceful multiracial society. The policy implications of this naturalized explanation would constitute a blatant expression of racist politics which the media would claim to discredit. The fact remains that its overt articulation is not necessary. The message to black citizens is already loud and clear.

Notes

1 I think it is important to draw attention here to Husbands' observation that despite the demise of the NF it would 'be excessively sanguine to dismiss the possibility of a future electoral resurgence of a similarly organised and oriented political party' (1983, p. ix). As I hope I show in this chapter, media coverage of the NF in the 1970s is of more than historical interest. It is exemplary of how racism, developed within the formal channels of parliamentary democracy, is covered routinely in the media.
2 The disastrous performance of the NF in the 1979 General Election did presage a new phase in NF strategy where 'the politics of intimidation' assumed more prominence. I have discussed this 'new phase' in my work with E. E. Cashmore (Cashmore and Troyna, 1983) and G. Murdock (1981).
3 Despite differences in presentation and style, press reporting of these disturbances was remarkably similar and transcended 'left'/'right', popular/quality distinctions in the daily national press.
4 Media coverage of the 1980, 1981 and 1985 civil disturbances also showed an overwhelming concern with the illegitimacy of violence as a mode of protest and only a cursory interest in the justification for protest (see Joshua and Wallace, 1983; Murdock, 1984).
5 Gale's article was subsequently posted on the windows of the NF's election campaign headquarters at Ladywood, Birmingham in August 1977.
6 See Errol Lawrence's excellent analysis of how common-sense racism was used by journalists to 'explain' the 1980 and 1981 disorders (1982).

References

Barker, M. (1981), *The New Racism*, Junction Books

Billig, M. (1978), *Fascists: A Social Psychological View of the National Front*, Academic Press

Cashmore, E. and Troyna, B. (1983), *Introduction to Race Relations*, Routledge and Kegan Paul

Clare, J. (1984), 'Eyewitness in Brixton' in J. Benyon (ed.), *Scarman and After*, Pergamon Press, pp. 46–53

Cohen, P. and Gardner, C. (eds), (1982), *It Ain't Half Racist Mum: Fighting Racism in the Media*, Comedia Publishing Group

Curran, C. (1974), 'Broadcasting and public opinion', *The Listener* (20 June), pp. 780–2

Davis, H. and Walton, P. (1983), 'Death of a Premier: consensus and closure in international news', in H. Davis and P. Walton (eds), *Language, Image, Media*, Basil Blackwell, pp. 8–49

Edgar, D. (1977), 'Racism, fascism and the politics of the National Front', *Race and Class*, vol. 19, no. 2, pp. 111–31

Edgar, D. (1978), 'Why the National Front is beyond the pale', *The Sunday Times* (1 October), p. 15

Evans, P. (1978), *Publish and Be Damned?* Runnymede Trust

Fielding, N. (1981), *The National Front*, Routledge and Kegan Paul

Foster-Carter, O. (1985), 'The struggle at Drummond Middle School', *Critical Social Policy*, no. 12, pp. 74–8

Gitlin, T. (1977), 'Spotlights and shadows: television and the culture of politics' *College English*, vol. 38, no. 8, pp. 789–801

Hall, S. (1974), 'Deviance, politics and the media', in P. Rock and M. McIntosh (eds), *Deviance and Social Control*, Tavistock, pp. 261–305

Hall, S. (1981), 'The whites of their eyes', in G. Bridges and R. Brunt (eds), *Silver Linings*, Lawrence and Wishart, pp. 28–52

Halloran, J. D. (1981), 'Preface' in B. Troyna, *Public Awareness and the Media: A Study of Reporting on Race*, Commission for Racial Equality, pp. 6–9

Halloran, J. D., Elliot, P. and Murdock, G. (1970), *Demonstrations and Communications: A Case Study*, Penguin

Hartmann, P. and Husband, C. (1974), *Racism and the Mass Media*, Davis-Poynter

Honeyford, R. (1984), 'Education and race – an alternative view', *The Salisbury Review*, Winter, pp. 30–2

Husbands, C. T. (1983), *Racial Exclusionism and the City: The Urban Support for the National Front*, Allen and Unwin

Joshua, H. and Wallace, T. (1983), *To Ride the Storm*, Heinemann Educational Books

Knopf, T. A. (1970), 'Media myths on violence', *New Society* (12 November), pp. 856–9

Lawrence, E. (1982), 'Just plain common sense: the "roots" of racism', in CCCS, *The Empire Strikes Back*, Hutchinson, pp. 47–94

Miliband, R. (1973), *The State in Capitalist Society*, Quartet Books

Morell, J. (1980), 'Arnold Leese and the Imperial Fascist League' in K. Lunn and R. C. Thurlow (eds), *British Fascism*, Croom Helm, pp. 57–75

Morrison, L. (1975), 'A black journalist's experience of British journalism', in C. Husband (ed.), *White Media and Black Britain*, Arrow Books, pp. 165–79

Murdock, G. (1983), 'Reporting the riots: images and impact', in J. Benyon (ed.), *Scarman and After*, Pergamon Press, pp. 73–95

Murdock, G. and Troyna, B. (1981), 'Recruiting racists', *Youth in Society*, no. 60, pp. 13–15

Robertson, G. (1979), 'Racists get T.V. election platform', *New Statesman*, (13 April), p. 510

Schlesinger, P., Murdock, G. and Elliot, P. (1983), *Televising 'Terrorism': Political Violence in Popular Culture*, Comedia Publishing Group

Seymour-Ure, C. (1974), *The Political Impact of Mass Media*, Constable Books

Swann, M. (1978), *Lecture to the Royal Television Society*, Yorkshire Centre, Leeds (17 May)

Taylor, S. (1978), 'The National Front: a contemporary evaluation', *University of Warwick Occasional Papers*, no. 16

Taylor, S. (1982), *The National Front in English Politics*, Macmillan

Tracey, M. and Troyna, B. (1979), 'What would the BBC do about the NF?' *Broadcast* (30 April), pp. 12–14

Troyna, B. (1980), 'The media and the electoral decline of the National Front', *Patterns of Prejudice*, vol. 14, no. 3, pp. 25–30

Troyna, B. (1981), *Public Awareness and the Media: A Study of Reporting on Race*, Commission for Racial Equality

Troyna, B. (1986), 'Raymond Honeyford: rebel without a pause', *Social Studies Review*, vol. 1, no. 3

16 Racism and nationalism in Britain*

Robert Miles

Introduction

It is a commonplace that there is a 'race relations' problem in Britain. Yet, in Scotland, this comment is rare. Indeed, in Scotland, it is commonly said that 'race relations' is an English problem. Common-sense conclusions might be that there cannot be any 'black people' in Scotland and that one should refer to 'race relations' as solely an English problem. However, there are 'black people' living in Scotland: these are migrants who came from India and Pakistan in the late 1950s and 1960s and their British-born children. The largest number live in Glasgow, although small numbers live in many of the smaller towns in the central lowland belt (Jones and Davenport, 1972; Kearsley and Srivastava, 1974; Scottish Office, 1983). So what are we to make of this common-sense conclusion? Are there really 'races' and 'race relations' in Scotland, but people just do not see them? Or is that these 'black people' are not really 'a problem' as they are in England. The questions multiply very quickly and are not easily answered, even in commonsense terms.

The questions arise from the way in which we begin to analyse the situation, from the concepts that we use. If the questions that arise seem to lead to senseless or contradictory answers, there might be good reason to look again at the concepts. It might be that they do not adequately grasp the reality, with the result that we should consider using new concepts. Using the above example, I shall argue that we should dispense with the concepts of 'race' and 'race relations' and substitute for them a different perspective and concepts. This perspective should consider the basis upon which ideologies are constructed and reproduced by and within different classes. With such a perspective, it is possible to analyse political and ideological processes in England and Scotland within the same analytical parameters and so identify important similarities as well as divergencies. Indeed, with this perspective it will be possible to demonstrate that a similar economic process underlies apparently dissimilar political and ideological processes in

* I would like to thank Michael Banton, Rohit Barot, Charles Husband and Annie Phizacklea for their comments on an earlier draft of this chapter. Their advice was useful, even if I have ignored some of it. Any errors are my own.

England and Scotland. The same argument applies to the case of Wales but there is not the space here to deal with what is in other respects a different case (for example see Hechter, 1975; Nairn, 1977).

The problem of the 'race relations' problematic

My starting point is the summary of an argument which I have developed at much greater length elsewhere (Miles, 1982, 1984a, 1984/85; Miles and Spoonley, 1985). The argument sets out from the fact that 'race relations' is a notion which is applied by people in their everyday lives and by sociologists to certain social processes which may or may not give rise to an enduring structure of social relations. For example, when the Special Patrol Group carries out a high-profile policing and arrest policy in Brixton, London, the local population, political commentators and academics will define this as a 'race relations' issue, claiming that the policy will result in the unnecessary harassment of innocent black youths which will, in turn, result in a deterioration of 'race' relations'. The logic of the claim lies in the argument that the two groups involved in the social interaction either are, or define themselves as, 'races' (cf. Rex, 1970). Hence, there are 'race relations', that is, a situation in which 'races' are relating or interacting. I want to suggest that this is a misleading interpretation.

There are no 'races' in the biological sense of there being distinct and discrete biological groups, distinguished by phenotypical (physical) or genetic characteristics and organized in some hierarchical fashion. This is not to deny the fact that there are phenotypical and genetic variations between human beings. Rather, the claim is that there is no scientific basis for both systematically categorizing the human population by such phenotypical and genetic factors and for attributing these supposedly biological groups with fixed cultural attributes (e.g. Montagu, 1964, 1972; Banton and Harwood, 1975; Banton, 1977; Bodmer and Cavalli-Sforza, 1976; Rose *et al.*, 1984). This is generally accepted by social scientists.

However, this has had little impact on everyday social life and ideology: people of all classes in Britain continue to believe and act as if there are 'races'. They do so when they take note of and give social significance to certain forms of phenotypical variation (e.g. skin colour, hair type). Most orthodox sociological reasoning attempts to construct a sociology of 'race relations' from this social process of categorization (e.g. Rex, 1970, 1973; Rex and Tomlinson, 1979; Van den Berghe, 1967). The method is to establish a set of criteria by which such socially defined relations differ from other social relations. The authors then attempt to generate explanations for the way in which these relations have developed. The limitation of such an enterprise is made evident by pointing to the fact that such relations are phenomenally 'different' from other social relations *only* in that people *believe* that biological differences (real or imagined) are of significance, despite the fact that such a belief has no foundation in scientific fact.

The case against this direction of inquiry can be made both analytically and by analogy (Miles, 1982). First, I wish to pursue the point by analogy. Sociological analysis purports both to describe and analyse social relations and social structures. One important dimension in the analysis of those relations and structures is the beliefs that people have about their social world. People often act consistently with the way in which they define a situation, but it does not follow that any independent scientific analysis is obliged to accept that definition as valid. Let it be admitted that this is an area of philosophical controversy but I do not wish to pursue the argument in that direction in this context. I am content to point out that sociological analysis does tend to proceed, but not consistently, by means of critically examining the validity of such definitions and tends not to incorporate everday definitions of phenomena into analytical reasoning (the example of ethnomethodology is an important exception). One may cite here the example of class: sociological definitions of class are not necessarily determined by everyday definitions of class. Weber, for example, defined class by reference to actual market situation and not by persons' beliefs about that situation or, indeed, by their beliefs about anything (1974, pp 424–9).

Similarly, sociologists of 'race relations' have not been disposed to develop and utilize a concept of racial discrimination which is measured solely by reference to what people believe is the extent of racial discrimination (e.g. Rex, 1979, p. 76). Indeed, the evidence clearly shows that black people in Britain underestimate the extent of racial discrimination (Smith, 1977, pp 127–39). Additionally, sociologists of 'race relations' have been at pains to stress that the beliefs of the 'indigenous' population of Britain about the scale of immigration from the New Commonwealth do not accord with the facts of immigration control (see for example, Deakin, 1970; Rex and Tomlinson, 1979; Runnymede Trust, 1980). In sum, people's beliefs can be, and are, mistaken. Their mistaken conceptions should not be incorporated into an analysis which purports to be scientific.

My point is that these sociologists must of necessity and actually do employ a set of criteria by which to establish and measure their analytical categories independently of the beliefs of the people they study. They are, therefore, equipped to prevent the everyday and mistaken notions of 'race' and 'race relations' from becoming incorporated into their analytical reasoning, but the fact is that they do not do so consistently. Indeed, they actively construct a discrete field of inquiry primarily on the basis of those everyday notions.

But why, in addition to the fact of analytical inconsistency, do I wish to reject such an enterprise? First, the very fact of giving the notions of 'race' and 'race relations' analytical status gives implicit scientific credibility to what are, *in fact*, scientifically inaccurate and discredited terms. Put in other words, there should be no ambiguity about the rejection of the scientific racism of the nineteenth and twentieth centuries and this is best achieved by ensuring a complete break with those terms which, however much they are redefined, by their continued usage nevertheless reproduce notions which are both false and politically unacceptable.

Second, if those relations socially defined as 'race relations' are different from other social relations only in that they are so defined, then there is little reason to expect that the determination or outcome of those relations involve factors and require explanation in terms which do not apply to other social relations. There is, then, little point in attempting to define a 'special' area of inquiry which will, in fact, draw upon extant concepts and reasoning.

Third, and derived from the previous point, the construction of 'race relations' as the focus of analytical attention tends to give explanatory primacy to supposedly 'race' related factors. Within the sociology of 'race relations', 'race' comes to be uncritically accorded identical analytical status with other factors (for example, class) without first considering whether it is possible to attribute to 'race' any analytical status at all (cf. Miles, 1980). Hence, within the sociology of 'race relations' there is a preoccupation with the extent and impact of racial discrimination and other factors are attributed with only secondary significance. With Annie Phizacklea, I have elsewhere (Phizacklea and Miles, 1980) shown empirically the limitations of such an analysis.

In sum, I do not believe it is defensible or worthwhile to attempt to construct or pursue a sociology of 'race relations'. I believe it is preferable to use Marxist theory which has the capacity to distinguish between the phenomenal appearance of the world and the essential relations which, in turn, can be used to explain why the social world appears as it does (e.g. see Sayer, 1979). For example, Marxists argue that the appearance of 'a fair day's work for a fair day's pay' (i.e. the wage form) obscures an underlying and essential process of exploitation (Geras, 1972). On the basis of this distinction we can recognize in contemporary Britain that people of all classes believe that people's physical appearance is indicative of their intellectual and cultural abilities and standards. This attribution of social significance to physical appearance can be understood as *racial categorization*. Thus, in the social world certain types of interaction between people and groups who are so categorized *appear* as 'race relations'. This can be understood as a phenomenal appearance because, although the beliefs and the activity really occur, as social constructions (which have no scientific validity in themselves), they cannot be fully analysed and understood without drawing upon the underlying essential factors or relations. A Marxist analysis permits a critical break with the way in which the social world appears immediately to the observer and allows us to form and use concepts which do not have their origin in these immediate appearances (cf. Geras, 1972). The task is not to analyse 'race relations' but to explain, *inter alia*, why the category of 'race relations' came to be used to categorize a certain group of social relations which, once examined from a different perspective, cannot be shown to be essentially distinct from other social relations.

The generation and reproduction of ideology

In the remainder of this paper, I shall follow through the implications of these arguments by reference to the example of the generation and reproduction of racism and nationalism, conceived as ideologies, in Britain. I am not trying to provide a complete and authentic account of the examples in question, but rather I want to cite particular findings and arguments to demonstrate the different perspective and greater scope offered by an analysis which proceeds from a different starting point from that suggested by the sociology of 'race relations'.

The concept of ideology is the object of critical debates (e.g. Althusser, 1969, 1971; Seliger, 1977; Centre for Contemporary Studies, 1978; Larrain, 1979) which must be put on one side in this context. I here use the concept to refer to a combination of assorted facts and explanations which have no necessary consistency or logical structure but which are articulated by individuals (seen as members of classes and class fractions) as a means of interpreting and acting upon the social world. An ideology is not necessarily articulated in the same form and manner by all individuals who constitute the class or class fraction. I do not presuppose that any particular element in an ideology is necessarily false, but I do argue that as a totality an ideology is either incomplete and/or inaccurate. Such an argument must not be interpreted to mean that the ideology cannot nevertheless be articulated to make sense 'successfully' of the social world (e.g. Gramsci, 1971, pp 376–7; Sayer, 1979, pp 8–9).

By referring to generation *and* reproduction, I signal the existence of an analytical distinction between what might be otherwise described as the origin of an ideology and the way in which the ideas are passed on both within and across different social contexts and historical periods. There has been a onesided emphasis upon explaining the absolute origin of ideas (an emphasis which seems to correlate with the predominant Marxist explanation for racism, e.g. Cox, 1970 and for a critique see Gabriel and Ben-Tovim, 1978, and Miles, 1980) and a failure to recognize the significance of *ideological reproduction*. The notion of reproduction is fundamental because it allows us to grasp the dynamic process by which ideas get taken up in certain situations by different class fractions, the ideas then undergoing some necessary but not necessarily consciously planned transformation. Conversely, we must also be aware of the possibility that essentially the same activity may be conceived by different classes and class fractions using different ideas in different contexts, as is evident in the history of the category of 'mugging' (see Hall *et al.*, 1977). In sum, ideologies should not be viewed as static collections of ideas but as always undergoing transformation in the course of their continued reproduction. This reproduction is not so much a function of ideas themselves but of the material context (which includes not simply the 'economic' but also the political and the ideological) in which they are reproduced. Our attention should, therefore, be less upon the structure of the ideas and more upon the situation and purposes of those (re)articulating the ideas (Marx and Engels, 1965).

Taking Britain in the second half of the twentieth century, the ideologies of racism and nationalism were not and are not newly articulated 'for the first time'. What is therefore required is an *historical analysis* of the generation and reproduction of these ideologies. The analytical task is less to explain their origin in the absolute sense than why they have been reproduced in the way that they were (and are). Put in other words, why do these ideologies continue to be used to make sense of the social world?

Nationalism and racism

For both nationalism and racism, various pre-existing sentiments, attitudes and loyalties were systematically organized and structured in the late eighteenth and early nineteenth centuries by sections of the intelligentsia, and were given political articulation by fractions of the ruling class in Western Europe. The specific manner of this systematization varied considerably from country to country (e.g. Minogue, 1967; Smith, 1971; Banton, 1977), but the fact that it is possible to identify certain core themes in both cases does allow us to identify these as distinct ideologies.

In the case of nationalism, the core themes are that: (a) the world's population is naturally divided into separate nations, each of which has its own specific character; (b) the national provides the only parameters for the exercise of political power and so individual identification with the nation is essential to ensure human freedom and self-realization; (c) consequently, each nation must have its own territory and state; and (d) the nation-state must maintain the absolute loyalty of its citizens and must be strong in order to maintain world peace (Smith, 1971, p. 21). These core doctrines support a number of key ideas which give rise to a particular political programme. These ideas are that the nation must be free from external influence and should be able to determine its own collective future; and that each nation has its own unique history and characteristics. These characteristics are usually identified as cultural in nature, e.g. religion, language, customs and values (Minogue, 1967, pp 10–11; Smith, 1971, pp 185–6; Nairn, 1977, pp 141, 335–40). Thus, the ideology of nationalism involves an appeal to the past (real and/or imagined) to construct ideas about current reality which have a political projection ('destiny') for the future of the defined nation (Smith, 1971, p 22; Nairn, 1977, pp 141, 348). Those who are included within the parameters of the 'nation' are constituted as an 'imagined community' (Anderson, 1983, pp 14–16).

As important as the *content* of nationalism is the *class position* of those who articulate and reproduce the ideology and the historical place of the ideology in relation to the development of the world capitalist economy. Both Gellner (1964, pp 166–9, 1983, pp 39–52) and Nairn (1977, pp 41–3, 70–3, 96–102, 335–40) have argued in their different ways that the generation and reproduction of nationalism can be explained in relation to the uneven development of capitalism. For these writers, nationalism constituted the ideology by which an emergent bourgeoisie attempts the political and ideological construction and mobilization of a 'nation' in order to provide the economic and political basis for their entry into competitive commodity production. Once the possibility of capitalist production within the boundaries of a nation-state had been demonstrated, other aspiring bourgeoisies wished to follow that example, to catch up and even surpass those who had gone before. Anderson has shown that the roots of this process precede the spread of capitalist relations of promotion through Western Europe during the nineteenth century and are to be found in the cultural transformation that accompanied the collapse of feudalism (1983, pp 17–40).

The systematization of the ideology of racism in the course of the late eighteenth and early nineteenth centuries utilized imagery and themes which had a long history in Western Europe, some being in existence before those events which initiated the slow rise of the capitalist mode of production (see Part One of this text; also, Miles, 1982, ch. 5). The resulting ideology can be considered to have the following major themes and arguments: (a) the world's population is naturally divided into biologically distinct 'races'; (b) each 'race' has its own specific and biologically ordered (e.g. Banton, 1977, p. 47). In the context of political violence in Jamaica and India in the mid nineteenth century and of colonial expansion in the late nineteenth century, this ideology could be and was used in Britain to justify the political and economic domination of territory populated by supposedly inferior 'races'. Let it be acknowledged here that the precise relationship between these and other events is the subject of debate (e.g. Cox, 1970; Bolt, 1971; Cairns, 1965; Curtin, 1965; Walvin, 1973; Lorimer, 1978; Banton, 1977; Gabriel and Ben-Tovim, 1978; Miles, 1980). However, it is undeniable that amateur scientists played a major role in the systematization of the ideology (e.g. Banton, 1977) but they did so in a particular economic and political context and their arguments were taken up and developed by dominant fractions of the British bourgeoisie (e.g. Eldridge, 1973).

Up to this point, I have spoken of racism and nationalism as discrete ideologies. This is because the central premises and themes of the two ideologies are, in abstract, quite distinct. Some writers have concluded from this that there is no overlap or relationship between the two ideologies and that they should always be carefully distinguished (e.g. Smith, 1979, pp 87–93; Anderson, 1983, pp 129–32). Thus, it is a common political argument that it is a people's 'race' that constitutes the heart and defining characteristic of a nation. At least three inter-related factors account for this: first, as previously mentioned, the systematization of the two ideologies occurred coincidentally in Western Europe (Banton, 1977, pp 3–4; Smith, 1979, p 90); second, both purport to identify a natural and inevitable social classification; and third, the ideologies are structured in such a way that there is a crucial overlap in their content, if not their presuppositions. It is this third factor which Smith and Anderson under-emphasize when arguing that it is an error to confuse the two. They incorrectly suggest that racism, as an ideology, is a purely biological doctrine and has no cultural referent.

In fact, it is a central characteristic of racist ideology that it maintains a deterministic relationship between biological characteristics and cultural attributes: for example, the nineteenth-century arguments which were used to support British imperialist expansion claimed that the 'inferior African races' lacked the capacity for self-government because of their supposedly inherent savagery and childishness (e.g. Curtin, 1965). In this instance, the attributed inferiority was both cultural and biological, with the former determined by the latter.

It is true that the early formulations of nationalist ideology stressed that 'nations' were to be identified by cultural characteristics, but, given that these were defined as *natural*, and that racism claimed this *deterministic* relation between biology and culture, the possibility of defining a 'nation' in terms of 'race' was a real one. I am not suggesting that this was a logically necessary consequence. Rather, I am arguing that the fact that it has happened (and continues to happen) has to be explained by reference to not only the structure of the ideologies but also to the historical context in which they are generated and reproduced. As we shall see later, contemporary expressions of nationalism in Scotland make little or no reference to 'race', while contemporary expressions of racism in England often contain within them a notion of 'nation'. And from any other examples. For instance, the idea of 'race' (and the idea of 'white superiority') with control to the development of Australian nationalism and to the formation of a racist immigration policy in the late nineteenth century (McQueen, 1970, pp 42–55; Huttenback, 1976; Miles, 1985).

The continued reproduction of ideologies has real, material effects by virtue of, *inter alia*, shaping political strategies and struggles. In the case of nationalism, when allied with specific economic interests, it has led to the construction of territorial boundaries and the formation of state institutions within those boundaries to exercise political power. Thereby, the 'nation' comes to have a phenomenal reality: but it is socially constructed and reproduced and is not the reflection of the 'natural'. As already suggested, the same argument applies with racism: the articulation of the ideology has been used to justify the exclusion of certain groups of the human population with certain phenotypical characteristics to certain sectors of the economy. Thereby, their alleged inferiority is given a phenomenal reality. For example, throughout Western Europe, migrant labour, which is in almost all cases phenotypically distinguishable from the indigenous population, is employed predominantly in the semi- and unskilled sectors of the economy (Castles and Kosack, 1972, 1973; Bohning, 1972). This is so, not because of their 'race' but, *inter alia*, because *beliefs about* 'race' structure the position that the migrants occupy in the process of material production, bringing about an apparent correlation between phenotypical variation and position in production relations.

Thus, the constructed, phenomenal realities of 'race' and 'nation' reflect back the ideologies of racism and nationalism, appearing to validate and verify them. These 'realities' become the material for people's everyday experience, with the result that the categories of 'nation' and 'race' come to play a useful interpretative role in their attempt to make sense of and act within the social world. Put in other words, the notions of 'race' and 'nation' remain available to classes and class fractions as a means of structuring their interpretation of the material problems that they face. These notions can therefore become the means by which class interests, which have a material basis, are expressed and pursued.

Consequently, we can view the articulation of racism and nationalism as having real effects at two levels: first, historically, in having assisted in the social construction of current realities; and second, in being available as means of interpreting that reality and structuring subsequent political action (which, in turn, can structure future realities). In the next section, I shall be concerned with the second of these when I consider the way in which the political significance attached to the categories of 'race' and 'nation' by the working class varies according to the circumstances of the historical conjuncture.

Racism and nationalism in Britain

Since the early 1960s, nationalism and racism have been articulated within all classes and have had substantial effects upon the political process and political struggles in Britain. It would seem that the significance of nationalism is confined to Scotland (e.g. the rise of the Scottish National Party) while the significance of racism is confined to England (e.g. the rise of the National Front). I shall briefly outline the evidence which supports these contentions and related problems of explanation, and then suggest that in both instances it is misleading to assume that the other ideology is without political significance.

Before doing this, two explanatory points are required. First, in distinguishing between England and Scotland, I am referring to the geographical basis of two distinct identities which can be called national and which receive political expression within territorial boundaries. These political identities of 'Englishness' and 'Scottishness' are historical products and are reproduced by, *inter alia*, the continued existence of different institutional structures. For example, church, banking, law and education are organized separately and distinctly in England and Scotland, as anyone who has tried to use a bank note in England which was issued by the Clydesdale Bank in Scotland will know. But these national identities are not equivalents, partly because of the nature of the incorporation of Scotland into what became the legal unity of Britain in 1707. The economic, political and ideological centre of the 'new' society was firmly located in the south of England (cf. Hechter, 1975) and this has remained so for over two and a half centuries.

For those living in England, this has meant that national identity is fluid and imprecise, floating between 'Englishness' and 'Britishness' because the centre of economic, political and ideological power in Britain is in London (and so England). It is therefore difficult to disentangle what is distinctly 'English' from what is 'British'. In Scotland, there is much less ambiguity over the nature of the national identity. Most of the available evidence shows that a large majority of the population of Scotland identify themselves as Scottish and not British (e.g. Budge and Urwin, 1966; but see Kearns, 1984). Thus, while in England, 'Englishness' and 'Britishness' tends to be overlapping and equally positive political identities, in Scotland 'Scottishness' and 'Britishness' are distinct and not equally positive political identities. Moreover, when defining themselves as Scottish, such persons are distancing themselves from both Britishness and 'the English'. Some of the significance of this will become apparent shortly.

Secondly, in what follows, I shall deal primarily with the expressions of racism and nationalism within the working class. This should not be interpreted to mean that the working class has an exclusive claim to the expression of these ideologies, not least because, historically, they have come to be central elements in the political beliefs of at least fractions of the ruling class. By concentrating upon the working class, I want to suggest that the expression of these ideas within this class should be explained not solely as a simple product of 'brainwashing' by the ruling class but partly as a result of independent economic and political processes which structure working-class political consciousness.

So, my focus is not upon 'race relations' in England or, indeed, in Britain, but upon the political articulation of racism and nationalism within the British working class in the 1960s and 1970s. It is my intention to shift the analytical terrain away from that constructed by the sociology of 'race relations' with its obsession with 'race' in England and so suggest that racism and nationalism are important components in *British* politics. In analysing those politics, including the ideology and political practice of the working class, we should have full regard for both the basis of the identifiable parallels in English and Scottish developments and the separate historical characteristics which structure and give an idiosyncratic character to each.

England and racism

What evidence is there for the claim that racism has increasingly become a means by which at least some sections of the English working class have come to interpret its social world and to structure its political activity since the early 1960s? First, there is the evidence of the involvement of the working class in the formation and subsequent activities of anti-immigration associations in London, the Midlands and Yorkshire in the early 1960s (e.g. Foot, 1975). Second, there is the evidence of the defeat of the Labour Party's designate Foreign Secretary, Patrick Gordon Walker, at Smethwick in the 1964 General Election as a consequence of the racist campaign by the Conservative candidate (e.g. Foot, 1965). Third, there is the evidence of increasing working-class support for Enoch Powell in the period immediately after his 'major' speeches in support of stronger controls over immigration and repatriation in 1968 (Schoen, 1977). And fourth, there is the evidence of working-class electoral support for the National Front in the early mid 1970s (Husband, 1979, 1983; Taylor, 1979; Fielding, 1981).

The significance of this evidence follows from the fact that the agitation against immigration was not against immigration *per se*, but against the immigration from the Caribbean and the Indian sub-continent of people who had black and brown skins. In the same period, there was little or no agitation to control immigration from the Irish Republic, Canada, Australia, Zimbabwe (then Rhodesia) and South Africa. The agitation was followed by the placing of increasingly restrictive controls over immigration from the New Commonwealth by successive Labour and Conservative Governments (e.g. Patterson, 1969; Moore and Wallace, 1975; Sivanandan, 1976; Runnymede Trust, 1980); the precise relationship between political agitation, politicians' response and legislative action being a matter for dispute (e.g. Foot, 1965; Humphry and Ward, 1974; Deakin, 1970; Studlar, 1980). Consequently, in contemporary English political life, to talk of immigration control is in fact to talk of the control only over the entry into Britain of people with black and brown skins, while black and brown skin denotes immigrant status irrespective of the place of birth.

Moreover, we should note that although not all electoral support for the National Front is explicable in terms of racist sentiment, the available evidence concerning the justifications given for voting for the National Front, the special distribution of National Front voting and the emphasis of National Front propaganda suggests that this is a major dynamic (e.g. Husband, 1975, 1979, 1980; Nugent and King, 1979; Taylor, 1979; Billig, 1979). Finally, we must take account of the evidence and arguments which suggest that racist beliefs are commonly and widely articulated within the working class irrespective of any related political agitation to express those beliefs (e.g. Deakin, 1970; Lawrence, 1974; Rex and Tomlinson, 1979; Miles and Phizacklea, 1979, 1981; Phizacklea and Miles, 1980), and that the mass media have played a crucial role in this by presenting racist interpretations of particular events and processes (e.g. Hartmann and Husband, 1974; Husband, 1975; Evans, 1976; Hall *et al.*, 1978).

Perhaps surprisingly, there has not been a lot of attention paid to *explaining* the reproduction of racism in England since the 1950s. Sociological analysis has been preoccupied with a dispute over the definition of the concept of racism (Banton, 1970, 1977; Rex, 1970, 1973; for a critique see Miles, 1982) or with the extent and effects of racial discrimination (see Daniel, 1968; Rex and Moore, 1967; Lawrence, 1974; Smith, 1977; Rex and Tomlinson, 1979). Within Marxism, much of the effort has been expended on reproducing economistic definitions of racism (e.g. Castles and Kosack, 1972, 1973; Nikolinakos, 1973; Sivanandan, 1973) which tend to claim that contemporary racism originates from a purposive strategy of the bourgeoisie to divide the working class.

One dominant strand of sociological argument maintains that racism is the product of the dominant culture which has as one of its components the colonial imagery of black and brown people (Lawrence, 1974; Rex, 1970, 1973; Rex and Tomlinson, 1979). A similar argument is found within Marxist writing, with considerable stress being placed on explaining the origin of the ideology in terms of colonial expansion (e.g. Sivanandan, 1973). The central claim is indisputable but, by itself, it only provides a partial explanation for the increasing political expression of racism in England (cf. Hall, 1978, p. 26; 1980, pp. 366–7). The argument assumes, but does not attempt to demonstrate, that the extent and content of racist belief is similar for all fractions of the working class throughout England. Moreover, if the English dominant culture is so pervasive and influential, there is little obvious scope for explaining the generation and reproduction of anti-racist ideas and political activity.

While not denying the general validity of this argument, Annie Phizacklea and I (see 1981 for a summary) have suggested that a further set of factors be considered. We used evidence from a small part of NW London to show that racist beliefs were common amongst the working class but we were equally interested in the *content* of those beliefs. We found references to colonial stereotypes but the vast majority of racist references were concrete and materialistic, focusing on problems of day-to-day living. In particular, there were references to black labour as illegitimate competitors in the struggle for access to the scarce resources of council houses and jobs. Our argument is that the articulation of much of this racism has a specific impetus generated in the nature of working-class experience of material decline. Particularly significant, we argued, was the fact that the industrial and social decline of the area occurred simultaneously with the settlement in the same area of black migrant labour from the Caribbean.

Hence, at the level of phenomenal relations, it *appeared* to the locally born working class that the arrival of black labour was associated with, if not the cause of, material decline. Moreover, it *appeared* to that same working class that since the arrival of the migrants, they were confronted with competitors for access to jobs and houses. That these 'competitors' were clearly distinguishable by certain of their physical characteristics and that the dominant culture contained negative evaluations of some of these characteristics (e.g. black skin) ensured that they were socially categorized as a distinct 'race'. All of these appearances were directly experienced with the result that the dynamic for the expression of racism must be considered to lie with the actual experience of material decline and not with a purposive decision of the ruling class to induce a division within what would otherwise be a unified working class. However, we have also argued that the nature of working-class experience also generates quite contradictory beliefs, some implicitly and others explicitly anti-racist, with the result that there is an ideological struggle within the working class, although it is a struggle in which the racist perspective tends to dominate (Miles and Phizacklea, 1981).

Assuming that this argument has validity outside of NW London, we have gone on to suggest that the articulation of racism becomes an important ideological element in the fractionalization of the English working class through the racialization of migrant labour (Phizacklea and Miles, 1980; Miles and Phizacklea, 1984; Miles, 1984b). It is also testimony to the fact that in the political and ideological struggle arising out of capitalist decline, the Labour Movement has not been successful in stimulating and developing the socialist elements in the political consciousness of the working class, although that is perhaps not surprising in the light of its recent history (see Nairn, 1977 and below). The point is that the open expression of racism means that working-class political identity comes to focus upon a black/white dichotomy which at least partly displaces or takes up the space that might otherwise be occupied by a political identity of belonging to a working class whose interests contradict those of the ruling class. 'We' comes to be defined by reference to physical characteristics (i.e. whiteness) and in opposition to the physical appearance of 'the coloureds' and their supposed intellectual inferiority, laziness, loud music, violence, and capacity to consume drink and other drugs, etc. Thus, the proposed solution to housing shortage, low wages and unemployment can come to be seen in terms of preventing competition with 'the (inferior) coloureds' for access to these scarce resources, if necessary by compulsory repatriation and not in terms of some sort of struggle for a socialist redistribution of economic resources and political power.

Scotland and nationalism

Nationalism was not newly created in Scotland in the 1960s but has deep roots in the history of the Scottish social formation (see Kellas, 1968; Nairn, 1977; Harvie, 1977). The continued existence of distinct institutions has constituted a political foundation for the maintenance of a Scottish identity and national sentiment. Arguably, this identity has also been maintained by the dependent and secondary development of Scottish capitalism (see Hechter, 1975; Dickson, 1980). The Scottish working class was therefore formed and developed in a distinct economic, political and ideological context, with the consequence that it is distinguished from the English working class by a number of cultural characteristics (Young, 1979).

In the 1960s the Scottish working class had available to it an historically constructed notion of a distinctive Scottish 'nation'. The parallel with England lies in that there was available to the English working class a nation of 'race'. But what requires explanation is not only the historical construction and availability of these notions of 'nation' and 'race' but also the reasons why these notions came to be drawn on to mediate working-class experience and to provide the basis for political action.

In Scotland, the political expression of nationalism in an organizational form can be dated to the formation of the National Association for the Vindication of Scottish Rights in 1853 and in the period up to the 1930s, a number of different organizations were formed, dissolved and merged. Scottish revolutionary socialists were involved in the various organizations, arguing for the establishment of an independent Scottish socialist republic as a step towards international socialism (e.g. Keating and Bleiman, 1979; Young, 1979), although they were rarely the dominant force. The Scottish National Party (SNP) was formed out of these schisms in 1934 and, after a split in 1942, it pursued independence from England as its main political goal. In the post-1945 period, the SNP participated in most General Elections but with little success. It remained a small and almost irrelevant political organization. The first sign of a reversal in electoral fortune came in the 1961 by-election in Bridgeton when the SNP gained 18.7 per cent of the vote (Brand, 1978, p. 258). Limited electoral success and membership growth followed, culminating in the winning of the Hamilton by-election in 1967. Despite significant reversals, particularly in 1969–70, the SNP went on to further electoral success and in the October 1974 General Election, polled 30 per cent of the Scottish vote and won eleven seats at Westminster (Harvie, 1977, p. 263).

Various explanations for this increase in the number of Scots giving political expression and significance to the notion of their being part of a separate 'nation' have been advanced (see Webb, 1978, for a summary). One explanation lays great stress upon the process of material decline of a dependent Scottish capitalism and the failure (or inability) of the Labour Party to propose and carry out an alternative socialist programme. This explanation takes a number of different forms (e.g. Hechter, 1975; Nairn, 1977; Brand, 1978) and what follows is only a brief summary.

It is argued that the development of Scottish capitalism was dependent on and limited by English capitalism, creating material disadvantages in Scotland which exceeded those in England. The failure to diversify adequately the Scottish economy ensured that, in the context of slump and increased world competition, the crisis of the capital goods industries created more serious and widespread economic and political problems in Scotland than was so in England after 1918. The related upsurge in working-class militancy was expressed in the 1920s and 1930s in support for socialist politics which came to be translated in the major urban, industrial areas into electoral support for the Labour Party, despite nationalist agitation by a number of revolutionary groups. Industrial and social decline continued but it was not until 1964 that the Labour Party's political commitments were tested in practice and found wanting. It proved itself incapable of reversing that decline, and a proportion of its supporters began to reconsider elements of their political consciousness. The result was that an increasing proportion of the Scottish population came to see their national identity as a means of identifying an alternative political solution to real, material problems. Sections of the Scottish working class, defining themselves as Scottish, attributed this identity with political significance by voting for a nationalist political party rather than a working-class party which had as its focus the 'British nation' (e.g. Brand and McCrone, 1975; Brand, 1978, pp. 144–66). The predominant object of their political identity became their Scottishness and the object of their hostility became English Governments, both Labour and Conservative.

It should be noted that this explanation faces a number of factual problems. For example, it has not been clearly established to what extent increased support for the SNP has been drawn from the previously Labour-voting manual working class (Mansbach, 1973). There exists the problem of explaining the substantial support for the SNP in those rural constituencies which were won from the Conservative Party (e.g. Argyllshire, Nairn and Banff, Galloway, South Angus). Finally, the fact that the 1979 General Election saw the dramatic electoral defeat of the SNP suggests that if any reconstruction of the political consciousness of the Scottish working cass had been taking place, it was not yet a long-lasting one.

But although it is not yet clear to what *extent* the Scottish working class gave political expression to the idea of 'nation' there is evidence which shows that some part of the Scottish working class, by changing its electoral allegiance, did contribute to the electoral success of the SNP (e.g. Hechter, 1975, p. 308; Mansbach, 1973, p. 188; Brand, 1978, p. 146; Bochel and Denver, 1972, p. 315). This can be explained in materialistic terms as outlined above, as can the historically parallel increased political articulations of racism by sections of the working class in England. In both instances, sections of the working class have reconstructed their political consciousness to explain their experience of economic and social decline in, to them, phenomenally adequate terms: in England, 'race' appears to sections of the working class to be an adequate explanatory idea, while in Scotland the idea of 'nation' is appropriated for similar reasons.

Nationalism and racism in Britain

But the parallel can be overdrawn: the fact that *different* ideas have been appropriated and given new meaning by sections of the working class in the two social formations testifies to the existence of historically specific features in both cases. The parallels and divergencies need careful historical analysis and Nairn's work (1977; for a critique see Hobsbawn, 1977) is an important contribution to that task. I want to show that this is a necessary and fruitful task by exploring further some parallels and divergencies. In order to suggest again that nationalism in Scotland and racism in England should not be analysed without reference to the other, I now want to argue briefly that, despite appearances, nationalism is an important element in the political consciousness of the working class in England and that a form of racism is an important element in the political consciousness of the working class in Scotland. The explanation for this illuminates the distinctness of the development of the two societies.

Most of the influential sociological studies of working-class political consciousness in England pay little, if any, attention to the possibility of nationalism being an important component (e.g. Goldthorpe *et al.*, 1969; Bulmer, 1975). This has been a blind spot of Marxist analyses too (Westergaard and Resler, 1975; Nichols and Armstrong, 1976; Beynon, 1973). There is therefore little empirical work upon which to draw and some of what follows is rather speculative.

My previous research with Annie Phizacklea led us to begin to appreciate the ideological significance of nationalism for at least the small section of the working class that we interviewed (Miles and Phizacklea, 1979, pp. 115–19). For a minority of our sample, the racialization of fellow black workers was linked to a notion of themselves as members of a distinct and separate 'nation', to which 'the coloureds' could never belong by virtue of their 'race'. For these workers, the very presence of West Indians in Britain was seen as related to Britain's declining world position, both economically and politically: joining the 'Common Market' and the giving of aid to the Third World were common objects of disfavour in this connection, while the economic superiority of Germany after defeat in the Second World War was a source of envy which, in a small minority of cases, had led to a re-evaluation of the validity of the war against fascism. Implicit in these ideological constructions was a conception of Britain's historically dominant position in the world. This was favourably evaluated in the context of their experience of material decline, both direct and indirectly mediated by media and politicians. The ideological construction of the 'nation' came to be expressed in terms of and ultimately fused into the idea of 'race'. The conception of being working class tended to become submerged by a notion of 'us' as *English/British* and *white* because of the way in which they had interpreted their experience of living with the effects of material decline and the settlement of migrant labour that could easily be typified as 'race' (cf. Nairn, 1977; Pearson, 1976; Birch, 1977, pp. 134–42). In other words, 'we' becomes less the working class and more the English/British 'nation' which is defined in conflict with 'the coloureds', the 'inferior races'. This nationalist/racist political identity is then able to draw upon the imagery of Empire and domination by the superior 'white race' of large sections of the world's inferior 'races'.

The nature of our sample did not allow us to comment on the extent of this ideological construction amongst the working class as a whole. Nevertheless, the fact that both Enoch Powell (see Powell, 1969, 1972) and the National Front (see Nugent and King, 1979; Billig, 1979; Fielding, 1981, pp. 76–104), have, in different ways, made a political appeal in terms of an idea of 'nation' and received political support from the working class, suggests that this is an ideological construction which is of some considerable significance. Moreover, one should also note that the notion of 'the national interest' has been widely and regularly used by both Labour and Conservative Governments since 1945 in appeals for political support. For these reasons alone, I would argue that the idea of 'nation' is an important component of working-class political consciousness, not only by itself but also in close relation to the idea of 'race'. Nairn (1977) takes the argument a stage further and argues that English nationalism can only be expressed in the negative and limiting terms of 'race' because of the nature of the origin of the English bourgeois state and the mode of incorporation of the working class.

In Scotland, working-class articulation of nationalism seems not to have been expressed in terms of the idea of 'race'. although there is an undercurrent of anti-English sentiment in Scotland, most writers seem to agree that this is not articulated in terms of arguments about the biological inferiority of a supposed English 'race' (e.g. Brand, 1978, pp. 16–18). On the other hand, there is good reason to believe that racism has been generated and reproduced within Scotland, and some evidence is available to sustain such an argument (Miles and Muirhead, 1986). I shall comment on two aspects of this. First, in so far as there is a relationship between colonialism and the articulation of racism, one is encouraged to investigate the Scottish role in the construction and maintenance of the British Empire. One of the consequences of the Act of Union of 1707 for the emergent Scottish merchant class was that it was permitted to intervene in what had previously been exclusively English trade routes and infant colonies of settlement. During the eighteenth century, the Scottish merchant class took advantage of this and Glasgow developed as a major port as a consequence of trade (particularly in tobacco and linen) with North America and the Caribbean. Out of the profits of this trade, manufacturing enterprises were funded in Scotland. Scots were also involved in trade with India, both within and outside the East India Company, and during the nineteenth century a number of Scottish companies came to dominate parts of the Indian economy.

Scottish involvement in colonialism was not limited to trade for Scots were prominent amongst the explorers, administrators, soldiers and missionaries who played a role in imperial expansion. All of these activities involved direct and indirect contact with the relations of exploitation utilized in that expansion and with the populations of the Caribbean, India and Africa, as a result of which information and imagery about them were channelled back to Scotland (e.g. National Library of Scotland, 1982). Only literary records remain available for analysis today and are under-researched, although a brief review of some of this material reveals that a racist image was reproduced in Scotland. In addition, there was a Scottish contribution to the development of scientific racism during the nineteenth century (e.g. Lord Kames, George Combe), and these ideas and arguments circulated in Scotland in journals such as Blackwoods *Edinburgh Magazine*. In sum, processes which sustained the historical generation and reproduction of racism in England were present in Scotland, and there is therefore good reason to believe that the Scottish population has been socialized in a culture which contains at least elements of racism. Indeed, there have been celebrations of the specifically Scottish contribution to the British Empire (Gibb, 1937).

Second, although Scotland tends to be regarded, and correctly, as a society of emigration, there have been a number of migrations into Scotland, the most significant and the largest being from Ireland. Both the reasons for, and the political and ideological reaction to, this migration are of direct relevance here. The development of industrial capitalism in Scotland required a substantial migration of labour into the western Lowlands, beginning in the late eighteenth and continuing through the nineteenth century. Much of this labour came from the surrounding rural areas and from the Highlands, but a significant proportion came from Ireland, with the result that by the middle of the nineteenth century, it was estimated that about a quarter of the population in this area was Irish-born or of Irish descent (Handley, n.d.). The early migrants were seasonal labourers who migrated for the summer to help with the Scottish harvest and so supplemented their own meagre living from the soil in Ireland. A proportion of these seasonal migrants gradually entered industrial production and became more permanent migrants (e.g. Handley, n.d.; Johnson, 1967). To these were added the Irish cotton handloom weavers whose trade was being destroyed as a result of competition from cheaper cotton products from Scotland; they migrated to Scotland to continue their trade in apparently more advantageous circumstances (Green, 1944). These connections between Ireland and Scotland were part of the first link in a migration chain (cf. MacDonald and MacDonald, 1964; Watson, 1977): once the link had been established, and so long as a demand for labour in the west of Scotland continued and the economic circumstances of the Irish peasantry worsened, the migration continued (Miles, 1982).

Irish migrant labour became an object of Scottish working-class hostility. This was partly because employers used Irish labour to break strikes and reduce wages (see Handley, n.d.; Young, 1979; Dickson, 1980). The search for profit thereby assured that at least sections of the new Scottish proletariat had a real material reason to be hostile to the presence of Irish labour. But this was not the only element involved. The majority of Irish migrants were adherents to the Catholic religion, a fact which greatly concerned the Presbyterian Kirk. Presbyterianism was founded in part on a militant anti-Catholicism, had recently faced the possibility of the restoration of a Catholic monarchy as a result of the Jacobite rebellion in 1745 and had been awarded the status of the 'state' religion of Scotland by the Act of Union (and, in the absence of distinctly Scottish political institutions, had come partially to play that role) (e.g. Reid, 1960; Donaldson, 1972). For these reasons, ministers of the Kirk were actively involved in stimulating and encouraging anti-Irish feeling because of the perceived threat to their own religion and its institutional position and significance (Handley, n.d., pp. 81, 141).

The continued fears and agitation of ministers of the Kirk of Scotland, combined with the agitation of the Orange Lodges, has led most commentators to identify anti-Irish agitation as anti-Catholic and therefore sectarian. On the other hand, 'race relations' theorists' obsession with the social significance attributed to skin colour has ensured that they have paid little or no attention to a situation which in many essentials has a parallel with that of England in the 1950s and 1960s. In both instances, capital required labour and the labour was supplied from territories which were, or had been, economically dependent upon Britain; a migration chain was established and the migrants were faced with a hostile reaction from the working class which they were joining to sell their labour power. Moreover, the Irish in Scotland in the nineteenth century were categorized as a separate 'race' and one measure of their supposed inferiority was said to be their adherence to Catholicism (cf. Miles, 1982, pp. 140–5). This racist imagery was reproduced in the 1920s and 1930s. In 1923, a Committee of the Church of Scotland reported on what it was as the consequences of continuing Irish migration to Scotland. The Irish and the Scots were identified as distinct and antagonistic 'races' and 'racial conflict' was predicted as a result of the attributed negative consequences of the Irish presence in Scotland. The Irish were accused of forcing Scots to leave Scotland, or moving into positions of power and influence in Scotland and of undermining the high moral character of the Scottish 'race' (see Miles and Muirhead, 1986). Similar views were expressed by a Professor of Law at the University of Glasgow who, *inter alia*, claimed that the Irish in Scotland had a monopoly of criminal activity, violence and sexual deviance (Gibb, 1930, p. 55). Thus, racism has been one of the ideological strands expressed in the Scottish reaction to Irish migration and an element in the fractionalism of the Scottish working class (cf. Young, 1979).

But if racism has had an active influence in Scottish political relations before 1945, we seem to be confronted with a paradox in so far as its subsequent influence has been comparatively weak. Certainly, the racialization of domestic politics that developed in England from the mid 1950s has not occurred in Scotland. Thus, the 'common-sense' definition of Scotland as not having a 'race relations' problem reflects a combination of absences in Scotland, the absence of an 'anti-immigration' campaign, of widespread and active support for Enoch Powell, of electoral and ideological support for the National Front, and an absence of a sustained and continuous growth of racist violence since the late 1970s. A large part of the explanation for this is historical and structural. The political reaction to postwar economic decline has been decisively shaped by nationalism, reflecting the secondary and dependent position of Scotland within the United Kingdom as a whole, while the prior fractionalization of the working class, particularly in the west of lowland Scotland, preserves a focus for internal class conflicts. But conjunctural factors are also relevant. Comparatively, fascist parties have had very limited success in Scotland since the 1930s while the Conservative Party has experienced a long period of electoral and political decline in Scotland since 1950, reducing its ability to mobilize the Scottish electorate on any issue. The Conservative Party and fascist groups played a major role in the racialization of politics in England but have been too weak in Scotland to have had the same influence, and therefore the Labour Party in Scotland has not faced the same pressures to capitulate to racism as happened in England (Miles, 1986).

But one cannot conclude that racism has been absent from Scotland since 1945. For the historical reasons outlined above, racism is one of the elements which has shaped the conceptualization of Asian migrants by Scottish people. Certainly, in the recent past, there have been more visible indications of its presence and influence on behaviour (Miles and Muirhead, 1986). Asian people and their property have been attacked, racist grafitti has become more common, fascist groups have maintained a more consistent and active presence, racist literature is more commonly distributed around housing estates and outside schools and there has been racist chanting at football matches. Thus, although racism has not had such a central influence on political processes in Scotland, to the extent of effecting a racialization of politics, it does have the capacity to influence the lives of Asian people who live in Scotland.

Conclusion

My concern in this chapter has been with working-class political consciousness in England and Scotland and not with 'race relations'. Political consciousness contains a picture and an evaluation of the way in which social relations are organized and the position of the individual in those relations. It therefore contains a political self-identity and thereby imagery of the groups to which the individual sees himself/herself belonging. The fact of selling one's labour power for a wage is a crucial determinant of a political identity but there are other processes which lead to the construction of additional identities. Those can co-exist or even displace an identity of belonging to a working class. I have been particularly concerned here with the political identities of belonging to a 'race' and/or 'nation' and with the circumstances in which such an identity might be given active political expression. Thus, in England we have seen sections of the working class demonstrating in support of Enoch Powell's racist anti-immigration speeches and so identifying themselves with an idea of a British 'race' and 'nation'. And in Scotland, we have witnessed sections of the working class giving political expression to their identity of Scottishness by voting for the Scottish National Party instead of the *British* Labour Party. In order to begin to understand why these events have occurred I have argued that we should consider the ways in which the ideas of 'race' and 'nation' can come to have phenomenal adequacy for sections of the working class in different situations of material decline in England and Scotland. This requires in turn an historical analysis of the inter-relationship between the development of capitalist production and the reproduction of the ideologies of racism and nationalism.

References

Althusser, L. (1969), *For Marx*, Allen Lane
Althusser, L. (1971), *Lenin and Philosophy and Other Essays*, New Left Books
Anderson, B. (1983), *Imagined Communities: Reflections on the Origins and Spread of Nationalism*, Verso
Banton, M. (1970), 'The concept of racism', S. Zubaida (ed.), *Race and Racialism*, Tavistock
Banton, M. and Harwood, J. (1975), *The Race Concept*, Newton Abbot: David & Charles
Banton, M. (1977), *The Idea of Race*, Tavistock
Benyon, H. (1973), *Working for Ford*, Penguin
Billig, M. (1979), *Fascists*, Harcourt Brace Jovanovich
Birch, H. H. (1977), *Political Integration and Disintegration in the British Isles*, Allen & Unwin
Bodmer, W. F. and Cavalli-Sforza L. L. (1976), *Genetics, Evolution and Man*, San Francisco: Freeman & Co.
Bohning W. R. (1972), *The Migration of Workers in the United Kingdom and the European Community*, Oxford University Press
Bolt, C. (1971), *Victorian Attitudes to Race*, Routledge & Kegan Paul
Brand, J. (1978), *The National Movement in Scotland*, Routledge & Kegan Paul
Budge, I. & Urwin D. W. (1966), *Scottish Political Behaviour*, Longman
Bulmer, M. (ed) (1975), *Working Class Images of Society*, Routledge & Kegan Paul
Cairns, H. A. C. (1965), *Prelude to Imperialism: British Reactions to Central African Society 1840-1890*, Routledge & Kegan Paul
Castles, S. and Kosack, G. (1972), 'The function of labour immigration in Western European capitalism', *New Left Review*, no. 73, pp. 3-21
Castles, S. and Kosack, G. (1973), *Immigrant Workers and the Class Structure*, Oxford University Press
Cox, O. C. (1970), *Caste, Class and Race*, New York: Monthly Review Press
Curtin, P. D. (1965), *The Image of Africa: British Ideas and Action 1780-1850*, Macmillan
Daniel W. W. (1968), *Racial Discrimination in England*, Penguin
Deakin, N. (1970), *Colour, Citizenship and British Society*, Panther
Dickson, T. (ed.) (1980), *Scottish Capitalism*, Lawrence & Wishart
Donaldson, G. (1972), *Scotland: Church and Nation through Sixteen Centuries*, Edinburgh: Scottish Academic Press
Eldridge, C. C. (1973), *England's Mission: The Imperial Idea in the Age of Gladstone and Disraeli, 1868-1880*, Macmillan
Evans, P. (1976), *Publish and be Damned?*, Runnymede Trust

Fielding, N. (1981), *The National Front*, Routledge & Kegan Paul

Foot, P. (1965), *Immigration and Race in British Politics*, Penguin

Gabriel, J. and Ben-Tovim, G. (1978), 'Marxism and the concept of racism', *Economy and Society*, vol. 7, no. 2, pp 118–54

Gellner, E. (1964), *Thought and Change*, Weidenfield & Nicolson

Gellner, E. (1983), *Nations and Nationalism*, Basil Blackwell

Geras, N. (1972), 'Marx and the critique of political economy' in R. Blackburn (ed.) *Ideology in Social Science*, Fontana

Gibb, A. D. (1930), *Scotland in Eclipse*, Toulmin

Gibb, A. D. (1937), *Scottish Empire*, Maclehose

Goldthorpe, J. *et al*. (1969), *The Affluent Worker in the Class Structure*, Cambridge University Press

Gramsci, A. (1971), *Selections from the Prison Notebooks*, Lawrence & Wishart

Green, E. R. R. (1944), 'The cotton hand-loom weavers in the northeast of Ireland', *Ulster Journal of Archaeology*, vol. 7, pp. 30–41

Hall, S. *et al*. (1978), *Policing the Crisis*, Macmillan

Hall, S. (1978), 'Racism and reaction', in Commission for Racial Equality, *Five Views of Multi-Racial Britain*, CRE

Hall, S. (1980), 'Race, articulation and societies structured in dominance', in UNESCO, *Sociological Theories: Race and Colonialism*, Paris: UNESCO

Handley, J. E. (n.d.), *The Irish in Scotland*, Glasgow: John S. Burns & Sons

Hartmann, P. and Husband, C. (1974), *Racism and the Mass Media*, Davis-Poynter

Harvie, C. (1977), *Scotland and Nationalism*, Allen & Unwin

Hechter, M. (1975), *Internal Colonialism*, Routledge & Kegan Paul

Hobsbawm, E. (1977), 'Some reflections on "The break-up of Britain"', *New Left Review*, no. 105, pp. 3–23

Humphry, D. and Ward, M. (1974), *Passports and Politics*, Penguin

Husband, C. (ed.) (1975), *White Media and Black Britain*, Arrow Books

Husband, C. (1975), 'The National Front: a response to crisis', *New Society* (15 May), pp 403–5

Husband, C. (1979), 'The "threat" hypothesis and racist voting in England and the United States', in R. Miles and A. Phizacklea (eds), *Racism and Political Action in Britain*, Routledge and Kegan Paul

Husband, C. (1980), 'The National Front: what happens to it now?, *Marxism Today* (September), pp 268–75

Husband, C. T. (1983), *Racial Exclusionism and the City: the urban support of the National Front*, George Allen and Unwin

Huttenback, R. A. (1976), *Racism and Empire: White Settlers and Coloured Immigrants in the British Self-governing Colonies 1830–1910*, Cornell University Press

Johnson, J. H. (1967), 'Harvest migration from nineteenth century Ireland', *Transactions of the Institute of British Geographers*, vol XLI, pp. 97–112

Jones, H. R. & Davenport, M. (1972), 'The Pakistani Community in Dundee: a study of its growth and demographic structure', *Scottish Geographical Magazine*, 88(2), pp. 75–86

Keating, M. and Bleiman, P. (1979), *Labour and Scottish Nationalism*, Macmillan

Kearsley, G. W. & Srivastava, S. R. (1974), 'The Spatial Evolution of Glasgow's Asian Community', *Scottish Geographical Magazine*, 90(2)

Kellas, J. (1968), *Modern Scotland: The Nation Since 1870*, Pall Mall

Kellas, J. (1984), *The Scottish Political System*, Cambridge University Press

Larrain, J. (1979), *The Concept of Ideology*, Hutchinson

Lawrence, D. (1974), *Black Migrants: White Natives*, Cambridge University Press

Lorimer, D. A. (1978), *Colour, Class and the Victorians*, Leicester University Press

MacDonald, J. S. and MacDonald, L. B. (1964), 'Chain migration, ethnic neighbourhood formation and social networks', *Millbank Memorial Fund Quarterly*, vol. 42, pp. 82–92

McQueen, H. (1970), *A New Brittania: an argument concerning the social origins of Australian radicalism and nationalism*, Penguin Books

Mansbach, R. W. (1973), 'The Scottish National Party': a revised political profit', *Comparative Politics*, vol. 5, no. 2, pp. 185–210

Marx, K. and Engels, F. (1965), *The German Ideology*, Lawrence & Wishart

Miles, R. (1980), 'Class, race and ethnicity: a critique of Cox's theory', *Ethnic and Racial Studies*, vol. 3, no. 2, pp 169–87

Miles, R. (1982), *Capitalism, Racism and Migrant Labour*, Routledge & Kegan Paul

Miles, R. (1984a), 'Marxism versus the Sociology of "Race Relations"?', *Ethnic and Racial Studies*, 7(2), pp 217–37

Miles, R. (1984b), 'The Riots of 1958: The Ideological Construction of "Race Relations" as a Political Issue in Britain', *Immigrants and Minorities*, 3(3), pp. 252–75

Miles, R. (1984/85), 'Racism and the Political Economy of Labour Migration: a reply to Brotz', *New Community*, 12(1).

Miles, R. (1985), 'Recent Marxist Theories of Nationalism and the Problem of Racism', Paper presented to a Colloquium on Marxist Perspectives on Ethnicity and Nationalism at the University of Belgrade, 2/3 September

Miles, R. & Muirhead, L. (1986), 'Racism in Scotland: a matter for further investigation?' in D. McCrone (ed.), *Scottish Government Yearbook*, 1986, Edinburgh

Miles, R. and Phizacklea, A. (eds) (1979), *Racism and Political Action in Britain*, Routledge & Kegan Paul

Miles, R. and Phizacklea, A. (1981), 'Racism and capitalist decline', in M. Harloe (ed.), *New Perspectives in Urban Change and Conflicts*, Heinemann

Miles, R. & Phizacklea, A. (1984), *White Man's Country: Racism in British Politics*, Pluto Press

Miles, R. & Spoonley, P. (1985), 'The Political Economy of Labour Migration:

an alternative to the sociology of "race" and "ethnic relations" in New Zealand', *Australia and New Zealand Journal of Sociology*, 21(1), pp. 3–26

Minogue, K. (1967), *Nationalism*, Batsford

Montagu, A., (ed.) (1964), *The Concept of Race*, New York: Free Press

Montagu, A., (ed.), (1972), *Statement on Race*, Oxford University Press

Moore, R. and Wallace, T. (1975), *Slamming the Door*, Martin Robertson

National Library of Scotland (1982), *Scotland and Africa*, National Library of Scotland

Nichols, T. and Armstrong, P. (1976), *Workers Divided*, Fontana

Nikolinakos, N. (1973), 'Notes on an economic theory of racism', *Race*, vol. XIV, No. 4, pp. 365–81

Nugent, N. and King, R. (1979), 'Ethnic minorities, scape-goating and the extreme right', in R. Miles and A. Phizacklea (eds) *Racism and Political Action in Britain*

Patterson, S. (1969), *Immigration and Race Relations in Britain 1960–76*, Oxford University Press

Pearson, G. (1976), ' "Paki-bashing" in a North-East Lancashire cotton town: a case study in its history', in G. Mungham and G. Pearson (eds), *Working Class Youth Culture*, Routledge & Kegan Paul

Phizacklea, A. and Miles, R. (1980), *Labour and Racism*, Routledge & Kegan Paul

Powell, E. (1969), *Freedom and Reality*, Surrey: Elliott Right Way Books

Powell, E. (1972), *Still to Decide*, Surrey: Elliot Right Way Books

Reid, J. M. (1970), *Kirk and Nation*, Skeffington

Rex, J. and Moore, R. (1967), *Race, Community and Conflict*, Oxford University Press

Rex, J. (1970), *Race Relations in Sociological Theory*, Weidenfeld & Nicolson

Rex, J. (1973), *Race, Colonialism and the City*, Routledge & Kegan Paul

Rex, J. (1979), 'Black militancy and class conflict', in R. Miles and A. Phizacklea (eds) *Racism and Political Action in Britain*

Rex, J. and Tomlinson, S. (1979), *Colonial Immigrants in a British City*, Routledge & Kegan Paul

Rose, S. *et. al.* (1984), *Not In Our Genes*, Penguin

Runnymede Trust and Radical Statistics Race Group (1980), *Britain's Black Population*, Heinemann

Sayer, D. (1979), *Marx's Method*, Brighton: Harvester Press

Schoen, D. S. (1977), *Enoch Powell and the Powellites*, Macmillan

Seliger, M. (1977), *The Marxist Conception of Ideology*, Cambridge University Press

Sivanandan, A. (1973), 'Race, class and power: an outline for study', *Race*, vol. 14, no. 4, pp. 3838–9

Sivanandan, A. (1967), 'Race, class and the state: the black experience in Britain', *Race and Class*, vol. XVII, no. 4, pp. 347–68

Smith, A. D. (1971), *Theories of Nationalism*, Duckworth

Smith, A. D. (1979), *Nationalism in the Twentieth Century*, Oxford: Martin Robertson

Smith, D. (1977), *Racial Disadvantage in Britain*, Penguin

Studlar, D. (1980), 'Elite responsiveness or elite autonomy: British immigration policy reconsidered', *Ethnic and Racial Studies*, vol. 3, no. 2, pp. 207–23

Taylor, S. (1979), 'The National Front: anatomy of a political movement', in R. Miles and A. Phizacklea (eds) *Racism and Political Action in Britain*

Van den Berghe, P. L. (1967), *Race and Racism*, New York: Wiley

Walvin, J. (1973), *Black and White: The Negro and English Society 1555–1945*, Allen Lane

Watson, J. (1977), *Between Two Cultures*, Oxford: Blackwell

Webb, K. (1978), *The Growth of Nationalism in Scotland*, Penguin

Weber, M. (1964), *The Theory of Social and Economic Organization*, New York: Free Press

Westergaard, J. and Resler, H. (1976), *Class in a Capitalist Society*, Penguin

Young, J. D. (1979), *The Rousing of the Scottish Working Class*, Croom Helm

Part Five

The 'new racism'

The purpose of this final section is to refer back to my introductory chapter and to link together some of the different levels of analysis that have been presented in the previous chapters. In doing this I am not attempting an overview. That is a task that would require much more space, and in the context of a text such as this it is one which is appropriately left to each reader.

In different chapters the reader has been invited to examine the nature of 'race' in Britain from quite varied perspectives. Some have focused upon the structure of contemporary British society, others on the politics of 'race'; Tajfel provides an explicitly social psychological analysis, and Part Three points to the importance of experiential data. In this concluding chapter I return to the nature of race-thinking that was explored in my introductory chapter, initially written for the 1982 edition, and examine the development of the 'New Racism'. In doing this I discuss racism as ideology and hope to provide a simple, but not simplistic, account of what this might mean for our understanding of contemporary events. In particular I wish to indicate that while employing different levels of analysis is analytically appropriate as a strategy for understanding racism, in reality racism exists as a complex interaction of consciousness and structure. I have tried to indicate this complexity in a way which allows for racism to be understood as being *simultaneously* an individual and a social phenomenon. There is a burgeoning literature on 'race relations' policies which makes it all the more important that we should have a clear understanding of what we understand 'race' and 'racism' to be.

17 British racisms: the construction of racial ideologies

Charles Husband

In this final chapter I would like to refer back to my introductory chapter on the concept of 'race' and to discuss some of the developments which have taken place since 1982. In that chapter I refer to the identification by Barker (1981) of *The New Racism* as being a major change in the construction of race thinking. In his book he argues that within this new theorization of race the belief in the inferiority of the outgroup is not crucial to their exclusion. Rather, he argues, it is the non-negotiable nature of their cultural difference which sets them apart:

> This, then, is the character of the new racism. It is a theory that I shall call biological, or better, pseudo-biological culturalism.Nations on this view are not built out of politics and economics, but out of human nature. It is in our biology, our instincts, to defend our way of life, traditions and customs against outsiders – not because they are inferior but because they are part of different cultures. This is a non-rational process; and none the worse for it. For we are soaked in, made up out of, our traditions and our culture. [Barker, 1981, p. 23]

It should not be thought that this 'new racism' is a coherent theory which has been systematically developed and set down in a definitive text. Rather it is an assemblage of ideas which have been generated by a loosely structured coterie of right-wing politicians, academics and journalists who have had the personal status and hence access to political and media discourses to be in Hall *et al.*'s (1978) terms 'primary definers'. They have been able to introduce concepts and issues which have been taken up in wider circles. These ideas are not new or unique to their contemporary sources. Indeed it is the fact that they refer back to notions that already exist in common-sense, taken for granted, popular belief that enables the elements of the new racism to cohere in a seemingly rational, and more importantly *reasonable*, package (see Gordon and Klug, 1986 and Seidel, 1985, for accounts of the development and content of the new racism).

As Barker has indicated above the core of new racist theory is the naturalness of ingroup preference and outgroup hostility: it is human nature to prefer your own. This invocation of 'human nature' is an idea which was already given scientific legitimacy by the 1960s and 1970s ethologists such as Lorenz and Morris whom I mentioned in my introductory chapter. It has more recently been given further academic support in the theoretical developments of sociobiology, which have for example been applied directly to 'race relations' by Van den Berghe, 1981 and 1986. Were these ideas confined to academic debates their political significance would be considerably lessened. Rather it is that through the mass media the popular belief in 'human nature' can be invoked to underpin statements about group preference; which is then additionally reinforced by the 'independent' support derived from scientific evidence. After all the legitimating power of 'science' is rehearsed daily in the subliminal agendas of advertising to promote the utility and reliability of everything from compact discs to washing powders. Thus in evaluating its success we must note the success of new right idealogues in gaining direct access to the national press, and in establishing a language which is echoed there by other journalists. For example, Gordon and Klug (1986, p. 14) give examples such as these:

> . . . a *Daily Express* editorial claimed that 'it is equally wrong not to recognise that racial selectivity – a natural human preference for one's own kind – is deeply ingrained in ALL peoples, whatever their colour or creed.' (20.4.81). Or again, *Daily Star's* commentator Robert McNeill argues that: 'Any fool knows (though some fools would rather not know) that the process which Darwin called natural selection means that, on the whole, people prefer their "ain folk" – their own ethnic stock. It's in our genes. It is part of every person's nature, black or white.' [18.4.84]

To refer back again to Barker, we can note that he identifies the linkage between this pseudo-biological definition of 'race' and the definition of nation. Both are made of 'one's own kind' who share a common culture, a way of life. The concept of nation is crucial in providing a linkage between the political and economic concerns of 'the new right' and the racist discourse of new racism. It is a 'natural' boundary for the organization of cultural and economic life; and as such it provides a point of convergence for the 'neo-liberal' and the 'neo-conservative' forces within 'new right' politics. The 'neo-liberal position' is essentially concerned with minimizing state intervention in the free operation of the economy, while the 'neo-conservatives' are more concerned with securing the continuity of traditional authority, culture, and morality. As one observer has commented:

> New Right political practice, such as Thatcherism, involves both sides. On the one hand it draws on the conservative discourse of authority and discipline and on the other on the liberal discourse of freedom and justice. The two sides seem quite distinct, but in political practice there is much cross-over and no clear separation can be made. It is mistake to ignore either side and the intermingling in practice. [Belsey, 1986, p. 173]

The presentation of the natural homogeneity of nations not only defines those who belong, it also reciprocally defines the criteria for the identification of aliens. From Enoch Powell's 1968 statement that a West Indian or Asian born in England did not thereby become an 'Englishman', through the nationalist fervour of the Falklands crisis, to the militarist language and nationalist sentiments of the 1987 Conservative Party election campaign national identity and national integrity have enjoyed a high visibility in British politics. Thus as Seidel (1985) has outlined, the ideas of nation and nationality have provided a language which has allowed for a coded vicarious discussion of race: what Reeves (1983) has called discursive deracialization, by which he means – 'persons speak purposely to their audiences about racial matters, while avoiding the overt deployment of racial descriptions, evaluations and prescriptions' (Reeves, 1983, p. 4). Thus the new racism has acquired a theory and a range of styles of argumentation which are enveloped in a self-evident reasonableness, which renders them superficially unobjectionable. At one level 'race' and ethnic self interest may be talked of as a normal expression of human nature, and at another one may speak of national culture and be understood in 'race' terms.

The importance of this is that the new racism avoids the explicit superiority claims of earlier social-Darwinist informed racism, *and* it benefits from comparison with its immediate forerunner. Thus proponents of the new racism are quick to deny that their utterances or policies are racist. Rather, by pivoting their concerns on the non-negotiability of cultural differences they have coopted and exploited the ground won by the liberal multiculturalists over the last two decades. After all it was they who asserted the moral importance of recognizing cultural differences, and rejected assimilation as a racist option. Effectively then all the new right is doing is to recognize, and extend, the validity of this argument by inflecting it with the new 'insights' on human nature. Therefore, the new right would argue that their policies are based upon a recognition of the 'genuine fears' of a national or cultural group. From this base it is then possible to move on to identify the genuine fears of the majority; that *they* may be threatened by the unreasonable demands of a number of minorities. In identifying the left in British politics as the agents of minority interests the new right has thus been able to fuse further elements of its political platform. In a Government led by a leader, Margaret Thatcher, who explicitly wants to rid British politics of socialism forever there is a double benefit from making this linkage. To the extent that the left is discredited then their association with anti-racist strategies brings such strategies into disrepute. To the extent that the success of new racism has enabled the definition of anti-racist strategies as being a politically motivated threat to the genuine interests of the white majority then this is damaging to the left's cause. It is a formula which has been successfully orchestrated over the last decade, and which was most successful in the pillorying of the 'looney left' in Brent and elsewhere during the last few years (see Murray, 1986; Gordon and Klug 1986, ch. 3; and Searle, 1987; for accounts of the new racist presence in the popular press and in pressure group publications). Since the essence of anti-racist analysis is to go beyond the recognition of cultural variation within Britain in order to expose the class and politically structured inequalities between different ethnic groups, then it inevitably provides a critique of the social philosophy of the contemporary Conservative Party leadership. Hence anti-racism is objectionable to the right not only in its opposition to new racist theory, but also in its political critique of new right philosophies and policies.

There is then as Barker (1981) and Gordon and Klug (1986) have illustrated an inherent inter-relation in the core concepts and values of the new right and the new racism. The fact that there is not a unitary definitive statement of the new racism, nor indeed a homogeneously unified absolute consensus among the personnel of the new right, ironically constitutes one of their strengths. For the arguments which are constructed around particular issues such as education, welfare or moral standards have an ad hoc, contingent, quality in their specifics; whilst echoing the general themes of 'human nature' and the 'genuine fears' of the majority in relation to *their* legitimate rights. Hence one of the strengths of the fusion of new racist thinking into new right politics is the frequent reiteration of the underlying 'reasonable' assumptions, rather than the coherence or defensibility of specific arguments. When you add to that the *discursive deracialization* of much of the debates on for example education, immigration or cultural standards then the new racism is a very potent ideological phenomenon. However, we should not leap to seeing it as universally shared, or uniformly employed. Let me make a few qualifying statements.

We could usefully ask, has the new racism usurped the old-fashioned vulgar social-Darwinist biological racism and the explicit claims of racial superiority that went with it? To anyone who travels by public transport the answer must by self-evidently no. Indeed the racist backwoodsmen in the House of Commons are not beyond invoking Anglo-Saxon blood in defence of an argument. Perhaps we should be clear about how we understand individuals to 'possess' racist ideologies. The first thing to dismiss is the assumption, widespread in social science, and in popular belief that individuals are consistent. The idea of prejudiced *personalities* did much to promote the expectation of individuals being more or less stable in their degree of racism. At a general level Billig (1982) has done much to challenge the assumed consistency of individual belief and action. And in the specific case of 'race-thinking' Potter and Wetherell (1987) have demonstrated the individual's ability to employ conflicting positions within the same conversation! Hence, whatever racist ideology is, it is not an overlearned set of beliefs that are passively acquired and routinely elicited in some mindless knee-jerk reflex to a social cue. The essence of Tajfel's (1981, 1982, 1984) work on social identification theory has been to try to depict the ego-involved way in which individuals incorporate values and beliefs associated with group membership. While social identity theory itself may be a flawed attempt, it does point to the necessity of conceiving of individuals as active agents who in constructing *their* meanings incorporate socially constructed concepts and values which have ideological properties.

We may now ask the necessary question – whence the ideology, or ideologies? Let me in gross terms state two alternative formulations which I think of as top-down and bottom-up. However, it is important that these are understood as being two different aspects of the same fundamental process, and as such are interactive, not mutually exclusive. By top-down I am referring to the conception of ideology being imposed by the control of ideas by a ruling elite, so that individuals are contained in a world of dominant images and values, and are denied access to cognitive alternatives. For example, as I write this I am able to consider my body image and reflect upon the regrettable truth that I do not have all the right muscles in the right place and that my body fat seems less than adequately distributed over my total frame. In fact I am fortunate in having a healthy and functionally adequate body, and yet I cannot detach myself from what I know to be entirely historically contingent notions of the ideal male body. That for me is the power of top-down ideological penetration of my consciousness, and I could also illustrate it in relation to notions of class, age, nationality, race, as well as gender identity.

In sociological terms this is consistent with Marx's view that the base determines the superstructure: namely that the superstructure of ideas and values are in a fundamental way determined by the (im)balance of power represented in the mode of production which prevails in any particular society. Thus in each society there will be a dominant class which will generate a dominant ideology. It is often related to the phrase from Marx and Engels' *The German Ideology* that the ideas of

the ruling class are in every epoch the ruling ideas, i.e. the class which is the ruling material force of society, is at the same time its ruling intellectual force.

In neo-Marxist writing this perspective has often in recent years been extended by the use of the concept of the Ideological State Apparatuses, of for example, education, law, the church and the media as being important vehicles for the transmission of 'the dominant' ideology. This in turn has led to a concern with the extent to which in a Parliamentary social democracy like Britain the state is neutral, or an agent of the dominant bloc in a society which operates within a capitalist mode of production. Hence for example, both the left and right argue over the ideological function of the education system (Troyna and Williams, 1986; O'Keeffe, 1986). Similar attention has been focused on the extent to which the institutions of the state guarantee neutrality in the administration of the law and of policing, and in the regulation and operation of the mass media (see McLennan *et al.*, 1984, for a useful critical discussion). The essence of top-down ideology is the winning of consent for the status quo by control over the definition of what is 'normal'. Hence in analysing the construction and the maintenance of a dominant ideology there is a necessary focusing of attention upon the control of the channels of information dissemination.

In comparison my notion of 'bottom-up' ideology is akin to the statement from the *Preface* (Marx, 1970) that:

It is not the consciousness of men that determines their being, but on the contrary, their social being that determines their consciousness.

Here Marx is reminding us that we do not live in a world of ideas alone, but also in a material world which imposes constraints on our existence, and hence on our experience. For Marx individual material existence was determined by class; defined by each person's relationship to the means of production. Hence, out of common material existences each class was seen as generating a culture which gave expression to its material existence. Given that classes have different experiences, and different class interests then it was expected that oppositional cultures would reflect in consciousness the opposed material conditions of existence. Let me then define bottom-up ideology as 'experience grounded in material existence determines consciousness', and illustrate this in relation to my gender identity once more. While it is true that in terms of top-down ideology I am aware of the ubiquity of *images* of male dominance over women in the mass media, and am likely to have incorporated some element of that into my identity, my capacity to incorporate such images is very significantly facilitated by the fact that since childhood I have been enabled *to practice* dominance over females. The research literature has demonstrated how in the home and in school young males are privileged in relation to young females. They are taught to assume dominance (Sharp, 1976; Delamont, 1980). Hence although thanks to feminist critiques of gender relations I am now more able to identify sexist *imagery*, and to *intellectually* comprehend aspects of male strategies of dominance I find a great difficulty in identifying the internal cognitive and behavioural routines that are the end product of forty-two years of practice.

Ideology then does not only exist in the imposition of imagery, concepts and values; it also exists in the structured patterning of behaviour. Sennett and Cobb (1973) in their book *The Hidden Injuries of Class* give the touching example of working-class parents whose children succeed academically and professionally. They are proud of their children's achievement but cannot value their skills. In terms of a shared dominant ideology of ideas the parents can identify with the status hierarchy within which their child has achieved. In terms of individuals who have come, through practice, to value manual skills they cannot truly comprehend wherein lies their child's prowess. As Sennett and Cobb (1973, p. 22) say of one person in their study:

> Capturing respect in the larger America, then, means to Frank getting into an educated position: but capturing that respect means that he no longer respects himself. This contradiction ran through every discussion we held, as an image either of what people felt compelled to do with their own lives or of what they ought for their sons. If the boys could get educated, anybody in America would respect them; and yet . . . the fathers felt education would lead the young into work not as 'real' as their own.

> In Frank's words: 'These jobs aren't real work where you make something – it's just pushing papers.' [Sennett and Cobb, 1973, p. 21]

What this example illustrates is the potential tension between the top-down ideology of ideas and imagery, and the bottom-up consciousness that rises from shared materially structured experience.

So too there are contradictions and consistencies within the ideologies of racism. The initial triumph, and fundamental necessity for its existence, is the establishing of 'race' as a *social fact* (see my introduction in this book). To believe that races are valid categories is to endorse an ideology that is racism. The new racism then does represent a transition in the dominant ideology. It is a good example of a dominant historical bloc within a nation state introducing an ideological transformation, which many observers see as fundamentally linked to the class interests of that class. For example in the Centre for Contemporary Cultural Studies' *The Empire Strikes Back* it is argued that:

The parallel growth of repressive state structures and new racisms has to be located in a non-reductionist manner, within the dynamics of both the international crisis of the capitalist world economy, and the deep-seated structural crisis of the British social formation. [CCCS 1982, p. 9: see Solomos, 1986]

Clearly the industrial base of Britain has undergone a dramatic transformation in the last two decades and finance capital has become a more dominant force within the British economy. If in 1968 anyone had predicted that Britain would in the mid 1980s have an *official* three million unemployed I suspect very few would have believed that it would have been possible without major public unrest, and governments would have been expected to fall. That the Conservative Government has been elected for a third term is not a triumph of ideology alone, the material class interests of many would favour their re-election. However, the fusion of the new racism, with the politics of the new right must be understood in relation to the legitimation of the reconstruction of the institutions of the state to meet the structural changes that have occurred in Britain. In that sense the new racism is functional in normalizing the objective disadvantage which the majority of black persons in Britain continue to experience (Brown, 1984).

However, living with that inequity is also part of the racializing experience of the white majority. The experience of an essentially white mass media (Troyna in this volume; Husband and Chouhan, 1985; Cohen and Gardner, 1982), of a racially demarcated labour force and significant segregation in housing (Brown, 1984) constructs a material experience in which racism is lived. There is a congruity between the experienced world and the world of the dominant culture. For those who unself-consciously have incorporated aspects of the new racism this is a stable basis for continued racism in Britain. For those white liberals who would espouse a rejection of racism, it is often the case that structurally they continue to benefit from the material inequalities of racism in Britain. For this reason some black analysts see only a limited basis for complete cooperation between black and white groups in opposing racism. The interests of whites as a class, it is argued, are not compatible with the interests of blacks as a class. Allen in this book has discussed how this has been reflected in feminist politics.

Hence it becomes clear that we should not talk of British racism, but of British racism*s*. We should recognize that elements of the dominant ideology (top-down) mesh differently with the existential consciousness of people in different material conditions. This is exactly what Phizacklea and Miles (1980) were demonstrating in their examination of racism in a London borough. Also we should remember that we have already sketched above the links between new right philosophies and the core ideas of the new racism, and hence we should note the way relatively independent belief systems may interlock. For example, I not only experience myself in terms of gender but also in relation to, among other things, my *de facto* middle-class status, my region of origin, my age, my nationality *and* my 'race'. The fact that I have been socialized within a dominant culture which transmits racist ideologies does not accurately reflect *my* particular experience of 'race'. As an adult, middle-class, male, the dominant images of age, class and gender all contain implicit status hierarchies. There is a degree of congruity between the images of superiority, authority, 'natural' claims to resources et cetera which are to be found in the ideologies of class, age and gender. Hence if as a white person I operate within the racist hierarchy of white–black ideologies this is not an entirely unique claim to privileged status: as an adult, middle-class male I routinely do this in relation to the personal politics defined by those ideologies. Note that in this last sentence I refer to *routinely doing* this; namely there is a rehearsal in practice of the ideologies. There is then a degree of congruence between the dominant ideological categories which define me, and within which I to a degree understand myself; *and* also there is a degree of congruence between those dominant ideologies and my *experience* of myself in action. We cannot assume that there is always such a meshing of ideological forces.

In fact my regional identity contains within it a strong current of working-class culture which sits uneasily with my *de facto* middle-class status. And for example a white, middle-class, female might experience the implied dominance of the first two identities as being inconsistent with her experience of the top-down and bottom-up ideologies of gender. We should not therefore see racist ideologies, new or otherwise, as being cognitive implants which have the same meaning or behavioural consequences in all who have incorporated them as beliefs.

It may be useful here to refer back to an important article of almost a decade ago by Abercrombie and Turner (1978) in which they argued that the classical Marxist view of the dominant ideology as the successful imposition by a ruling class upon subordinate classes 'of the truth and moral relevance of a set of beliefs which are contrary to the interests of a subordinate class' was over-simplistic and misconceived. They argued that such a situation would require 'an extremely powerful set of agencies which transmit beliefs downwards from the dominant classes' and they questioned historical evidence for such an impact. Indeed in contemporary academic literature there is a very considerable body of literature which attests to the 'cultures of resistance' of class and ethnic minorities (e.g. Willis, 1977; Clarke *et al.*, 1979; Fryer, 1984; Gilroy, 1987). This leads them to propose a challenging hypothesis:

We do not of course wish to exaggerate our argument with the claim that the coercion of the workplace or the routine of everyday life is a complete explanation of working class quiescence and that ideology is completely irrelevant. However, we *do* wish to suggest that the importance of ideological compliance is exaggerated and that the real significance of the dominant ideology lies in the organization of the dominant class rather than in the subordination of dominated classes. [Abercrombie and Turner, 1978, p. 161]

In suggesting that it is the dominant classes rather than the dominated classes who are most influenced by the dominant ideology Abercrombie and Turner present us with a useful challenge to the assumed logic of the top-down model of ideology. The implication is that the main function of this ideological production is to sustain the structures of the elite. At one level it would function in Tajfel's (1981) terms to prevent the intrusion of 'insecure social comparisons'; namely to maintain the *dominant classes*' perception of their advantage as being 'natural', inevitable and/or for the greater good of the nation. It suggests the importance of the dominant ideology for maintaining the cohesion of the historically specific class alliance of economic and political interests which constitute the current ruling elite. As both Levitas (1986) and Gordon and Klug (1986) have argued the 'new right' is not a homogeneous grouping and the competing interests within this group, and the interests they represent, must be contained. As Held says:

Political order is not achieved through common value systems, or general respect for the authority of the state, or legitimacy, or, by contrast, simple brute force: rather, it is the outcome of a complex web of interdependencies between political, economic and social institutions and activities which divide power centres and which create multiple pressures to comply. [Held, 1984, p. 361]

Hence we may begin to discern in the new racism a theory which permeates different fields of policy and which forms a linking discourse within the factions of the dominant classes. Certainly the overlapping activities of new right pressure groups sketched by Gordon and Klug (1986) would fit with the view that a great deal of their effort is directed toward the dominant elite as their primary target. This would be a logical strategy given that this group constitute the primary definers who set the agenda for popular debates through their control of political and mass media debates. Hence the racism of the dominant ideology is a binding belief system of and for the dominant classes. And, as we have seen earlier, the diffuse formulation and transmission of the new racism facilitates its ubiquitous melding with the disparate interests represented within the dominant bloc.

However, we should not minimize the significance of the dominant ideology for the subordinated groups, which in Abercrombie and Turner's terms may have a 'dualistic' consciousness, involving some accommodation with the dominant ideology. The dominant ideologies of 'race' and nationalism have proved powerful agents of dominant interests as has been illustrated by such recent phenomena as

Powellism in the early 1970s, the jingoism of the Falklands crisis and the continuing power of the, barely, discursive deracialization of *immigration* as a political issue. These instances allow for the tracing of common ideological themes across class boundaries. They also illustrate the ways in which the apparently same content of 'top-down' ideas may be incorporated into different 'bottom-up' consciousness. The anti-'immigrant' sentiments of a working-class, white, male may be concretely focused upon competition for jobs, whereas for an affluent, white, middle-class person they may be concentrated around a concern for 'English' culture. The material position of particular groups will lead them to experience their inequality *vis-à-vis* other groups in relation to particular areas of their life. Whether it be class, gender, ethnic or regional identities that are being negotiated the fractured, *ad hoc*, nature of the new racism gives it a flexible capacity to be attached to a range of disparate issues. Its subsequent appearance over a range of issues, and across group boundaries, consequently lends it a spurious coherence as a discourse which binds disparate groups.

In relation to the role of racism in legitimating the status quo it sometimes seems to be the case that it is invoked as *the* ideological weapon *par excellence* which maintains the viability of existing class relations. Where this is the case there are two obvious flaws. One is the exaggeration of the mystificatory power of racism alone. The other is the exaggeration of the radicalism of the 'cultures of resistance'. The oppositional cultures which express the social being of the oppressed groups may well contain alternative values which are compatible with the reproduction of the status quo. Certainly this is apparent in Willis' account of *Learning To Labour*: an analysis of the working classes' relation to education and employment. We can therefore be cautious in evaluating the *ideological work* which racism may be expected to do in contemporary Britain. Ideologies of domination feed off each other, and racism should not be analysed in a manner which excludes awareness of the significance of these other ideologies. Williams (1985), for example, has sought to demonstrate in relation to the operation of institutional racism the way in which a wide range of ideologies may have racial outcomes through legitimating routine aspects of institutional structures and prac- tices which are *de facto* discriminatory in their outcomes. Nor should we believe that the status quo is only achieved by the winning of consent, for in recent years we have seen the increasing visibility of centralized state power creating an environment of coercion to impose compliance on sections of the population who have resisted the dominant ideology (see for example, Gordon, 1983 and Wallington, 1984). In a social democracy the exercise of such force is itself pro- blematic and fuels the creation of moral panics, and the definition of scapegoats whose existence legitimates (necessitates) strong measures. The responses to the civil disturbances of 1980 and 1981 are indicative of this process (see Joshua *et al.*, 1983 and Benyon, 1984). They also demonstrate that racism can be disfunctional to the dominant interests in challenging the image of benign liberalism which is so central to much of the British self-image. We need therefore to be careful, and critical, in examining the claims made about the nature and role of racism in contemporary Britain.

It has been my purpose in this chapter, to extend the discussion of racism from that set out in my introductory chapter and to comment upon the significance of the analysis of 'the new racism' which has followed its initial publication. In doing that I hope to have raised questions about how the ideological significance of racism should be understood, for there is a danger of concepts such as 'the new racism' being taken up with more enthusiasm than insight; and resulting in a form of explanation by labelling. Racism must be understood in its complexity, being constructed through top-down and bottom-up processes which therefore allow for the existing social structure of society to be reflected through *both*, the structural position of each group determining their 'social being', and hence consciousness; and though the dominant bloc in that structure constructing a dominant ideology. I have tried to indicate something of the potency of 'the new racism', but also have sought to indicate that it exists alongside earlier racist theory. I have stressed, too, that racism is not an ideological package which has its effects independently of other ideologies of, for example, class, or gender, or age. Thus I have argued that we should speak of the reality of British racisms, which represent the variety of ways in which racism is integrated into personal biographies and consciousness, which are themselves determined by people's structured material existences.

Thus while racism, as a dominant ideology, *should* possess common core features, at the same time the unique multiple social identity of individuals makes the incorporation of the different elements of racist ideologies a unique configuration. We should not, therefore, look for 'the new racism', or any other racism, as a common cognitive package imposed by an all powerful dominant group throughout a homogeneous subordinate class. Part of the strength of racism is its unique incorporation into a variety of sites within individual consciousness. Hence, as we noted above, racism is reproduced in individual discourse in inconsistent and flexible codes. Racism remains a major feature of contemporary Britain, perpetuating discrimination and disadvantage for those group who are given subordinate status through the power of 'race' discourses. Racism has also become an integral element in 'new right' politics and is incorporated into ideologies of nation and class, where these ideologies of domination feed off each other.

References

Abercrombie, N., and Turner, B. S. (1978), 'The dominant ideology thesis', *British Journal of Sociology*, vol. 29, no. 2, June

Barker, M. (1981), *The New Racism*, London: Junction Books

Belsey, A. (1986), 'The new right social order and civil liberties' in Ruth Levitas (ed.), *The Ideology of the New Right*

Benyon, J. (1984), *Scarman and After*, Oxford: Pergamon

Billig, M. (1982), *Ideology and Social Psychology*, Oxford: Basil Blackwell

Brown, C. (1984), *Black and White Britain*, London: Heinemann

Centre for Contemporary Cultural Studies (1982), *The Empire Strikes Back*, London: Hutchinson

Clarke, J., Critcher, C. and Johnson, R. (1979), *Working Class Culture*, London: Hutchinson

Cohen, P. and Gardner, C. (1982), *It ain't half racist mum: Fighting racism in the media*, London: Comedia

Delamont, S. (1980), *Sex Roles and The School*, London: Methuen

Fryer, P. (1984), *Staying Power*, London: Pluto Press

Gilroy, P. (1987), *There Ain't No Black in the Union Jack*, London: Hutchinson

Gordon, P. (1983), *White Law*, London: Pluto Press

Gordon, P. and Klug, F. (1986), *New Right New Racism*, London: Searchlight Publications

Hall, S., Critcher, C., Jefferson, T., Clark, J. and Roberts, B. (1978), *Policing The Crisis*, London: Macmillan

Held, D. (1984), 'Power and legitimacy in contemporary Britain' in G. McLennan *et al.*, *State and Society in Contemporary Britain*

Husband, C. and Chouhan, J. M. (1985), 'Local Radio in the Communication Environment of Ethnic Minorities in Britain' in Teun A. van Dijk (ed.), *Discourse and Communication*, Berlin: Walter de Gruyter

Joshua, H., and Wallace, T. (1983), *To Ride The Storm*, London: Heinemann

Levitas, R. (1986), *The Ideology of the New Right*, London: Polity Press

Lorenz, K. (1966), *On Aggression*, London: Methuen

McLennan, G., Held, D., and Hall, S. (1984), *State and Society in Contemporary Britain*, Cambridge: Polity Press

Marx, K. (1970), 'Preface to a Contribution to the Critique of Political Economy' in K. Marx and F. Engels, *Selected Works*, London: Lawrence and Wishart

Marx, K. and Engels, F. (1970), *The German Ideology*, London: Lawrence and Wishart

Morris, D. (1967), *The Naked Ape*, London: Cape

Murray, N. (1986), 'Anti-racists and other demons: the press and ideology in Thatcher's Britain', *Race and Class*, vol. XXVII, Winter, no. 3, pp 1–20

O'Keefe, D. (1986), *The Wayward Curriculum*, London: Social Affairs Unit

Phizacklea, A. and Miles, R. (1980), *Labour and Racism*, London: Routledge and Kegan Paul

Potter, J. and Wetherell, M. (1987), *Discourse and Social Psychology*, London: Sage

Reeves, F. (1983), *British Racial Discourse*, Cambridge: Cambridge University Press

Rex, J. and Mason, D. (1986), *Theories of Race and Ethnic Relations*, Cambridge: Cambridge University Press

Searle, C. (1987), 'Your daily dose: racism and the SUN', *Race and Class*, vol. XXIX, no. 1, Summer, pp 55–71

Seidel, G. (1986), 'Culture, Nation and "Race" in the British and French New Right' in Ruth Levitas (ed.) *The Ideology of the New Right*

Sennett, R. and Cobb, J. (1976), *The Hidden Injuries of Class*, New York: Vintage Books

Sharpe, S. (1976), *Just Like a Girl*, Harmondsworth: Penguin

Solomos, J. (1986), 'Varieties of Marxist conceptions of "race", class and the state: a critical analysis' in John Rex and David Mason (eds) *Theories of Race*

Tajfel, H. (1981), *Human Groups and Social Categories*, Cambridge: Cambridge University Press

Tajfel, H. (1982), *Social Identity and Intergroup Relations*, Cambridge: Cambridge Univeristy Press

Tajfel, H. (1984), *The Social Dimension*, Cambridge: Cambridge University Press

Troyna, B. and Williams, J. (1986), *Racism, Education and the State*, Beckenham: Croom Helm

Van den Berghe, P. L. (1981), *The Ethnic Phenomenon*, New York: Elsevier

Van den Berghe, P. L. (1986), 'Ethnicity and the socio-biology debate' in John Rex and David Mason (eds), *Theories of Race*

Wallington, P. (1984), *Civil Liberties 1984*, Oxford: Martin Robertson

Williams, J. (1985), 'Redefining institutional racism', *Ethnic and Racial Studies*, vol. 8, no. 3, July, pp 323–48

Willis, P. (1977), *Learning to Labour*, Farnborough: Saxon House

Index

Smith, D. 294, 302
Smith, D. J. 180, 183
'social competition' 262–3
Social Darwinism 14–15, 17, 61
social psychology of minorities 232–74
social services 146, 155
Society for Individual Freedom 115, 128
sociobiology 17–18, 172
sociology: political sociology of race 158–62; and study of racial variation 15–16, 293–5
Solomos, J. 90, 97, 99
Sorensen, Reginald 118, 150
Soskice, Frank 118, 119, 121, 127, 130
South Africa 36, 234, 238, 262, 264
Soweto 264
Spain 28, 30, 38
Spanish America 33, 35
Standing Conference of Afro-Caribbean and Asian Councillors 163
state racism 91–6, 142–57
stereotyping, racial 59–71, 191 ff., 236, 276
Stevens, A. 81
Stokes, D. 162
strikes 163–4, 178–9
Studlar, D. 301
Styron, William 244
Sumner, William Graham 248
'Sus' campaign 165
Swann, Sir Michael 284
Sylheti immigrants 230

TUC and racism 160, 161
Tajfel, Henri 245, 247, 258, 271, 322, 327
Tasmania 15
Taylor, S. 280, 282, 301, 302
Teachers Against Racism 160
television 16, 118, 156
Tennyson, Alfred Lord 69
Thatcher, Margaret 100, 321
'theory' of race 13–20
Thompson, E. P. 21
Tomlinson, S. 162, 184
Topsell, Edward 51
Tracey, M. and Troyna, B. 283

trade unions and racism 157, 158, 159, 163–4, 178–9
Trades Unionists Against Racism 160
Treaty of Rome 135
Trethowan, Ian 283
Trollope, Anthony 60, 65, 68–9, 70
Troyna, Barry 101, 276, 282, 283
Troyna, B. and Williams, J. 323
Turkey 27, 28, 32, 33, 35, 37–8
Turner, J. and Brown, R. 245, 268
typology, racial 13–14
Tyson, Edward 52

UN 135
UNESCO 15, 74
USA 15, 33, 35, 38–9, 60, 75, 256, 262, 263
Ugandan Asians 148, 158
Ukrainians 88, 199
unemployment 21, 160, 207; and immigration controls 144, 146
'Unemployment and Homelessness' (1974) 162
universities and CDPs 155
urban deprivation 149, 153–5, 156
Urban Programme 98, 151, 153–4

Vagrancy Act (1824) 165
Van den Berghe, P. L. 293, 320
Vaughan, Graham 251
Vernant, J. 87, 88
Vietnam 36
vigilantes 205
violence: against blacks 143, 158, 202, 205–8; defence committees 165
virginity tests 143
Vizram, R. 174
voting patterns, immigrant 163–4
vouchers *see* employment vouchers

Wagley, C. and Harris, M. 234
Wales: race relations 293; Welsh language and nationalism 267
Walker, M. 157
Wallington, P. 328
Wallman, S. 177, 216, 221, 223
Walvin, J. 11, 298
Ward, Michael 74
Wasserstein, B. 83, 84
Watson, J. D. 265
Webb, K. 304
Weber, M. 294